Quick notes

BIBLE CONCORDANCE

GEORGE W. KNIGHT

ISBN 978-1-60260-443-8

All Scripture quotations are taken from the King James Version of the Bible.

Published by Barbour Publishing, Inc., P.O. Box 719, Uhrichsville, Ohio 44683, www.barbourbooks.com

Our mission is to publish and distribute inspirational products offering exceptional value and biblical encouragement to the masses.

Printed in the United States of America.

Introduction

What do you get when you combine the best features of a biblical concordance, a Bible dictionary, and a guide to the major events and key passages of the Bible into one handy book? You get the book you are now holding. . .the *QuickNotes Bible Concordance.* Based on the familiar King James Version, its purpose is to provide essential biblical information to lay students of the Bible in a format that is compact, convenient, and easy to use and understand.

The heart of this book is the concordance, which helps you find full passages in the Bible by looking under key words which the passages contain. Only selected Bible words, included because of their biblical significance, are listed as concordance entries. Under each concordance entry, only the most important verses from the Bible that contain these key words appear. This selective process makes the *QuickNotes Bible Concordance* easier to use than an exhaustive concordance such as *Strong's,* which tends to overwhelm lay Bible students with too much information.

Another handy feature of this book's concordance is the listing of all forms of the same root word under one entry. For example, see the entry **CONVERT [ED, ETH, ING].** Bible verses containing the words *Convert, Converted, Converteth,* and *Converting* are listed under this one concordance entry. Key phrases from the Bible, such as **BEAR FALSE WITNESS, ETERNAL LIFE,**

PREACH THE GOSPEL, and **SEEK THE LORD,** also appear as concordance entries throughout the book.

The names of important people and places in the Bible appear as dictionary entries in this book. Most of these people or places have brief, thumbnail definitions, followed by passages in the Bible where pertinent information about these people or places can be found. Bible passages printed in **bold type** identify the most important sources of information about this biblical person or place. For a more complete narrative description of important people, places, and theological concepts in the Bible, see the companion volume to this book, the *QuickNotes Bible Concordance,* issued by Barbour Publishing in 1998.

Throughout the *QuickNotes Bible Concordance,* you will also find many key Bible events and major biblical passages listed for your convenience. For example, let's assume you are looking for the "Fruit of the Spirit" passage in the New Testament. Perhaps you cannot recall any of the key words in this passage from the King James Version that would help you find it through the concordance route. You simply look under **FRUIT OF THE SPIRIT** in this book, and it directs you to the passage in question: Galatians 5:22–26. Other important biblical passages and events that can be located through this same approach include **BURNING BUSH REVEALED TO MOSES, FAITH CHAPTER OF THE BIBLE,** and **PLAGUES AGAINST EGYPT.**

My thanks to Paul Muckley of Barbour Publishing for his encouragement and counsel in this book project. I am also grateful to my wife, Dorothy, for her assistance with the word processing and proofreading of the manuscript. I send the book forth with the prayer that it will help lay Bible students in the important work of studying and teaching God's Word.

George W. Knight
Nashville, Tennessee

Abbreviations Used for Books of the Bible

Old Testament

Abbreviation	*Bible Book*	*Abbreviation*	*Bible Book*
Gen	Genesis	Eccl	Ecclesiastes
Ex	Exodus	Song	Song of Solomon
Lev	Leviticus	Isa	Isaiah
Num	Numbers	Jer	Jeremiah
Deut	Deuteronomy	Lam	Lamentations
Josh	Joshua	Ezek	Ezekiel
Judg	Judges	Dan	Daniel
Ruth	Ruth	Hos	Hosea
1 Sam	1 Samuel	Joel	Joel
2 Sam	2 Samuel	Amos	Amos
1 Kgs	1 Kings	Obad	Obadiah
2 Kgs	2 Kings	Jon	Jonah
1 Chr	1 Chronicles	Mic	Micah
2 Chr	2 Chronicles	Nah	Nahum
Ezra	Ezra	Hab	Habakkuk
Neh	Nehemiah	Zeph	Zephaniah
Esth	Esther	Hag	Haggai
Job	Job	Zech	Zechariah
Ps, Pss	Psalm(s)	Mal	Malachi
Prov	Proverbs		

Abbreviations Used for Books of the Bible

New Testament

Abbreviation	*Bible Book*	*Abbreviation*	*Bible Book*
Matt	Matthew	1 Tim	1 Timothy
Mark	Mark	2 Tim	2 Timothy
Luke	Luke	Titus	Titus
John	John	Phlm	Philemon
Acts	Acts	Heb	Hebrews
Rom	Romans	Jas	James
1 Cor	1 Corinthians	1 Pet	1 Peter
2 Cor	2 Corinthians	2 Pet	2 Peter
Gal	Galatians	1 John	1 John
Eph	Ephesians	2 John	2 John
Phil	Philippians	3 John	3 John
Col	Colossians	Jude	Jude
1 Thes	1 Thessalonians	Rev	Revelation
2 Thes	2 Thessalonians		

-A-

AARON (brother of Moses and first high priest of Israel). For a description of Aaron's life and work, see **Ex 4:14; 5:1; 7:10–20; 17:12; 28:1; 32:3–5,35 • Lev 8:2–27; 10:8 • Num 4:19; 16:3; 17:3–10; 20:12,28.** Aaron is also mentioned in 1 Chr 6:49 • Pss 105:26; 133:2 • Luke 1:5 • Acts 7:40 • Heb 5:4; 7:11; 9:4.

ABANA RIVER (a river of Syria). 2 Kgs 5:12.

ABASE [D]

Ezek 21:26 exalt him that is low, and ***a*** him that is high

Luke 18:14 every one that exalteth himself shall be ***a'd***

Phil 4:12 I [Paul] know...how to be ***a'd***...how to abound

ABATED

Gen 8:3 hundred and fifty days the waters were ***a***

Deut 34:7 his [Moses'] eye was not dim, nor...natural force ***a***

ABBA (an Aramaic word for "Father"). Mark 14:36 • Rom 8:15 • Gal 4:6.

ABDON (a judge of Israel). Judg 12:13,15.

ABED-NEGO (a companion of Daniel). Dan 2:49; 3:12–30. *Azariah:* Dan 1:7.

ABEL (a son of Adam). **Gen 4:2–25** • Matt 23:35 • Luke 11:51 • Heb 11:4; 12:24.

ABIA. See *Abijah.*

ABIATHAR (a high priest in David's time). 1 Sam 22:20–22; 23:6,9; 30:7 • 2 Sam 8:17; 15:24–35; 17:15; 19:11; 20:25 • 1 Kgs 1:7–42; 2:22–35; 4:4 • 1 Chr 15:11; 18:16; 24:6; 27:34 • Mark 2:26.

ABIDE [ING, TH]

1 Kgs 8:13 the earth a settled place for thee [God] to ***a*** in

Ps 15:1 LORD, who shall ***a*** in thy tabernacle?

Ps 91:1 ***a*** under the shadow of the Almighty

Ps 119:90 thou [God] hast established the earth...it ***a'th***

Eccl 1:4 another generation cometh...earth ***a'th*** for ever

Nah 1:6 who can ***a*** in...fierceness of his [God's] anger?

Luke 2:8 shepherds ***a'ing*** in the field, keeping watch

Luke 9:4 whatsoever house ye enter into, there ***a***

Luke 19:5 Zacchaeus...to day I [Jesus] must ***a*** at thy house

John 3:36 believeth not the Son...wrath...***a'th*** on him

John 12:46 whosoever believeth on me [Jesus]...not ***a*** in darkness
John 14:16 another Comforter...may ***a*** with you for ever
John 15:4 **A** in me [Jesus], and I in you
John 15:5 He that ***a'th*** in me [Jesus]...bringeth...fruit
John 15:10 keep my [Jesus'] commandments...***a*** in my love
1 Cor 3:14 any man's work ***a*** which he hath built
1 Cor 13:13 ***a'th*** faith, hope, charity...greatest...is charity
Phil 1:25 I [Paul] shall ***a***... with you all for your...joy
1 Pet 1:23 Born...by the word of God...***a'th*** for ever
1 John 2:10 He that loveth his brother ***a'th*** in the light
1 John 2:17 but he that doeth the will of God ***a'th*** for ever
1 John 2:28 ***a*** in him [Jesus]... confidence...at his coming
1 John 3:14 He that loveth not his brother ***a'th*** in death
1 John 3:15 no murderer hath eternal life ***a'ing*** in him

ABIGAIL (a wife of David). 1 Sam 25:3–42; 27:3; 30:5 • 2 Sam 2:2; 3:3 • 1 Chr 3:1.

ABIJAH (son and successor of Rehoboam as king of Judah). 2 Chr 11:20–22. *Abia:* Matt 1:7. *Abijam:* 1 Kgs 14:31; **15:1–8.**

ABIJAM. See *Abijah.*

ABILENE (a Roman section of Palestine). Luke 3:1.

ABIMELECH

1. A Philistine king in Abraham's time. Gen 20:2–18; 21:22–32; 26:1–31.

2. A son of Gideon. Judg 8: 31; **9:1–56;** 10:1 • 2 Sam 11:21.

ABIRAM (leader of a rebellion against Moses). **Num 16:1–27;** 26:9 • Deut 11:6 • Ps 106:17.

ABISHAG (David's nurse in his old age). 1 Kgs 1:3–4,15; 2:17,21–22.

ABISHAI (deputy commander in David's army). 1 Sam 26:6–9 • 2 Sam 2:18,24; 3:30; 10:10–14; 16:9–11; 18:2–12; 19:21; 20: 6,10; 21:17; 23:18 • 1 Chr 2:16; 11:20; 18:12; 19:11,15.

ABISHALOM. See *Absalom.*

ABLE TO DELIVER

Isa 36:14 Let not Hezekiah deceive...not be ***a-t-d*** you
Ezek 7:19 gold...not be ***a-t-d*** them in the day of the... LORD

Dan 3:17 God...is ***a-t-d*** us [Daniel's friends]

ABNER (commander of King Saul's army). 1 Sam 14:50–51; 17:55–57; 20:25; 26:5–15 • 2 Sam 2:8–30; 3:6–37; 4:1,12 • 1 Kgs 2:5,32 • 1 Chr 26:28; 27:21.

ABOLISH [ED]

Isa 2:18 the idols he [God] shall utterly ***a***

Isa 51:6 my [God's] righteousness shall not be ***a'ed***

Eph 2:15 ***a'ed*** in his [Jesus'] flesh...enmity...making peace

2 Tim 1:10 Jesus Christ, who hath ***a'ed*** death

ABOMINATION OF DESOLATION

Matt 24:15 see the ***a-o-d***... stand in the holy place

Mark 13:14 see the ***a-o-d***... standing where it ought not

ABOMINATION TO THE LORD, THINGS CONSIDERED AN

1. Graven images (Deut 7:25)
2. The froward, or wicked (Prov 3:32)
3. A false balance (Prov 11:1)
4. Lying lips (Prov 12:22)
5. Sacrifice of the wicked (Prov 15:8)
6. Thoughts of the wicked (Prov 15:26)
7. Every one that is proud in heart (Prov 16:5)

ABOUND [ED]

Rom 5:15 the grace of God... hath ***a'ed*** unto many

Rom 5:20 sin ***a'ed,*** grace did much more ***a***

Rom 6:1 Shall we continue in sin, that grace may ***a?***

Rom 15:13 ***a*** in hope, through the power of the Holy Ghost

2 Cor 8:7 in your love...see that ye ***a*** in this grace also

Eph 1:8 he [God] hath ***a'ed*** toward us in all wisdom

Phil 4:12 I [Paul] know...how to be abased...how to ***a***

1 Thes 3:12 increase and ***a*** in love one toward another

ABOVE

Gen 1:7 God...divided the waters...***a*** the firmament

Ex 19:5 a peculiar treasure unto me [God] ***a*** all people

Ex 20:4 not make...likeness of any thing...in heaven ***a***

Deut 7:6 chosen thee to be a special people...***a*** all people

1 Kgs 8:23 no God like thee, in heaven ***a,*** or on earth beneath

1 Chr 16:25 great is the LORD... to be feared ***a*** all gods

1 Chr 29:11 thou [God] art exalted as head ***a*** all

2 Chr 2:5 for great is our God ***a*** all gods
Esth 2:17 the king loved Esther ***a*** all the women
Ps 8:1 who [God] hast set thy glory ***a*** the heavens
Ps 57:5 Be thou exalted, O God, ***a*** the heavens
Ps 95:3 For the LORD is...a great King ***a*** all gods
Ps 99:2 The LORD...is high ***a*** all the people
Prov 31:10 a virtuous woman? For her price is far ***a*** rubies
Jer 17:9 The heart is deceitful ***a*** all things
Dan 6:3 Daniel was preferred ***a*** the...princes
Matt 10:24 The disciple is not ***a*** his master
John 8:23 Ye are from beneath; I [Jesus] am from ***a***
1 Cor 10:13 God...not suffer you...tempted ***a***...ye are able
Eph 1:21 Far ***a*** all principality, and power, and might
Eph 3:20 unto him [Jesus]... able to do...***a*** all that we ask
Eph 4:6 One God...who is ***a*** all, and through all
Eph 6:16 ***A*** all, taking the shield of faith
Phil 2:9 given him [Jesus] a name...***a*** every name
Col 3:1 seek those things which are ***a***
Col 3:2 Set your affection on things ***a***, not on...the earth
Jas 1:17 Every good...and... perfect gift is from ***a***
Jas 3:17 Wisdom...from ***a*** is first pure, then...gentle

ABRAHAM (father of the nation of Israel). Also known as *Abram*. See **Gen 11:26–25:10** for a sketch of Abraham.

1. Called by the Lord to a new land (Gen 12:1–6)
2. Promised many descendants (Gen 12:1–7; 13:14–18; 15:5–21; 17:1–9; 22:15–19)
3. Separated from Lot (Gen 13:1–12)
4. Blessed by Melchizekek (Gen 14:17–20)
5. Son Ishmael born to Hagar (Gen 16:15–16)
6. Name changed from Abram to Abraham (Gen 17:5)
7. Circumcised with his household (Gen 17:10–27)
8. Interceded for Sodom and Gomorrah (Gen 18:23–33)
9. Son Isaac born to Sarah (Gen 21:1–8)
10. Prevented from sacrificing Isaac (Gen 22:1–14)
11. Death of Sarah (Gen 23:1–20)
12. Death of Abraham (Gen 25:7–10)

Abraham is mentioned several times in the New Testament: Matt 1:1–2,17; 3:9; 8:11; 22:32 • Mark 12:26 • Luke 1:55,73; 3:8,34; 13:16,28; 16:23–25, 29–30; 19:9; 20:37 •

John 8:39–58 • Acts 3:13,25; 7:2–32; 13:26 • Rom 4:1–16; 9:7; 11:1 • 2 Cor 11:22 • Gal 3:6–18; 4:22 • Heb 2:16; 6:13; 7:1–9; 11:8,17 • Jas 2:21,23 • 1 Pet 3:6.

ABRAM. See *Abraham*.

ABSALOM (a son of King David who tried to seize his father's throne). 2 Sam 3:3; 13:1,4,20–39; 14:1–33; **15:1–18:33;** 19:1–10; 20:6 • 1 Kgs 1:6; 2:7 • 1 Chr 3:2 • 2 Chr 11:20–21. *Abishalom:* 1 Kgs 15:2–10.

ABUNDANCE

1 Kgs 18:41 Elijah said...there is a sound of ***a*** of rain

Ps 37:11 meek shall...delight... in the ***a*** of peace

Eccl 5:12 ***a*** of the rich will not suffer him to sleep

Matt 12:34 out of the ***a*** of the heart the mouth speaketh

Luke 12:15 life consisteth not in the ***a***...he possesseth

ABUNDANT

1 Cor 12:24 more ***a*** honour to that part which lacked

2 Cor 4:15 ***a*** grace might... redound to the glory of God

2 Cor 11:23 in labours more ***a,*** in stripes above measure

1 Tim 1:14 grace of our Lord was exceeding ***a*** with faith

1 Pet 1:3 according to his [God's] ***a*** mercy...hath begotten us...a lively hope

ACCEPT [ED]

Job 42:9 the LORD also ***a'ed*** Job

Jer 14:12 I [God] will not ***a*** them...consume them by the sword

Jer 37:20 let my supplication... be ***a'ed*** before thee [God]

Amos 5:22 burnt offerings...I [God] will not ***a*** them

Mal 1:10 neither will I [God] ***a*** an offering at your hand

Luke 4:24 No prophet is ***a'ed*** in his own country

Acts 10:35 feareth him [God]... is ***a'ed*** with him

ACCEPTABLE

Ps 19:14 meditation of my heart...***a*** in thy [God's] sight

Prov 21:3 To do justice...is more ***a***...than sacrifice

Isa 61:2 To proclaim the ***a*** year of the LORD

Luke 4:19 To preach the ***a*** year of the Lord

Rom 12:1 bodies a living sacrifice...***a*** unto God

Eph 5:10 Proving what is ***a*** unto the Lord

1 Tim 2:3 good and ***a*** in the sight of God

1 Pet 2:5 spiritual sacrifices, ***a*** to God by Jesus Christ

ACCESS

Rom 5:2 By whom [Jesus]...we have ***a***...into this grace

Eph 2:18 through him [Jesus] we...have ***a***...unto the Father

Eph 3:12 In whom [Jesus] we have...***a*** with confidence

ACCOMPLISHED

Isa 40:2 Speak...to Jerusalem...her warfare is ***a***

Jer 25:12 seventy years are ***a,*** that I [God] will punish the king of Babylon

Luke 2:6 days were ***a*** that she [Mary] should be delivered

Luke 12:50 how am I [Jesus] straitened till it be ***a***

Luke 18:31 things...concerning the Son of man shall be ***a***

John 19:28 Jesus knowing that all things were now ***a***

ACCORD

Acts 1:14 These all continued with one ***a*** in prayer

Acts 2:1 Pentecost was...come, they were all with one ***a***

Acts 2:46 one ***a***...and breaking bread from house to house

Phil 2:2 having the same love, being of one ***a***

ACCOUNT [ED]

Ps 144:3 the son of man, that thou makest ***a*** of him!

Matt 12:36 idle word that men...speak, they shall give ***a***

Luke 16:2 ***a*** of thy stewardship...thou mayest be no longer steward

Luke 20:35 ***a'ed*** worthy...neither marry, nor are given in marriage

Luke 21:36 ***a'ed*** worthy to...stand before the Son of man

Luke 22:24 strife among them, which...be ***a'ed*** the greatest

Rom 14:12 every one...shall give ***a*** of himself to God

Gal 3:6 Abraham believed God...***a'ed***...for righteousness

Phil 4:17 I [Paul] desire fruit that may abound to your ***a***

Phlm 1:18 oweth thee ought, put that on mine [Paul's] ***a***

1 Pet 4:5 give ***a*** to him...ready to judge...the dead

ACCURSED

Josh 6:18 keep yourselves from the ***a*** thing

Josh 7:1 For Achan...took of the ***a*** thing

Rom 9:3 myself [Paul] were ***a*** from Christ for...kinsmen

1 Cor 12:3 no man speaking by the Spirit...calleth Jesus ***a***

ACCUSATION

Matt 27:37 over his head his ***a***...JESUS THE KING OF THE JEWS

Luke 6:7 Pharisees watched him [Jesus]...find an ***a*** against him

John 18:29 Pilate...said, What ***a*** bring ye against this man?

ACCUSE [D]

Matt 12:10 heal on the sabbath day...they might ***a*** him [Jesus]

Matt 27:12 ***a'd*** of the chief priests...he [Jesus] answered nothing

Luke 3:14 neither ***a*** any falsely...content with... wages

Luke 11:54 catch something out of his [Jesus'] mouth, that they might ***a*** him

Luke 23:2 ***a*** him [Jesus]...We found this fellow perverting the nation

ACELDAMA (a burial ground purchased with Judas's betrayal money). Acts 1:19.

ACHAIA (a Roman province of Greece visited by Paul). Acts 18:12,27; **19:21** • Rom 15:26; 16:5 • 1 Cor 16:15 • 2 Cor 1:1; 9:2; 11:10 • 1 Thes 1:7–8.

ACHAN (a warrior under Joshua executed for his disobedience). **Josh 7:1–26;** 22:20. *Achar:* 1 Chr 2:7.

ACHAZ. See *Ahaz.*

ACHISH (a Philistine king who aided David). 1 Sam 21:10–14; 27:2–12; 28:1–2; 29:6–9.

ACKNOWLEDGE

Ps 51:3 I ***a*** my transgressions...my sin is ever before me

Prov 3:6 ways ***a*** him [God], and he shall direct thy paths

Jer 3:13 ***a*** thine iniquity...that thou hast transgressed against the LORD

Jer 14:20 ***a,*** O LORD, our wickedness...sinned against thee

ACQUAINTED

Ps 139:3 Thou [God]...art ***a*** with all my ways

Isa 53:3 a man of sorrows, and ***a*** with grief

ACTS

Deut 11:7 eyes have seen all the great ***a*** of the LORD

1 Sam 12:7 reason with you... righteous ***a*** of the LORD

Ps 103:7 his [God's] ***a*** unto the children of Israel

Ps 106:2 ***a*** of the LORD? who can show forth all his praise?

Ps 145:4 One generation shall declare thy [God's] mighty ***a***

Ps 150:2 Praise him [God] for his mighty ***a***

ACTS OF THE APOSTLES, BOOK OF. The one book of history in the New Testament that traces the expansion of the early church from the ascension of Jesus to Paul's imprisonment in Rome—a period of about thirty-five years. Acts shows how the Christian witness spread in accordance with the Great Commission of Jesus (see Acts 1:8).

ADAM (the first person created by God). **Gen 2:19–5:5** • Deut 32:8 • 1 Chr 1:1 • Job 31:33 • Luke 3:38 • Rom 5:14 • 1 Cor 15:22,45 • 1 Tim 2:13–14 • Jude 14.

ADMAH (a city destroyed with Sodom and Gomorrah). Gen 10:19; 14:2,8 • Deut 29:23 • Hos 11:8.

ADMONISH [ING]

Rom 15:14 ye also are...able also to ***a*** one another

Col 3:16 ***a'ing*** one another in psalms and hymns

2 Thes 3:15 not as an enemy, but ***a*** him as a brother

ADONIJAH (a son of King David and rival of Solomon for the throne). 2 Sam 3:4 • **1 Kgs 1:5–53;** 2:13–28 • 1 Chr 3:2.

ADOPTION

Rom 8:15 Spirit of ***a,*** whereby we cry, Abba, Father

Rom 8:23 waiting for the ***a***... the redemption of our body

Gal 4:5 them...under the law...receive the ***a*** of sons

Eph 1:5 predestinated us unto the ***a*** of children by Jesus

ADRIA (the Adriatic Sea). Acts 27:27.

ADULTERY

Ex 20:14 Thou shalt not commit ***a***

Lev 20:10 ***a***...neighbour's wife...adulterer...put to death

Deut 5:18 Neither shalt thou commit ***a***

Prov 6:32 whoso committeth ***a***...destroyeth his own soul

Jer 7:9 and commit ***a***...and walk after other gods

Matt 5:28 looketh on a woman to lust...hath committed ***a***

Mark 10:11 put away his wife, and marry another, committeth ***a***

John 8:3 brought unto him [Jesus] a woman taken in ***a***

Gal 5:19 works of the flesh are...***A,*** fornication

2 Pet 2:14 eyes full of ***a***...cannot cease from sin

ADVERSARY [IES]

Deut 32:43 he [God] will...render vengeance to his ***a'ies***

1 Sam 2:10 ***a'ies*** of the LORD shall be broken

1 Kgs 5:4 hath given me rest... there is neither ***a*** nor evil

Esth 7:6 The ***a*** and enemy is this wicked Haman

Ps 69:19 mine ***a'ies*** are all before thee [God]

Ps 74:10 how long shall the ***a*** reproach?

Ps 109:29 Let mine ***a'ies*** be clothed with shame

Nah 1:2 LORD will take vengeance on his ***a'ies***

Matt 5:25 Agree with thine ***a***... in the way with him

Luke 18:3 widow...came...saying, Avenge me of mine ***a***

Luke 21:15 wisdom, which all your ***a'ies*** shall not...resist

1 Cor 16:9 great door...is opened...many ***a'ies***

1 Pet 5:8 ***a*** the devil...seeking whom he may devour

ADVERSITY

Ps 35:15 mine ***a*** they rejoiced, and gathered...together

Prov 17:17 a brother is born for ***a***

Prov 24:10 faint in the day of ***a,*** thy strength is small

Isa 30:20 bread of ***a,*** and the water of affliction

ADVOCATE

1 John 2:1 we have an ***a*** with the Father, Jesus Christ

AFFECTION

Rom 1:31 Without understanding...without natural ***a***

Col 3:2 Set your ***a*** on things above, not...on the earth

Col 3:5 uncleanness, inordinate ***a,*** evil concupiscence

2 Tim 3:3 Without natural ***a,*** trucebreakers, false accusers

AFFLICT [ED]

Ex 1:11 taskmasters to ***a*** them [Israelites] with their burdens

Ex 1:12 more they ***a'ed*** them [Israelites]...more they... grew

Ex 22:22 not ***a*** any widow, or fatherless child

Ruth 1:21 Almighty hath ***a'ed*** me [Naomi]

1 Kgs 11:39 I [God] will for this ***a*** the seed of David

2 Kgs 17:20 LORD rejected... Israel, and ***a'ed*** them

Job 34:28 he [God] heareth the cry of the ***a'ed***

Ps 44:2 thou [God] didst ***a*** the people, and cast them out

Ps 88:15 I am ***a'ed*** and ready to die

Ps 90:15 the days wherein thou [God] hast ***a'ed*** us

Ps 119:71 I have been ***a'ed***... learn thy [God's] statutes

Ps 140:12 maintain the cause of the ***a'ed***

Isa 49:13 the LORD...will have mercy upon his ***a'ed***

Isa 53:4 esteem him [God's servant] stricken...smitten... ***a'ed***

Lam 1:12 LORD hath ***a'ed*** me in...his fierce anger

Lam 3:33 he [God] doth not ***a*** willingly nor grieve

Nah 1:12 Though I have ***a'ed*** thee [God], I will ***a*** thee no more

Matt 24:9 ***a'ed,*** and shall kill you...for my [Jesus']...sake

Heb 11:37 wandered about in sheepskins...***a'ed,*** tormented

Jas 4:9 Be ***a'ed***...your laughter be turned to mourning

Jas 5:13 ***a'ed?*** let him pray. Is any merry...sing psalms

AFFLICTION [S]

Gen 29:32 the LORD hath looked upon my [Leah's] ***a***

Ex 3:7 I [God] have...seen the ***a*** of my people

Deut 16:3 unleavened bread... the bread of ***a***

Deut 26:7 the LORD...looked on our ***a***...and our oppression

Job 30:16 days of ***a*** have taken hold upon me

Ps 25:18 Look upon mine ***a*** and my pain

Ps 34:19 Many are the ***a's*** of the righteous

Ps 119:153 mine ***a***...for I do not forget thy [God's] law

Ps 132:1 LORD, remember David, and all his ***a's***

Isa 30:20 bread of adversity, and the water of ***a***

Lam 1:3 Judah is gone into captivity because of ***a***

2 Cor 4:17 light ***a***...worketh for us...exceeding...glory

Col 1:24 fill up that...behind of the ***a's*** of Christ

2 Tim 4:5 endure ***a's***...make full proof of thy ministry

Jas 1:27 visit the fatherless and widows in their ***a***

AFRAID

Gen 3:10 I [Adam] was ***a***...and I hid myself

Gen 28:17 he [Jacob] was ***a***... How dreadful is this place

Ex 3:6 Moses...was ***a*** to look upon God

Ex 14:10 Egyptians marched after them [Israelites]... they were sore ***a***

Num 22:3 Moab was sore ***a*** of the people [Israelites]

Deut 7:18 not be ***a***...remember what the LORD...did

Deut 31:6 nor be ***a***...thy God... will not fail thee

Josh 1:9 be not ***a***...for the LORD...is with thee

1 Sam 18:12 Saul was ***a*** of David...the LORD was with him

Esth 7:6 Haman was ***a*** before the king and the queen

Job 3:25 that which I was ***a*** of is come unto me

Job 5:21 neither shalt thou be ***a*** of destruction

Ps 27:1 LORD...strength of my life; of whom shall I be ***a?***

Ps 56:3 What time I am ***a,*** I will trust in thee [God]

Ps 56:11 In God have I put my trust...I will not be ***a*** what man can do unto me
Ps 91:5 Thou shalt not be ***a*** for the terror by night
Isa 12:2 not be ***a***...Jehovah is my strength
Jer 1:8 be not ***a***...I [God] am with thee to deliver thee
Jer 2:12 Be astonished...be horribly ***a***...saith the LORD
Jer 42:11 not ***a*** of the king of Babylon...I [God]...with you
Jer 42:16 famine, whereof ye were ***a***, shall follow
Dan 4:5 a dream...made me [Daniel] ***a***...visions...troubled me
Jon 1:5 mariners were ***a***, and cried every man unto his god
Matt 14:27 Jesus spake...it is I; be not ***a***
Matt 17:7 Jesus...said, Arise, and be not ***a***
Matt 25:25 I was ***a***, and...hid thy talent in the earth
Matt 28:10 Be not ***a***: go tell my [Jesus'] brethren that they go into Galilee
Mark 6:50 Be of good cheer: it is I [Jesus]; be not ***a***
Mark 9:32 they [the disciples] understood not...and were ***a*** to ask him [Jesus]
Luke 2:9 and they [shepherds] were sore ***a***
Luke 12:4 Be not ***a*** of them that kill the body
John 14:27 not your heart be troubled, neither let it be ***a***
Acts 9:26 they [apostles] were all ***a*** of him [Paul]
Gal 4:11 I [Paul] am ***a*** of you, lest I...labour in vain

AGABUS (a prophet who warned of a famine and foretold Paul's arrest in Jerusalem). Acts 11:28; 21:10.

AGAG (a king of Amalek who was killed by Samuel). Num 24:7 • **1 Sam 15:8–33.**

AGAR. See *Hagar.*

AGREE [D]
Amos 3:3 Can two walk together, except they be ***a'd***
Matt 5:25 ***A*** with...adversary quickly...in the way with him
Matt 20:13 didst not thou ***a*** with me for a penny?
Mark 14:56 false witness against him [Jesus], but their witness ***a'd*** not

AGRIPPA (a ruler before whom Paul made his defense at Caesarea). Acts 25:13–26; **26:1–32.**

AHAB (a king of Israel whose wicked reign led to idol worship). **1 Kgs 16:28–22:40** • 2 Kgs 1:1; 3:1,5; 9:7–29;

10:1–30; 21:3,13 • **2 Chr 18:1–34;** 21:6,13; 22:3–8 • Mic 6:16.

AHASUERUS (a king of Persia who married Esther). Esth 1:1–3:12; 6:2–10:3.

AHAVA (a town or river in Babylonia). Ezra 8:15,21,31.

AHAZ (a king of Judah who practiced idol worship). **2 Kgs 15:38–16:20 • 2 Chr 28:1–27** • Isa 1:1; 7:1–3,10–12; 14:28; 38:8 • Hos 1:1 • Mic 1:1. *Achaz:* Matt 1:9.

AHAZIAH

1. A king of Israel who worshiped the pagan god Baal. 1 Kgs 22:40,49–51 • 2 Kgs 1:2,18 • 1 Chr 3:11 • 2 Chr 20:35–37.

2. A king of Judah who fell into idol worship. 2 Kgs 8:24–9:28 • 2 Chr 22:1–9. *Azariah:* 2 Chr 22:6.

AHIJAH (a prophet in Solomon's time who foretold the division of the kingdom). **1 Kgs 11:29–39;** 14:2,18; 15:29 • 2 Chr 9:29; 10:15.

AHIMAAZ (a person who kept David informed about Absalom's rebellion). **2 Sam 15:27,36;** 17:17,20; 18:19–29 • 1 Chr 6:8–9,53.

AHIMELECH (high priest during King Saul's reign). 1 Sam 21:1–2,8; 22:9–20; 23:6 • 2 Sam 8:17 • 1 Chr 24:3,6,31.

AHITHOPHEL (one of David's aides who joined Absalom's rebellion against the king). 2 Sam 15:12–34; **16:15–23; 17:1–23** • 2 Sam 23:34 • 1 Chr 27:33–34.

AI (a Canaanite city captured by Joshua). **Josh 7:2–8:29;** 9:3; 10:1–2; 12:9 • Ezra 2:28 • Neh 7:32 • Jer 49:3. *Aiath:* Isa 10:28. *Aija:* Neh 11:31. *Hai:* Gen 12:8.

AIATH. See *Ai.*

AIJA. See *Ai.*

ALARM

Jer 4:19 the sound of the trumpet, the ***a*** of war

Joel 2:1 an ***a***...for the day of the LORD cometh

ALIEN

Ex 18:3 I have been an ***a*** in a strange land

Job 19:15 a stranger: I [Job] am an ***a*** in their sight

Ps 69:8 stranger...***a*** unto my mother's children

ALIVE

Gen 7:23 Noah only remained ***a,*** and they...with him

Ps 41:2 The LORD will preserve him, and keep him ***a***
Mark 16:11 heard that he [Jesus] was ***a***...had been seen
Luke 15:24 my son was dead, and is ***a*** again
Acts 1:3 he [Jesus] showed himself ***a*** after his passion
Rom 6:11 dead...unto sin, but ***a*** unto God through Jesus
1 Cor 15:22 even so in Christ shall all be made ***a***
1 Thes 4:17 are ***a***...caught up together...to meet the Lord
Rev 1:18 I [Jesus] am ***a***...and have the keys...of death
Rev 2:8 first and the last, which was dead, and is ***a***

ALMIGHTY GOD
Gen 17:1 I am the ***A-G***...be thou perfect
Rev 19:15 treadeth the winepress of the...wrath of ***A-G***

ALMS
Matt 6:1 do not your ***a*** before men, to be seen of them
Luke 12:33 give ***a;*** provide...a treasure...that faileth not
Acts 10:4 thine [Cornelius's] ***a*** are come up...before God

ALONE
Gen 2:18 not good that the man should be ***a***
Gen 32:24 Jacob was left ***a***... wrestled a man with him
Ex 24:2 Moses ***a*** shall come near the LORD
Num 11:14 I [Moses] am not able to bear all this people ***a***
Job 7:16 let me ***a;*** for my [Job's] days are vanity
Ps 86:10 thou art great...thou art God ***a***
Ps 148:13 praise the...LORD... his name ***a*** is excellent
Eccl 4:10 woe to him that is ***a*** when he falleth
Isa 2:11 the LORD ***a*** shall be exalted
Dan 10:7 And I Daniel ***a*** saw the vision
Matt 4:4 It is written, Man shall not live by bread ***a***
Matt 14:23 a mountain...to pray...he [Jesus] was there ***a***
Mark 1:24 Let us ***a;*** what have we to do with thee...Jesus
Mark 14:6 Let her ***a***...she hath wrought a good work
Luke 5:21 Who can forgive sins, but God ***a?***
John 12:24 a corn of wheat fall...and die, it abideth ***a***
John 17:20 Neither pray I [Jesus] for these ***a***
Jas 2:17 faith, if it hath not works, is dead, being ***a***

ALPHA AND OMEGA (the first and last letters of the Greek alphabet). Rev 1:8,11; 21:6; 22:13.

ALPHAEUS. See *Cleophas.*

ALTAR [S]

1 Kgs 1:50 Adonijah...caught hold on the horns of the ***a***

1 Kgs 8:22 Solomon stood before the ***a***...in the presence of all... Israel

Ezek 6:4 ***a's*** shall be desolate, and...images...broken

Luke 1:11 angel...standing on the right side of the ***a***

Acts 17:23 an ***a*** with this inscription, TO THE UNKNOWN GOD

ALTARS BUILT BY OLD TESTAMENT PERSONALITIES

1. Noah (Gen 8:20)
2. Abraham (Gen 12:7)
3. Isaac (Gen 26:25)
4. Jacob at Shalem (Gen 33:20)
5. Jacob at Bethel (Gen 35:7)
6. Moses (Ex 17:15)
7. Joshua (Josh 8:30)
8. Gideon (Judg 6:24)
9. Saul (1 Sam 14:35)
10. David (2 Sam 24:25)

ALWAYS

Gen 6:3 My [God's] spirit shall not ***a*** strive with man

1 Chr 16:15 mindful ***a*** of his [God's] covenant

Ps 16:8 LORD ***a*** before me...he is at my right hand

Ps 103:9 He [God] will not ***a*** chide: neither...keep his anger for ever

Prov 5:19 be thou ravished ***a*** with her love

Mark 14:7 the poor with you ***a***...me [Jesus] ye have not ***a***

Luke 18:1 men ought ***a*** to pray, and not to faint

Acts 7:51 ye do ***a*** resist the Holy Ghost

Rom 1:9 I [Paul] make mention of you ***a*** in my prayers

1 Cor 1:4 I [Paul] thank my God ***a*** on your behalf

1 Cor 15:58 ***a*** abounding in the work of the Lord

2 Cor 4:10 **A** bearing about... the dying of the Lord

Eph 5:20 Giving thanks ***a*** for all things unto God

AMALEKITES (tribal enemies of the Israelites). Gen 14:7 • Num 13:29; 14:25,43–45 • Judg 6:3,33; 7:12; 10:12; 12:15 • 1 Sam 14:48; 15:6–8,15–32; 27:8; 30:1,18 • 2 Sam 1:1 • 1 Chr 4:43.

AMASA (commander of Absalom's rebel army). 2 Sam 17:25; 19:13; 20:4–12 • 1 Kgs 2:5,32 • 2 Chr 2:17.

AMAZED

Ex 15:15 dukes of Edom shall be ***a***...inhabitants of Canaan shall melt away

Matt 12:23 people were ***a***...Is not this the son of David?
Matt 19:25 disciples heard it, they were exceedingly ***a***
Mark 1:27 all ***a,*** insomuch that they questioned
Mark 2:12 all ***a***...We never saw it on this fashion
Mark 6:51 they were sore ***a***... beyond measure
Mark 9:15 people...were...***a,*** and...saluted him [Jesus]
Mark 10:32 Jesus went before them: and they were ***a***
Luke 9:43 they were all ***a*** at the...power of God
Acts 2:7 they were all ***a***...are not all these...Galilaeans?
Acts 2:12 were all ***a***...saying... What meaneth this?

AMAZIAH (a king of Judah who worshiped the false gods of Edom). 2 Kgs 12:21; 13:12; 14:1–20 • **2 Chr 25:1–28.**

AMMONITES (tribal enemies of the Israelites). Deut 2:20 • 1 Sam 11:11 • 1 Kgs 11:1,5 • 2 Chr 20:1; 26:8; 27:5 • Ezra 9:1 • Neh 4:7 • Jer 27:3; 40:11,14; 41:10,15; 49:1–2 • Ezek 21:20,28; 25:2–10.

AMNON (a son of David who was murdered by his half brother Absalom). 2 Sam 3:2; **13:1–39.**

AMON (an evil king of Judah who was assassinated by his own servants). **2 Kgs 21:18–25 • 2 Chr 33:20–25** • Jer 1:2; 25:3 • Zeph 1:1 • Matt 1:10.

AMORITES (tribal enemies of the Israelites). Gen 10:16; 14:13; 15:16,21; 48:22 • Ex 3:8,17; 13:5; 23:23; 33:2; 34:11 • Num 13:29; 21:13–34; 22:2; 32:33,39; • Deut 1:4–44; 2:24; 3:2–9; 4:46–47; 7:1; 20:17; 31:4 • Josh 2:10; 3:10; 5:1; 7:7; 9:1,10; 10:5–12; 12:2,8; 13:4,10,21; 24:8–18 • Judg 1:34–36; 3:5; 6:10; 10:8,11; 11:19–23 • 1 Sam 7:14 • 2 Sam 21:2 • 1 Kgs 4:19; 9:20; 21:26 • 2 Kgs 21:11 • 1 Chr 1:14 • 2 Chr 8:7 • Ezra 9:1 • Neh 9:8 • Pss 135:11; 136:19 • Ezek 16:3,45 • Amos 2:9,10.

AMOS (a prophet against the Northern Kingdom and author of the book that bears his name). Amos is not mentioned outside the Book of Amos.

AMOS, BOOK OF. A prophetic book of the Old Testament written to call the people of the Northern Kingdom (Israel) back to worship of the one true God. According to Amos, true religion consists of following God's commands and treating others with justice (see Amos 5:24).

AMRAPHEL (a king of Shinar in Abraham's time). Gen 14:1,9.

ANAK (ancestor of a tribe of giants). **Num 13:22–33** • Deut 9:2 • Josh 15:13–14; 21:11 • Judg 1:20.

ANAKIMS (a tribe of giants). Deut 1:28; 2:10–11,21; 9:2 • Josh 11:21–22; 14:12,15.

ANAMMELECH (a pagan god of the Babylonians). 2 Kgs 17:31.

ANANIAS

1. A believer in the early church struck dead for lying. Acts 5:1–5.

2. A believer who befriended Paul after his conversion. Acts 9:10–17; 22:12.

ANATHOTH (a village north of Jerusalem). Josh 21:18 • 1 Kgs 2:26 • 1 Chr 6:60 • Ezra 2:23 • Neh 7:27; 11:32 • Isa 10:30 • Jer 1:1; 11:21,23; 29:27; 32:7–9.

ANCIENT OF DAYS (a title of God). Dan 7:9,13,22.

ANDREW (one of the twelve disciples of Jesus). Matt 4:18; 10:2 • Mark 1:16,29; 3:18; 13:3 • Luke 6:14 • John 1:40,44; 6:8; 12:22 • Acts 1:13.

ANGEL APPEARANCES

1. To Hagar during her pregnancy with Ishmael (Gen 16:7–11)

2. To Lot (Gen 19:1)

3. To Hagar and Ishmael in the wilderness (Gen 21:17)

4. To Abraham (Gen 22: 11,15)

5. To Jacob at Haran (Gen 28:12; 31:11)

6. To Jacob at Mahanaim (Gen 32:1)

7. To Moses (Ex 3:2)

8. To Balaam (Num 22:22–35)

9. To Gideon (Judg 6:11–22)

10. To Samson's mother and father (Judg 13:3–21)

11. To Elijah (1 Kgs 19:5,7 • 2 Kgs 1:3,15)

12. To David (1 Chr 21:16)

13. To Gad (1 Chr 21:18)

14. To Ornan (1 Chr 21:20,27)

15. To Shadrach, Meshach, and Abed-nego (Dan 3:24–28)

16. To Zechariah (Zech 1:9)

17. To Joseph in Nazareth (Matt 1:20)

18. To Joseph in Bethlehem (Matt 2:13)

19. To Joseph in Egypt (Matt 2:19)

20. To Zacharias (Luke 1: 11–29)

21. To Mary (Luke 1:26–38)

22. To shepherds at Jesus' birth (Luke 2:9–14)

23. To Jesus in the Garden of Gethsemane (Luke 22:43)

24. To Jesus at the resurrection (Matt 28:2)
25. To women at the tomb (Matt 28:5)
26. To Mary Magdalene at the empty tomb (John 20:11–12)
27. To the apostles (Acts 5:19)
28. To Philip (Acts 8:26)
29. To Cornelius (Acts 10:3)
30. To Peter in prison (Acts 12:7–11)
31. To Paul (Acts 27:23–24)
32. To John on the isle of Patmos (Rev 1:1)

ANGELS

Ps 8:5 thou [God] hast made him [man] a little lower than the ***a***
Ps 148:2 Praise ye him, all his [God's] ***a***
Matt 22:30 nor are given in marriage, but are as the ***a***
Matt 25:31 Son of man shall come...holy ***a*** with him
Luke 15:10 joy in the presence of the ***a***...over one sinner that repenteth
Rom 8:38 death, nor life, nor ***a,*** nor principalities
1 Cor 13:1 tongues of men and of ***a,*** and have not charity
Heb 13:2 some have entertained ***a*** unawares

ANGER

Gen 30:2 Jacob's ***a*** was kindled against Rachel
1 Sam 11:6 spirit of God came upon Saul...***a*** was kindled
1 Sam 20:30 Saul's ***a*** was kindled against Jonathan
2 Sam 12:5 David's ***a*** was... kindled against the man
Ps 6:1 O LORD, rebuke me not in thine ***a,*** neither chasten
Ps 30:5 For his [God's] ***a*** endureth but a moment
Ps 78:58 provoked him [God] to ***a*** with their high places
Ps 103:8 LORD is merciful and gracious, slow to ***a***
Prov 15:1 but grievous words stir up ***a***
Prov 16:32 He that is slow to ***a*** is better than the mighty
Prov 21:14 A gift...pacifieth ***a:*** and a reward...wrath
Isa 63:6 I [God] will tread down the people in mine ***a***
Jer 4:8 the fierce ***a*** of the LORD is not turned back
Lam 4:16 the ***a*** of the LORD hath divided them
Mic 5:15 I [God] will execute vengeance in ***a*** and fury upon the heathen
Nah 1:3 LORD is slow to ***a***...will not...acquit the wicked
Mark 3:5 he [Jesus] looked... with ***a***...for the hardness of their hearts
Eph 4:31 wrath, and ***a***...and evil speaking, be put away
Col 3:8 put off all these; ***a,*** wrath, malice
Col 3:21 Fathers, provoke not your children to ***a***

ANGER OF THE LORD

Ex 4:14 the ***a-o-t-L*** was kindled against Moses

Num 11:10 ***a-o-t-L*** was kindled...Moses also was displeased

Num 25:3 the ***a-o-t-L*** was kindled against Israel

2 Sam 6:7 the ***a-o-t-L*** was kindled against Uzzah

2 Sam 24:1 the ***a-o-t-L*** was... against Israel and he moved David against them

2 Kgs 24:20 through the ***a-o-t-L***...Zedekiah rebelled against...Babylon

2 Chr 25:15 the ***a-o-t-L*** was kindled against Amaziah

Jer 4:8 the fierce ***a-o-t-L*** is not turned back

Jer 12:13 be ashamed...because of the fierce ***a-o-t-L***

Jer 51:45 deliver ye every man his soul from the...***a-o-t-L***

ANGUISH

Job 15:24 ***a*** shall make him afraid; they shall prevail

Ps 119:143 ***a*** have taken...me: yet thy [God's] commandments are my delights

John 16:21 delivered of the child, she remembereth no more the ***a***

Rom 2:9 and ***a,*** upon every soul of man that doeth evil

2 Cor 2:4 and ***a***...I [Paul] wrote...with many tears

ANNA (a prophetess who praised the infant Jesus). Luke 2:36–38.

ANNAS (a high priest during Jesus' ministry). Luke 3:2 • John 18:13,24 • Acts 4:6.

ANNUNCIATION OF JESUS' BIRTH TO JOSEPH. Matt 1:18–25.

ANNUNCIATION OF JESUS' BIRTH TO MARY. Luke 1:26–38.

ANOINT [ED, EST, ING]

Ex 30:30 ***a*** Aaron and his sons, and consecrate them

Ex 40:15 ***a*** them [Aaron's sons]...that they may minister...in the priest's office

Lev 8:10 Moses...***a'ed*** the tabernacle...and sanctified them

Lev 8:12 the ***a'ing*** oil upon Aaron's head...sanctify him

Judg 9:8 trees went forth...to ***a*** a king over them

1 Sam 15:1 LORD sent me [Samuel] to ***a*** thee [Saul]

1 Sam 16:13 Samuel...***a'ed*** him [David] in the midst of his brethren

2 Sam 2:4 they ***a'ed*** David king over the house of Judah

1 Kgs 19:15 ***a*** Hazael to be king over Syria

2 Chr 6:42 turn not away... thine ***a'ed:*** remember... David

Ps 20:6 LORD saveth his ***a'ed;*** he will hear...from... heaven

Ps 23:5 thou [God] ***a'est*** my head with oil

Isa 45:1 Thus saith the LORD to his ***a'ed,*** to Cyrus

Isa 61:1 LORD hath ***a'ed*** me [God's servant]...to proclaim liberty

Mark 14:8 come...to ***a*** my [Jesus'] body to...burying

Mark 16:1 bought...spices, that they [women] might... ***a*** him [Jesus]

Luke 7:46 this woman hath ***a'ed*** my [Jesus'] feet

John 9:6 he [Jesus] ***a'ed*** the eyes of the blind man

John 12:3 Mary...***a'ed*** the feet of Jesus

Heb 1:9 hath ***a'ed*** thee with the oil of gladness

Jas 5:14 ***a'ing*** him with oil in the name of the Lord

ANSWER

Job 31:35 that the Almighty would ***a*** me [Job]

Ps 27:7 have mercy...upon me, and ***a*** me

Ps 86:7 I will call upon thee [God]...thou wilt ***a*** me

Prov 15:1 A soft ***a*** turneth away wrath

Prov 26:4 **A** not a fool according to his folly

Jer 33:3 I [God] will ***a*** thee, and show thee great... things

Luke 21:14 not to meditate before what ye shall ***a***

1 Pet 3:15 give an ***a*** to every man that asketh you a reason

1 Pet 3:21 baptism...the ***a*** of a good conscience toward God

ANTICHRIST (the archenemy of Christ). 1 John 2:18,22; 4:3 • 2 John 7.

ANTIOCH

1. A city in Syria. Acts 6:5; 11:19–27; 13:1; 14:26; 15:22–35; 18:22 • Gal 2:11.

2. A city in Pisidia. Acts 13:14; 14:19,21 • 2 Tim 3:11.

APOLLOS (a Jewish believer from Alexandria, Egypt). Acts 18:24; 19:1 • 1 Cor 3:4–6,22; 4:6; 16:12 • Titus 3:13.

APOSTLE [S]

Matt 10:2 names of the twelve ***a's*** are these

Mark 6:30 ***a's*** gathered...and told him [Jesus] all things

Luke 6:13 he [Jesus] chose twelve...he named ***a's***

Acts 1:26 Matthias...numbered with the eleven ***a's***

Acts 2:42 they continued stedfastly in the ***a's'*** doctrine

Acts 2:43 many wonders and signs were done by the ***a's***

Acts 5:18 laid their hands on the ***a's***...put them in... prison
Acts 8:1 they [believers] were... scattered...except the ***a's***
Rom 1:1 Paul, a servant... called to be an ***a***
Rom 11:13 I [Paul] am the ***a*** of the Gentiles
1 Cor 1:1 Paul, called to be an ***a*** of Jesus Christ
1 Cor 9:1 Am I [Paul] not an ***a?*** am I not free?
1 Cor 12:28 in the church, first ***a's,*** secondarily prophets
1 Cor 12:29 Are all ***a's?*** are all prophets? are all teachers?
1 Cor 15:9 I [Paul] am the least of the ***a's***
2 Cor 11:13 transforming themselves into...***a's*** of Christ
2 Cor 12:12 signs of an ***a*** were wrought among you
Eph 2:20 built upon the foundation of the ***a's***
Eph 4:11 gave some, ***a's;*** and some, prophets
Heb 3:1 ***A*** and High Priest of our profession, Christ Jesus

APPEAR [ED, ETH, ING]
Gen 1:9 let the dry land ***a:*** and it was so
Gen 12:7 the LORD ***a'ed*** unto Abram...Unto thy seed will I give this land
Gen 35:9 God ***a'ed*** unto Jacob...and blessed him
Ex 3:2 Angel...***a'ed*** unto him [Moses] in a flame
Ex 16:10 the glory of the LORD ***a'ed*** in the cloud
1 Sam 3:21 LORD ***a'ed*** again... revealed himself to Samuel
1 Kgs 9:2 LORD ***a'ed*** to Solomon...as he had...at Gibeon
2 Kgs 2:11 ***a'ed*** a chariot...Elijah went...by a whirlwind
Ps 42:2 when shall I come and ***a*** before God?
Ps 102:16 the LORD...shall ***a*** in his glory
Song 2:12 The flowers ***a*** on the earth
Mal 3:2 who shall stand when he [God] ***a'eth?***
Matt 2:13 ***a'eth***...take the... child...and flee into Egypt
Matt 2:19 Herod was dead... the Lord ***a'eth***...to Joseph
Matt 17:3 ***a'ed***...Moses and Elias talking with him [Jesus]
Matt 23:27 whited sepulchres, which...***a*** beautiful outward
Matt 24:30 then shall ***a*** the sign of the Son of man
Mark 16:9 Jesus...***a'ed*** first to Mary Magdalene
Mark 16:12 he [Jesus] ***a'ed*** in another form...two of them
Mark 16:14 he [Jesus] ***a'ed*** unto...eleven as they sat at meat
Luke 1:11 there ***a'ed*** unto him [Zacharias] an angel
Luke 24:34 The Lord...hath ***a'ed*** to Simon

Acts 2:3 there ***a'ed*** unto them cloven tongues like as of fire
2 Cor 5:10 all ***a*** before the judgment seat of Christ
Col 3:4 then shall ye also ***a*** with him [Jesus]
1 Tim 6:14 keep this commandment...until the ***a'ing*** of our Lord Jesus Christ
2 Tim 1:10 made manifest by the ***a'ing*** of our Saviour
2 Tim 4:1 judge the quick and the dead at his ***a'ing***
2 Tim 4:8 unto all them...that love his [Jesus'] ***a'ing***
Titus 2:13 the glorious ***a'ing*** of...our Saviour
Jas 4:14 It [life] is...a vapour, that ***a'eth*** for a little time
1 Pet 5:4 chief Shepherd shall ***a***, ye shall receive a crown

APPII FORUM (a place south of Rome where believers greeted Paul). Acts 28:15.

APPOINT [ED]
Num 1:50 ***a*** the Levites over the tabernacle of testimony
Josh 20:2 **A** out for you cities of refuge
Job 14:5 thou hast ***a'ed*** his bounds that he cannot pass
Ps 104:19 He [God] ***a'ed*** the moon for seasons
Isa 1:14 your ***a'ed*** feasts my [God's] soul hateth
Luke 10:1 Lord ***a'ed*** other... and sent them two and two
Acts 6:3 seven men...whom we may ***a*** over this business
1 Thes 5:9 God hath not ***a'ed*** us to wrath, but to... salvation
2 Tim 1:11 I [Paul] am ***a'ed*** a preacher, and an apostle
Heb 1:2 whom he [God] hath ***a'ed*** heir [Jesus] of all things
Heb 9:27 ***a'ed***...once to die, but after this the judgment

APPROVED
Acts 2:22 Jesus of Nazareth, a man ***a***...by miracles
2 Tim 2:15 Study to show thyself ***a*** unto God

AQUILA (a believer who worked with Paul at Corinth). Acts 18:2,18,26 • Rom 16:3 • 1 Cor 16:19 • 2 Tim 4:19.

ARABAH (the Jordan River valley). Josh 18:18.

ARAM. See *Syria*.

ARARAT (a mountainous region in Armenia where Noah's ark came to rest). **Gen 8:4** • Jer 51:27.

ARAUNAH (a Jebusite from whom David bought a threshing floor). 2 Sam 24:16–24. *Ornan:* 1 Chr 21:15–28 • 2 Chr 3:1.

ARCHANGEL (a chief angel). 1 Thes 4:16 • Jude 9.

AREOPAGUS (a meeting place in Athens). Acts 17:19.

ARIEL (a name for Jerusalem). Isa 29:1–7.

ARIMATHAEA (a city northwest of Jerusalem). Matt 27:57 • Mark 15:43 • Luke 23:51 • John 19:38.

ARISE

Josh 1:2 now therefore ***a,*** go over this Jordan

Ps 7:6 **A,** O LORD...because of the rage of mine enemies

Ps 82:8 **A,** O God, judge the earth...inherit all nations

Prov 31:28 Her children ***a*** up, and call her blessed

Isa 60:1 **A,** shine; for thy light is come

Jer 18:2 **A**...go down to the potter's house...hear my [God's] words

Dan 7:17 Beasts...are four kings...***a*** out of the earth

Jon 1:2 **A,** go to Nineveh, that great city...cry against it

Mal 4:2 shall the Sun of righteousness ***a*** with healing in his wings

Matt 2:13 angel...appeareth to Joseph...saying, **A**...take the young child

Matt 24:24 there shall ***a*** false Christs, and false prophets

Mark 5:41 Damsel, I [Jesus] say unto thee, ***a***

Luke 5:24 I [Jesus] say...**A**... take up thy couch

Luke 15:18 ***a*** and go to my father...I have sinned

Luke 17:19 he [Jesus] said... **A,** go thy way: thy faith hath made thee whole

Acts 11:7 **A,** Peter; slay and eat

Acts 20:30 men ***a,*** speaking perverse things

ARISTARCHUS (a companion of Paul). Acts 19:29; 20:4; 27:2 • Col 4:10 • Phlm 24.

ARK OF MOSES (a basket in which the infant Moses was placed). Ex 2:3,5.

ARK OF NOAH (a wooden ship in which Noah's family escaped from the flood). **Gen 6:12–9:18** • Matt 24:38 • Luke 17:27 • 1 Pet 3:20.

ARK OF THE COVENANT (a wooden chest containing a pot of manna, Aaron's rod that budded, and stone tablets on which the Ten Commandments were inscribed). **Ex 25:10–22** • Num 10:33 • Deut 10:8; 31:9,25 • Josh 3:3–17; 4:7–18; 6:6–8; 8:33 • Judg 20:27 • 1 Sam 4:3–5 • 2 Sam 15:24 • 1 Kgs 3:15; 6:19; 8:1,6 • 1 Chr 15:25–29; 16:6,37; 17:1; 22:19; 28:2,18 • 2 Chr 5:2–7 • Jer

3:16. *Ark of the testimony:* Ex 25:22 • Num 7:89 • Josh 4:16.

ARK OF THE TESTIMONY. See *Ark of the Covenant.*

ARM OF THE LORD
Isa 51:9 O ***a-o-t-L;*** awake, as in the ancient days
Isa 53:1 to whom is the ***a-o-t-L*** revealed?

ARMAGEDDON (scene of the final conflict between God and the forces of evil). Rev 16:16.

ARNON (a river in southern Palestine). Num 21:13–28; 22:36 • Deut 2:24,36; 3:12,16; 4:48 • Josh 12:1–2; 13:9,16 • Judg 11:13–26 • 2 Kgs 10:33 • Isa 16:2 • Jer 48:20.

ARTAXERXES I (the Persian king in whose court Ezra and Nehemiah served). Ezra 4:7–23; 8:1 • Neh 2:1; 5:14; 13:6.

ASA (a king of Judah who led a religious revival). 1 Kgs 15:8–33; 16:8–29 • **2 Chr 14:1–13;** 15:2–19; 16:1–13 • Jer 41:9 • Matt 1:7–8.

ASAHEL (a captain in David's army). 2 Sam 2:18–32; 3:27,30; 23:24 • 1 Chr 2:16; 11:26; 27:7.

ASCEND [ED, ING]
Gen 28:12 ladder...the angels... ***a'ing*** and descending
Josh 10:7 Joshua ***a'ed*** from Gilgal, he...all the people of war
Ps 24:3 who shall ***a*** into the hill of the LORD
Ps 68:18 Thou hast ***a'ed*** on high...led captivity captive
Luke 19:28 he [Jesus] went before, ***a'ing*** up to Jerusalem
John 1:51 angels of God ***a'ing***...upon the Son of man
John 6:62 see the Son of man ***a*** up where he was before
John 20:17 I [Jesus] am not yet ***a'ed*** to my Father
Eph 4:8 he [Jesus] ***a'ed*** up on high, he led captivity captive

ASCENSION OF JESUS. See *Jesus, Life and Ministry of.*

ASENATH (Joseph's Egyptian wife). Gen 41:45,50; 46:20.

ASER. See *Asher.*

ASHAMED
Gen 2:25 both naked, the man and his wife, and were not ***a***
Ps 31:17 Let me not be ***a***...for I have called upon thee [God]
Joel 2:27 your God...and my people shall never be ***a***
Mark 8:38 of him also shall the Son of man be ***a***

Rom 1:16 I [Paul] am not ***a*** of the gospel of Christ
Rom 10:11 Whosoever believeth on him [Jesus] shall not be ***a***
2 Tim 2:15 a workman that needeth not to be ***a***
1 John 2:28 not be ***a*** before him [Jesus] at his coming

ASHDOD (a major Philistine city). Josh 11:22; 15:46–47 • 1 Sam 5:1–7; 6:17 • 2 Chr 26:6 • Neh 13:23–24 • Isa 20:1 • Jer 25:20 • Amos 1:8; 3:9 • Zeph 2:4 • Zech 9:6.

ASHER (a son of Jacob and ancestor of one of the twelve tribes of Israel). Gen 30:13; 35:26; 46:17; 49:20 • Ex 1:4 • Num 26:46 • 1 Chr 2:2; 7:30,40. The tribe of Asher settled in northern Canaan. Josh 19:24–31. *Aser:* Luke 2:36.

ASHES
Job 2:8 he [Job] took...a potsherd to scrape himself... among the ***a***
Isa 61:3 to give unto them beauty for ***a***
Jer 25:34 Howl, ye shepherds... and wallow...in the ***a***

ASHIMA (a pagan god of Hamath). 2 Kgs 17:30.

ASHKELON (a major Philistine city). Judg 14:19 • Jer 25:20; 47:5,7 • Amos 1:8 • Zeph 2:4,7 • Zech 9:5. *Askelon:* Judg 1:18.

ASHTAROTH (a pagan goddess of the Philistines). Judg 2:13; 10:6 • 1 Sam 7:3–4; 12:10; 31:10. *Ashtoreth:* 1 Kgs 11:33.

ASIA (a Roman province in Asia Minor). Acts 2:9; 6:9; 16:6; 19:10,22,26–27,31; 20:4,16,18 • 1 Cor 16:19 • 2 Cor 1:8 • 2 Tim 1:15 • 1 Pet 1:1 • Rev 1:4,11.

ASK [ED]
Josh 4:6 your children ***a***... What mean...these stones?
Judg 1:1 Israel ***a'ed***...Who shall go up...against the Canaanites
1 Kgs 3:5 LORD appeared to Solomon in a dream...***A*** what I shall give thee
Ps 105:40 people ***a'ed,*** and he [God] brought quails
Jer 37:17 king ***a'ed*** him [Jeremiah]...Is there any word from the LORD
Matt 6:8 Father knoweth what...ye...need...before ye ***a***
Matt 7:7 ***A,*** and it shall be given you
Matt 7:9 if his son ***a*** bread, will he give him a stone
Matt 18:19 any thing...they shall ***a,*** it shall be done
Matt 21:22 ye shall ***a***...believing, ye shall receive

Mark 14:61 high priest ***a'ed*** him [Jesus]...Art thou the Christ

Mark 15:2 Pilate ***a'ed*** him [Jesus], Art thou the King of the Jews

Luke 11:13 Your...Father give the Holy Spirit to them that ***a*** him

John 14:14 ***a*** any thing in my [Jesus'] name, I will do it

John 16:24 ***a,*** and ye shall receive...your joy may be full

Eph 3:20 exceeding abundantly above all that we ***a***

Jas 1:5 If any of you lack wisdom, let him ***a*** of God

Jas 4:2 yet ye have not, because ye ***a*** not

1 John 5:14 ***a***...according to his [God's] will, he heareth

ASKELON. See *Ashkelon.*

ASNAPPER (an Assyrian king). Ezra 4:10.

ASSHUR. See *Assyria.*

ASSUR. See *Assyria.*

ASSYRIA (a dominant power in the ancient world which overthrew the Northern Kingdom, enslaved many of its inhabitants, and resettled the region with foreigners). **2 Kgs 18:9–37;** 19:35–37 • Isa 7–8; 10:12; 14:24–25 • Hos 10:6 • Nah 3:1–19. *Asshur:* Gen 10:11; Num 24:22–24. *Assur:* Ezra 4:2.

ATHALIAH (a daughter of Ahab and Jezebel who seized the throne as queen of Judah). 2 Kgs 8:26; **11:1–20** • 2 Chr 22:2–12; 23:12–21.

ATHENS (capital city of ancient Greece and the idolatrous city where Paul preached to the philosophers). **Acts 17:15–22;** 18:1 • 1 Thes 3:1.

ATONEMENT

Ex 29:36 offer...a bullock for a sin offering for ***a***

Num 15:25 priest shall make an ***a*** for all...Israel

ATTAIN [ED]

Ps 139:6 knowledge is too wonderful...I cannot ***a***...it

Phil 3:11 I [Paul] might ***a*** unto the resurrection of the dead

Phil 3:12 as though I [Paul] had already ***a'ed***

Phil 3:16 already ***a'ed,*** let us walk by the same rule

1 Tim 4:6 nourished up in... faith and of good doctrine whereunto thou hast ***a'ed***

ATTEND

Ps 17:1 O LORD, ***a*** unto my cry, give ear unto my prayer

Ps 86:6 O LORD...***a*** to...my supplications

Prov 4:1 Hear...the instruction of a father, and ***a*** to know understanding

AUGUSTUS (emperor of the Roman Empire at the time when Jesus was born). **Luke 2:1** • Acts 25:21,25; 27:1.

AUTHORITY

Prov 29:2 When the righteous are in ***a,*** the people rejoice

Matt 8:9 I am a man under ***a,*** having soldiers under me

Matt 20:25 they that are great exercise ***a*** upon them

Matt 21:23 who gave thee [Jesus] this ***a***

Matt 21:27 Neither tell I you by what ***a*** I [Jesus] do these things

Mark 1:22 he [Jesus] taught them as one that had ***a***

Luke 9:1 he [Jesus] called his... disciples...gave them...***a*** over all devils

1 Cor 15:24 when he [Jesus] shall have put down... all ***a***

1 Tim 2:12 suffer not a woman...to usurp ***a*** over the man

AVEN. See *On,* No. 2.

AZARIAH. See *Abed-nego; Ahaziah,* No. 2; *Uzziah.*

AZZAH. See *Gaza.*

-B-

BAAL (a pagan Canaanite god of rain thought to provide fertility for crops and livestock and worshiped on occasion during Old Testament times by the Israelites). Num 22:41 • Judg 2:13; 6:25–32 • 1 Kgs 16:31–32; 18:19–40; 19:18; 22:53 • 2 Kgs 10:18–28; 11:18; 17:16; 21:3–4 • 2 Chr 23:17 • Jer 2:8; 7:9; 11:13,17; 12:16; 19:5; 23:13; 32:29,35 • Hos 2:8; 13:1 • Zeph 1:4. *Baalim:* 1 Sam 12:10.

BAALAH. See *Kirjath-jearim.*

BAAL-BERITH (a name under which the Canaanite god Baal was worshiped at Shechem). Judg 8:33; 9:4. *Berith:* Judg 9:46.

BAAL-PEOR (a name under which the Canaanite god Baal was worshiped by the Moabites). Num 25:1–9 • Deut 4:3–4 • Ps 106:28–29 • Hos 9:10. *Peor:* Num 31:1–18 • Josh 22:17.

BAAL-ZEBUB (a name under which the Canaanite god Baal was worshiped by the Philistines). 2 Kgs 1:2–16. *Beelzebub:* Matt 10:25; 12:24.

BAASHA (a king of the Northern Kingdom who gained the throne by murdering the heirs of King Jeroboam). **1 Kgs 15:16–33;** 16:1–13 • 2 Kgs 9:9 • 2 Chr 16:1–6 • Jer 41:9.

BABEL, TOWER OF. See *Tower of Babel.*

BABE [S]

Ps 8:2 Out of the mouth of ***b's*** and sucklings hast thou [God] ordained strength

Matt 21:16 Out of the mouth of ***b's*** and sucklings thou [God] hast perfected praise

Luke 1:41 when Elisabeth heard...Mary, the ***b*** leaped in her womb

Luke 2:16 Mary, and Joseph, and the ***b*** lying in a manger

1 Pet 2:2 As newborn ***b's,*** desire the...milk of the word

BABYLON (capital city of the Babylonian Empire). Citizens of the Southern Kingdom (Judah) were taken to Babylon as captives after the fall of Jerusalem in 587 B.C. (2 Chr 36:5–21). Most references to Babylon appear in the books of 2 Kings, Jeremiah, Ezekiel, and Daniel. In the Book of Revelation, Babylon is a symbol of evil and wickedness (Rev 14:8; 16:19; 17:5; 18:2,10,21).

BABYLONIA (a powerful nation that carried the Southern Kingdom [Judah] into exile about 587 B.C.). The Babylonians were defeated by the Persians about 539 B.C., fulfilling the prophecies of Isaiah and Jeremiah. **2 Chr 36:5–21** • Isa 14:22 • Jer 50:9. *Land of the Chaldeans:* Ezek 12:13. *Sheshach:* Jer 25:26. *Shinar:* Isa 11:11.

BACK [S]

Gen 19:26 But his [Lot's] wife looked ***b***...and she became a pillar of salt
Ex 14:21 LORD caused the sea to go ***b*** by a strong...wind
Josh 7:8 Israel turneth their ***b's*** before their enemies
2 Sam 12:23 can I [David] bring him [David's child] ***b***
Neh 9:26 they [the Israelites] were disobedient...cast thy [God's] law behind their ***b's***
Job 39:22 neither turneth he [God] ***b*** from the sword
Ps 35:4 let them be turned ***b*** and brought to confusion
Ps 44:18 Our heart is not turned ***b***
Prov 10:13 a rod is for the ***b*** of him...void of understanding
Prov 26:3 a bridle for the ass, and a rod for the fool's ***b***
Isa 14:27 who shall turn it [God's hand] ***b***
Isa 38:17 thou [God] hast cast all my sins behind thy ***b***
Jer 4:8 anger of the LORD is not turned ***b*** from us
Ezek 23:35 thou hast...cast me [God] behind thy ***b***
Dan 7:6 a leopard, which had upon the ***b*** of it four wings
Matt 24:18 Neither let him... return ***b*** to take his clothes
Luke 9:62 No man...looking ***b,*** is fit for the kingdom
John 6:66 many of his [Jesus'] disciples went ***b***
Acts 20:20 I [Paul] kept ***b*** nothing...profitable unto you

BACKSLIDER

Prov 14:14 The ***b*** in heart shall be filled with his own ways

BACKSLIDING [S]

Jer 3:14 Turn, O ***b*** children, saith the LORD
Jer 14:7 our ***b's*** are many; we have sinned
Hos 4:16 For Israel slideth back as a ***b*** heifer
Hos 14:4 I [God] will heal their ***b***...love them freely

BALAAM (a soothsayer or wizard hired by King Balak of Moab to curse the Israelites). **Num 22:1–24:25** • Deut 23:4–5 • Josh 13:22; 24:9–10 • Mic 6:5 • 2 Pet 2:15 • Jude 11 • Rev 2:14.

BALAC. See *Balak.*

BALAK (a king of Moab who hired Balaam the soothsayer to curse the Israelites). **Num 22:1–24:25** • Josh 24:9 • Judg 11:25 • Mic 6:5. *Balac:* Rev 2:14.

BALANCE [S]

Lev 19:36 Just ***b's,*** just weights, a just ephah

Job 31:6 Let me be weighed in an even ***b***

Prov 11:1 A false ***b*** is abomination to the LORD

Isa 40:12 Who [God] hath measured...the hills in a ***b***

Dan 5:27 Thou [Belshazzar] art weighed in the ***b's,*** and art found wanting

Amos 8:5 making the ephah small...falsifying the ***b's***

Rev 6:5 he that sat on him [a black horse] had a pair of ***b's*** in his hand

BALM OF GILEAD (an aromatic gum, used for medicinal purposes, exported from Gilead in Arabia). Jer 8:22.

BAND [S]

Lev 26:13 I [God] have broken the ***b's*** of your yoke

Ps 119:61 The ***b's*** of the wicked have robbed me

Jer 2:20 I [God] have broken thy yoke, and burst thy ***b's***

Hos 11:4 I [God] drew them... with ***b's*** of love

Matt 27:27 the soldiers...gathered unto him [Jesus] the whole ***b*** of soldiers

Luke 8:29 he [wild man among the tombs] brake the ***b's***

John 18:12 the ***b***...took Jesus, and bound him

Acts 10:1 Cornelius, a centurion of the ***b*** called...Italian ***b***

Acts 16:26 prison...doors were opened, and every one's ***b's*** were loosed

BAPTISM

Matt 20:22 Are ye [James and John] able...to be baptized with the ***b*** that I [Jesus] am baptized with

Matt 21:25 The ***b*** of John, whence was it

Mark 1:4 John did...preach the ***b*** of repentance

Luke 12:50 I [Jesus] have a ***b*** to be baptized with

Rom 6:4 we are buried with him [Jesus] by ***b*** into death

Eph 4:5 One Lord, one faith, one ***b***

Col 2:12 Buried with him [Jesus] in ***b***

1 Pet 3:21 The like figure whereunto even ***b*** doth also now save us

BAPTISM OF JESUS. See *Jesus, Life and Ministry of.*

BAPTISM OF REPENTANCE

Luke 3:3 he [John the Baptist] came...preaching the ***b-o-r*** for the remission of sins

Acts 13:24 John...preached... the ***b-o-r*** to all the people

Acts 19:4 Then said Paul, John verily baptized with the ***b-o-r***

BAPTIZE [D, ING]

Matt 3:11 he [Jesus] shall ***b*** you with the Holy Ghost

Matt 3:13 Then cometh Jesus... unto John, to be ***b'd*** of him

Matt 28:19 Go...and teach all nations, ***b'ing*** them in the name of the Father

Mark 1:8 but he [Jesus] shall ***b*** you with the Holy Ghost

Mark 16:16 He that believeth and is ***b'd*** shall be saved

Luke 3:7 Then said he [John the Baptist] to the multitude that came forth to be ***b'd***

John 1:28 Bethabara beyond Jordan...John was ***b'ing***

John 3:22 he [Jesus] tarried... and ***b'd***

John 3:23 John also was ***b'ing*** in Aenon near to Salim

John 4:1 Jesus made and ***b'd*** more disciples than John

Acts 1:5 ye shall be ***b'd*** with the Holy Ghost

Acts 2:38 Repent, and be ***b'd***... in the name of Jesus

Acts 2:41 they that gladly received his [Peter's] word were ***b'd***

Acts 8:12 they [the Samaritans] were ***b'd,*** both men and women

Acts 8:36 what doth hinder me [the eunuch] to be ***b'd***

Acts 9:18 he [Paul] received sight...arose, and was ***b'd***

Acts 16:15 she [Lydia] was ***b'd,*** and her household

Acts 16:33 he [Philippian jailer]...was ***b'd,*** he and all his

Acts 22:16 arise, and be ***b'd,*** and wash away thy sins

Rom 6:3 so many of us as were ***b'd*** into Jesus Christ were ***b'd*** into his death

1 Cor 1:13 or were ye ***b'd*** in the name of Paul

1 Cor 1:17 Christ sent me [Paul] not to ***b,*** but to preach the gospel

1 Cor 12:13 by one Spirit are we all ***b'd*** into one body

1 Cor 15:29 what shall they do which are ***b'd*** for the dead

Gal 3:27 as many of you as have been ***b'd*** into Christ have put on Christ

BARABBAS (a notorious murderer and insurrectionist released by Pilate during the trial of Jesus). Matt 27:16–26 • Mark 15:7–15 • Luke 23:18 • John 18:40.

BARAK (a general who led the judge Deborah to victory over the Canaanites). **Judg 4:1–24** • Heb 11:32.

BARBARIAN (a word used by the Greeks to designate uncouth foreigners or citizens of other nations besides Greece). Acts 28:4 • Rom 1:14 • 1 Cor 14:11 • Col 3:11.

BAR-JESUS (a false prophet who opposed Paul and Silas). Acts 13:6–12. *Elymas:* Acts 13:8.

BARNABAS (a believer who befriended Paul and accompanied him on the first missionary journey). Acts 4:36–37; 9:27; 11:22–30; 12:25; **13:1–14:28;** 15:2–39 • 1 Cor 9:6 • Gal 2: 1,9,13. *Joses:* Acts 4:36.

BARREN

Gen 11:30 But Sarai was ***b;*** she had no child

Gen 29:31 he [God] opened her [Leah's] womb...Rachel was ***b***

Ps 113:9 He [God] maketh the ***b*** woman to keep house

Luke 1:7 Elisabeth was ***b,*** and...well stricken in years

Luke 23:29 Blessed are the ***b***... wombs that never bare

2 Pet 1:8 ye shall neither be ***b*** nor unfruitful in the knowledge of our Lord

BARTHOLOMEW (one of the twelve apostles of Jesus). Matt 10:3 • Mark 3:18 • Luke 6:14 • Acts 1:13. Probably the same person as *Nathanael:* John 1:45–46.

BARTIMAEUS (a blind beggar healed by Jesus). Mark 10:46–52.

BARUCH (friend and scribe of the prophet Jeremiah). Jer 32:12–16; 36:4–32; 43:1–7; 45:1–2.

BARZILLAI (a friend who helped King David during his flight from Absalom). **2 Sam 17:27–29;** 19:31–39 • 1 Kgs 2:7.

BASHAN (a fertile plain east of the Jordan River allotted to the half-tribe of Manasseh after the conquest of Canaan). Num 21:33–35 • Deut 3:13; 29:7 • Josh 13:11–12 • 2 Kgs 10:32–33 • Neh 9:22 • Ps 22:12 • Ezek 39:18 • Amos 4:1.

BASKET [S]

Gen 40:18 Joseph answered... The three ***b's*** are three days

Jer 24:2 One ***b*** had very good figs...like...figs...first ripe

Amos 8:1 and behold a ***b*** of summer fruit

Matt 14:20 they [the disciples] took up of the fragments

that remained twelve ***b's*** full

Mark 8:20 how many ***b's*** full of fragments took ye [the disciples] up

Acts 9:25 the disciples...let him [Paul] down...in a ***b***

BATH-SHEBA (wife of Uriah who committed adultery with David and became his wife). **2 Sam 11:1–27;** 12:24 • 1 Kgs 1:11,15–31; 2:13–25. *Bath-shua:* 1 Chr 3:5.

BATH-SHUA. See *Bath-sheba.*

BE STRONG

Deut 31:6 ***B-s*** and of a good courage, fear not

Josh 10:25 Joshua said...***b-s*** and of good courage

1 Chr 28:10 chosen thee [Solomon] to build an house for the sanctuary: ***b-s***...do it

Isa 35:4 ***B-s***...your God will come with vengeance

Hag 2:4 **b-s,** all ye people of the land, saith the LORD

1 Cor 16:13 stand fast in the faith...***b-s***

Eph 6:10 ***b-s*** in the Lord, and in the power of his might

2 Tim 2:1 ***b-s*** in the grace that is in Christ Jesus

BEAM

1 Sam 17:7 the staff of his [Goliath's] spear was like a weaver's ***b***

Matt 7:3 why...considerest not the ***b***...in thine own eye

Luke 6:42 cast out first the ***b*** out of thine own eye

BEAR [ETH, ING]

Gen 4:13 Cain said unto the LORD, My punishment is greater than I can ***b***

Gen 16:11 thou [Hagar]...shalt ***b*** a son...Ishmael

Gen 17:19 Sarah thy [Abraham's] wife shall ***b***...a son

Ex 20:16 shalt not ***b*** false witness against thy neighbour

Ex 37:5 he [Bezaleel] put... staves into...rings by... sides of...ark, to ***b*** the ark

Lev 16:22 the goat shall ***b*** upon him all their iniquities

Lev 19:18 Thou shalt not avenge, nor ***b*** any grudge

Num 11:14 I [Moses] am not able to ***b*** all this people alone

Num 14:27 How long shall I [God] ***b*** with this evil congregation

Deut 5:20 Neither shalt thou ***b*** false witness against thy neighbour

Deut 32:11 As an eagle...***b'eth*** them [her young] on her wings

Ps 91:12 They shall ***b*** thee up... lest thou dash thy foot against a stone

Ps 126:6 goeth forth and weepeth, ***b'ing*** precious seed

Prov 25:18 A man that ***b'eth*** false witness against his neighbour is a maul

Isa 7:14 a virgin shall...***b*** a son...call his name Immanuel

Isa 46:4 I [God] will ***b***...and will deliver you

Ezek 4:6 thou [Ezekiel] shalt ***b*** the iniquity of...Judah

Ezek 18:20 neither shall the father ***b***...iniquity of the son

Ezek 36:7 the heathen...shall ***b*** their shame

Mic 7:9 I will ***b*** the indignation of the Lord

Matt 3:11 whose [Jesus'] shoes I [John the Baptist] am not worthy to ***b***

Mark 15:21 compel one Simon...to ***b*** his [Jesus'] cross

Luke 4:11 they [angels] shall ***b*** thee [Jesus] up, lest...thou dash thy foot against a stone

Luke 13:9 if it ***b*** fruit, well: and if not...cut it down

Luke 14:27 whosoever doth not ***b*** his cross...cannot be my disciple

Luke 22:10 there shall a man meet you [the disciples], ***b'ing*** a pitcher

John 1:7 came for a witness, to ***b*** witness of the Light

John 5:31 If I [Jesus] ***b*** witness of myself, my witness is not true

John 8:18 Father that sent me [Jesus] ***b'eth*** witness of me

John 10:25 the works that I [Jesus] do...***b*** witness of me

John 15:8 Herein is my [Jesus'] Father glorified, that ye ***b*** much fruit

John 16:12 many things to say unto you, but ye cannot ***b*** them

John 19:17 he [Jesus] ***b'ing*** his cross went forth into...the place of a skull

Acts 9:15 he [Paul] is a chosen vessel...to ***b*** my [Jesus'] name before the Gentiles

Rom 8:16 The Spirit itself ***b'eth*** witness with our spirit

Rom 15:1 We then that are strong ought to ***b*** the infirmities of the weak

1 Cor 13:7 [charity] ***b'eth*** all things, believeth all things

2 Cor 4:10 ***b'ing*** about...the dying of the Lord Jesus

2 Cor 11:1 Would to God ye could ***b*** with me [Paul] a little in my folly

Gal 6:2 ***B*** ye one another's burdens, and so fulfil the law of Christ

Gal 6:17 I [Paul] ***b*** in my body the marks of the Lord Jesus

Heb 9:28 Christ was once offered to ***b*** the sins of many

Heb 13:13 Let us go forth... ***b'ing*** his [Jesus'] reproach

1 John 5:6 it is the Spirit that ***b'eth*** witness, because the Spirit is truth

1 John 5:7 three that ***b*** record in heaven, the Father, the Word, and the Holy Ghost

BEAR FALSE WITNESS

Ex 20:16 Thou shalt not ***b-f-w*** against thy neighbour

Deut 5:20 Neither shalt thou ***b-f-w*** against thy neighbour

Matt 19:18 Thou shalt not steal, Thou shalt not ***b-f-w***

Rom 13:9 Thou shalt not ***b-f-w,*** Thou shalt not covet

BEAR FRUIT

Isa 37:31 remnant...of the house of Judah shall...***b-f***

Luke 13:9 if it ***b-f,*** well: and if not...cut it down

John 15:4 branch cannot ***b-f*** of itself, except it abide in... vine

BEAT [ETH, ING]

Prov 23:14 ***b*** him with the rod...deliver his soul from hell

Isa 2:4 they shall ***b*** their swords into plowshares

Isa 3:15 What mean ye that ye ***b*** my [God's] people to pieces...grind the...poor

Joel 3:10 ***B*** your plowshares into swords

Jon 4:8 the sun ***b*** upon the head of Jonah

Matt 7:25 the winds blew, and ***b*** upon that house

Mark 4:37 the waves ***b*** into the ship, so that it was now full

Mark 12:5 him they killed, and many others; ***b'ing*** some

Acts 16:22 the magistrates... commanded to ***b*** them [Paul and Silas]

Acts 22:19 I [Paul] imprisoned and ***b***...them that believed on thee [Jesus]

1 Cor 9:26 so fight I [Paul], not as one that ***b'eth*** the air

BEATITUDES. Matt 5:3–11.

BEAUTIFUL

1 Sam 16:12 he [David] was... of a ***b*** countenance

2 Sam 11:2 David...saw a woman...and the woman was very ***b***

Eccl 3:11 He [God] hath made every thing ***b*** in his time

Isa 52:7 How ***b*** upon the mountains are the feet of him that bringeth good tidings

Matt 23:27 ye [scribes and Pharisees]...indeed appear ***b*** outward

Rom 10:15 as it is written, How ***b*** are the feet of them

BECKONED

Luke 5:7 they ***b*** unto their partners...in the other ship

Acts 21:40 Paul...***b*** with the hand unto the people

Acts 24:10 Paul, after that the governor had ***b*** unto him to speak, answered

BEELZEBUB. See *Baal-zebub.*

BEER-SHEBA (a well that Abraham and Abimelech dug to seal their covenant and a city that grew up around the well). **Gen 21:31–33;** 26:32–33 • Judg 20:1 • 2 Sam 3:10 • Amos 5:5.

BEFOREHAND

Mark 13:11 take no thought ***b*** what ye shall speak

1 Tim 5:25 the good works of some are manifest ***b***

BEGAN

Gen 6:1 men ***b*** to multiply on the face of the earth

2 Sam 5:4 David was thirty years old when he ***b*** to reign

2 Chr 3:1 Solomon ***b*** to build the house of the LORD

Jon 3:4 Jonah ***b*** to enter into the city a day's journey

Matt 4:17 Jesus ***b*** to preach, and to say, Repent

Matt 26:22 they [the disciples]... ***b*** every one of them to say unto him, Lord, is it I

Mark 6:7 he [Jesus] called... the twelve...***b*** to send them forth

Mark 8:31 he [Jesus] ***b*** to teach them, that the Son of man must suffer

Luke 14:18 they all with one consent ***b*** to make excuse

Luke 15:14 famine...and he [the prodigal son] ***b*** to be in want

Luke 19:45 he [Jesus]...***b*** to cast out them that sold therein

John 13:5 he [Jesus]...***b*** to wash the disciples' feet

BEGINNING [S]

Gen 1:1 In the ***b*** God created the heaven and the earth

Job 42:12 the LORD blessed the latter end of Job more than his ***b***

Ps 111:10 The fear of the LORD is the ***b*** of wisdom

Prov 1:7 The fear of the LORD is the ***b*** of knowledge

Eccl 7:8 Better is the end of a thing than the ***b*** thereof

Isa 40:21 hath it not been told you from the ***b***

Isa 48:3 I have declared the former things from the ***b***

Matt 19:4 Have ye not read... he which made them at the ***b*** made them male and female

Matt 20:8 give them their hire, ***b*** from the last unto the first

Mark 13:8 famines and troubles: these are the ***b's*** of sorrows

Luke 24:27 ***b*** at Moses...he [Jesus] expounded...the things concerning himself

John 1:1 In the ***b*** was the Word...Word was with God
John 6:64 Jesus knew from the ***b*** who...believed not
Col 1:18 he [Jesus] is the ***b,*** the firstborn from the dead
2 Thes 2:13 God hath from the ***b*** chosen you to salvation
Heb 7:3 [Melchisedec] having neither ***b*** of days
2 Pet 3:4 all things continue as they were from the ***b***
1 John 1:1 That which was from the ***b***...we have heard
1 John 2:13 ye have known him [Jesus] that is from the ***b***
1 John 3:11 heard from the ***b***... we should love one another
Rev 1:8 Alpha and Omega, the ***b*** and the ending
Rev 22:13 Alpha and Omega, the ***b*** and the end

BEGOTTEN
Ps 2:7 Thou art my Son; this day have I ***b*** thee
John 1:14 we beheld his [Jesus'] glory, the glory as of the only ***b*** of the Father
John 1:18 the only ***b*** Son...he hath declared him [God]
John 3:16 God so loved the world...gave his only ***b*** Son
1 Cor 4:15 for in Christ Jesus I [Paul] have ***b*** you through the gospel
1 Pet 1:3 God...hath ***b*** us again unto a lively hope

BEHAVE [D]
1 Sam 18:14 David ***b'd*** himself wisely...LORD was with him
Ps 101:2 I will ***b*** myself wisely in a perfect way
Ps 131:2 I have ***b'd*** and quieted myself, as a child
1 Cor 13:5 [charity] doth not ***b*** itself unseemly
2 Thes 3:7 we ***b'd*** not ourselves disorderly among you

BEHIND
Matt 9:20 behold, a woman... with an issue of blood... came ***b*** him [Jesus]
Matt 16:23 he [Jesus]...said unto Peter, Get thee ***b*** me
Phil 3:13 forgetting those things which are ***b***
Col 1:24 fill up that which is ***b*** of the afflictions of Christ
Rev 1:10 I was in the Spirit... and heard ***b*** me a great voice

BEHOLD [EST, ETH, ING]
Gen 1:31 God saw every thing that he had made, and, ***b,*** it was very good
Ps 33:13 The LORD...***b'eth*** all the sons of men
Ps 119:18 that I may ***b*** wondrous things out of thy [God's] law
Ps 133:1 ***B,*** how...pleasant it is for brethren to dwell together in unity

Prov 15:3 The eyes of the LORD are in every place, ***b'ing*** the evil and the good
Isa 7:14 ***B,*** a virgin shall conceive, and bear a son
Isa 40:26 ***b*** who hath created these things
Isa 42:1 ***B*** my [God's] servant, whom I uphold
Isa 59:1 ***B,*** the LORD's hand is not shortened, that it cannot save
Jer 32:27 ***B,*** I am the LORD, the God of all flesh
Jer 44:11 ***B,*** I [God] will set my face against you for evil
Mal 4:5 ***B,*** I [God] will send you Elijah the prophet
Matt 10:16 ***B,*** I [Jesus] send you forth as sheep in the midst of wolves
Matt 12:18 ***B*** my [God's] servant, whom I have chosen
Matt 12:49 ***B*** my [Jesus'] mother and my brethren
Mark 10:21 Then Jesus ***b'ing*** him [young ruler] loved him
Luke 1:38 Mary said, ***B*** the handmaid of the Lord
Luke 6:41 why ***b'est*** thou the mote...in thy brother's eye
John 1:36 he [John the Baptist] saith, ***B*** the Lamb of God
John 19:14 and he [Pilate] saith unto the Jews, ***B*** your King
1 Cor 15:51 ***B***...We shall not all sleep...shall all be changed
2 Cor 5:17 ***b,*** all things are become new
Jas 1:23 a hearer...and not a doer...is like...a man ***b'ing*** his...face in a glass
1 John 3:1 ***B,*** what manner of love the Father hath bestowed upon us
Rev 3:11 ***B,*** I [Jesus] come quickly: hold...fast
Rev 3:20 ***B,*** I [Jesus] stand at the door, and knock
Rev 21:5 ***B,*** I [Jesus] make all things new

BELA. See *Zoar.*

BELIAL. See *Satan.*

BELIEVE [D, ING, TH]
Gen 15:6 he [Abraham] ***b'd*** in the LORD; and he counted it to him for righteousness
Ex 4:1 they will not ***b*** me [Moses], nor hearken unto my voice
Ps 119:66 I have ***b'd*** thy [God's] commandments
Jon 3:5 the people of Nineveh ***b'd*** God...put on sackcloth
Matt 18:6 whoso shall offend one of these little ones which ***b*** in me
Matt 21:22 whatsoever ye shall ask in prayer, ***b'ing,*** ye shall receive
Mark 5:36 he [Jesus] saith... Be not afraid, only ***b***
Mark 9:23 If thou canst ***b,*** all things are possible
Mark 9:24 Lord, I ***b;*** help thou mine unbelief

Mark 11:24 ***b*** that ye receive them, and ye shall have them

Luke 24:25 O fools, and slow of heart to ***b***

John 3:12 how shall ye ***b,*** if I tell you of heavenly things

John 3:16 whosoever ***b'th*** in him [Jesus] should not perish

John 3:18 he hath not ***b'd*** in the name of the only begotten Son of God

John 3:36 He that ***b'th*** on the Son hath everlasting life

John 4:48 Except ye see signs and wonders, ye will not ***b***

John 6:29 This is the work of God, that ye ***b*** on him whom he hath sent

John 6:35 he that ***b'th*** on me [Jesus] shall never thirst

John 6:64 Jesus knew...who they were that ***b'd*** not

John 9:36 Who is he, Lord, that I might ***b*** on him

John 11:25 he that ***b'th*** in me [Jesus], though he were dead, yet shall he live

John 11:26 whosoever...***b'th*** in me [Jesus] shall never die

John 11:27 Yea, Lord: I ***b*** that thou art the Christ

John 12:46 whosoever ***b'th*** on me [Jesus] should not abide in darkness

John 14:1 ye ***b*** in God, ***b*** also in me [Jesus]

John 20:25 Except I [Thomas]... thrust my hand into his [Jesus'] side, I will not ***b***

John 20:29 blessed are they that have not seen, and yet have ***b'd***

John 20:31 that ye might ***b*** that Jesus is the Christ

Acts 4:32 multitude of them that ***b'd*** were of one heart

Acts 8:37 And he [the eunuch] said, I ***b*** that Jesus Christ is the Son of God

Acts 16:31 ***B*** on the Lord Jesus Christ...thou shalt be saved

Rom 1:16 it [the gospel] is the power of God unto salvation to every one that ***b'th***

Rom 4:3 Abraham ***b'd*** God, and it was counted unto him for righteousness

Rom 6:8 we ***b*** that we shall also live with him [Jesus]

Rom 10:4 Christ is the end of the law for righteousness to every one that ***b'th***

Rom 10:9 ***b***...that God hath raised him [Jesus] from the dead, thou shalt be saved

Rom 10:14 How then shall they call on him in whom they have not ***b'd***

Rom 13:11 now is our salvation nearer than when we ***b'd***

Rom 15:13 the God of hope fill you with all joy...in ***b'ing***

1 Cor 1:21 it pleased God by the foolishness of preaching to save them that ***b***
1 Cor 13:7 [charity] beareth all things, ***b'th*** all things
2 Tim 1:12 I [Paul] know whom I have ***b'd***
Heb 11:6 he that cometh to God must ***b*** that he is
Jas 2:19 thou doest well: the devils also ***b,*** and tremble
1 John 3:23 we should ***b*** on the name of his Son Jesus
1 John 5:1 Whosoever ***b'th*** that Jesus is the Christ is born of God
1 John 5:10 He that ***b'th*** on the Son of God hath the witness in himself

BELIEVERS
Acts 5:14 ***b*** were the more added to the Lord
1 Tim 4:12 be thou an example of the ***b,*** in word...faith

BELONG [ED, ETH]
Ps 3:8 Salvation ***b'eth*** unto the LORD
Ps 94:1 O LORD God, to whom vengeance ***b'eth,*** show thyself
Dan 9:9 To the Lord our God ***b*** mercies and forgivenesses
Luke 23:7 he [Pilate] knew that he [Jesus] ***b'ed*** unto Herod's jurisdiction
1 Cor 7:32 He that is unmarried careth for the things that ***b*** to the Lord

BELOVED SON
Matt 3:17 This is my ***b-S,*** in whom I am well pleased
Matt 17:5 This is my ***b-S,*** in whom I am well pleased; hear ye him
Mark 1:11 Thou art my ***b-S,*** in whom I am well pleased
Mark 9:7 This is my ***b-S:*** hear him
Luke 3:22 Thou art my ***b-S;*** in thee I am well pleased
Luke 9:35 This is my ***b-S:*** hear him
Luke 20:13 send my ***b-s:*** it may be they will reverence him
1 Cor 4:17 I [Paul] sent unto you Timotheus, who is my ***b-s***
2 Tim 1:2 To Timothy, my [Paul's] dearly ***b-s:*** Grace, mercy

BELSHAZZAR (last king of the Babylonian Empire whose fall was foretold by a mysterious hand writing on the wall). **Dan 5:1–31;** 7:1; 8:1.

BELTESHAZZAR. See *Daniel.*

BENAIAH (a loyal supporter of David who later became commander-in-chief of Solomon's army). 2 Sam 8:18; 20:23; 23:20,22 • 1 Kgs 1:8–44; 2:25–46; 4:4 • 1 Chr 11:22,24; 18:17; 27:5–6.

BEN-AMMI (a son of Lot and ancestor of the Ammonites). Gen 19:30–38.

BENEFITS
Ps 68:19 Blessed be the Lord, who daily loadeth us with ***b***
Ps 103:2 Bless the LORD, O my soul...forget not all his ***b***
Ps 116:12 What shall I render unto the LORD for all his ***b***

BEN-HADAD (a title for three different kings of Damascus, Syria).

1. Ben-hadad I, who invaded the Northern Kingdom in league with King Asa of Judah. 1 Kgs 15:18–21 • 2 Chr 16:2–4.
2. Ben-hadad II, who waged war against King Ahab of Israel. 1 Kgs 20:1–34 • 2 Kgs 6:24; 8:7–9.
3. Ben-hadad III, who was defeated by the Assyrians, as the prophet Amos predicted. 2 Kgs 13:3,24–25 • Amos 1:4.

BENJAMIN (a son of Jacob and ancestor of one of the twelve tribes of Israel). Gen 35:18,24; 42:4,36; 43:14–29; 45:12–14,22; 46:19,21 • Ex 1:3 • 1 Chr 2:2; 7:6; 8:1. The tribe of Benjamin settled in central Canaan. Josh 18:11–28.

BEREA (a city of Macedonia visited by Paul). Acts 17:10–14.

BEREAVE [D]
Gen 42:36 Me [Jacob] have ye ***b'd*** of my children
Jer 15:7 I [the LORD] will ***b*** them of children
Jer 18:21 let their wives be ***b'd*** of their children

BERITH. See *Baal-berith.*

BERNICE (a sister of Herod Agrippa II, Roman governor of Palestine before whom Paul appeared). Acts 25:13,23; 26:1–32.

BERODACH-BALADAN (a king of Babylon whose ambassadors viewed the treasures of King Hezekiah of Judah). 2 Kgs 20:12–19. *Merodach-baladan:* Isa 39:1.

BESEECH [ING]
1 Chr 21:8 ***b*** thee [God], do away...iniquity of thy servant
Ps 116:4 O LORD, I ***b*** thee, deliver my soul
Isa 64:9 see, we ***b*** thee [God], we are all thy people
Jer 38:20 Obey, I [Jeremiah] ***b*** thee, the voice of the LORD
Dan 9:16 I [Daniel] ***b*** thee [God], let thine anger...be turned away
Jon 4:3 O LORD, take, I [Jonah] ***b*** thee, my life from me

Matt 8:5 came unto him [Jesus] a centurion, ***b'ing*** him
Luke 7:3 he sent unto him [Jesus]...***b'ing*** him that he would...heal his servant
Luke 9:38 Master, I ***b*** thee, look upon my son
Rom 12:1 I [Paul] ***b*** you therefore, brethren
1 Cor 4:16 I [Paul] ***b*** you, be ye followers of me
2 Cor 2:8 I [Paul] ***b*** you...confirm your love toward him
2 Cor 5:20 we are ambassadors for Christ, as though God did ***b*** you by us
Eph 4:1 I [Paul]...***b*** you that ye walk worthy of the vocation wherewith ye are called
Phlm 10 I [Paul] ***b*** thee for my son Onesimus
1 Pet 2:11 I [Peter] ***b*** you...abstain from fleshly lusts

BEST
1 Sam 8:14 he [the king] will take your fields...the ***b*** of them
Luke 15:22 Bring forth the ***b*** robe, and put it on him
1 Cor 12:31 But covet earnestly the ***b*** gifts

BESTOW [ED]
Luke 12:17 What shall I do...no room where to *b* my fruits
John 4:38 I [Jesus] sent you to reap that whereon ye ***b'ed*** no labour
1 Cor 13:3 though I [Paul] ***b*** all my goods to feed the poor
Gal 4:11 I [Paul] am afraid of you, lest I have ***b'ed*** upon you labour in vain
1 John 3:1 what manner of love the Father hath ***b'ed*** upon us

BETHABARA (a place along the Jordan River where John the Baptist baptized). John 1:28.

BETHANY (a village outside Jerusalem where Lazarus, Mary, and Martha lived and the site from which Jesus ascended to heaven). Matt 21:17; 26:6 • Mark 11:1,11–12; 14:3 • Luke 19:29; 24:50–51 • John 11:1,18; 12:1.

BETHEL (a city where Jacob had a vision of angels on a staircase). Gen 12:8; 13:3–4; **28:10–19;** 35:1–15 • Josh 16:2 • 1 Sam 7:15–16; 10:3 • 1 Kgs 12:28–33 • 2 Kgs 23:4,15–20 • Jer 48:13 • Hos 10:15 • Amos 7:10–13. *El-bethel:* Gen 35:7. *Luz:* Gen 28:19.

BETHESDA (a pool in Jerusalem where Jesus healed a lame man). John 5:2–8.

BETH-HORON (twin towns—Upper and Lower—in the territory of Ephraim which served as important military outposts). Josh 10:10–14; 16:3–5 • 1 Sam 13:18 • 1 Chr 7:24 • 2 Chr 8:5.

BETHLEHEM (a town in southern Palestine near Jerusalem where Jesus was born in fulfillment of prophecy). Gen 35:19; 48:7 • Ruth 1:19,22; 2:4; 4:11 • 1 Sam 16:4; 17:15; 20:6,28 • 2 Sam 2:32; 23:14–16,24 • 1 Chr 11:16–26 • 2 Chr 11:6 • Ezra 2:21 • Neh 7:26 • **Mic 5:2** • Matt 2:1–16 • **Luke 2:4–7.** *Beth-lehem-judah:* Judg 19:18. *Ephratah:* Ruth 4:11. *Ephrath:* Gen 35:16–19.

BETH-LEHEM-JUDAH. See *Bethlehem.*

BETHPHAGE (a village outside Jerusalem mentioned in connection with Jesus' triumphal entry into the city). Matt 21:1 • Mark 11:1 • Luke 19:29.

BETHSAIDA (a fishing village on the Sea of Galilee; the home of Andrew, Peter, and Philip—apostles of Jesus). Matt 11:21 • Mark 6:45 • Luke 10:13 • **John 1:44; 12:21.**

BETRAY [ED, EST, ETH]

Matt 17:22 Son of man shall be ***b'ed*** into the hands of men

Matt 26:2 the Son of man is ***b'ed*** to be crucified

Matt 26:16 he [Judas] sought opportunity to ***b*** him [Jesus]

Matt 26:45 the Son of man is ***b'ed*** into the hands of sinners

Mark 14:10 Judas...went unto the chief priests, to ***b*** him [Jesus] unto them

Mark 14:21 but woe to that man by whom the Son of man is ***b'ed***

Luke 22:21 the hand of him that ***b'eth*** me [Jesus] is with me on the table

Luke 22:48 Judas, ***b'est*** thou the Son of man with a kiss

John 6:64 Jesus knew...who should ***b*** him

1 Cor 11:23 the Lord Jesus the same night in which he was ***b'ed*** took bread

BETTER

1 Sam 15:22 Behold, to obey is ***b*** than sacrifice

2 Kgs 5:12 Are not Abana and Pharpar...***b*** than all the waters of Israel

Ps 37:16 A little that a righteous man hath is ***b*** than the riches of many wicked

Ps 84:10 a day in thy [God's] courts is ***b*** than a thousand

Ps 118:8 ***b*** to trust in the LORD than to put confidence in man

Prov 8:11 For wisdom is ***b*** than rubies

Prov 15:16 ***B*** is little with the fear of the LORD than great treasure and trouble

Prov 16:16 How much ***b*** is it to get wisdom than gold

Prov 19:22 a poor man is ***b*** than a liar

Prov 27:5 Open rebuke is ***b*** than secret love

Prov 27:10 ***b*** is a neighbour... near than a brother far off

Eccl 4:9 Two are ***b*** than one; because they have a good reward for their labour

Eccl 4:13 ***B*** is a poor and a wise child than an old and foolish king

Eccl 6:9 ***B*** is the sight of the eyes than the wandering of the desire

Eccl 7:1 A good name is ***b*** than precious ointment

Eccl 7:8 ***B*** is the end of a thing than the beginning thereof

Eccl 9:18 Wisdom is ***b*** than weapons of war

Song 4:10 how much ***b*** is thy love than wine

Dan 1:20 found them [Daniel and his friends] ten times ***b*** than all the magicians

Jon 4:8 Jonah...said, It is ***b*** for me to die than to live

Matt 12:12 How much then is a man ***b*** than a sheep

Matt 18:8 it is ***b*** for thee to enter into life halt or maimed

1 Cor 7:9 for it is ***b*** to marry than to burn

Phil 1:23 having a desire...to be with Christ; which is far ***b***

Heb 1:4 Being made so much ***b*** than the angels

Heb 7:22 was Jesus made a surety of a ***b*** testament

BEULAH (a symbolic name for Israel after the Exile in Babylon when the nation would be in a fruitful relationship with God). Isa 62:4.

BEZER (a city of refuge in the territory of Reuben). Deut 4:43 • Josh 20:8; 21:36 • 1 Chr 6:78.

BILDAD (one of the three friends who comforted Job). His speeches appear in Job 8:1–22; 18:1–21; 25:1–6.

BILHAH (a wife of Jacob and mother of two of his sons, Dan and Naphtali). Gen 29:29; 30:3–7; 35:22,25; 37:2; 46:25 • 1 Chr 7:13.

BIND [ETH, ING]

Gen 37:7 we [Joseph and his brothers] were ***b'ing*** sheaves in the field

Deut 6:8 thou shalt ***b*** them for a sign upon thine hand

Ps 147:3 He [God] healeth the broken in heart, and ***b'eth*** up their wounds

Prov 3:3 ***b*** them [mercy and truth] about thy neck

Isa 61:1 the LORD...hath sent me to ***b*** up the broken-hearted

Dan 3:20 he [the king] commanded...to ***b*** Shadrach, Meshach, and Abednego

Matt 12:29 how can one enter into a strong man's house... except he first ***b***...man

Matt 16:19 whatsoever thou shalt ***b*** on earth shall be bound in heaven

Matt 23:4 they [Pharisees] ***b*** heavy burdens

Mark 5:3 no man could ***b*** him [demon-possessed man]

Acts 22:4 I [Paul] persecuted... ***b'ing*** and delivering...both men and women

BIRTH

Eccl 7:1 good name is better than...ointment...day of death than...day of...***b***

Matt 1:18 the ***b*** of Jesus Christ was on this wise

John 9:1 Jesus...saw a man which was blind from his ***b***

Rev 12:2 she being with child cried, travailing in ***b***

BIRTH OF JESUS. See *Jesus, Life and Ministry of.*

BIRTHRIGHT

Gen 25:31 Jacob said, Sell me this day thy [Esau's] ***b***

Heb 12:16 Esau, who for one morsel of meat sold his ***b***

BISHOP [S]

Phil 1:1 to all the saints...at Philippi, with the ***b's***

1 Tim 3:1 If a man desire the office of a ***b,*** he desireth a good work

1 Tim 3:2 A ***b*** then must be blameless...husband of one wife

Titus 1:7 a ***b*** must be blameless, as the steward of God

1 Pet 2:25 ye are now returned unto the Shepherd and ***B*** of your souls

BITHYNIA (a Roman province of Asia Minor that Paul was prevented from entering). Acts 16:7.

BITTER

Ex 1:14 they [the Egyptians] made...lives ***b*** with... bondage

Ex 12:8 with ***b*** herbs they shall eat it [the Passover meal]

Ex 15:23 could not drink of the waters of Marah...they were ***b***

Isa 24:9 strong drink shall be ***b*** to them that drink it

Jer 31:15 A voice was heard in Ramah...***b*** weeping

Hab 1:6 I raise up the Chaldeans, that ***b*** and hasty nation

Jas 3:11 Doth a fountain send forth...sweet water and ***b***

BITTER HERBS (herbs eaten by the Israelites during their Passover celebrations to help them remember their enslavement years in Egypt). Ex 12:8 • Num 9:11.

BITTERNESS

Job 9:18 He [God]...filleth me [Job] with ***b***

Job 21:25 another dieth in the ***b*** of his soul

Acts 8:23 thou art in the gall of ***b,*** and in the bond of iniquity

Rom 3:14 Whose mouth is full of cursing and ***b***

Eph 4:31 Let all ***b,*** and wrath... be put away from you

BLAMELESS

1 Cor 1:8 ye may be ***b*** in the day of our Lord Jesus

1 Tim 3:2 A bishop then must be ***b,*** the husband of one wife

1 Tim 3:10 use the office of a deacon, being found ***b***

Titus 1:7 a bishop must be ***b,*** as the steward of God

BLASPHEME [D]

Ps 74:10 shall the enemy ***b*** thy [God's] name for ever

Ps 74:18 the foolish people have ***b'd*** thy [God's] name

Mark 3:29 he that shall ***b*** against the Holy Ghost hath never forgiveness

Rev 13:6 he opened his mouth... against God, to ***b*** his name

BLASPHEMY [IES]

Matt 12:31 ***b*** against the Holy Ghost shall not be forgiven

Matt 26:65 He [Jesus] hath spoken ***b;*** what further need have we of witnesses

Mark 2:7 Why doth this man [Jesus] thus speak ***b'ies***

Col 3:8 put off all these; anger, wrath, malice, ***b***

Rev 13:1 I [John]...saw a beast...and upon his heads the name of ***b***

BLESS [ED, ING, INGS]

Gen 1:22 God ***b'ed*** them...Be fruitful, and multiply

Gen 2:3 God ***b'ed*** the seventh day, and sanctified it

Gen 9:1 And God ***b'ed*** Noah and his sons

Gen 12:2 I [God] will ***b*** thee [Abraham], and make thy name great

Gen 22:18 in thy [Abraham's] seed shall all the nations of the earth be ***b'ed***

Gen 27:34 Esau...said unto his father, ***B*** me, even me also

Gen 39:5 the LORD ***b'ed*** the Egyptian's house for Joseph's sake

Ex 20:11 the LORD ***b'ed*** the sabbath day, and hallowed it

Num 6:24 The LORD ***b*** thee, and keep thee

Num 24:1 Balaam saw that it pleased the LORD to ***b*** Israel

Deut 8:10 thou shalt ***b*** the LORD...for the good land... he hath given thee

Deut 11:26 I set before you this day a ***b'ing*** and a curse

Deut 33:1 Moses...***b'ed*** the children of Israel

Job 1:21 the LORD hath taken away; ***b'ed*** be the name of the LORD

Job 42:12 the LORD ***b'ed*** the latter end of Job more than his beginning

Ps 1:1 ***B'ed*** is the man that walketh not in the counsel of the ungodly

Ps 28:6 ***B'ed*** be the LORD, because he hath heard...my supplications

Ps 29:11 the LORD will ***b*** his people with peace

Ps 32:1 ***B'ed*** is he whose transgression is forgiven

Ps 33:12 ***B'ed*** is the nation whose God is the LORD

Ps 41:13 ***B'ed*** be the LORD God...from everlasting

Ps 66:20 ***B'ed*** be God, which hath not turned away my prayer, nor his mercy

Ps 67:1 God...***b*** us; and cause his face to shine upon us

Ps 84:4 ***B'ed*** are they that dwell in thy [God's] house

Ps 94:12 ***B'ed*** is the man whom thou [God] chastenest

Ps 96:2 Sing unto the LORD, ***b*** his name

Ps 106:48 ***B'ed*** be the LORD God of Israel from everlasting to everlasting

Ps 115:18 we will ***b*** the LORD from this time forth

Ps 119:2 ***B'ed*** are they that keep his [God's] testimonies

Ps 128:1 ***B'ed*** is every one that feareth the LORD

Ps 145:1 I will ***b*** thy [God's] name for ever and ever

Prov 10:6 ***B'ings*** are upon the head of the just

Prov 31:28 Her children arise up, and call her ***b'ed***

Ezek 34:26 there shall be showers of ***b'ing***

Matt 5:3 ***B'ed*** are the poor in spirit

Matt 5:4 ***B'ed*** are they that mourn

Matt 5:5 ***B'ed*** are the meek

Matt 5:6 ***B'ed*** are they which do hunger...after righteousness

Matt 5:7 ***B'ed*** are the merciful

Matt 5:8 ***B'ed*** are the pure in heart

Matt 5:9 ***B'ed*** are the peacemakers

Matt 5:10 ***B'ed*** are they which are persecuted for righteousness' sake

Matt 5:11 ***B'ed*** are ye, when men shall revile you, and persecute you

Matt 5:44 Love your enemies, ***b*** them that curse you

Matt 16:17 ***B'ed*** art thou, Simon Barjona

Matt 26:26 Jesus took bread, and ***b'ed*** it, and brake it

Mark 10:16 he [Jesus]...put his hands upon them [the children], and ***b'ed*** them

Luke 1:28 ***b'ed*** art thou [Mary] among women

Luke 11:28 Yea rather, ***b'ed*** are they that hear the word of God, and keep it

John 20:29 ***b'ed*** are they that have not seen, and yet have believed

Rom 12:14 ***B*** them which persecute you: ***b,*** and curse not

1 Cor 4:12 being reviled, we ***b***

1 Cor 10:16 The cup of ***b'ing***... is it not the communion of the blood of Christ

Gal 3:9 they which be of faith are ***b'ed*** with...Abraham

Eph 1:3 who [God] hath ***b'ed*** us with all spiritual ***b'ings***

1 Tim 6:15 who [Jesus] is the ***b'ed*** and only Potentate

Titus 2:13 that ***b'ed*** hope, and the glorious appearing of... our Saviour

Jas 1:12 ***B'ed*** is the man that endureth temptation

Jas 3:10 Out of the same mouth proceedeth ***b'ing*** and cursing

Rev 1:3 ***B'ed*** is he that readeth, and they that hear the words of this prophecy

Rev 5:12 Worthy is the Lamb... to receive...honour, and glory, and ***b'ing***

Rev 22:7 ***b'ed*** is he that keepeth the sayings of the prophecy of this book

BLESS THE LORD

Ps 16:7 I will ***b-t-L,*** who hath given me counsel

Ps 34:1 I will ***b-t-L*** at all times: his praise shall continually be in my mouth

Ps 103:1 ***B-t-L,*** O my soul: and all that is within me, bless his holy name

Ps 103:2 ***B-t-L,*** O my soul, and forget not all his benefits

Ps 134:2 Lift up your hands in the sanctuary, and ***b-t-L***

BLIND [ED]

Job 29:15 I was eyes to the ***b,*** and feet was I to the lame

Ps 146:8 The LORD openeth the eyes of the ***b***

Isa 35:5 the eyes of the ***b*** shall be opened

Isa 42:7 To open the ***b*** eyes, to bring out the prisoners

Isa 43:8 Bring forth the ***b*** people that have eyes

Lam 4:14 They have wandered as ***b*** men in the streets

Mal 1:8 if ye offer the ***b*** for sacrifice, is it not evil

Matt 11:5 The ***b*** receive their sight, and the lame walk

Matt 20:30 two ***b*** men sitting by the way side...cried out

Matt 23:24 Ye ***b*** guides [Pharisees], which strain at a gnat

Mark 8:22 they bring a ***b*** man unto him [Jesus], and besought him
Mark 10:46 ***b*** Bartimaeus, the son of Timaeus, sat by the highway
Luke 4:18 Spirit...anointed me [Jesus] to preach... recovering of sight to the ***b***
Luke 6:39 Can the ***b*** lead the ***b***
Luke 7:22 tell John...that the ***b*** see, the lame walk
John 9:2 who did sin, this man, or his parents, that he was born ***b***
John 12:40 He [God] hath ***b'ed*** their eyes...hardened their heart
Acts 13:11 thou [Elymas the sorcerer]...shalt be ***b***
1 John 2:11 he that hateth his brother is in darkness, and...darkness hath ***b'ed*** his eyes

BLINDNESS
Gen 19:11 they [angels] smote the men...with ***b,*** both small and great
2 Kgs 6:18 And he [God] smote them with ***b*** according to the word of Elisha
Eph 4:18 being alienated from the life of God...because of the ***b*** of their heart

BLOOD
Gen 4:10 the voice of thy [Cain's] brother's ***b*** crieth unto me [God]
Gen 9:6 Whoso sheddeth man's ***b,*** by man shall his ***b*** be shed
Ex 7:21 there was ***b*** throughout all the land of Egypt
Ex 12:23 when he seeth the ***b*** upon the lintel...the LORD will pass over the door
Ex 24:8 Moses took the ***b,*** and sprinkled it on the people
Lev 7:27 Whatsoever soul eateth...***b***...shall be cut off
Lev 15:19 if...her issue in her flesh be ***b,*** she shall be put apart seven days
Lev 17:11 For the life of the flesh is in the ***b***
Lev 20:9 he hath cursed his father or his mother; his ***b*** shall be upon him
Num 35:19 The revenger of ***b***... shall slay the murderer
1 Kgs 18:28 they [the priests of Baal]...cut themselves... till the ***b*** gushed out
1 Kgs 22:38 the dogs licked up his [Ahab's] ***b***
2 Kgs 9:33 her [Jezebel's] ***b*** was sprinkled on the wall
1 Chr 22:8 thou [David] hast shed much ***b*** upon the earth
Ps 30:9 What profit is there in my ***b,*** when I go...to the pit
Prov 1:16 their feet...make haste to shed ***b***
Prov 6:17 a lying tongue, and hands that shed innocent ***b***
Isa 1:11 I [God] delight not in the ***b*** of bullocks
Isa 1:15 I [God] will not hear: your hands are full of ***b***

Isa 59:3 hands are defiled with ***b***...fingers with iniquity

Ezek 9:9 land is full of ***b***, and the city full of perverseness

Joel 2:31 The sun shall be turned into darkness, and the moon into ***b***

Matt 9:20 a woman...with an issue of ***b*** twelve years, came behind him [Jesus]

Matt 16:17 for flesh and ***b*** hath not revealed it unto thee [Peter]

Matt 26:28 this is my [Jesus'] ***b*** of the new testament, which is shed for many

Matt 27:8 that field was called, The field of ***b***, unto this day

Matt 27:24 Pilate...washed his hands...saying, I am innocent of the ***b*** of this... person [Jesus]

Matt 27:25 Then answered all the people...His [Jesus'] ***b*** be on us

Luke 11:50 the ***b*** of all the prophets...may be required of this generation

Luke 22:44 his [Jesus'] sweat was as...great drops of ***b***

John 6:53 Except ye...drink his [Jesus'] ***b***, ye have no life

John 19:34 one of the soldiers...pierced his [Jesus'] side...came there out ***b*** and water

Acts 2:20 sun shall be turned into darkness...moon into ***b***

Acts 17:26 And [God] hath made of one ***b*** all nations of men

Acts 18:6 Your ***b*** be upon your own heads

Acts 20:28 feed the church of God, which he [Jesus] hath purchased with his own ***b***

Rom 5:9 now justified by his [Jesus'] ***b***, we shall be saved from wrath

1 Cor 10:16 The cup of blessing...is it not the communion of the ***b*** of Christ

1 Cor 15:50 flesh and ***b*** cannot inherit the kingdom of God

Eph 2:13 ye who sometimes were far off are made nigh by the ***b*** of Christ

Eph 6:12 we wrestle not against flesh and ***b***

Col 1:14 In whom we have redemption through his [Jesus'] ***b***

Heb 9:12 by his [Jesus'] own ***b*** he entered in once into the holy place

Heb 10:4 not possible that the ***b*** of bulls...should take away sins

Heb 13:12 he [Jesus] might sanctify...with his own ***b***

1 John 1:7 the ***b*** of Jesus Christ his Son cleanseth us from all sin

Rev 6:12 the sun became black...and the moon became as ***b***

Rev 7:14 they...have washed their robes, and made them white in the ***b*** of the Lamb
Rev 16:3 the sea...became as the ***b*** of a dead man

BLOT [TED, TETH]
Ex 32:33 Whosoever hath sinned against me [God], him will I ***b*** out of my book
Ps 51:1 according unto...thy [God's] tender mercies ***b*** out my transgressions
Ps 51:9 Hide thy [God's] face from my sins, and ***b*** out all mine iniquities
Ps 69:28 Let them be ***b'ted*** out of the book of the living
Isa 43:25 I [God], even I, am he that ***b'teth*** out thy transgressions for mine own sake
Isa 44:22 I [God] have ***b'ted*** out...thy transgressions
Acts 3:19 Repent...that your sins may be ***b'ted*** out
Rev 3:5 I [God] will not ***b*** out his name out of the book of life...will confess his name

BOANERGES (a name, meaning "sons of thunder," given by Jesus to His disciples James and John). Mark 3:17.

BOAST [ETH, ING, INGS]
Ps 44:8 In God we ***b*** all the day long
Prov 25:14 Whoso ***b'eth*** himself of a false gift is like clouds... without rain
Prov 27:1 ***B*** not thyself of tomorrow
2 Cor 9:3 lest our ***b'ing*** of you should be in vain
Eph 2:9 Not of works, lest any man should ***b***
Jas 3:5 the tongue is a little member...***b'eth*** great things
Jas 4:16 ye rejoice in your ***b'ings:*** all such rejoicing is evil

BOAZ (the husband of Ruth and an ancestor of Christ). Ruth 2:1–23; 3:2,7; 4:1–21 • 1 Chr 2:11–12. *Booz:* Matt 1:5 • Luke 3:32.

BODY
Num 19:11 He that toucheth the dead ***b***...shall be unclean
Deut 21:23 His ***b*** shall not remain all night upon the tree
Mic 6:7 give...the fruit of my ***b*** for the sin of my soul
Matt 6:23 eye be evil, thy whole ***b*** shall be full of darkness
Matt 26:26 Jesus took bread... Take, eat; this is my ***b***
Mark 15:43 Joseph of Arimathaea...craved the ***b*** of Jesus
Luke 12:22 Take no thought... for the ***b,*** what ye...put on
Luke 23:55 the women... beheld...how his [Jesus'] ***b*** was laid
Rom 6:12 Let not sin therefore reign in your mortal ***b***

Rom 7:24 who shall deliver me from the ***b*** of this death
Rom 12:5 we, being many, are one ***b*** in Christ
1 Cor 6:18 he that committeth fornication sinneth against his own ***b***
1 Cor 10:17 we being many are one bread, and one ***b***
1 Cor 12:12 the ***b*** is one, and hath many members
1 Cor 13:3 though I [Paul] give my ***b*** to be burned
1 Cor 15:44 It is sown a natural ***b;*** it is raised a spiritual ***b***
2 Cor 5:8 absent from the ***b***... present with the Lord
Gal 6:17 I [Paul] bear in my ***b*** the marks of the Lord Jesus
Phil 1:20 Christ shall be magnified in my [Paul's] ***b***
Col 1:18 he [Christ] is the head of the ***b,*** the church
Jas 3:6 it [the tongue] defileth the whole ***b***
1 Pet 2:24 Who [Jesus]...bare our sins in his own ***b*** on the tree

BODY OF CHRIST
Rom 7:4 ye also are become dead to the law by the ***b-o-C***
1 Cor 10:16 The bread which we break, is it not the communion of the ***b-o-C***
1 Cor 12:27 ye are the ***b-o-C,*** and members in particular
Eph 4:12 for the work of the ministry...edifying of the ***b-o-C***

BOLD [LY]
Prov 28:1 The wicked flee... righteous are ***b*** as a lion
Acts 9:29 he [Paul] spake ***b'ly*** in the name of the Lord Jesus
Acts 19:8 he [Paul] went into the synagogue, and spake ***b'ly***
Phil 1:14 many of the brethren...are much more ***b*** to speak the word without fear
Heb 4:16 Let us...come ***b'ly*** unto the throne of grace

BOLDNESS
Acts 4:13 they saw the ***b*** of Peter and John
Acts 4:31 they [the apostles]... prayed...spake the word of God with ***b***
Eph 3:12 In whom [Jesus] we have ***b***...with confidence
Phil 1:20 with all ***b***...Christ... magnified in my [Paul's] body
1 John 4:17 that we may have ***b*** in the day of judgment

BOND [S]
Ps 116:16 thou [God] hast loosed my ***b's***
Jer 27:2 Make thee ***b's*** and yokes, and put them upon thy [Jeremiah's] neck
Acts 26:29 that...all that hear me this day, were...such as I [Paul] am, except these ***b's***

Gal 3:28 There is neither Jew nor Greek...***b*** nor free
Eph 4:3 keep the unity of the Spirit in the ***b*** of peace
Eph 6:20 I [Paul] am an ambassador in ***b's***
Phil 1:13 my [Paul's] ***b's*** in Christ are manifest in... palace
Col 3:11 there is neither...***b*** nor free: but Christ is all
Col 3:14 put on charity, which is the ***b*** of perfectness
Phlm 10 son Onesimus, whom I [Paul] have begotten in my ***b's***

BONDAGE
Ex 1:14 they [the Egyptians] made...lives bitter with hard ***b***
Ex 6:6 I [God] will rid you [the Israelites] out of their ***b***
John 8:33 We be Abraham's seed...never in ***b*** to any man
Rom 8:15 ye have not received the spirit of ***b*** again to fear
Gal 4:9 how turn ye...to... desire again to be in ***b***
Gal 5:1 be not entangled again with the yoke of ***b***

BOOK OF LIFE
Phil 4:3 help those...fellowlabourers, whose names are in the ***b-o-l***
Rev 3:5 I will not blot out his name out of the ***b-o-l***
Rev 20:12 another book was opened, which is the ***b-o-l***
Rev 20:15 whosoever was not found written in the ***b-o-l*** was cast into the lake of fire

BOOZ. See *Boaz.*

BORN
Gen 17:17 Shall a child be ***b*** unto him [Abraham] that is an hundred years old
Gen 21:5 Abraham was an hundred years old, when his son Isaac was ***b***
Job 3:3 Let the day perish wherein I [Job] was ***b***
Job 5:7 man is ***b*** unto trouble, as the sparks fly upward
Job 14:1 Man that is ***b*** of a woman is of few days
Ps 58:3 The wicked...go astray as soon as they be ***b***
Prov 17:17 A friend loveth at all times, and a brother is ***b*** for adversity
Eccl 3:2 A time to be ***b,*** and a time to die
Isa 9:6 unto us a child is ***b,*** unto us a son is given
Jer 20:14 Cursed be the day wherein I [Jeremiah] was ***b***
Matt 2:1 when Jesus was ***b*** in Bethlehem of Judaea
Luke 1:35 that holy thing...***b*** of thee [Mary] shall be called the Son of God
Luke 2:11 unto you is ***b*** this day...a Saviour
Luke 7:28 Among those...***b*** of women...not a greater

prophet than John the Baptist

John 9:2 sin, this man, or his parents, that he was ***b*** blind

John 18:37 Thou sayest that I [Jesus] am a king. To this end was I ***b***

Acts 22:28 And Paul said, But I was free ***b***

1 Cor 15:8 he [Jesus] was seen of me [Paul] also, as of one ***b*** out of due time

1 John 3:9 Whosoever is ***b*** of God doth not commit sin

1 John 4:7 every one that loveth is ***b*** of God

BORN AGAIN

John 3:3 Jesus...said...Except a man be ***b-a,*** he cannot see the kingdom of God

John 3:7 Marvel not that I [Jesus] said unto thee [Nicodemus], Ye must be ***b-a***

1 Pet 1:23 ***b-a,*** not of corruptible seed, but of incorruptible

BOSOM

Ex 4:6 he [Moses] put his hand into his ***b:*** and...his hand was leprous as snow

Prov 5:20 why wilt thou... embrace the ***b*** of a stranger

Isa 40:11 He [God] shall... carry them [lambs] in his ***b***

Luke 16:22 the beggar died... carried...into Abraham's ***b***

John 1:18 the only begotten Son...in the ***b*** of the Father

John 13:23 leaning on Jesus' ***b*** one of his disciples

BOTTLE [S]

Job 32:19 my belly...is ready to burst like new ***b's***

Ps 56:8 put thou my tears into thy [God's] ***b***

Luke 5:37 no man putteth new wine into old ***b's***

BOTTOMLESS PIT

Rev 9:1 to him was given the key of the ***b-p***

Rev 11:7 the beast that ascendeth out of the ***b-p*** shall make war

Rev 20:1 I saw an angel... having the key of the ***b-p***

BOUGHT

Lev 27:24 the field shall return unto him of whom it was ***b***

Jer 32:9 I [Jeremiah] ***b*** the field of Hanameel

Matt 13:46 he [merchant]... sold all...he had, and ***b*** it [pearl]

Mark 11:15 Jesus...began to cast out them that sold and ***b*** in the temple

Luke 14:18 I have ***b*** a piece of ground, and I must needs go and see it

1 Cor 6:20 ye are ***b*** with a price...glorify God

1 Cor 7:23 Ye are ***b*** with a price; be not ye the servants of men

BOUND

Gen 22:9 Abraham...laid the wood...and ***b*** Isaac his son

Judg 16:21 the Philistines took him [Samson]...and ***b*** him with fetters of brass

Dan 3:23 Shadrach, Meshach, and Abednego, fell down ***b*** into the...fiery furnace

Matt 14:3 Herod had laid hold on John, and ***b*** him

Matt 18:18 Whatsoever ye shall bind on earth shall be ***b*** in heaven

Mark 5:4 he [a demon-possessed man] had been often ***b***

Luke 10:34 ***b***...wounds... took care of him [wounded traveler]

John 11:44 he [Lazarus] came forth, ***b***...with graveclothes

Acts 20:22 I [Paul] go ***b*** in the spirit unto Jerusalem

2 Tim 2:9 but the word of God is not ***b***

Rev 20:2 he [an angel] laid hold on the dragon...and ***b*** him a thousand years

BOUNTIFUL [LY]

Ps 13:6 the LORD...hath dealt ***b'ly*** with me

Prov 22:9 He that hath a ***b*** eye shall be blessed

2 Cor 9:6 he which soweth ***b'ly*** shall reap also ***b'ly***

BOWED

Ps 38:6 I am troubled; I am ***b*** down greatly

Ps 57:6 They...prepared a net for my steps...soul is ***b*** down

Isa 2:11 the haughtiness of men shall be ***b*** down

Matt 27:29 they ***b*** the knee before him [Jesus]...mocked him

Luke 13:11 a woman which had a spirit of infirmity... was ***b*** together

John 19:30 Jesus...***b*** his head, and gave up the ghost

BOZRAH (ancient capital of Edom). Gen 36:33 • 1 Chr 1:44 • Isa 34:6; 63:1 • Jer 49:13,22 • Amos 1:12 • Mic 2:12.

BREAD OF LIFE, JESUS AS. See *"I Am" Statements of Jesus.*

BREAK [EST, ETH, ING]

Gen 32:24 there wrestled a man with him [Jacob] until the ***b'ing*** of the day

Job 9:17 For he [God] ***b'eth*** me with a tempest

Job 19:2 How long will ye [God]...***b*** me...with words

Job 34:24 He [God] shall ***b*** in pieces mighty men

Ps 2:9 Thou shalt ***b*** them with a rod of iron

Ps 29:5 the LORD ***b'eth*** the cedars of Lebanon

Ps 46:9 he [God] ***b'eth*** the bow, and cutteth the spear

Ps 48:7 Thou [God] ***b'est*** the ships of Tarshish
Ps 58:6 ***b*** out the great teeth of the young lions, O LORD
Ps 89:34 My covenant will I [God] not ***b***
Ps 94:5 They ***b*** in pieces thy people, O LORD
Eccl 3:3 a time to ***b*** down, and a time to build up
Isa 14:7 The whole earth is at rest...***b*** forth into singing
Isa 42:3 A bruised reed shall he [God's servant] not ***b***
Jer 1:14 Out of the north an evil shall ***b*** forth
Jer 19:11 Even so will I [God] ***b*** this people and this city
Jer 23:29 Is not my [God's] word like...a hammer that ***b'eth*** the rock
Hos 1:5 I [God] will ***b*** the bow of Israel
Matt 6:20 lay up...treasures in heaven...where thieves do not ***b*** through nor steal
Matt 12:20 A bruised reed shall he [Jesus] not ***b***
Luke 24:35 he [Jesus] was known of them in ***b'ing*** of bread
Acts 2:42 they [believers] continued stedfastly in the apostles' doctrine...***b'ing*** of bread
1 Cor 10:16 The bread which we ***b,*** is it not the communion of the body of Christ

BRIBE [S]

1 Sam 12:3 of whose hand have I received any ***b***
Ps 26:10 and their right hand is full of ***b's***
Amos 5:12 they afflict the just, they take a ***b***

BUILDER [S]

Ps 118:22 stone which the ***b's*** refused is become the head stone of the corner
Mark 12:10 The stone which the ***b's*** rejected is become the head of the corner
Acts 4:11 This is the stone... set at nought of you ***b's***
Heb 11:10 he [Abraham] looked for a city...whose ***b*** and maker is God
1 Pet 2:7 the stone which the ***b's*** disallowed...is made the head of the corner

BUILDING [S]

1 Kgs 7:1 Solomon was ***b*** his own house thirteen years
2 Chr 3:3 Solomon was instructed for the ***b*** of the house of God
Mark 13:2 Seest thou these great ***b's?*** there shall not be left one stone upon another
1 Cor 3:9 ye are God's husbandry, ye are God's ***b***
2 Cor 5:1 we have a ***b*** of God, an house not made with hands, eternal

Eph 2:21 the ***b*** fitly framed together groweth unto an holy temple

BURDEN [S]

Ex 1:11 they [the Egyptians] did set over them taskmasters to afflict them with their ***b's***

Ps 38:4 as an heavy ***b*** they [sins] are too heavy for me

Ps 55:22 Cast thy ***b*** upon the LORD...he shall sustain thee

Jer 17:22 Neither carry forth a ***b***...on the sabbath day

Matt 11:30 my [Jesus'] yoke is easy, and my ***b*** is light

Matt 20:12 we have borne the ***b*** and heat of the day

Matt 23:4 they [the Pharisees] bind heavy ***b's***

Gal 6:2 Bear ye one another's ***b's***...fulfil the law of Christ

Gal 6:5 For every man shall bear his own ***b***

BURIAL OF JESUS. See *Jesus, Life and Ministry of.*

BURN [ED, ETH, ING]

Ex 3:2 the bush ***b'ed*** with fire, and...was not consumed

Ex 30:8 when Aaron lighteth the lamps...shall ***b*** incense

Neh 2:17 the gates [of Jerusalem] thereof are ***b'ed***

Job 30:30 my [Job's] bones are ***b'ed*** with heat

Job 41:19 Out of his [God's] mouth go ***b'ing*** lamps

Ps 79:5 shall thy [God's] jealousy ***b*** like fire

Ps 97:3 A fire goeth before him [God], and ***b'eth*** up his enemies round about

Prov 6:27 Can a man take fire in his bosom, and his clothes not be ***b'ed***

Jer 7:9 Will ye steal, murder... and ***b*** incense unto Baal

Jer 20:9 his [God's] word was in mine [Jeremiah's] heart as a ***b'ing*** fire

Jer 39:8 the Chaldeans ***b'ed*** the king's house

Dan 3:17 our God...is able to deliver us from the ***b'ing*** fiery furnace

Luke 3:17 the chaff he [God] will ***b*** with fire

Luke 24:32 Did not our heart ***b*** within us

Rom 1:27 the men...***b'ed*** in their lust one toward another

1 Cor 3:15 If any man's work shall be ***b'ed***...suffer loss

1 Cor 7:9 for it is better to marry than to ***b***

1 Cor 13:3 though I [Paul] give my body to be ***b'ed,*** and have not charity

2 Pet 3:10 the earth also and the works...shall be ***b'ed*** up

Rev 19:20 beast...false prophet ...were cast...into a lake... ***b'ing*** with brimstone

BURNING BUSH REVEALED TO MOSES. Ex 3:1–5.

BURNT OFFERING, INSTRUCTIONS FOR. Lev 1:1–17.

BUY [ETH]

Gen 42:3 Joseph's ten brethren went...to ***b*** corn in Egypt

Prov 23:23 ***B*** the truth, and sell it not; also wisdom

Prov 31:16 She considereth a field, and ***b'eth*** it

Amos 8:6 ***b*** the poor for silver... needy for a pair of shoes

Matt 13:44 a man...selleth all...he hath, and ***b'eth*** that field

John 6:5 he [Jesus] saith... Whence shall we ***b*** bread, that these may eat

BUYER

Isa 24:2 as with the ***b,*** so with the seller

Ezek 7:12 let not the ***b*** rejoice, nor the seller mourn

BYWORD

Deut 28:37 thou shalt become... a ***b,*** among all nations

1 Kgs 9:7 Israel shall be...a ***b*** among all people

Job 17:6 He [God] hath made me [Job] also a ***b***

Ps 44:14 Thou [God] makest us a ***b*** among the heathen

-C-

CAESAREA (a city of Judah on the coast of the Mediterranean Sea where Paul was held as a prisoner). Acts 8:40; 9:30; 10:1,24; 11:11; 12:19; 18:22; 21:8–16; **23:23,33; 25:1–16.**

CAESAREA PHILIPPI (a city in northern Palestine where Peter confessed Jesus as the Messiah). Matt 16:13–20.

CAIAPHAS (high priest of the Jews before whom Jesus and the apostles Peter and John appeared). Matt 26:3,57 • Luke 3:2 • John 11:49; 18:13–14,24, 28 • Acts 4:6.

CAIN (oldest son of Adam and Eve who murdered his brother Abel). **Gen 4:1–25** • Heb 11:4 • 1 John 3:12 • Jude 11.

CAINAN. See *Kenan.*

CALEB (one of the twelve spies who scouted Canaan and recommended that Israel attack the Canaanites). **Num 13:6,30;** 14:6,24,30,38; 26:65; 32:12; 34:19 • Deut 1:36 • Josh 14:6,13–14; 15:13–18; 21:12 • Judg 1:12–20 • 1 Sam 25:3; 30:14 • 1 Chr 4:15; 6:56.

CALF

Ex 32:24 I [Aaron] cast it into the fire...there came out this ***c***

Deut 9:16 ye had sinned...and had made you a molten ***c***

Ps 106:19 They made a ***c*** in Horeb, and worshipped the molten image

Isa 11:6 shall lie down with... ***c*** and the young lion

Jer 34:18 they cut the ***c*** in twain, and passed between the parts thereof

Luke 15:23 bring hither the fatted ***c,*** and kill it

Acts 7:41 they made a ***c***...and offered sacrifice unto the idol

CALL [ED, EST, ING]

Gen 1:5 God ***c'ed*** the light Day...the darkness...Night

Gen 2:19 whatsoever Adam ***c'ed*** every living creature, that was the name

Gen 12:8 he [Abraham] builded an altar...and ***c'ed*** upon the name of the LORD

Gen 17:5 Neither shall thy name any more be ***c'ed*** Abram, but...Abraham

Gen 17:19 thou [Abraham] shalt ***c*** his name Isaac

Gen 32:30 Jacob ***c'ed*** the name of the place Peniel

Gen 35:10 thy name shall not be ***c'ed*** any more Jacob

Gen 49:1 Jacob ***c'ed*** unto his sons, and said, Gather yourselves together
Ex 2:7 ***c*** to thee a nurse of the Hebrew women
Ex 2:10 she ***c'ed*** his name Moses...Because I drew him out of the water
Ex 3:4 God ***c'ed*** unto him [Moses] out of the midst of the bush
Ex 19:20 the LORD ***c'ed*** Moses up to the top of the mount
Deut 4:26 I [Moses] ***c*** heaven... to witness against you
Deut 28:10 all people...shall see that thou art ***c'ed*** by the name of the LORD
Judg 16:25 ***C*** for Samson, that he may make us sport
1 Sam 3:8 the LORD ***c'ed*** Samuel again the third time
1 Sam 12:18 So Samuel ***c'ed*** unto the LORD
1 Kgs 18:25 Elijah said...***c*** on the name of your gods, but put no fire under
2 Kgs 5:11 I [Naaman] thought, He [Elisha] will surely...***c*** on...the LORD
1 Chr 11:7 they ***c'ed*** it [Jerusalem] the city of David
1 Chr 16:8 ***c*** upon his [God's] name, make known his deeds
2 Chr 7:14 If my [God's] people, which are ***c'ed*** by my name, shall...pray
Job 27:10 will he always ***c*** upon God
Ps 4:1 Hear me when I ***c,*** O God of my righteousness
Ps 18:3 ***c*** upon the LORD, who is worthy to be praised
Ps 18:6 In my distress I ***c'ed*** upon the LORD
Ps 50:15 ***c*** upon me [God] in the day of trouble
Ps 72:17 all nations shall ***c*** him [God] blessed
Ps 86:5 thou, Lord, art...plenteous in mercy unto all them that ***c*** upon thee
Ps 105:1 give thanks unto the LORD; ***c*** upon his name
Ps 145:18 The LORD is nigh unto all them that ***c*** upon him
Prov 31:28 Her children arise up, and ***c*** her blessed
Isa 7:14 and bear a son, and shall ***c*** his name Immanuel
Isa 9:6 his [Messiah's] name shall be ***c'ed*** Wonderful
Isa 45:3 I, the LORD, which ***c*** thee by thy name, am the God of Israel
Isa 49:1 The LORD hath ***c'ed*** me from the womb
Isa 55:6 ***c*** ye upon him [God] while he is near
Isa 62:2 thou shalt be ***c'ed*** by a new name
Isa 62:4 but thou shalt be ***c'ed*** Hephzibah, and thy land Beulah
Isa 65:24 before they ***c,*** I [God] will answer

Jer 3:17 they shall ***c*** Jerusalem the throne of the LORD

Jer 33:3 ***C*** unto me [God], and I will answer thee

Dan 2:2 the king commanded to ***c*** the magicians

Hos 1:6 God said unto him [Hosea], ***C*** her name Loruhamah

Hos 11:1 then I [God]...***c'ed*** my son out of Egypt

Joel 1:14 Sanctify ye a fast, ***c*** a solemn assembly

Joel 2:32 whosoever shall ***c*** on the name of the LORD shall be delivered

Jon 1:6 O sleeper [Jonah]? arise, ***c*** upon thy God

Matt 1:21 thou [Joseph] shalt ***c*** his name JESUS

Matt 1:25 and he [Joseph] ***c'ed*** his name JESUS

Matt 2:23 He [Jesus] shall be ***c'ed*** a Nazarene

Matt 5:9 the peacemakers... shall be ***c'ed***...children of God

Matt 9:13 I [Jesus] am not come to ***c*** the righteous, but sinners to repentance

Matt 11:16 children sitting in the markets, and ***c'ing*** unto their fellows

Matt 18:2 Jesus ***c'ed*** a little child unto him

Matt 19:17 Why ***c'est*** thou me [Jesus] good

Matt 20:16 many be ***c'ed,*** but few chosen

Matt 21:13 My [God's] house shall be ***c'ed***...house of prayer

Matt 23:9 ***c*** no man your father upon the earth

Matt 27:22 What shall I [Pilate] do then with Jesus which is ***c'ed*** Christ

Luke 1:13 thou [Zacharias] shalt ***c*** his name John

Luke 1:32 He [Jesus]...shall be ***c'ed***...Son of the Highest

Luke 6:46 And why ***c*** ye me, Lord, Lord

Luke 9:1 he [Jesus] ***c'ed*** his twelve disciples together, and gave them...authority

Luke 14:13 ***c*** the poor, the maimed, the lame

Luke 15:21 I [prodigal son] have sinned...no more worthy to be ***c'ed*** thy son

John 1:42 thou [Peter] shalt be ***c'ed*** Cephas...a stone

Acts 2:21 whosoever shall ***c*** on...the Lord shall be saved

Acts 10:15 What God hath cleansed, that ***c*** not thou [Peter] common

Acts 11:26 disciples were ***c'ed*** Christians first in Antioch

Acts 13:2 Separate me Barnabas and Saul for the work whereunto I have ***c'ed*** them

Rom 1:1 Paul, a servant...***c'ed*** to be an apostle

Rom 8:28 all things work together for good...to them who are the ***c'ed***

Rom 10:12 the same Lord...is rich unto all that ***c*** upon him
Rom 10:13 whosoever shall ***c*** upon...the Lord shall be saved
Rom 10:14 How then shall they ***c*** on him in whom they have not believed
1 Cor 1:26 not many mighty, not many noble, are ***c'ed***
1 Cor 7:20 Let every man abide in the same ***c'ing***
Gal 5:13 brethren, ye have been ***c'ed*** unto liberty
Eph 4:1 walk worthy of the vocation...ye are ***c'ed***
Phil 3:14 I [Paul] press toward the mark for the prize of the high ***c'ing*** of God
1 Thes 4:7 For God hath not ***c'ed*** us unto uncleanness, but unto holiness
2 Tim 2:22 follow righteousness...with them that ***c*** on the Lord out of a pure heart
Heb 11:8 Abraham, when he was ***c'ed***...obeyed
Jas 5:14 Is any sick among you? let him ***c*** for the elders
1 Pet 2:9 the praises of him [Jesus] who hath ***c'ed*** you out of darkness
1 John 3:1 that we should be ***c'ed*** the sons of God

CALL ON THE LORD
2 Sam 22:4 I will ***c-o-t-L,*** who is worthy to be praised
2 Tim 2:22 follow righteousness...with them that ***c-o-t-L*** out of a pure heart

CALVARY (a hill near Jerusalem where Jesus was crucified). Luke 23:33. The word is from a Latin word which means "skull," thus "place of the skull." *Golgotha:* Mark 15:22 • John 19:17.

CANA OF GALILEE (a village where Jesus performed His first miracle—the turning of water into wine). **John 2:1–11;** 4:46–54; 21:2.

CANAAN
1. A son of Ham whose descendants founded several tribal peoples in and around Palestine. Gen 9:18–27; 10:6,15–18 • 1 Chr 1:8,13.
2. The region where Canaan's descendants settled and the territory that God promised to Abraham. Gen 15:3–7. *Chanaan:* Acts 7:11.

CANDACE (a title of the queens of Ethiopia in New Testament times). Acts 8:27.

CANDLE
Ps 18:28 For thou [God] wilt light my ***c***
Matt 5:15 Neither do men light a ***c,*** and put it under a bushel

Rev 22:5 they need no **c,** neither light of the sun

CAPERNAUM (a city on the shore of the Sea of Galilee which served as the headquarters for Jesus during His Galilean ministry). **Matt 4:13–17;** 8:5; 11:23; 17:24 • Mark 1:21; 2:1; 9:33 • Luke 4:23,31; 7:1; 10:15 • John 2:12; 4:46; 6:17,24,59.

CAPHTOR (the original home of the Philistines, probably the island of Crete). Deut 2:23 • Jer 47:4 • Amos 9:7.

CAPPADOCIA (a Roman province of Asia Minor). Acts 2:9 • 1 Pet 1:1.

CAPTIVE [S]
Ps 68:18 Thou hast ascended on high, thou hast led captivity ***c***
Isa 61:1 LORD hath anointed me [God's servant]...to proclaim liberty to the ***c's***
Jer 13:19 Judah shall be carried away ***c***
Jer 39:9 Nebuzaradan...carried away ***c*** into Babylon the remnant of the people
Ezek 1:1 as I [Ezekiel] was among the ***c's*** by the river
Luke 4:18 he [God] hath anointed me [Jesus]...to preach deliverance to the ***c's***
Eph 4:8 When he [Jesus] ascended...he led captivity ***c***

CARCHEMISH (an ancient city in Mesopotamia where the Assyrian army defeated the Egyptians). Isa 10:9 • Jer 46:2. *Charchemish:* 2 Chr 35:20–24.

CARE [S, ST, TH]
Mark 4:19 the ***c's*** of this world...choke the word
Mark 4:38 ***c'st*** thou [Jesus] not...we [the disciples] perish
John 10:13 he is an hireling, and ***c'th*** not for the sheep
1 Cor 7:33 he that is married ***c'th*** for the things that are of the world
2 Cor 11:28 that which cometh upon me [Paul] daily, the ***c*** of all the churches
1 Tim 3:5 how shall he take ***c*** of the church of God
1 Pet 5:7 all your ***c*** upon him [Jesus]; for he ***c'th*** for you

CARMEL, MOUNT (a mountain where the prophet Elijah demonstrated the authority of God over the priests of the pagan god Baal). Josh 12:22; 19:26 • 1 Sam 15:12 • **1 Kgs 18:19–45** • 2 Kgs 2:25; 4:25; 19:23 • 2 Chr 26:10 • Song 7:5 • Isa 33:9; 35:2; 37:24 • Jer 46:18; 50:19 • Amos 1:2; 9:3 • Mic 7:14 • Nah 1:4.

CASLUHIM (an ancient people descended from Mizraim, son of Ham; Casluhim was the Hebrew word for Egypt). Gen 10:14 • 1 Chr 1:12.

CAST [ING]

Gen 37:20 slay him [Joseph], and ***c*** him into some pit

Ex 4:3 he [Moses] ***c*** it [his rod] on the ground, and it became a serpent

Ex 32:24 I [Aaron] ***c*** it into the fire...there came out this calf

Lev 16:8 Aaron shall ***c*** lots upon the two goats

Josh 18:10 Joshua ***c*** lots for them in Shiloh

Job 8:20 God will not ***c*** away a perfect man

Job 30:19 He [God] hath ***c*** me into the mire

Ps 37:24 Though he fall, he shall not be utterly ***c*** down

Ps 42:11 Why art thou ***c*** down, O my soul

Ps 51:11 ***C*** me not away from thy [God's] presence

Ps 55:22 ***C*** thy burden upon the LORD...he shall sustain thee

Ps 71:9 ***C*** me not off in the time of old age

Ps 77:7 Will the Lord ***c*** off for ever...be favourable no more

Ps 94:14 the LORD will not ***c*** off his people

Eccl 3:5 A time to ***c*** away stones, and a time to gather

Eccl 11:1 ***C*** thy bread upon the waters

Isa 31:7 every man shall ***c*** away his idols of silver

Jer 7:15 I [God] will ***c*** you out of my sight

Dan 3:21 these men...were ***c*** into the...fiery furnace

Dan 6:16 brought Daniel... ***c*** him into the den of lions

Jon 1:15 they [mariners]...***c*** him [Jonah] forth into the sea

Zech 11:13 thirty pieces of silver, and ***c*** them to the potter

Matt 3:10 tree...bringeth not forth good fruit is...***c*** into the fire

Matt 15:26 take the children's bread, and ***c*** it to dogs

Matt 21:12 Jesus...***c*** out all them that sold and bought in the temple

Matt 27:5 And he [Judas] ***c*** down the pieces of silver

Matt 27:35 crucified him [Jesus], and parted his garments, ***c'ing*** lots

Mark 1:39 he [Jesus] preached...throughout all Galilee, and ***c*** out devils

Mark 12:43 this poor widow hath ***c*** more in

Luke 9:49 Master, we saw one ***c'ing*** out devils in thy name

John 8:7 He that is without sin...let him first ***c*** a stone

Rom 13:12 let us therefore ***c*** off the works of darkness

1 Pet 5:7 ***C'ing*** all your care upon him [Jesus]; for he careth for you

Rev 12:9 the great dragon was ***c*** out, that old serpent

Rev 20:15 not found...in the book of life was ***c*** into the lake of fire

CASTOR AND POLLUX
(pagan gods who were considered protectors of sailors). Paul's ship to Rome featured a carving of these two gods. Acts 28:11.

CAUGHT

2 Sam 18:9 his [Absalom's] head ***c*** hold of the oak

Eccl 9:12 as the birds...***c*** in the snare; so are the sons of men

Matt 14:31 Jesus stretched... his hand, and ***c*** him [Peter]

Acts 8:39 the Spirit of the Lord ***c*** away Philip

1 Thes 4:17 we...shall be ***c*** up together...in the clouds

CEASE [D, ING]

Gen 8:22 While the earth remaineth...day and night shall not ***c***

Josh 5:12 And the manna ***c'd*** on the morrow

Neh 6:3 why should the work ***c***...I [Nehemiah] leave it

Job 32:1 these three men ***c'd*** to answer Job

Ps 37:8 ***C*** from anger, and forsake wrath

Ps 85:4 O God...cause thine anger toward us to ***c***

Prov 23:4 Labour not to be rich: ***c*** from thine...wisdom

Eccl 12:3 the grinders ***c*** because they are few

Ezek 26:13 I will cause the noise of thy songs to ***c***

Jon 1:15 they...cast him [Jonah] forth...and the sea ***c'd*** from her raging

Mark 4:39 the wind ***c'd,*** and there was a great calm

Acts 5:42 they [the apostles] ***c'd*** not to teach and preach Jesus Christ

Acts 12:5 prayer was made without ***c'ing*** of the church unto God for him [Peter]

Rom 1:9 without ***c'ing*** I [Paul] make mention of you always in my prayers

1 Cor 13:8 whether there be tongues, they shall ***c***

Col 1:9 since the day we heard it, do not ***c*** to pray for you

1 Thes 5:17 Pray without ***c'ing***

CEDARS OF LEBANON

Judg 9:15 let fire come out... and devour the ***c-o-L***

Ps 29:5 yea, the LORD breaketh the ***c-o-L***

Ps 104:16 trees...are full of sap; the ***c-o-L,*** which he [God] hath planted

Isa 2:13 upon all the ***c-o-L,*** that are high and lifted up

Isa 14:8 the fir trees rejoice at thee, and the ***c-o-L***

CEDRON. See *Kidron.*

CENCHREA (a harbor of Corinth through which Paul passed during his second missionary journey). **Acts 18:18** • Rom 16:1.

CHALDEANS, LAND OF THE. See *Babylonia.*

CHANAAN. See *Canaan,* No. 2.

CHANGE [D, TH]

Jer 2:11 Hath a nation ***c'd*** their gods, which are...no gods

Jer 13:23 Can the Ethiopian ***c*** his skin...the leopard his spots

Dan 2:21 he [God] ***c'th*** the times and the seasons

Dan 5:6 the king's countenance was ***c'd***

Hos 4:7 therefore will I [God] ***c*** their glory into shame

Rom 1:23 ***c'd*** the glory of the uncorruptible God

Rom 1:26 their women did ***c*** the natural use into that which is against nature

1 Cor 15:51 We shall not all sleep, but we shall all be ***c'd***

Phil 3:21 Who shall ***c*** our vile body...like...his glorious body

CHARCHEMISH. See *Carchemish.*

CHARGE [D]

Deut 3:28 ***c*** Joshua, and encourage him

1 Kgs 2:1 David...***c'd*** Solomon his son

Ps 91:11 For he [God] shall give his angels ***c*** over thee

Matt 16:20 Then ***c'd*** he...that they should tell no man that he was Jesus the Christ

Mark 8:15 And he [Jesus] ***c'd*** them, saying...beware of the leaven of the Pharisees

Luke 8:56 he [Jesus] ***c'd*** them... tell no man what was done

Acts 7:60 Lord, lay not this sin to their ***c***

1 Tim 6:17 ***C*** them that are rich...they be not highminded

CHARITY

1 Cor 13:3 and have not ***c,*** it profiteth me nothing

Col 3:14 And above all these things put on ***c***

1 Tim 4:12 be thou an example...in conversation, in ***c***

1 Pet 4:8 ***c*** shall cover the multitude of sins

Rev 2:19 I [Jesus] know thy works, and ***c,*** and service

CHARRAN. See *Haran.*

CHASTEN [ED, EST, ETH, ING]

Ps 38:1 O LORD, rebuke me not...neither ***c*** me in thy hot displeasure

Ps 73:14 all the day long have I been...***c'ed*** every morning

Ps 94:12 Blessed is the man whom thou ***c'est,*** O LORD

Prov 3:11 My son, despise not the ***c'ing*** of the LORD

1 Cor 11:32 we are judged, we are ***c'ed*** of the Lord

Heb 12:6 whom the Lord loveth he ***c'eth***

Rev 3:19 As many as I love, I rebuke and ***c***

CHEBAR (a river or canal of Babylonia where the prophet Ezekiel received his visions during the Exile). Ezek 1:1,3; 3:15,23; 10:15,20,22; 43:3.

CHEDORLAOMER (a king of Elam who invaded Canaan in Abraham's time). Gen 14:1–17.

CHEER

Matt 9:2 Son [man with palsy], be of good ***c***

John 16:33 be of good ***c;*** I [Jesus] have overcome the world

Acts 23:11 Be of good ***c,*** Paul... so must thou bear witness also at Rome

CHEERFUL

Prov 15:13 A merry heart maketh a ***c*** countenance

Zech 9:17 corn shall make the young men ***c***

2 Cor 9:7 let him give...for God loveth a ***c*** giver

CHEMOSH (chief pagan god of the Moabites and Ammonites to which children were sacrificed). Num 21:29 • Judg 11:24 • 1 Kgs 11:7,33 • 2 Kgs 23:13 • Jer 48:7,13,46.

CHERETHIMS. See *Cherethites.*

CHERETHITES (a tribe of the Philistines in southwest Palestine). 1 Sam 30:14 • Zeph 2:5. *Cherethims:* Ezek 25:16.

CHERITH (a brook where the prophet Elijah was fed by ravens during a famine). 1 Kgs 17:3–6.

CHILD

Gen 17:17 a ***c*** be born unto him...an hundred years old

Ex 22:22 Ye shall not afflict any widow, or fatherless ***c***

1 Kgs 3:25 king [Solomon] said, Divide the living ***c*** in two

1 Kgs 17:22 the soul of the ***c*** came into him...he revived

2 Kgs 5:14 his [Naaman's] flesh came again like unto the flesh of a little ***c***

Prov 22:6 Train up a ***c*** in the way he should go
Isa 9:6 unto us a ***c*** is born, unto us a son is given
Jer 1:6 behold, I [Jeremiah] cannot speak: for I am a ***c***
Hos 11:1 When Israel was a ***c,*** then I [God] loved him
Matt 1:23 a virgin shall be with ***c***...bring forth a son
Matt 2:21 he [Joseph]...took the young ***c***...and came into the land of Israel
Matt 18:4 Whosoever...shall humble himself as this little ***c,*** the same is greatest
Mark 10:15 not receive the kingdom...as a little ***c,*** he shall not enter
Luke 2:17 they made known abroad the saying...concerning this ***c***
Luke 2:40 the ***c*** [Jesus] grew, and waxed strong in spirit
1 Cor 13:11 When I [Paul] was a ***c,*** I spake as a ***c***
2 Tim 3:15 from a ***c*** thou [Timothy] hast known the holy scriptures

CHILDREN

Gen 3:16 in sorrow thou [Eve] shalt bring forth ***c***
Gen 37:3 Israel loved Joseph more than all his ***c***
Ex 1:7 the ***c*** of Israel were fruitful, and increased
Ex 12:26 when your ***c*** shall say...What mean ye by this service
Ex 20:5 visiting the iniquity of the fathers upon the ***c***
Num 8:17 the firstborn of the ***c*** of Israel are mine [God's]
Deut 24:16 The fathers shall not be put to death for the ***c***
Josh 4:6 when your ***c*** ask their fathers...What mean ye by these stones
Josh 18:10 Joshua divided the land unto the ***c*** of Israel
Job 19:18 Yea, young ***c*** despised me [Job]
Ps 14:2 The LORD looked down...upon the ***c*** of men
Ps 34:11 Come, ye ***c***...I will teach...the fear of the LORD
Ps 103:7 He [God] made known...acts unto the ***c*** of Israel
Ps 103:13 as a father pitieth his ***c,*** so the LORD pitieth them that fear him
Ps 115:14 The LORD shall increase...you and your ***c***
Ps 127:3 Lo, ***c*** are an heritage of the LORD
Ps 127:4 As arrows are in the hand of a mighty man; so are ***c*** of the youth
Prov 4:1 Hear, ye ***c,*** the instruction of a father
Prov 13:22 A good man leaveth an inheritance to his children's ***c***
Prov 20:7 his ***c*** are blessed after him [the just man]
Prov 31:28 Her ***c*** arise up, and call her blessed

Isa 54:13 all thy ***c*** shall be taught of the LORD
Jer 3:22 Return, ye backsliding ***c***...I [God] will heal
Jer 31:15 Rahel weeping for her ***c*** refused to be comforted
Lam 1:16 my ***c*** are desolate, because the enemy prevailed
Hos 2:4 they be the ***c*** of whoredoms
Matt 2:16 Herod...slew all the ***c***...in Bethlehem
Matt 7:11 know how to give good gifts unto your ***c***
Matt 18:3 Except ye...become as little ***c,*** ye shall not enter into the kingdom
Matt 23:37 how often would I [Jesus] have gathered thy ***c***
Matt 27:25 His [Jesus'] blood be on us, and on our ***c***
Mark 10:13 they brought young ***c*** to him [Jesus]
Luke 16:8 the ***c*** of this world... wiser than the ***c*** of light
John 8:39 If ye were Abraham's ***c,*** ye would do the works of Abraham
John 12:36 that ye may be the ***c*** of light
1 Cor 14:20 Brethren, be not ***c*** in understanding
Gal 4:28 we, brethren...are the ***c*** of promise
Eph 4:14 That we henceforth be no more ***c***
Eph 6:1 ***C,*** obey your parents in the Lord
Eph 6:4 fathers, provoke not your ***c*** to wrath
1 Thes 5:5 Ye are all the ***c*** of light...children of the day
1 John 2:1 My little ***c***...write I unto you, that ye sin not
1 John 3:18 little ***c,*** let us not love in word...but in deed
1 John 5:21 Little ***c,*** keep yourselves from idols
3 John 4 no greater joy than to hear that my [John's] ***c*** walk in truth

CHILDREN OF GOD
Matt 5:9 Blessed are the peacemakers: for they shall be called the ***c-o-G***
Rom 8:16 The Spirit...beareth witness...we are the ***c-o-G***
Gal 3:26 ye are all the ***c-o-G*** by faith in Christ Jesus
1 John 5:2 know that we love the ***c-o-G,*** when we love God

CHILDREN WELCOMED BY JESUS. Matt 19:13–15 • Mark 10:13–16 • Luke 18:15–17.

CHINNEROTH, SEA OF. See *Galilee, Sea of.*

CHITTIM. See *Cyprus.*

CHLOE (a believer in Corinth). 1 Cor 1:11.

CHOOSE [ING]

Deut 7:7 The LORD did not...***c*** you, because ye were more in number

Deut 30:19 ***c*** life, that both thou and thy seed may live

Josh 24:15 ***c*** you this day whom ye will serve

Neh 9:7 Thou art the LORD the God, who didst ***c*** Abram

Phil 1:22 yet what I [Paul] shall ***c*** I wot not

Heb 11:25 ***C'ing*** rather to suffer affliction

CHORAZIN (a city near the Sea of Galilee upon which Jesus pronounced a woe because of its unbelief). Matt 11:21 • Luke 10:13.

CHOSEN

Deut 7:6 God hath ***c*** thee to be a special people

Judg 10:14 Go and cry unto the gods which ye have ***c***

1 Chr 16:13 ye children of Jacob, his [God's] ***c*** ones

1 Chr 28:5 he [God] hath ***c*** Solomon my [David's] son to sit upon the throne

Ps 33:12 Blessed is...the people whom he [God] hath ***c*** for his own inheritance

Prov 22:1 A good name is rather to be ***c*** than great riches

Isa 43:10 Ye are...my [God's] servant whom I have ***c***

Matt 12:18 Behold my [God's] servant, whom I have ***c***

Matt 20:16 for many be called, but few ***c***

Luke 10:42 Mary hath ***c*** that good part

John 15:16 Ye have not ***c*** me [Jesus], but I have ***c*** you

Acts 9:15 he [Paul] is a ***c*** vessel unto me [Jesus]

1 Cor 1:27 God hath ***c*** the foolish things of the world to confound the wise

2 Thes 2:13 God hath...***c*** you to salvation

1 Pet 2:9 ye are a ***c*** generation, a royal priesthood

CHRONICLES, BOOKS OF FIRST AND SECOND. Two historical books of the Old Testament that cover several centuries of history, beginning with a genealogy of Adam and his descendants (1 Chr 1–9) and ending with the return of Jewish captives to their homeland about 538 B.C. following a period of exile (2 Chr 36).

CHURCH [ES]

Matt 16:18 thou art Peter, and upon this rock I [Jesus] will build my ***c***

Matt 18:17 if he shall neglect to hear them, tell it unto the ***c***

Acts 2:47 Lord added to the ***c*** daily such as should be saved

Acts 5:11 great fear came upon all the ***c***

Acts 8:3 As for Saul, he made havock of the ***c***

Acts 14:23 when they [Paul and Barnabas] had ordained them elders in every ***c***

Acts 20:28 the Holy Ghost hath made you overseers, to feed the ***c*** of God

Rom 16:16 The ***c'es*** of Christ salute you

1 Cor 14:4 he that prophesieth edifieth the ***c***

1 Cor 14:35 it is a shame for women to speak in the ***c***

2 Cor 11:28 cometh upon me [Paul] daily, the care of all the ***c'es***

Gal 1:13 I [Paul] persecuted the ***c*** of God

Eph 3:21 Unto him be glory in the ***c*** by Christ Jesus

Eph 5:25 Christ also loved the ***c,*** and gave himself for it

Col 1:18 he [Christ] is the head of the body, the ***c***

1 Tim 3:5 how shall he take care of the ***c*** of God

1 Tim 3:15 ***c*** of the living God... pillar and ground of...truth

Jas 5:14 elders of the ***c;*** and let them pray over him

Rev 1:4 John to the seven ***c'es*** which are in Asia

Rev 2:1 Unto the angel of the ***c*** of Ephesus

Rev 2:8 unto the angel of the ***c*** in Smyrna

Rev 2:12 to the angel of the ***c*** in Pergamos

Rev 2:18 unto the angel of the ***c*** in Thyatira

Rev 3:1 unto the angel of the ***c*** in Sardis

Rev 3:7 to the angel of the ***c*** in Philadelphia

Rev 3:14 unto the angel of the ***c*** of the Laodiceans

CHUSHAN-RISHATHAIM (a king of Mesopotamia who was defeated by the judge Othniel). Judg 3:8–10.

CILICIA (a province of Asia Minor whose major city was Tarsus, the apostle Paul's hometown). Acts 6:9; 15:23,41; 21:39; 22:3; 23:34; 27:5 • Gal 1:21.

CIRCUMCISE [D]

Gen 17:11 ye shall ***c*** the flesh of your foreskin

Gen 17:24 Abraham was ninety years old and nine, when he was ***c'd***

Lev 12:3 eighth day the flesh of his foreskin shall be ***c'd***

Josh 5:2 ***c*** again the children of Israel the second time

Jer 4:4 ***C*** yourselves to the LORD, and take away the foreskins of your heart

Acts 15:1 certain men...from Judaea...said, Except ye be ***c'd***...ye cannot be saved

Gal 5:2 if ye be ***c'd,*** Christ shall profit you nothing

Phil 3:5 ***C'd*** the eighth day, of the stock of Israel

CIRCUMCISION

Acts 10:45 they of the ***c*** which believed were astonished

Rom 3:1 or what profit is there of ***c***

Rom 15:8 Christ was a minister of the ***c*** for the truth of God

1 Cor 7:19 ***C*** is nothing, and uncircumcision is nothing

Col 3:11 neither Greek nor Jew, ***c*** nor uncircumcision

CITIES OF REFUGE (six cities—Bezer, Golan, Hebron, Kedesh, Ramoth-gilead, and Shechem—set aside as sanctuaries for those who killed other persons by accident). Num 35:11,14 • Josh 20:2,8; 21:13, 21,27,32,38 • 1 Chr 6:57,67.

CLAUDA (a small island near Crete where Paul's ship anchored during a storm). Acts 27:16.

CLAUDIUS LYSIAS (a Roman military officer who protected Paul from his enemies). Acts 21:30–35; 23:22–30.

CLEAN AND UNCLEAN ANIMALS. Lev 11:1–47.

CLEANSE [D, TH]

Lev 16:30 shall the priest make an atonement...to ***c*** you

Neh 13:22 I [Nehemiah] commanded the Levites that they should ***c*** themselves

Ps 51:2 Wash me thoroughly... and ***c*** me from my sin

Ps 73:13 Verily I have ***c'd*** my heart in vain

Matt 11:5 the lepers are ***c'd,*** and the deaf hear

Matt 23:26 ***c*** first that which is within the cup

Mark 1:42 the leprosy departed...and he was ***c'd***

Luke 17:17 Were there not ten ***c'd?*** but where are the nine

Acts 10:15 What God hath ***c'd,*** that call not thou [Peter] common

2 Cor 7:1 let us ***c*** ourselves from all filthiness

1 John 1:7 the blood of Jesus Christ...***c'th*** us from all sin

1 John 1:9 he [Jesus] is faithful and just...to ***c*** us from all unrighteousness

CLEAVE [D, TH]

Gen 2:24 shall a man leave his father and his mother, and shall ***c*** unto his wife

Deut 10:20 to him [God] shalt thou ***c***...swear by his name

Josh 23:8 But ***c*** unto the LORD your God

Job 19:20 My bone ***c'th*** to my skin and to my flesh

Job 29:10 their tongue ***c'd*** to the roof of their mouth
Ps 102:5 By reason...of my groaning my bones ***c*** to my skin
Ps 137:6 let my tongue ***c*** to the roof of my mouth; if I prefer not Jerusalem
Mark 10:7 shall a man leave his father and mother, and ***c*** to his wife
Rom 12:9 Abhor that which is evil; ***c*** to that which is good

CLEOPAS (a Christian believer to whom the resurrected Christ appeared on the road to Emmaus). Luke 24:18.

CLEOPHAS (the husband of Mary, one of the women who was present at the crucifixion of Jesus). John 19:25. *Alphaeus:* Matt 10:3.

CLOTHE [D, ING]
Gen 3:21 Unto Adam...wife did...God make coats of skins, and ***c'd*** them
2 Chr 6:41 O LORD God, be ***c'd*** with salvation
Job 7:5 My [Job's] flesh is ***c'd*** with worms
Ps 93:1 The LORD...is ***c'd*** with majesty
Ps 132:9 Let thy priests be ***c'd*** with righteousness
Prov 31:25 Strength and honour are her ***c'ing***
Isa 50:3 I [God] ***c*** the heavens with blackness
Isa 61:10 For he [God] hath ***c'd*** me with the garments of salvation
Matt 7:15 Beware of false prophets...in sheep's ***c'ing***
Matt 25:36 Naked, and ye ***c'd*** me; sick...ye visited me
Mark 1:6 John was ***c'd*** with camel's hair
Mark 12:38 the scribes...love to go in long ***c'ing***
Mark 15:17 they ***c'd*** him [Jesus] with purple
Luke 12:28 how much more will he [God] ***c*** you, O ye of little faith
Luke 16:19 a certain rich man...***c'd*** in purple
1 Pet 5:5 be subject one to another...***c'd*** with humility
Rev 19:13 he was ***c'd*** with a vesture dipped in blood

CLOTHES
Gen 37:34 Jacob rent his ***c***... put sackcloth upon his loins
Num 8:21 the Levites were purified...washed their ***c***
Josh 7:6 Joshua rent his ***c,*** and fell to the earth
1 Kgs 1:1 covered him [David] with ***c,*** but he gat no heat
Prov 6:27 Can a man take fire in his bosom, and his ***c*** not be burned
Mark 5:28 she [woman with issue of blood] said, If I...

touch but his [Jesus'] ***c,*** I shall be whole

Luke 2:7 wrapped him [Jesus] in swaddling ***c***

John 19:40 wound it [Jesus' body] in linen ***c***

Acts 7:58 laid down...***c*** at a young man's [Paul's] feet

CLOUD [S]

Gen 9:13 I [God] do set my bow in the ***c***

Ex 13:21 LORD went before them [Israel]...pillar of a ***c***

Ex 40:34 a ***c*** covered the tent of the congregation

1 Kgs 8:10 the ***c*** filled the house of the LORD

1 Kgs 18:44 there ariseth a little ***c*** out of the sea

Job 26:8 He [God] bindeth up the waters in his thick ***c's***

Ps 78:14 he [God] led them [Israel] with a ***c***

Ps 108:4 and thy [God's] truth reacheth unto the ***c's***

Prov 3:20 By his [God's] knowledge...the ***c's*** drop down the dew

Isa 14:14 I will ascend above the heights of the ***c's***

Isa 19:1 the LORD rideth upon a swift ***c***

Isa 44:22 I [God] have blotted out, as a thick ***c,*** thy transgressions

Lam 3:44 Thou [God] hast covered thyself with a ***c***

Joel 2:2 A day of darkness and...gloominess, a day of ***c's***

Matt 24:30 the Son of man coming in the ***c's***

Mark 9:7 voice came out of the ***c,*** saying, This is my beloved Son [Jesus]

Luke 21:27 Son of man coming in a ***c*** with power and great glory

Acts 1:9 he [Jesus] was taken up; and a ***c*** received him out of their sight

1 Thes 4:17 we...shall be caught up together with them in the ***c's***

Heb 12:1 we also are compassed about with so great a ***c*** of witnesses

Rev 1:7 Behold, he [Jesus] cometh with ***c's;*** and every eye shall see him

COCK

Matt 26:34 before the ***c*** crow, thou [Peter] shalt deny me [Jesus] thrice

Mark 14:68 he [Peter] went out...and the ***c*** crew

Luke 22:61 Peter remembered...Before the ***c*** crow, thou shalt deny me [Jesus]

COLD

Ps 147:17 who can stand before his [God's] ***c***

Prov 25:25 As ***c*** waters to a thirsty soul, so is good news

Matt 24:12 the love of many shall wax ***c***

Rev 3:15 thou [church at Laodicea] art neither ***c*** nor hot

COLOSSE (a city near Ephesus and the site of a church to which Paul wrote one of his epistles). Col 1:2.

COLOSSIANS, EPISTLE TO THE. A short epistle of the apostle Paul on the theme of Christ's glory and majesty and His work of redemption (chaps. 1–2). Paul also challenged the Colossian Christians to express the love of Christ in their relationships with others (chaps. 3–4).

COMFORT [ED, ETH]

Job 2:11 Job's three friends... came...to ***c*** him

Ps 23:4 thy [God's] rod and thy staff they ***c*** me

Isa 40:1 **C** ye, ***c*** ye my people, saith your God

Isa 49:13 the LORD hath ***c'ed*** his people

Isa 61:2 To proclaim the acceptable year of the LORD...to ***c*** all that mourn

Jer 31:15 Rahel weeping for her children refused to be ***c'ed*** for her children

Lam 1:21 there is none to ***c*** me

Matt 5:4 Blessed are they that mourn: for they shall be ***c'ed***

Luke 8:48 be of good ***c***...faith hath made thee [woman with issue of blood] whole

2 Cor 1:3 Blessed be God...the Father of mercies, and the God of all ***c***

2 Cor 1:4 Who ***c'eth*** us in all our tribulation

Phil 2:1 If there be therefore any consolation in Christ, if any ***c*** of love

1 Thes 4:18 ***c*** one another with these words

COMFORTER

John 14:26 the **C**...shall teach you all things

John 15:26 the **C**...shall testify of me [Jesus]

John 16:7 if I [Jesus] go not away, the ***C*** will not come unto you

COMMAND [ED, ETH, ING]

Gen 7:5 Noah did...all that the LORD ***c'ed*** him

Gen 21:4 Abraham circumcised his son Isaac...as God had ***c'ed*** him

Gen 49:33 Jacob had made an end of ***c'ing*** his sons

Ex 19:7 Moses...laid before their faces all these words which the LORD ***c'ed***

Deut 4:2 Ye shall not add unto the word...I [God] ***c*** you

Deut 5:12 Keep the sabbath day to sanctify it, as the LORD...hath ***c'ed***

Josh 1:9 Have not I [God] ***c'ed*** thee? Be strong and of a good courage

1 Sam 13:13 thou [Saul] hast not kept the commandment...which he [God] ***c'ed*** thee

1 Chr 16:15 the word which he [God] ***c'ed*** to a thousand generations

Ps 33:9 he [God] ***c'ed,*** and it stood fast

Ps 105:8 He [God] hath remembered...the word...he ***c'ed***

Jer 1:17 speak unto them all that I [God] ***c*** thee [Jeremiah]

Dan 6:16 the king ***c'ed,*** and they...cast him [Daniel] into the den of lions

Matt 28:20 observe all things whatsoever I [Jesus] have ***c'ed*** you

Mark 1:27 with authority ***c'eth*** he [Jesus]...the unclean spirits

Mark 6:8 [Jesus] ***c'ed*** them that they should take nothing for their journey

Luke 4:3 ***c*** this stone that it be made bread

Luke 8:25 for he [Jesus] ***c'eth*** even the winds and water

John 8:5 Moses in the law ***c'ed*** us...such should be stoned

John 15:17 These things I [Jesus] ***c*** you...love one another

COMMANDMENT [S]

Ex 16:28 How long refuse ye to keep my [God's] ***c's***

Ex 34:28 he [Moses] wrote upon the tables...the ten ***c's***

Lev 27:34 These are the ***c's***... for the children of Israel in mount Sinai

Deut 28:9 thou shalt keep the ***c's*** of the LORD thy God

1 Kgs 2:3 keep his [God's]...***c's,*** and his judgments

2 Kgs 17:16 they left all the ***c's*** of the LORD

Ezra 9:10 for we have forsaken thy [God's] ***c's***

Ps 111:7 all his [God's] ***c's*** are sure

Ps 119:10 let me not wander from thy [God's] ***c's***

Ps 119:115 I will keep the ***c's*** of my God

Ps 147:15 He [God] sendeth forth his ***c*** upon earth

Prov 6:20 My son, keep thy father's ***c***

Prov 10:8 The wise in heart will receive ***c's:*** but a prating fool shall fall

Eccl 12:13 keep his [God's] ***c's***...this is the...duty of man

Amos 2:4 they have...not kept his [God's] ***c's***

Matt 15:3 ye [Pharisees] also transgress the ***c*** of God by your tradition

Matt 22:40 On these two ***c's*** hang...the law and the prophets

Mark 12:28 Which is the first ***c*** of all
Mark 12:29 The first of all the ***c's*** is...The Lord our God is one Lord
John 13:34 A new ***c*** I [Jesus] give unto you, That ye love one another
John 14:15 If ye love me [Jesus], keep my ***c's***
John 15:10 If ye keep my [Jesus'] ***c's,*** ye shall abide in my love
John 15:12 This is my [Jesus'] ***c***...love one another, as I have loved you
1 Cor 7:19 Circumcision is nothing...but the keeping of the ***c's*** of God
Eph 6:2 Honour thy father and mother; which is the first ***c*** with promise
1 John 2:3 we know him [Jesus], if we keep his ***c's***
2 John 6 this is love, that we walk after his [God's] ***c's***
Rev 22:14 Blessed are they that do his [God's] ***c's***

COMMANDMENT [S] OF THE LORD
Num 9:18 At the ***c-o-t-L*** the children of Israel journeyed
Num 14:41 Wherefore now do ye transgress the ***c-o-t-L***
Deut 4:2 keep the ***c's-o-t-L*** your God
Deut 8:6 thou shalt keep the ***c's-o-t-L*** thy God
1 Sam 15:24 I [Saul] have transgressed the ***c-o-t-L***
2 Kgs 17:16 they left all the ***c's-o-t-L***...and made them molten images
Ps 19:8 the ***c-o-t-L*** is pure, enlightening the eyes

COMMEND [ED, ETH]
Prov 12:8 A man shall be ***c'ed*** according to his wisdom
Luke 16:8 the lord ***c'ed*** the unjust steward, because he had done wisely
Luke 23:46 Father, into thy hands I [Jesus] ***c*** my spirit
Rom 5:8 God ***c'eth*** his love toward us...Christ died for us
Rom 16:1 I [Paul] ***c*** unto you Phebe our sister

COMMIT [TED, TETH]
Gen 39:22 the keeper of the prison ***c'ted*** to Joseph's hand all the prisoners
Ex 20:14 Thou shalt not ***c*** adultery
Lev 18:29 the souls that ***c*** them shall be cut off
Lev 20:10 the man that ***c'teth*** adultery...shall surely be put to death
Josh 22:20 Did not Achan the son of Zerah ***c*** a trespass
Ps 31:5 Into thine [God's] hand I ***c*** my spirit
Prov 6:32 whoso ***c'teth*** adultery with a woman lacketh understanding

Prov 16:3 **C** thy works unto the Lord
Jer 2:13 my [God's] people have ***c'ted*** two evils
Matt 5:28 whosoever looketh on a woman to lust after her hath ***c'ted*** adultery
Matt 5:32 whosoever shall marry her that is divorced ***c'teth*** adultery
Mark 10:11 Whosoever shall put away his wife, and marry another, ***c'teth*** adultery
Mark 10:19 Thou knowest the commandments, Do not ***c*** adultery, Do not kill
John 5:22 Father...hath ***c'ted*** all judgment unto the Son
John 8:34 Whosoever ***c'teth*** sin is the servant of sin
1 Cor 6:18 he that ***c'teth*** fornication sinneth against his own body
1 Cor 10:8 Neither let us ***c*** fornication, as some of them
2 Cor 5:19 God...in Christ... hath ***c'ted*** unto us the word of reconciliation
1 Tim 6:20 Timothy, keep that which is ***c'ted*** to thy trust
2 Tim 1:12 he [Jesus] is able to keep that which I [Paul] have ***c'ted***...against that day
2 Tim 2:2 the same ***c*** thou to faithful men
1 John 3:9 Whosoever is born of God doth not ***c*** sin

COMMON

Mark 12:37 the ***c*** people heard him [Jesus] gladly
Acts 2:44 all that believed... had all things ***c***
Acts 10:14 I [Peter] have never eaten any thing that is ***c*** or unclean
1 Cor 10:13 There hath no temptation taken you but such as is ***c*** to man

COMMUNICATION [S]

Matt 5:37 let your ***c*** be, Yea, yea; Nay, nay
Luke 24:17 What manner of ***c's*** are these
Eph 4:29 Let no corrupt ***c*** proceed out of your mouth

COMMUNION

1 Cor 10:16 cup of blessing which we bless, is it not the ***c*** of the blood of Christ
2 Cor 6:14 what ***c*** hath light with darkness
2 Cor 13:14 and the ***c*** of the Holy Ghost, be with you all

COMPASSION [S]

Ex 2:6 she had ***c*** on him [Moses], and said, This is one of the Hebrews' children
Ps 86:15 thou, O Lord, art a God full of ***c***
Ps 145:8 The LORD is gracious, and full of ***c***

Jer 12:15 I [God] will return, and have ***c*** on them

Zech 7:9 show mercy and ***c's*** every man to his brother

Matt 14:14 Jesus...was moved with ***c*** toward them

Matt 18:27 the lord of that servant was moved with ***c,*** and loosed him

Mark 9:22 if thou canst do any thing, have ***c*** on us

Luke 10:33 a certain Samaritan...when he saw him, he had ***c*** on him

Luke 15:20 his father...had ***c,*** and ran, and fell on his neck

1 Pet 3:8 be ye all of one mind, having ***c*** one of another

1 John 3:17 seeth his brother have need, and shutteth up his bowels of ***c*** from him

COMPEL

Matt 5:41 ***c*** thee to go a mile, go with him twain

Mark 15:21 they ***c*** one Simon a Cyrenian...to bear his [Jesus'] cross

Luke 14:23 Go out into the highways and hedges, and ***c*** them to come in

CONCEIT [S]

Prov 26:5 Answer a fool...lest he be wise in his own ***c***

Prov 28:11 The rich man is wise in his own ***c***

Rom 12:16 Be not wise in your own ***c's***

CONCEIVE [D]

Gen 21:2 Sarah ***c'd,*** and bare Abraham a son

Job 3:3 the day perish...in which it was said, There is a man child ***c'd***

Ps 51:5 shapen in iniquity, and in sin did my mother ***c*** me

Isa 7:14 a virgin shall ***c,*** and bear a son

Matt 1:20 that...***c'd*** in her [Mary] is of the Holy Ghost

Luke 1:31 thou [Mary] shalt ***c***...and bring forth a son

Luke 1:36 thy [Mary's] cousin Elisabeth, she hath also ***c'd*** a son in her old age

Heb 11:11 Sara herself received strength to ***c*** seed

CONCERNING

Luke 2:17 they [shepherds] made known abroad the saying...***c*** this child

Luke 18:31 all things that are written...***c*** the Son of man shall be accomplished

Luke 24:27 he [Jesus] expounded...the things ***c*** himself

Acts 28:22 for as ***c*** this sect...it is spoken against

1 Cor 12:1 Now ***c*** spiritual gifts, brethren

Eph 5:32 I [Paul] speak ***c*** Christ and the church

1 Thes 5:18 this is the will of God in Christ Jesus ***c*** you

1 Pet 4:12 ***c*** the fiery trial which is to try you

2 Pet 3:9 The Lord is not slack ***c*** his promise

CONDEMN [ED, ETH]

Job 15:6 Thine own mouth ***c'eth*** thee

Prov 12:2 a man of wicked devices will he [God] ***c***

Matt 12:37 by thy words thou shalt be ***c'ed***

Luke 6:37 ***c*** not, and ye shall not be ***c'ed***

John 3:17 God sent not his Son...to ***c*** the world

John 8:11 Neither do I [Jesus] ***c*** thee: go...sin no more

CONDEMNATION

John 3:19 the ***c***...men loved darkness rather than light

Rom 8:1 no ***c*** to them which are in Christ Jesus

Jas 3:1 knowing that we shall receive the greater ***c***

Jas 5:12 let your yea be yea... lest ye fall into ***c***

CONFESS [ETH, ING]

Ps 32:5 I will ***c*** my transgressions unto the LORD

Mark 1:5 were all baptized of him [John the Baptist]... ***c'ing*** their sins

Luke 12:8 him shall the Son of man also ***c***

Rom 10:9 if thou shalt ***c*** with thy mouth the Lord Jesus

Phil 2:11 every tongue should ***c*** that Jesus Christ is Lord

Jas 5:16 ***C*** your faults one to another

1 John 1:9 If we ***c*** our sins, he is faithful and just to forgive

1 John 4:2 Every spirit that ***c'eth*** that Jesus Christ is come in the flesh is of God

1 John 4:15 Whosoever shall ***c*** that Jesus is the Son of God, God dwelleth in him

Rev 3:5 I [Jesus] will ***c*** his name before my Father

CONFIDENCE

Ps 118:9 better to trust in the LORD than to put ***c*** in princes

Prov 14:26 In the fear of the LORD is strong ***c***

Isa 30:15 in quietness and in ***c*** shall be your strength

Mic 7:5 put ye not ***c*** in a guide

Eph 3:12 In whom [Jesus] we have...access with ***c***

1 John 2:28 when he [Jesus] shall appear, we may have ***c***

CONFIDENT

Prov 14:16 but the fool rageth, and is ***c***

2 Cor 5:8 We are ***c***...willing... to be absent from the body

Phil 1:6 Being ***c***...that he which hath begun a good work...will perform it

CONFIRM [ED, ETH, ING]

Deut 27:26 Cursed be he that ***c'eth*** not all the words of this law to do them

1 Chr 14:2 David perceived... LORD had ***c'ed*** him king
Mark 16:20 the Lord working with them, and ***c'ing*** the word with signs
Acts 15:41 And he [Paul] went through Syria and Cilicia, ***c'ing*** the churches
Rom 15:8 Jesus Christ was a minister...to ***c*** the promises made unto the fathers
1 Cor 1:6 as the testimony of Christ was ***c'ed*** in you
1 Cor 1:8 Who [Jesus] shall also ***c*** you unto the end
2 Cor 2:8 ***c*** your love toward him [Jesus]

CONFORMED
Rom 8:29 he [God] also did predestinate to be ***c*** to the image of his Son
Rom 12:2 be not ***c*** to this world: but be ye transformed

CONIAH. See *Jehoiachin.*

CONQUEST OF CANAAN BY ISRAEL. Josh 6–12.

CONSCIENCE
John 8:9 they [scribes and Pharisees]...being convicted by their own ***c,*** went out
Acts 23:1 I [Paul] have lived in all good ***c*** before God
1 Cor 8:12 when ye...wound their weak ***c,*** ye sin
1 Cor 10:27 eat, asking no question for ***c*** sake
1 Tim 1:5 charity out of a pure heart, and of a good ***c***
1 Tim 3:9 mystery of the faith in a pure ***c***
Heb 9:14 the blood of Christ... purge...***c*** from dead works

CONSENT [ING]
Prov 1:10 if sinners entice thee, ***c*** thou not
Luke 14:18 all with one ***c*** began to make excuse
Acts 8:1 Saul was ***c'ing*** unto his [Stephen's] death
Acts 22:20 I [Paul]...was... ***c'ing*** unto his [Stephen's] death
1 Cor 7:5 Defraud ye not... except it be with ***c*** for a time

CONSIDER [ED, EST, ETH, ING]
1 Sam 12:24 ***c*** how great things he [God] hath done
Job 1:8 Hast thou [Satan] ***c'ed*** my [God's] servant Job
Job 37:14 stand still, and ***c*** the wondrous works of God
Ps 8:3 When I ***c*** thy [God's] heavens, the work of thy fingers...moon and...stars
Ps 25:19 ***C*** mine enemies; for they are many
Ps 41:1 Blessed is he that ***c'eth*** the poor
Ps 119:153 ***C*** mine affliction, and deliver me

Prov 6:6 Go to the ant, thou sluggard; ***c*** her ways
Prov 31:16 She ***c'eth*** a field, and buyeth it
Isa 43:18 neither ***c*** the things of old
Hag 1:5 thus saith the LORD of hosts; ***C*** your ways
Matt 6:28 ***C*** the lilies of the field, how they grow
Matt 7:3 but ***c'est*** not the beam that is in thine own eye
Gal 6:1 ***c'ing*** thyself, lest thou also be tempted
Heb 3:1 ***c*** the...High Priest of our profession, Christ Jesus

CONSOLATION
Luke 2:25 man [Simeon] was just and devout, waiting for the ***c*** of Israel
Luke 6:24 But woe unto you that are rich! for ye have received your ***c***
Acts 4:36 Barnabas...being interpreted, The son of ***c***
Rom 15:5 the God of...***c*** grant you to be likeminded
Phil 2:1 If there be therefore any ***c*** in Christ

CONTENT
Phil 4:11 whatsoever state I [Paul] am, therewith to be ***c***
1 Tim 6:8 having food and raiment let us be therewith ***c***
Heb 13:5 be ***c*** with such things as ye have

CONTINUE [D, ING, TH]
Luke 6:12 he [Jesus]...***c'd*** all night in prayer
John 8:31 If ye ***c*** in my [Jesus'] word, then are ye my disciples indeed
John 15:9 so have I [Jesus] loved you: ***c*** ye in my love
Acts 1:14 These all ***c'd*** with one accord in prayer
Acts 2:46 they [the believers], ***c'ing*** daily with one accord
Acts 18:11 he [Paul] ***c'd*** there... teaching the word of God
Rom 6:1 Shall we ***c*** in sin, that grace may abound
Rom 12:12 patient in tribulation; ***c'ing*** instant in prayer
Gal 3:10 Cursed is every one that ***c'th*** not in all things... in the book of the law
Phil 1:25 I [Paul]...shall abide and ***c*** with you all for your... joy of faith
1 Tim 4:16 Take heed...unto the doctrine; ***c*** in them
Heb 13:1 Let brotherly love ***c***
2 Pet 3:4 all things ***c*** as they were from the beginning
1 John 2:19 they would no doubt have ***c'd*** with us

CONVERSATION
Gal 1:13 ye have heard of my [Paul's] ***c*** in time past
Phil 3:20 our ***c*** is in heaven; from whence also we look for the Saviour

1 Tim 4:12 be thou an example ...in ***c,*** in charity
Heb 13:5 Let your ***c*** be without covetousness
2 Pet 3:11 what manner of persons ought ye to be in all holy ***c*** and godliness

CONVERSION
Acts 15:3 they [Paul and Barnabas] passed through ...declaring the ***c*** of the Gentiles

CONVERSION OF PAUL. Acts 9:1–16.

CONVERT [ED, ETH, ING]
Ps 19:7 The law of the LORD is perfect, ***c'ing*** the soul
Ps 51:13 sinners shall be ***c'ed*** unto thee [God]
Matt 18:3 Except ye be ***c'ed,*** and become as little children
Acts 3:19 Repent ye therefore, and be ***c'ed***
Jas 5:19 if any of you do err... and one ***c*** him
Jas 5:20 he which ***c'eth*** the sinner...shall save a soul

CORE. See *Korah.*

CORINTH (a major city in Greece where Paul lived for eighteen months and established a church). **Acts 18:1–18;** 19:1 • 1 Cor 1:2 • 2 Cor 1:1,23 • 2 Tim 4:20.

CORINTHIANS, FIRST AND SECOND EPISTLES TO THE. Two letters of the apostle Paul to the church at Corinth, dealing mainly with problems in the church, including divisions (1 Cor. 1–4), sexual immorality (1 Cor. 5–6), and abuses of the Lord's Supper and spiritual gifts (1 Cor. 11–12; 14).

CORNELIUS (a Roman soldier who became one of the first Gentile converts to Christianity). Acts 10:1–48.

CORRUPT [ED]
Gen 6:11 The earth also was ***c*** before God
Ex 8:24 land [Egypt] was ***c'ed*** by...swarm of flies
Job 17:1 My [Job's] breath is ***c,*** my days are extinct
Matt 6:20 treasures in heaven ...neither moth nor rust doth ***c***
Luke 6:43 a good tree bringeth not forth ***c*** fruit
2 Cor 7:2 we have wronged no man, we have ***c'ed*** no man
Eph 4:29 no ***c*** communication proceed out of your mouth
Jas 5:2 Your riches are ***c'ed...*** garments are motheaten

CORRUPTION
Isa 38:17 thou [God] hast in love...delivered it [my soul] from the pit of ***c***

Rom 8:21 delivered from...***c*** into the glorious liberty of the children of God

1 Cor 15:42 It [the body] is sown in ***c***...raised in incorruption

Gal 6:8 he that soweth to his flesh shall of the flesh reap ***c***

COUNSEL OF THE LORD

Ps 33:11 The ***c-o-t-L*** standeth for ever

Prov 19:21 nevertheless the ***c-o-t-L,*** that shall stand

COUNT [ED, ETH]

Gen 15:6 and he [God] ***c'ed*** it... for righteousness

Job 31:4 Doth not he [God] see my ways...***c*** all my steps

Ps 44:22 we are ***c'ed*** as sheep for the slaughter

Prov 17:28 a fool, when he holdeth his peace, is ***c'ed*** wise

Luke 14:28 sitteth not down first, and ***c'eth*** the cost

Acts 5:41 ***c'ed*** worthy to suffer shame for his [Jesus'] name

Rom 4:3 it was ***c'ed*** unto him [Abraham] for righteousness

Phil 3:7 gain to me [Paul], those I ***c'ed*** loss for Christ

Phil 3:8 I [Paul] ***c*** all things but loss

Phil 3:13 I [Paul] ***c*** not myself to have apprehended

2 Thes 1:5 that ye may be ***c'ed*** worthy of the kingdom of God

1 Tim 5:17 Let the elders that rule well be ***c'ed*** worthy

Jas 1:2 ***c*** it all joy when ye fall into divers temptations

2 Pet 3:9 The Lord is not slack concerning his promise, as some men ***c*** slackness

COURAGE

Deut 31:6 Be strong and of a good ***c,*** fear not

Ps 31:24 Be of good ***c,*** and he [God] shall strengthen your heart

Isa 41:6 every one said to his brother, Be of good ***c***

COVENANT [S]

Gen 9:9 I [God] establish my ***c*** with you [Noah]

Gen 9:13 bow in the cloud... shall be for a token of a ***c***

Gen 15:18 the LORD made a ***c*** with Abram

Ex 2:24 God remembered his ***c*** with Abraham

Ex 19:5 keep my [God's] ***c,*** then ye shall be a peculiar treasure

Ex 34:28 he [Moses] wrote... the words of the ***c,*** the ten commandments

Deut 4:23 Take heed...lest ye forget the ***c*** of the LORD

Deut 29:9 Keep therefore the words of this ***c***

1 Sam 18:3 Jonathan and David made a ***c***

Jer 11:3 Cursed be the man that obeyeth not...this ***c***

Jer 31:31 I [God] will make a new ***c*** with...Israel

Ezek 16:62 I [God] will establish my ***c*** with thee

Rom 11:27 For this is my [God's] ***c***...when I shall take away their sins

Eph 2:12 aliens...and strangers from the ***c's*** of promise

Heb 8:6 he [Jesus] is the mediator of a better ***c***

Heb 13:20 through the blood of the everlasting ***c***

COVET [ED, ETH]

Ex 20:17 Thou shalt not ***c*** thy neighbour's house

Prov 21:26 He ***c'eth*** greedily all the day long

Acts 20:33 I [Paul] have ***c'ed*** no man's silver

1 Cor 12:31 But ***c*** earnestly the best gifts

1 Tim 6:10 some ***c'ed*** after... erred from the faith

COVETOUSNESS

Ps 119:36 Incline my heart unto thy [God's] testimonies, and not to ***c***

Luke 12:15 Take heed, and beware of ***c***

Heb 13:5 Let your conversation be without ***c***

CREATE [D]

Gen 1:1 In the beginning God ***c'd*** the heaven and the earth

Gen 1:27 God ***c'd*** man in his own image

Gen 6:7 I [God] will destroy man whom I have ***c'd***

Ps 51:10 **C** in me a clean heart, O God...renew a right spirit

Ps 148:5 for he [God] commanded, and they were ***c'd***

Isa 45:12 I [God] have made the earth...***c'd*** man upon it

Isa 65:17 I [God] ***c*** new heavens and a new earth

Jer 31:22 the LORD hath ***c'd*** a new thing in the earth

Mal 2:10 Have we not all one father? hath not one God ***c'd*** us

1 Cor 11:9 Neither was the man ***c'd*** for the woman

Eph 2:10 we are his workmanship, ***c'd*** in Christ Jesus

Col 1:16 all things were ***c'd*** by him [Jesus], and for him

Rev 4:11 for thou [God] hast ***c'd*** all things

CREATION

Mark 10:6 beginning of the ***c*** God made...male and female

Rom 1:20 invisible things of him [God] from the ***c*** of the world are clearly seen

Rom 8:22 the whole ***c*** groaneth and travaileth in pain

CREATION OF MAN. Gen 1:26–2:7.

CREATION OF WOMAN. Gen 2:18–25.

CREATION OF WORLD. Gen 1:1–25.

CROOKED

Deut 32:5 they are a perverse and ***c*** generation

Eccl 7:13 make that straight, which he [God] hath made ***c***

Isa 40:4 the ***c*** shall be made straight...rough places plain

Luke 3:5 the ***c*** shall be made straight...rough ways... smooth

Phil 2:15 sons of God...in the midst of a ***c***...nation

CROSS

Matt 27:32 they compelled [Simon] to bear his [Jesus'] ***c***

Matt 27:42 let him [Jesus] now come down from the ***c***

Luke 9:23 take up his ***c*** daily, and follow me [Jesus]

John 19:17 And he [Jesus] bearing his ***c*** went forth into...the place of a skull

1 Cor 1:18 the preaching of the ***c*** is to them that perish foolishness

Gal 6:14 forbid that I [Paul] should glory, save in the ***c***

Phil 2:8 he [Jesus]...became obedient unto...death of the ***c***

Heb 12:2 who [Jesus] for the joy that was set before him endured the ***c***

CROSSING OF JORDAN RIVER INTO CANAAN. Josh 3:1–17.

CROSSING OF RED SEA. Ex 14:21–31.

CROWN [ED, EDST]

Ps 8:5 thou [God]...hast ***c'ed*** him [man] with...honour

Prov 17:6 Children's children are the ***c*** of old men

Mark 15:17 platted a ***c*** of thorns, and put it about his [Jesus'] head

Phil 4:1 my joy and ***c,*** so stand fast in the Lord

2 Tim 4:8 laid up for me [Paul] a ***c*** of righteousness

Heb 2:7 thou ***c'edst*** him [Jesus] with glory and honour

Heb 2:9 But we see Jesus... ***c'ed*** with glory and honour

CROWN OF GLORY

Prov 16:31 The hoary head is a ***c-o-g***

Isa 28:5 shall the LORD of hosts be for a ***c-o-g***

Isa 62:3 Thou shalt...be a ***c-o-g*** in the hand of the LORD

1 Pet 5:4 chief Shepherd... appear, ye shall receive a ***c-o-g***

CROWN OF LIFE

Jas 1:12 when he is tried, he shall receive the ***c-o-l***

Rev 2:10 faithful unto death, and I will give thee a ***c-o-l***

CRUCIFIXION OF JESUS. See *Jesus, Life and Ministry of.*

CURSE [D, DST, ING, TH]

Gen 3:14 thou [the serpent] art ***c'd*** above all cattle

Gen 12:3 I [God] will...***c*** him that ***c'th*** thee [Abraham]

Lev 20:9 one that ***c'th*** his father...shall be...put to death

Num 23:11 I [Balak] took thee [Balaam] to ***c*** mine enemies

Deut 11:26 I [Moses] set before you [Israel] this day a blessing and a ***c***

Deut 27:15 ***C'd*** be the man that maketh any graven or molten image

Deut 30:19 I [Moses] have set before you life and death, blessing and ***c'ing***

Josh 6:26 ***C'd*** be the man... that...buildeth...Jericho

Job 2:9 Dost thou [Job] still retain thine integrity? ***c*** God, and die

Jer 20:14 ***C'd*** be the day...I [Jeremiah] was born

Matt 5:44 Love your enemies, bless them that ***c*** you

Matt 15:4 He that ***c'th*** father... let him die

Matt 25:41 Depart from me [Jesus], ye ***c'd,*** into everlasting fire

Mark 11:21 fig tree which thou [Jesus] ***c'dst*** is withered

Mark 14:71 But he [Peter] began to ***c***...saying, I know not this man [Jesus]

Acts 23:14 bound ourselves under a great ***c***...eat nothing until we have slain Paul

Rom 12:14 Bless them which persecute you: bless...***c*** not

Gal 3:13 Christ hath redeemed us from the ***c*** of the law

Jas 3:10 Out of the same mouth proceedeth blessing and ***c'ing***

CUSTOM

Matt 9:9 he [Jesus] saw... Matthew...at the receipt of ***c***

John 18:39 a ***c,*** that I [Pilate] should release unto you one at the passover

Rom 13:7 Render...to all their dues...***c*** to whom ***c***

CUTH (a Babylonian district whose citizens settled the Northern Kingdom [Israel] after it fell to the Assyrians). 2 Kgs 17:30. *Cuthah:* 2 Kgs 17:24.

CUTHAH. See *Cuth.*

CYPRUS (a large island in the Mediterranean Sea that Paul and Barnabas visited during the first missionary journey). Acts 4:36; 11:19–20; **13:4–13;** 15:39; 21:3,16; 27:4. *Chittim:* Jer 2:10. *Kittim:* Gen 10:4.

CYRENE (a city in Africa and home of the Simon who carried the cross of Jesus). Matt 27:32 • Mark 15:21 • Luke 23:26 • Acts 2:10; 6:9; 11:20; 13:1.

CYRENIUS (Roman governor of Syria at the time of Jesus' birth). Luke 2:1–4.

CYRUS (a king of the Persian empire who allowed the Jewish captives to return to their homeland about 536 B.C.). 2 Chr 36:22–23 • **Ezra 1:1–8;** 3:7; 4:3,5; 5:13–14,17; 6:3,14 • Isa 44:28; 45:1 • Dan 1:21; 6:28; 10:1.

-D-

DAGON (chief pagan god of the Philistines). Judg 16:23 • 1 Sam 5:1–7.

DALMANUTHA (a place near the Sea of Galilee visited by Jesus). Mark 8:10.

DALMATIA (a Roman province along the Adriatic Sea visited by Titus). 2 Tim 4:10.

DAMASCUS (capital city of Syria and the city to which Paul was traveling when he was converted). Gen 14:15 • 2 Sam 8:5–6 • 1 Kgs 15:18 • 2 Kgs 8:7–15 • Isa 8:4 • **Acts 9:1–8** • 2 Cor 11:32–33 • Gal 1:17. *Syria-damascus:* 1 Chr 18:6.

DAMNATION

Mark 3:29 blaspheme against the Holy Ghost...is in danger of eternal ***d***

John 5:29 that have done evil, unto the resurrection of ***d***

1 Cor 11:29 he...eateth and drinketh ***d*** to himself

DAN

1. A son of Jacob and ancestor of one of the twelve tribes of Israel. Gen 30:6; 35:25; 46:23; 49:16–17 • Ex 1:4 • Josh 19:47–48 • 1 Chr 2:2 • Ezek 27:19. The tribe of Dan settled in central Palestine and along the Mediterranean Sea. Judg 1:34; 5:17; 13:25; 18:2–30.

2. A village in the territory of Dan. Gen 14:14 • Judg 20:1 • 1 Chr 21:2 • 2 Chr 30:5. *Laish:* Isa 10:30.

DANIEL (a prophet who remained faithful to God among the pagan Babylonians and Persians). References to Daniel outside the Book of Daniel are found in Ezek 14:14, 20; 28:3 • Matt 24:15 • Mark 13:14. His Babylonian name was *Belteshazzar:* Dan 1:7.

DANIEL, BOOK OF. An apocalyptic book of the Old Testament known for its imagery that is similar to that in the Book of Revelation in the New Testament. The book describes the trials and tribulations suffered by Daniel and his three friends as captives of the Babylonians and Persians (Dan 1–7) and Daniel's visions and dreams about the future (Dan 8–12).

DARIUS (a title for four different kings of Persia).

1. Darius I or Darius the Great, who continued Cyrus's policy of restoring the Jewish people to their homeland. Ezra 6:1–12.

2. Darius II or Darius the Persian. Neh 12:22.

3. Darius III or Darius Codomannus, who is probably the "fourth" king of Persia mentioned by the prophet Daniel. Dan 11:2.

4. Darius the Mede, who made Daniel a ruler over several provincial leaders. Dan 6:1–2.

DARKENED

Isa 24:11 all joy is ***d,*** the mirth of the land is gone

Joel 3:15 The sun and the moon shall be ***d***

Mark 13:24 after that tribulation, the sun shall be ***d***

Rom 1:21 they [ungodly]... became vain...heart was ***d***

DARKNESS

Gen 1:2 and ***d*** was upon the face of the deep

Ex 10:22 a thick ***d*** in all the land of Egypt three days

2 Sam 22:29 the LORD will lighten my ***d***

Job 34:22 There is no ***d,*** nor shadow of death

Ps 18:9 He [God]...came down...***d*** was under his feet

Isa 5:20 Woe unto them that... put ***d*** for light, and light for ***d***

Isa 9:2 people that walked in ***d*** have seen a great light

Joel 2:31 sun shall be turned into ***d***...moon into blood

Matt 4:16 people which sat in ***d*** saw great light

Luke 23:44 a ***d*** over all the earth until the ninth hour

John 1:5 the ***d*** comprehended it [the light] not

John 3:19 men loved ***d*** rather than light

John 12:46 whosoever believeth...not abide in ***d***

Acts 2:20 The sun shall be turned into ***d***

Acts 26:18 To open their eyes, and to turn them from ***d*** to light

2 Cor 4:6 God, who commanded the light to shine out of ***d***... shined in our hearts

Eph 6:12 we wrestle...against the rulers...***d*** of this world

1 Pet 2:9 who [Jesus] hath called you out of ***d*** into his marvellous light

1 John 1:5 God is light, and in him is no ***d*** at all

1 John 2:11 he that hateth his brother is in ***d***

DAVID (a popular king of Judah and an earthly ancestor of the promised Messiah, Jesus Christ). See **1 Sam 16–31 • 2 Sam 1–24 • 1 Kgs 1:1–2:11 • 1 Chr 11–29** for a sketch of David.

1. Anointed as a boy by Samuel (1 Sam 16:1–13)

2. Musician and armorbearer for King Saul (1 Sam 16:14–23)

3. Killed the Philistine Goliath (1 Sam 17:1–54)

4. Hid from King Saul as a fugitive (1 Sam 19:1–30:31)

5. King over Judah (2 Sam 2:1–4:12)

6. Captured Jerusalem (Jebus) and turned it into his capital city (1 Chr 11:4–9)

7. King over all Israel (2 Sam 5:1–6:16)

8. His throne established by the Lord forever (2 Sam 7:1–29)

9. Committed adultery with Bathsheba (2 Sam 11:1–27)

10. Survived rebellion by his son Absalom (2 Sam 15:7–23)

11. Not allowed to build the temple (1 Chr 17:1–15)

12. Death of David (1 Kgs 2:10–11 • 1 Chr 29:26–28)

13. Succeeded by his son Solomon (1 Kgs 1:10–35)

The phrase "a psalm of David" appears in the titles of many psalms in the Book of Psalms, indicating either that David wrote these psalms or that they were written in his honor. Pss 2–9; 11–41; 51–65; 68–70; 86; 101–103; 108–110; 122; 124; 131–133; 138–145.

The prophets of the Old Testament often spoke of the promised Messiah who would fulfill God's promise to David. Isa 9:7; 55:3 • Jer 17:25; 33:17 • Ezek 37:24 • Zech 12:8.

In the New Testament, Jesus was called "the son of David" or "seed of David." Matt 9:27; 20:31 • Luke 18:38–39 • John 7:42 • Rom 1:3 • 2 Tim 2:8.

DAY

Gen 1:5 evening and the morning were the first ***d***

Ex 13:3 Remember this ***d***...ye came out from Egypt

Ex 20:11 LORD blessed the sabbath ***d,*** and hallowed it

Deut 4:4 ye that did cleave unto the LORD your God are alive...this ***d***

Deut 11:26 Behold, I [Moses] set before you this ***d*** a blessing and a curse

Josh 4:14 On that ***d*** the LORD magnified Joshua

Josh 10:13 the sun stood still... and hasted not to go down about a whole ***d***

Josh 24:15 choose you this ***d*** whom ye will serve

1 Kgs 18:36 known this ***d*** that thou art God in Israel

1 Chr 16:23 show forth from ***d*** to ***d*** his [God's] salvation

Job 3:3 the ***d*** perish wherein I [Job] was born

Job 19:25 he shall stand at the latter ***d*** upon the earth

Ps 1:2 in his [God's] law doth he meditate ***d*** and night

Ps 19:2 ***D*** unto ***d*** uttereth speech

Ps 50:15 call upon me [God] in the ***d*** of trouble

Ps 84:10 For a ***d*** in thy [God's] courts is better than a thousand

Ps 86:7 In the ***d*** of my trouble I will call upon thee [God]

Ps 91:5 shalt not be afraid... for the arrow that flieth by ***d***

Ps 118:24 This is the ***d*** which the LORD hath made

Ps 121:6 sun shall not smite thee by ***d***

Prov 27:1 knowest not what a ***d*** may bring forth

Isa 13:6 Howl ye, for the ***d*** of the LORD is at hand

Isa 60:19 sun shall be no more thy light by ***d***

Jer 1:10 I [God] have this ***d*** set thee over the nations

Jer 9:1 I [Jeremiah] might weep ***d*** and night for the slain of my people

Jer 20:14 Cursed be the ***d***...I [Jeremiah] was born

Joel 2:31 before...the terrible ***d*** of the LORD come

Amos 5:18 Woe unto you that desire the ***d*** of the LORD

Zech 2:11 many nations...be joined to the LORD in that ***d***

Zech 14:6 in that ***d,*** that the light shall not be clear

Mal 3:2 who may abide the ***d*** of his [God's] coming

Matt 6:11 Give us this ***d*** our daily bread

Matt 7:22 Many will say to me in that ***d,*** Lord, Lord

Matt 25:13 know neither the ***d*** nor the hour wherein the Son of man cometh

Mark 14:25 I [Jesus] will drink no more of the fruit of the vine, until that ***d***...I drink it new

Luke 2:11 born this ***d*** in the city of David a Saviour

Luke 9:22 Son of man must... be slain...raised the third ***d***

Luke 19:9 This ***d*** is salvation come to this house

Luke 24:46 it behoved Christ to suffer...to rise from the dead the third ***d***

John 9:4 I [Jesus] must work... while it is ***d***

John 11:24 he [Lazarus] shall rise again...at the last ***d***

1 Cor 16:2 Upon the first ***d*** of the week let every one of you lay by him in store

2 Cor 6:2 behold, now is the ***d*** of salvation

Phil 3:5 Circumcised the eighth ***d***...stock of Israel

2 Tim 1:12 keep that...committed unto him [Jesus] against that ***d***

Heb 13:8 Jesus Christ the same yesterday, and to ***d***

2 Pet 3:8 one ***d*** is with the Lord as a thousand years

Rev 1:10 I [John] was in the Spirit on the Lord's ***d***

Rev 6:17 the great ***d*** of his [God's] wrath is come

DAY OF ATONEMENT

Lev 23:27 a ***d-o-a:*** it shall be an holy convocation

Lev 23:28 a ***d-o-a,*** to make an atonement...before the LORD

Lev 25:9 in the ***d-o-a*** shall ye make the trumpet sound

DAY OF JUDGMENT

Matt 11:22 It shall be more tolerable for Tyre...at the ***d-o-j,*** than for you

Matt 12:36 every idle word... men...shall give account thereof in the ***d-o-j***

1 John 4:17 that we may have boldness in the ***d-o-j***

DAY OF THE LORD

Isa 2:12 the ***d-o-t-L*** of hosts... upon every one that is proud

Joel 1:15 Alas...for the ***d-o-t-L*** is at hand

Amos 5:20 Shall not the ***d-o-t-L*** be darkness, and not light? even very dark

Obad 15 the ***d-o-t-L*** is near upon all the heathen

Zech 14:1 Behold, the ***d-o-t-L*** cometh

Mal 4:5 send you Elijah the prophet before the...dreadful ***d-o-t-L***

Acts 2:20 sun shall be turned into darkness...before that great...***d-o-t-L*** come

1 Thes 5:2 the ***d-o-t-L*** so cometh as a thief in the night

2 Pet 3:10 the ***d-o-t-L*** will come as a thief in the night

DEACON [S]

1 Tim 3:10 use the office of a ***d,*** being found blameless

1 Tim 3:12 Let the ***d's*** be the husbands of one wife

1 Tim 3:13 used the office of a ***d*** well purchase to themselves a good degree

DEAD

Ex 12:30 great cry in Egypt... not a house where there was not one ***d***

Josh 1:2 Moses my [God's] servant is ***d***...therefore arise

2 Kgs 4:32 when Elisha was come into the house, behold, the child was ***d***

Eccl 9:5 but the ***d*** know not any thing

Jer 22:10 Weep ye not for the ***d,*** neither bemoan him

Matt 2:19 when Herod was ***d***... an angel...appeareth in a dream to Joseph

Matt 8:22 Follow me [Jesus]; and let the ***d*** bury their ***d***

Matt 10:8 Heal the sick, cleanse the lepers, raise the ***d***

Mark 6:16 I [Herod] beheaded: he [John the Baptist] is risen from the ***d***

Mark 15:44 Pilate marvelled if he [Jesus] were already ***d***

Luke 15:24 this my son was ***d,*** and is alive again

Luke 20:38 he is not a God of the ***d,*** but of the living
Luke 24:46 it behoved Christ to suffer...rise from the ***d***
John 11:25 though he were ***d,*** yet shall he live
John 20:9 they knew not... that he [Jesus] must rise again from the ***d***
Acts 17:32 when they heard of the resurrection of the ***d,*** some mocked
Acts 26:8 thought a thing incredible with you, that God should raise the ***d***
Rom 1:4 declared to be the Son of God with power...by the resurrection from the ***d***
Rom 6:4 Christ was raised up from the ***d*** by...the Father
Rom 10:9 if thou...shalt believe...that God hath raised him [Jesus] from the ***d***
1 Cor 15:13 no resurrection of the ***d,*** then is Christ not risen
Gal 2:19 I [Paul] through the law am ***d*** to the law
Eph 2:1 you hath he [Jesus] quickened, who were ***d*** in trespasses and sins
Col 1:18 who [Jesus] is...the firstborn from the ***d***
1 Thes 4:16 the ***d*** in Christ shall rise first
2 Tim 2:8 Jesus Christ...was raised from the ***d*** according to my gospel
Jas 2:17 Even so faith, if it hath not works, is ***d***
1 Pet 4:5 to him that is ready to judge the quick and the ***d***
Rev 1:17 I [John] saw him [Jesus], I fell at his feet as ***d***
Rev 14:13 Blessed are the ***d*** which die in the Lord

DEAD SEA. See *Salt Sea.*

DEAF
Isa 35:5 the ears of the ***d*** shall be unstopped
Mark 7:32 they bring unto him [Jesus] one that was ***d***
Luke 7:22 tell John...lepers are cleansed, the ***d*** hear

DEATH
Deut 30:15 I [Moses] have set before thee...***d*** and evil
Deut 33:1 Moses...blessed the children of Israel before his ***d***
2 Kgs 4:40 man of God, there is ***d*** in the pot
Job 16:16 on my [Job's] eyelids is the shadow of ***d***
Ps 13:3 lighten mine eyes, lest I sleep the sleep of ***d***
Ps 23:4 walk through the valley of the shadow of ***d***
Ps 48:14 For this God...will be our guide even unto ***d***
Ps 107:14 He [God] brought them out of...shadow of ***d***
Ps 116:15 Precious in the sight of the LORD...***d*** of his saints
Prov 14:12 but the end thereof are the ways of ***d***

Isa 9:2 they that dwell in...the shadow of ***d,*** upon them hath the light shined
Isa 53:9 he [God's servant] made his grave with the wicked, and...rich in his ***d***
Jer 21:8 I [God] set before you the way of life, and...***d***
Matt 4:16 to them which sat in the...shadow of ***d*** light is sprung up
Mark 14:34 My [Jesus'] soul is exceeding sorrowful unto ***d***
Luke 2:26 he [Simon] should not see ***d,*** before he had seen the Lord's Christ
John 5:24 He that...believeth... is passed from ***d*** unto life
John 11:4 sickness is not unto ***d,*** but for the glory of God
Acts 8:1 Saul was consenting unto his [Stephen's] ***d***
Rom 5:12 so ***d*** passed upon all men, for that all have sinned
Rom 6:4 we are buried with him [Jesus] by baptism into ***d***
Rom 6:23 the wages of sin is ***d***
Rom 7:24 who shall deliver me [Paul] from the body of...***d***
Rom 8:38 neither ***d,*** nor life, nor angels
1 Cor 11:26 ye do show the Lord's ***d*** till he come
1 Cor 15:26 The last enemy that shall be destroyed is ***d***
1 Cor 15:55 O ***d,*** where is thy sting
Phil 2:8 he [Jesus] humbled himself...obedient unto ***d***
Phil 3:10 being made conformable unto his [Jesus'] ***d***
Heb 11:5 Enoch was translated that he should not see ***d***
1 John 3:14 we have passed from ***d*** unto life, because we love the brethren
Rev 1:18 I [Jesus] am alive for evermore...and have the keys of hell and of ***d***
Rev 20:14 ***d*** and hell were cast into the lake of fire
Rev 21:4 there shall be no more ***d,*** neither sorrow

DEATH OF JESUS. See *Jesus, Life and Ministry of.*

DEBORAH (a prophetess and judge of Israel who defeated the Canaanites). **Judg 4:4–16;** 5:1–31.

DEBT [S]
Matt 6:12 forgive us our ***d's,*** as we forgive our debtors
Matt 18:27 the lord of that servant...forgave him the ***d***
Rom 4:4 to him that worketh is the reward...of ***d***

DEBTOR [S]
Rom 1:14 I [Paul] am ***d*** both to the Greeks, and to the Barbarians
Rom 8:12 we are ***d's,*** not to the flesh, to live after the flesh

DECAPOLIS (a district with a large Greek population east of the Jordan River). Jesus visited this area several times. Matt 4:25 • Mark 5:20; 7:31.

DECEIVE [D, ING, TH]

Deut 11:16 Take heed...that your heart be not ***d'd***

Prov 20:1 Wine is a mocker... and whosoever is ***d'd*** thereby is not wise

Luke 21:8 Take heed that ye be not ***d'd:*** for many shall come in my [Jesus'] name

Gal 6:3 think himself to be something, when he is nothing, he ***d'th*** himself

Gal 6:7 Be not ***d'd;*** God is not mocked

Eph 5:6 Let no man ***d*** you with vain words

Jas 1:22 be ye doers of the word, and not hearers only, ***d'ing*** your own selves

1 John 1:8 If we say that we have no sin, we ***d*** ourselves

DECEIVER [S]

Matt 27:63 ***d*** said...After three days I [Jesus] will rise again

2 John 7 many ***d's*** are entered into the world

DECLARE [D, ING]

1 Chr 16:24 ***D*** his [God's] glory among the heathen

Ps 9:11 ***d*** among the people his [God's] doings

Ps 19:1 The heavens ***d*** the glory of God

Ps 66:16 ***d*** what he [God] hath done for my soul

Ps 71:17 hitherto have I ***d'd*** thy [God's] wondrous works

Ps 96:3 ***D*** his [God's] glory among the heathen

Isa 12:4 Praise the LORD...***d*** his doings among the people

Isa 48:3 I have ***d'd*** the former things from the beginning

John 1:18 the only begotten Son...he hath ***d'd*** him [God]

Acts 15:12 ***d'ing*** what miracles...God had wrought among the Gentiles

Acts 17:23 Whom therefore ye ignorantly worship, him [God] ***d*** I [Paul] unto you

Rom 1:4 ***d'd*** to be the Son of God with power

1 Cor 15:1 I [Paul] ***d*** unto you the gospel...I preached

1 John 1:3 That which we have seen...***d*** we unto you

1 John 1:5 the message which we...***d*** unto you

DEED [S]

1 Chr 16:8 Call upon his [God's] name, make known his ***d's*** among the people

Luke 23:41 we receive the due reward of our ***d's***

John 3:19 men loved darkness... because their ***d's*** were evil

Rom 2:6 render to every man according to his ***d's***

Rom 3:28 justified by faith without the ***d's*** of the law

Col 3:17 And whatsoever ye do in word or ***d***

1 John 3:18 not love in word... but in ***d*** and in truth

DEFILE [D, TH]

Ezek 20:7 ***d*** not yourselves with the idols of Egypt

Dan 1:8 Daniel...would not ***d*** himself with...king's meat

Matt 15:20 to eat with unwashen hands ***d'th*** not a man

Mark 7:2 saw some of his [Jesus'] disciples eat bread with ***d'd***...hands

Mark 7:18 thing from without entereth into the man, it cannot ***d*** him

John 18:28 went not into the judgment hall, lest they [Pharisees] should be ***d'd***

1 Cor 3:17 If any man ***d*** the temple of God

Jas 3:6 the tongue...***d'th*** the whole body

DEHAVITES (a tribe which settled in Samaria after the Northern Kingdom fell to the Assyrians). Ezra 4:9–16.

DELILAH (a woman who betrayed Samson to the Philistines). Judg 16:4–21.

DELIVER [ED, EDST, ETH, ING]

Ex 18:10 Jethro said...the LORD...hath ***d'ed*** you out of the hand of the Egyptians

Deut 1:27 the LORD...hath brought us forth...to ***d*** us into the hand of the Amorites

Deut 9:10 LORD ***d'ed*** unto me [Moses] two tables of stone

Josh 10:8 I [God] have ***d'ed*** them into thine hand

Judg 6:1 the LORD ***d'ed*** them into the hand of Midian

Judg 10:13 ye have forsaken me [God] and served other gods...I will ***d*** you no more

1 Sam 17:37 he [God] will ***d*** me [David] out of the hand of this Philistine

Job 16:11 God hath ***d'ed*** me [Job] to the ungodly

Job 33:28 He [God] will ***d*** his [man's] soul from...the pit

Ps 17:13 O LORD, ***d*** my soul from the wicked

Ps 25:20 keep my soul and ***d*** me: let me not be ashamed

Ps 34:4 the LORD...***d'ed*** me from all my fears

Ps 34:17 the LORD...***d'eth*** them out of all their troubles

Ps 41:1 the LORD will ***d*** him in time of trouble

Ps 72:12 he [God] shall ***d*** the needy when he crieth

Ps 107:6 and he [God] ***d'ed*** them out of their distresses

Ps 116:8 thou [God] hast ***d'ed*** my soul from death
Ps 120:2 ***D*** my soul, O LORD, from lying lips
Prov 11:4 righteousness ***d'eth*** from death
Isa 19:20 he [God] shall send them a saviour...and he shall ***d*** them
Isa 46:4 even I [God] will carry, and will ***d*** you
Jer 1:8 I am with thee to ***d*** thee, saith the LORD
Jer 20:13 he [God] hath ***d'ed***... the poor from...evildoers
Dan 3:17 our God...is able to ***d*** us from the...furnace
Dan 6:20 is thy [Daniel's] God...able to ***d*** thee
Hos 11:8 how shall I [God] ***d*** thee, Israel
Joel 2:32 whosoever shall call on...the LORD shall be ***d'ed***
Zeph 1:18 nor their gold shall... ***d*** them in the day of the LORD'S wrath
Matt 6:13 lead us not into temptation...***d*** us from evil
Matt 24:9 Then shall they ***d*** you up to be afflicted
Matt 25:20 Lord, thou ***d'edst*** unto me five talents
Mark 10:33 Son of man shall be ***d'ed*** unto the chief priests
Mark 15:1 the chief priests... ***d'ed*** him [Jesus] to Pilate
Luke 2:6 days were accomplished that she [Mary] should be ***d'ed***
Luke 9:44 Son of man shall be ***d'ed*** into the hands of men
Acts 22:4 I [Paul] persecuted... ***d'ing*** into prisons both men and women
Rom 7:24 who shall ***d*** me [Paul] from...this death
Gal 1:4 he [Jesus] might ***d*** us from this present evil world
Col 1:13 Who [Jesus]...***d'ed*** us from the power of darkness
2 Tim 4:18 Lord shall ***d*** me from every evil work
2 Pet 2:9 Lord...knoweth how to ***d***...out of temptations

DEMAS (a believer who deserted Paul). Col 4:14 • 2 Tim 4:10 • Phlm 24.

DEMETRIUS

1. A silversmith at Ephesus who incited a riot against the apostle Paul. Acts 19:24–38.

2. A believer commended by the apostle John. 3 John 12.

DENY [IED, IETH, ING]

Matt 10:33 him will I also ***d*** before my Father
Matt 26:72 And again he [Peter] ***d'ied*** with an oath, I do not know the man [Jesus]
Mark 14:30 thou [Peter] shalt ***d*** me [Jesus] thrice
Luke 9:23 let him ***d*** himself, and take up his cross daily
Luke 12:9 he that ***d'ieth*** me [Jesus] before men shall be ***d'ied*** before...God

1 Tim 5:8 hath ***d'ied*** the faith, and is worse than an infidel
2 Tim 2:12 if we ***d*** him [Jesus], he also will ***d*** us
Titus 2:12 ***d'ing***...worldly lusts, we should live soberly
1 John 2:23 Whosoever ***d'ieth*** the Son...hath not the Father

DEPTH [S]
Ps 106:9 so he [God] led them through the ***d's***
Ps 130:1 Out of the ***d's*** have I cried unto thee, O LORD
Jon 2:5 the ***d*** closed me [Jonah] round about
Mic 7:19 thou [God] wilt cast... their sins into...***d's*** of the sea
Rom 8:39 Nor height, nor ***d***... shall be able to separate us from the love of God
Rom 11:33 ***d*** of the riches both of the wisdom and knowledge of God

DERBE (a village in the province of Lycaonia visited by Paul and Barnabas). **Acts 14:6–20;** 16:1; 20:4.

DESCEND [ED, ING]
Gen 28:12 and behold...angels of God ascending and ***d'ing*** on it [a ladder]
Prov 30:4 Who hath ascended up into heaven, or ***d'ed***
Matt 7:27 the rain ***d'ed,*** and the floods came
Matt 28:2 angel...***d'ed*** from heaven...rolled back the stone
Mark 15:32 Let Christ...***d*** now from the cross
Luke 3:22 Holy Ghost ***d'ed***... like a dove
John 1:32 I [John] saw the Spirit ***d'ing*** from heaven like a dove
Rom 10:7 Who shall ***d*** into the deep...to bring up Christ
Eph 4:10 He [Jesus] that ***d'ed***...also...ascended up far above all heavens
1 Thes 4:16 Lord himself shall ***d*** from heaven with a shout
Rev 21:10 that great city...holy Jerusalem, ***d'ing*** out of heaven from God

DESIRE [D, ING, S, TH]
Gen 3:16 ***d*** shall be to thy [Eve's] husband
Deut 5:21 Neither shalt thou ***d*** thy neighbour's wife
Ps 27:4 One thing have I ***d'd*** of the LORD
Ps 37:4 and he [God] shall give thee the ***d's*** of thine heart
Ps 38:9 all my ***d*** is before thee [God]...my groaning...not hid
Ps 73:25 none upon earth that I ***d*** beside thee [God]
Ps 145:16 Thou [God]...satisfiest the ***d*** of every living thing

Prov 21:25 The ***d*** of the slothful killeth him
Song 7:10 I am my beloved's, and his ***d*** is toward me
Isa 26:9 With my soul have I ***d'd*** thee [God] in the night
Ezek 24:16 I take away from thee the ***d*** of thine eyes
Hos 6:6 I [God] ***d'd*** mercy, and not sacrifice
Amos 5:18 Woe unto you that ***d*** the day of the LORD
Matt 12:46 his [Jesus'] mother ...stood without, ***d'ing*** to speak with him
Mark 9:35 any man ***d*** to be first, the same shall be last
Mark 11:24 What things soever ye ***d,*** when ye pray
Luke 22:31 Simon, behold, Satan hath ***d'd*** to have you
Rom 10:1 my [Paul's] heart's ***d*** ...for Israel is, that they might be saved
2 Cor 5:2 ***d'ing*** to be clothed upon with our house which is from heaven
Phil 1:23 having a ***d*** to depart, and to be with Christ
1 Tim 3:1 ***d*** the office of a bishop, he ***d'th*** a good work
Heb 11:16 now they ***d*** a better country, that is, an heavenly
1 Pet 2:2 As newborn babes, ***d*** the sincere milk of the word

DESTRUCTION [S]

Job 5:22 At ***d*** and famine thou shalt laugh
Ps 90:3 Thou [God] turnest man to ***d***
Ps 107:20 He [God]...delivered them from their ***d's***
Prov 16:18 Pride goeth before ***d,*** and a haughty spirit before a fall
Isa 13:6 day of the LORD... shall come as a ***d*** from the Almighty
Matt 7:13 broad is the way, that leadeth to ***d***

DEUTERONOMY, BOOK OF. An Old Testament book that contains a series of speeches delivered by Moses to the Israelites as they prepared to enter the land of Canaan. This book repeats many of the laws of God revealed to Moses on Mt. Sinai about two generations earlier—thus its name Deuteronomy, which means "second law."

DEVOUT

Luke 2:25 Simeon...was just and ***d,*** waiting for the consolation of Israel
Acts 2:5 there was dwelling at Jerusalem Jews, ***d*** men

DIANA (a pagan goddess to whom a shrine was erected at Ephesus, a center of Diana worship). Acts 19:24–35.

DIE [D, ST, TH] ***See also*** **DYING**

Gen 2:17 day that thou eatest thereof [the forbidden tree] thou shalt surely ***d***

Gen 45:28 I [Jacob] will...see him [Joseph] before I ***d***

Ex 16:3 Would to God we had ***d'd***...in the land of Egypt

Deut 4:22 I [Moses] must ***d*** in this land, I must not go over Jordan...ye shall go over

Deut 14:21 not eat of any thing that ***d'th*** of itself

Judg 16:30 Samson said, Let me ***d*** with the Philistines

Ruth 1:17 Where thou [Naomi] ***d'st,*** will I [Ruth] die

2 Sam 12:5 he [David] said... the man that hath done this thing shall surely ***d***

2 Chr 25:4 every man shall ***d*** for his own sin

Job 2:9 Dost thou [Job] still retain thine integrity? curse God, and ***d***

Job 3:11 Why ***d'd*** I [Job] not from the womb

Job 14:14 If a man ***d,*** shall he live again

Prov 10:21 but fools ***d*** for want of wisdom

Eccl 3:2 A time to be born, and a time to ***d***

Isa 6:1 In the year that king Uzziah ***d'd*** I [Isaiah] saw also the Lord

Jer 16:6 the great and the small shall ***d*** in this land

Jer 31:30 every one shall ***d*** for his own iniquity

Ezek 18:32 I [God] have no pleasure in the death of him that ***d'th***

Jon 4:3 it is better for me [Jonah] to ***d*** than to live

Matt 26:35 Though I [Peter] should ***d*** with thee [Jesus], yet will I not deny thee

John 6:50 bread...from heaven, that a man may eat...and not ***d***

John 11:16 said Thomas...Let us also go, that we may ***d*** with him [Jesus]

John 11:21 Lord, if thou hadst been here, my [Martha's] brother had not ***d'd***

John 11:50 it is expedient for us, that one man should ***d*** for the people

John 12:24 if it [grain of wheat] ***d,*** it bringeth forth much fruit

Acts 21:13 I [Paul] am ready... to ***d*** at Jerusalem for the name of...Jesus

Rom 5:6 in due time Christ ***d'd*** for the ungodly

Rom 5:7 scarcely for a righteous man will one ***d***

Rom 5:8 while we were yet sinners, Christ ***d'd*** for us

Rom 6:9 Christ being raised from the dead ***d'th*** no more

Rom 14:7 none...liveth to himself...no man ***d'th*** to himself

Rom 14:8 whether we live...or ***d,*** we are the Lord's
1 Cor 15:3 how that Christ ***d'd*** for our sins according to the scriptures
1 Cor 15:22 in Adam all ***d***...in Christ...all be made alive
2 Cor 5:14 if one ***d'd*** for all, then were all dead
2 Cor 5:15 he [Jesus] ***d'd*** for all, that they...should not... live unto themselves
Phil 1:21 to me [Paul] to live is Christ, and to ***d*** is gain
Heb 9:27 it is appointed unto men once to ***d***
Rev 14:13 Blessed are the dead which ***d*** in the Lord

DINAH (Jacob's daughter who was assaulted by Shechem). Gen 30:20–21; **34:1–31.**

DINAITES (a tribe which settled in Samaria after the Northern Kingdom fell to the Assyrians). Ezra 4:9–16.

DIOTREPHES (a believer condemned for his false teachings by the apostle John). 3 John 9–10.

DISCERN [ING]
1 Kgs 3:9 that I [Solomon] may ***d*** between good and bad
Ezek 44:23 cause them to ***d*** between...unclean and... clean
Matt 16:3 ye hypocrites, ye can ***d*** the face of the sky
1 Cor 11:29 drinketh damnation to himself, not ***d'ing*** the Lord's body
1 Cor 12:10 another prophecy; to another ***d'ing*** of spirits

DISCIPLE
Matt 10:24 The ***d*** is not above his master
Luke 14:26 If any man...hate not his father...he cannot be my [Jesus'] ***d***
John 19:38 Joseph of Arimathaea, being a ***d*** of Jesus

DISOBEDIENCE
Rom 5:19 For as by one man's [Adam's] ***d*** many were made sinners
Eph 5:6 cometh the wrath of God upon the children of ***d***

DISOBEDIENT
Acts 26:19 I [Paul] was not ***d*** unto the heavenly vision
2 Tim 3:2 boasters, proud, blasphemers, ***d*** to parents
Titus 1:16 they deny him [God], being abominable, and ***d*** and...reprobate
1 Pet 2:7 unto them which be ***d,*** the stone...is made the head of the corner

DISTRESS [ED, ES]
Ps 18:6 In my ***d*** I called upon the LORD

Ps 107:13 he [God] saved them out of their ***d'es***

Zeph 1:15 That day is...a day of trouble and ***d***

Luke 21:23 for there shall be great ***d*** in the land

Rom 8:35 shall separate us from the love of Christ? shall tribulation, or ***d***

2 Cor 4:8 troubled on every side, yet not ***d'ed***

2 Cor 12:10 I [Paul] take pleasure...in ***d'es*** for Christ's sake

1 Thes 3:7 comforted over you [Thessalonians] in all our... ***d*** by your faith

DIVIDE [D, ING, TH]

Gen 1:6 let it [the firmament] ***d*** the waters from the waters

Ex 14:16 stretch out thine [Moses'] hand over the sea, and ***d*** it

Ex 14:21 the LORD...made the sea dry land...waters were ***d'd***

Num 33:54 ye shall ***d*** the land by lot for an inheritance

Judg 7:16 he [Gideon] ***d'd***... men into three companies

Job 26:12 He [God] ***d'th*** the sea with his power

Ps 78:13 He [God] ***d'd*** the sea... caused them to pass through

Prov 16:19 Better it is to be... with the lowly, than to ***d*** the spoil with the proud

Dan 5:28 Thy [Belshazzar's] kingdom is ***d'd,*** and given to the Medes and Persians

Zech 14:1 thy spoil shall be ***d'd*** in the midst of thee

Matt 25:32 he [Jesus] shall separate them...as a shepherd ***d'd*** his sheep from the goats

Luke 11:17 kingdom ***d'd*** against itself is brought to desolation

Luke 12:13 speak to my brother, that he ***d*** the inheritance with me

Luke 12:53 The father shall be ***d'd*** against the son

Luke 15:12 And he [prodigal son's father] ***d'd*** unto them his living

1 Cor 1:13 Is Christ ***d'd?*** was Paul crucified for you

2 Tim 2:15 a workman...not... ashamed, rightly ***d'ing*** the word of truth

DIVISION [S]

Luke 12:51 I [Jesus] tell you, Nay; but rather ***d***

John 9:16 How can a man...do such miracles? And there was a ***d*** among them

Rom 16:17 mark them which cause ***d's*** and offences

1 Cor 3:3 there is among you envying, and strife, and ***d's***

DIVISION OF CANAAN AMONG THE ISRAELITE TRIBES. Josh 14:1–19:51.

DIVORCE [D]
Lev 21:14 a widow, or a ***d'd*** woman...these shall he [a priest] not take
Jer 3:8 I [God] had put her [Israel] away, and given her a bill of ***d***
Matt 5:32 whosoever shall marry her that is ***d'd*** committeth adultery

DOCTRINE [S]
Mark 11:18 the people was astonished at his [Jesus'] ***d***
John 7:16 My [Jesus'] ***d*** is not mine, but his that sent me
Acts 2:42 they continued stedfastly in the apostles' ***d***
Eph 4:14 be no more children... carried about with every wind of ***d***
1 Tim 4:13 give attendance to reading, to exhortation, to ***d***
2 Tim 3:16 All scripture is... profitable for ***d***
2 Tim 4:3 For the time will come when they will not endure sound ***d***
Heb 13:9 Be not carried about with divers and strange ***d's***
2 John 9 He that abideth in the ***d*** of Christ

DOEG (a shepherd for King Saul who betrayed David). 1 Sam 21:7; **22:9–22.**

DOER [S]
Prov 17:4 A wicked ***d*** giveth heed to false lips
Rom 2:13 the ***d's*** of the law shall be justified
Jas 1:22 be ye ***d's*** of the word, and not hearers only
Jas 1:23 if any be a hearer of the word, and not a ***d***

DOMINION [S]
Gen 1:28 God said...have ***d*** over the fish of the sea
Job 25:2 ***D*** and fear are with him [God]
Ps 8:6 Thou [God] madest him [man] to have ***d*** over the works of thy hands
Ps 72:8 He [God] shall have ***d*** also from sea to sea
Dan 4:3 his [God's] ***d*** is from generation to generation
Zech 9:10 and his [God's] ***d*** shall be from sea even to sea
Matt 20:25 princes of the Gentiles exercise ***d***
Rom 6:9 death hath no more ***d*** over him [Jesus]
Col 1:16 by him [Jesus] were all things created...whether they be thrones, or ***d's***
1 Pet 4:11 to whom [Jesus] be... ***d*** for ever and ever
Jude 25 To...God our Saviour, be...***d*** and power

DOOR OF THE SHEEP, JESUS AS. See *"I Am" Statements of Jesus.*

DORCAS. See *Tabitha.*

DOTHAN (a city where Joseph was sold into slavery by his brothers). **Gen 37:17–28** • 2 Kgs 6:8–23.

DOUBT [ED, ING]

Matt 14:31 thou of little faith, wherefore didst thou ***d***

Matt 28:17 they worshipped him [Jesus]: but some ***d'ed***

1 Tim 2:8 men pray every where lifting up holy hands, without wrath and ***d'ing***

DREAM

Gen 37:5 Joseph dreamed a ***d,*** and he told it his brethren

Gen 40:9 the chief butler told his ***d*** to Joseph

Gen 41:25 Joseph said...The ***d*** of Pharaoh is one

Dan 2:3 I [Nebuchadnezzar] have dreamed a ***d,*** and my spirit was troubled

Joel 2:28 pour out my [God's] spirit...old men shall ***d*** dreams

Acts 2:17 and your old men shall ***d*** dreams

DREAMS THROUGH WHICH GOD SPOKE TO PEOPLE

1. To Abimelech, king of Gerar (Gen 20:3)

2. To Jacob, son of Isaac (Gen 28:10–12)

3. To Laban, father-in-law of Jacob (Gen 31:24)

4. To Solomon, king of Judah (1 Kgs 3:5)

5. To Joseph, husband of Mary (Matt 1:20; 2:12–13,22)

DRINK [ETH, ING]

Ex 15:24 the people murmured against Moses, saying, What shall we ***d***

Job 1:13 when his [Job's] sons and his daughters were eating and ***d'ing*** wine

Ps 69:21 in my thirst they gave me vinegar to ***d***

Ps 78:15 He [God]...gave them ***d*** as out of the great depths

Prov 5:15 ***D*** waters out of thine own cistern

Prov 20:1 Wine is a mocker, strong ***d*** is raging

Prov 25:21 and if he [your enemy] be thirsty, give him water to ***d***

Eccl 2:24 There is nothing better for a man, than that he should eat and ***d***

Eccl 9:7 ***d*** thy wine with a merry heart

Isa 5:11 Woe unto them that rise up early...that they may follow strong ***d***

Ezek 12:18 ***d*** thy water with trembling

Dan 1:12 give us [Daniel and his friends] pulse to eat, and water to ***d***

Matt 6:31 What shall we eat? or, What shall we ***d***

Matt 25:42 I was thirsty, and ye gave me no ***d***

Mark 2:16 he [Jesus] eateth and ***d'eth*** with...sinners
Mark 10:38 can ye ***d*** of the cup that I [Jesus] ***d*** of
Mark 15:23 they gave him [Jesus] to ***d*** wine...with myrrh
Luke 5:30 Why do ye [Jesus] eat and ***d*** with publicans
Luke 7:33 John the Baptist came neither eating bread nor ***d'ing*** wine
Luke 10:7 eating and ***d'ing*** such things as they give
Luke 22:18 I [Jesus] will not ***d*** of the fruit...until the kingdom of God shall come
John 4:7 Jesus saith unto her [the Samaritan woman], Give me to ***d***
John 4:14 ***d'eth*** of the water that I [Jesus] shall give him shall never thirst
John 6:53 Except ye...***d*** his [Jesus'] blood, ye have no life in you
Acts 23:12 saying that they would neither eat nor ***d*** till they had killed Paul
Rom 12:20 if he [your enemy] thirst, give him ***d***
Rom 14:17 the kingdom of God is not meat and ***d***
1 Cor 10:31 Whether therefore ye eat, or ***d***...do all to the glory of God
1 Cor 11:25 as oft as ye ***d*** it, in remembrance of me [Jesus]
1 Cor 11:29 eateth and ***d'eth*** damnation to himself
1 Tim 5:23 **D** no longer water, but use a little wine
Rev 16:6 thou hast given them blood to ***d***

DRY BONES, EZEKIEL'S VISION OF. Ezek 37:1–14.

DUMB
Isa 53:7 as a sheep before her shearers is ***d***
Mark 7:37 he [Jesus] maketh... the ***d*** to speak
Luke 1:20 thou [Zacharias] shalt be ***d,*** and not able to speak
1 Cor 12:2 Ye know that ye were Gentiles, carried away unto these ***d*** idols

DURA (a plain where an image of the Babylonian king was set up). Dan 3:1.

DYING (*See also* **DIE**)
2 Cor 4:10 in the body the ***d*** of the Lord Jesus
Heb 11:21 Jacob, when he was a ***d,*** blessed both the sons of Joseph

-E-

EARTH [LY]

Gen 1:1 God created the heaven and the ***e***

Gen 6:6 it repented the LORD... he had made man on the ***e***

Gen 9:1 Be fruitful, and multiply, and replenish the ***e***

Gen 12:3 and in thee [Abraham] shall all families of the ***e*** be blessed

Deut 30:19 call heaven and ***e*** to record this day against you

1 Kgs 10:23 Solomon exceeded all the kings of the ***e***...for wisdom

Job 1:8 there is none like him [Job] in the ***e***

Job 19:25 he shall stand at the latter day upon the ***e***

Job 38:4 Where wast thou [Job] when I [God] laid the foundations of the ***e***

Ps 8:1 how excellent is thy [God's] name in all the ***e***

Ps 24:1 The ***e*** is the LORD'S, and the fulness thereof

Ps 37:11 But the meek shall inherit the ***e***

Ps 67:2 thy [God's] way may be known upon ***e***

Ps 82:8 Arise, O God, judge the ***e***...inherit all nations

Ps 96:1 O sing...a new song: sing unto the LORD, all the ***e***

Ps 108:5 Be thou exalted, O God...and thy glory above all the ***e***

Isa 6:3 the whole ***e*** is full of his [God's] glory

Isa 45:22 be ye saved, all the ends of the ***e***

Isa 55:9 higher than the ***e***, so are my [God's] ways higher than your ways

Isa 66:1 heaven is my [God's] throne...***e*** is my footstool

Joel 3:16 and the heavens and the ***e*** shall shake

Hab 2:20 let all the ***e*** keep silence before him [God]

Matt 5:13 Ye are...salt of the ***e***

Matt 6:10 Thy [God's] will be done in ***e***, as it is in heaven

Matt 12:40 shall the Son of man be...three nights in the heart of the ***e***

Matt 16:19 whatsoever thou shalt loose on ***e*** shall be loosed in heaven

Matt 24:35 Heaven and ***e*** shall pass away, but my [Jesus'] words shall not pass away

Matt 28:18 All power is given unto me [Jesus] in heaven and in ***e***

Luke 2:14 on ***e*** peace, good will toward men

Luke 23:44 darkness over all the ***e*** until the ninth hour

John 3:12 I [Jesus] have told you ***e'ly*** things, and ye believe not

John 12:32 if I [Jesus] be lifted up from the ***e***

Acts 1:8 ye shall be witnesses... the uttermost part of the ***e***

2 Cor 5:1 our ***e'ly*** house of this tabernacle were dissolved
Col 3:2 Set your affection on things above, not on things on the ***e***
Rev 7:1 four angels standing on the four corners of the ***e***
Rev 21:1 I [John] saw a new heaven and a new ***e***

EAST SEA. See *Salt Sea.*

EAT [EN, ER, ETH, ING]
Gen 2:17 the tree of...good and evil, thou shalt not ***e***
Gen 3:11 Hast thou ***e'en*** of the tree...thou shouldest not ***e***
Ex 16:35 the children of Israel did ***e*** manna
Lev 11:41 every creeping thing...shall not be ***e'en***
Judg 14:14 Out of the ***e'er*** came forth meat
Ps 102:9 For I have ***e'en*** ashes like bread
Eccl 2:24 nothing better for a man, than that he should ***e*** and drink
Jer 31:29 fathers have ***e'en*** a sour grape
Ezek 3:1 ***e*** that thou [Ezekiel] findest; ***e*** this roll
Ezek 12:18 ***e*** thy [Ezekiel's] bread with quaking
Matt 6:25 Take no thought for your life, what ye shall ***e***
Matt 9:11 Why ***e'eth*** your [disciples'] Master with publicans
Matt 15:20 to ***e*** with unwashen hands defileth not a man
Matt 26:26 they were ***e'ing,*** Jesus took bread...blessed it
Mark 7:28 dogs under the table ***e*** of the children's crumbs
Mark 14:18 One of you which ***e'eth*** with me [Jesus] shall betray me
Luke 5:30 Why do ye ***e*** and drink with...sinners
Luke 7:33 John the Baptist came neither ***e'ing*** bread nor drinking wine
Luke 15:23 bring...the fatted calf...let us ***e,*** and be merry
John 4:32 I [Jesus] have meat to ***e*** that ye know not of
John 6:50 This is...bread... from heaven, that a man may ***e***...and not die
Acts 10:13 there came a voice... Rise, Peter; kill, and ***e***
1 Cor 10:31 ye ***e,*** or drink...do all to the glory of God
1 Cor 11:26 as often as ye ***e*** this bread, and drink this cup
1 Cor 11:29 he that ***e'eth***... unworthily, ***e'eth***...damnation to himself
2 Thes 3:10 if any would not work, neither should he ***e***
Rev 2:7 him that overcometh will I give to ***e***...tree of life

EBAL (a mountain where Joshua built an altar after destroying the city of Ai). Deut 11:29; 27:4,13 • **Josh 8:30–35.**

EBED-MELECH (an Ethiopian eunuch who rescued Jeremiah from a dungeon). **Jer 38:7–13;** 39:15–18.

EBENEZER (a memorial site in Philistine territory that commemorated Israel's victory over the Philistines). 1 Sam 4:1–10; 5:1; **7:10–12.**

EBER (a great-grandson of Shem and ancestor of the Hebrew race). Gen 10:21–25; 11:14–17 • 1 Chr 1:18–23.

ECCLESIASTES, BOOK OF. A wisdom book in the Old Testament, probably written by King Solomon, which declares that life derives joy and meaning not from riches, fame, or work but from reverence for God and obedience to His commandments.

EDEN, GARDEN OF (the fruitful garden created specifically by the Lord as the home for Adam and Eve). **Gen 2:8–3:24;** 4:16 • Isa 51:3 • Ezek 28:13; 31:9,16–18; 36:35 • Joel 2:3.

EDIFY [IETH, ING]

1 Cor 14:4 speaketh in an unknown tongue ***e'ieth*** himself

Eph 4:12 for the ***e'ing*** of the body of Christ

1 Thes 5:11 comfort...and ***e*** one another

EDOM

1. The name given to Esau, Jacob's brother, after he traded away his birthright. Gen 25:30.

2. The land where the descendants of Esau settled. Gen 36:21,31–32,43 • Num 20:14–23; 34:3 • Josh 15:1,21 • Judg 11:17–18 • 2 Sam 8:14 • 2 Kgs 3:8–26 • Jer 25:21; 27:3; 40:11; 49:7–22 • Ezek 25:12–14 • Amos 1:6–11 • Obad 1,8. *Idumea:* Mark 3:8. See also *Esau.*

EGYPT (an ancient nation along the Nile River which held the Hebrew people in slavery before their miraculous deliverance). Gen 12:10; 37:28–36 • **Ex 1:7–14; 12:29–36** • Isa 19:3–25; 30:1–7; 36:6 • Jer 46:8 • Ezek 30:25 • Matt 2:13–15.

EHUD (a judge of Israel who killed King Eglon of Moab). Judg 3:15–26.

EKRON (a major Philistine city captured by Israel). Josh 13:3; 15:11,45–46; 19:43 • **Judg 1:18** • 1 Sam 5:10; 6:16–17; 7:14; 17:52 • 2 Kgs 1:2–6,16 • Jer 25:20 • Amos 1:8 • Zeph 2:4 • Zech 9:5,7.

ELAH

1. A valley where David killed the Philistine giant Goliath. **1 Sam 17:2,49;** 21:9.

2. A king of Israel who was assassinated and succeeded by Zimri. 1 Kgs 16:6–10.

ELAM (a son of Shem and ancestor of the Elamites). **Gen 10:22** • 1 Chr 1:17.

ELAMITES (descendants of Elam who lived in Mesopotamia in the area later populated by the Medes and Persians). Gen 14:1,9 • Ezra 4:9 • Isa 11:11; 21:2; 22:6 • Jer 25:25; 49:34–39 • Ezek 32:24 • Dan 8:2 • Acts 2:9.

EL-BETHEL. See *Bethel.*

ELDER [S]

Matt 15:2 Why do thy [Jesus'] disciples transgress the tradition of the ***e's***

Luke 15:25 his [father of prodigal son] ***e*** son was in the field

Acts 14:23 they [Paul and Barnabas] had ordained them ***e's***

Acts 20:17 he [Paul] sent to Ephesus, and called the ***e's***

1 Tim 5:1 Rebuke not an ***e,*** but entreat him as a father

1 Tim 5:17 Let the ***e's*** that rule well be counted worthy

Jas 5:14 call for the ***e's***...and let them pray over him

2 John 1 The ***e*** unto the elect lady and her children

Rev 4:10 four and twenty ***e's*** fall down before him [God]

ELEAZAR (a son of Aaron who succeeded his father as high priest). Ex 6:23–25; 28:1 • Lev 10:6–7 • Num 3:32; **20:25–28** • Josh 14:1; 24:33.

ELECT

Isa 42:1 mine [God's] ***e,*** in whom my soul delighteth

Mark 13:27 he [Jesus] shall gather together his ***e*** from the four winds

Col 3:12 Put on...as the ***e*** of God...bowels of mercies

1 Pet 1:2 ***E*** according to the foreknowledge of God

ELECTION

Rom 11:5 a remnant according to the ***e*** of grace

2 Pet 1:10 give diligence to make your calling and ***e*** sure

ELI (a high priest of Israel with whom the prophet Samuel lived during his boyhood years). **1 Sam 1:9–3:17;** 4:15–18; 14:3 • 1 Kgs 2:27.

ELIAKIM

1. An aide to King Hezekiah of Judah who mediated

peace with the invading Assyrian army. **2 Kgs 18:18–19:2 • Isa 22:20–25;** 36:3, 11,22; 37:2.

2. Another name for King Jehoiakim of Judah. See *Jehoiakim.*

ELIAS. See *Elijah.*

ELIHU (a man who criticized Job and his three friends). Job 32:2–6; 34:1; 35:1; 36:1.

ELIJAH (a courageous prophet who opposed King Ahab and his successor, Ahaziah, because of their encouragement of Baal worship throughout the Northern Kingdom). **1 Kgs 17–21 • 2 Kgs 1:1–18; 2:1–11;** 3:11; 9:36; 10:10,17 • 2 Chr 21:12 • Mal 4:5. *Elias:* Matt 17:3–4 • Mark 9:4–13 • Luke 9:30–54 • John 1:21,25 • Rom 11:2 • Jas 5:17.

ELIPHAZ

1. A son of Esau. Gen 36:10 • 1 Chr 1:35–36.

2. One of the three friends who comforted Job. His speeches appear in Job 4:1–5:27; 15:1–35; 22:1–30.

ELISABETH (mother of John the Baptist and a relative of Mary, earthly mother of Jesus). Luke 1:5–60.

ELISEUS. See *Elisha.*

ELISHA (a prophet selected and anointed by Elijah as his successor). 1 Kgs 19:16–19 • **2 Kgs 2:1–15;** 3:11–14; 4:1–38; 5:9–10,20,25; 6:1–32; 7:1; 8:1–14; 9:1; 13:14–21. *Eliseus:* Luke 4:27.

ELON (a minor judge of Israel). Judg 12:11–12.

ELOTH (a former Edomite city used as a port city by King Solomon). **1 Kgs 9:26** • 2 Chr 8:17; 26:2.

ELYMAS. See *Bar-jesus.*

EMMAUS (a village near Jerusalem where Jesus appeared to two of His followers after His resurrection). Luke 24:13–33.

END [ED, S]

Gen 2:2 on the seventh day God ***e'ed*** his work

Job 28:24 For he [God] looketh to the ***e's*** of the earth

Job 42:12 the LORD blessed the latter ***e*** of Job

Ps 22:27 the ***e's*** of the world shall...turn unto the LORD

Ps 39:4 make me to know mine ***e***...measure of my days

Ps 102:27 thy [God's] years shall have no ***e***

Prov 14:12 the ***e*** thereof are the ways of death
Eccl 7:8 Better is the ***e*** of a thing than the beginning
Eccl 12:12 of making many books there is no ***e***
Isa 9:7 Of...his [the Messiah's] ...peace...there shall be no ***e***
Jer 8:20 summer is ***e'ed,*** and we are not saved
Dan 12:9 words are...sealed till the time of the ***e***
Matt 10:22 he that endureth to the ***e*** shall be saved
Matt 24:6 all these things must come to pass...***e*** is not yet
Matt 28:20 I [Jesus] am with you alway, even unto the ***e*** of the world
John 18:37 Jesus answered... To this ***e*** was I born
Rom 10:4 Christ is the ***e*** of the law for righteousness
1 Cor 15:24 Then cometh the ***e***
Eph 3:21 be glory in the church by Christ Jesus...world without ***e***
1 Pet 4:7 But the ***e*** of all things is at hand
Rev 2:26 he that overcometh... keepeth my works unto the ***e***
Rev 22:13 Alpha and Omega, the beginning and the ***e***

END [S] OF THE EARTH

1 Sam 2:10 the LORD shall judge the ***e's-o-t-e***
Ps 48:10 so is thy [God's] praise unto the ***e's-o-t-e***
Ps 61:2 From the ***e-o-t-e*** will I cry unto thee [God]
Ps 67:7 all the ***e's-o-t-e*** shall fear him [God]
Isa 40:28 the Creator of the ***e's-o-t-e,*** fainteth not
Isa 42:10 Sing...his [God's] praise from the ***e-o-t-e***
Isa 45:22 be ye saved, all the ***e's-o-t-e***
Acts 13:47 thou [Paul] shouldest be for salvation unto the ***e's-o-t-e***

EN-DOR (a city where King Saul sought advice from a fortune teller). Josh 17:11 • **1 Sam 28:1–10** • Ps 83:9–10.

ENDUED

Luke 24:49 tarry ye in...Jerusalem, until...***e*** with power
Jas 3:13 Who is...***e*** with knowledge among you

ENDURE [D, ING, TH]

Ex 18:23 then thou [Moses] shalt be able to ***e***
1 Chr 16:34 his [God's] mercy ***e'th*** for ever
Esth 8:6 how can I [Esther] ***e*** to see the evil that shall come
Job 8:15 he shall hold it fast, but it shall not ***e***
Ps 9:7 LORD shall ***e*** for ever
Ps 19:9 The fear of the LORD is clean, ***e'ing*** for ever
Ps 30:5 For his [God's] anger ***e'th*** but a moment

Ps 89:36 His [David's] seed shall ***e*** for ever

Ps 102:12 But thou, O LORD, shalt ***e*** for ever

Ps 107:1 give thanks unto... LORD...his mercy ***e'th*** for ever

Ps 145:13 thy [God's] dominion ***e'th*** throughout all generations

Prov 27:24 doth the crown ***e*** to every generation

Matt 10:22 he that ***e'th*** to the end shall be saved

Mark 13:13 he that shall ***e*** unto the end...shall be saved

1 Cor 13:7 [charity] hopeth all things, ***e'th*** all things

2 Tim 2:3 ***e*** hardness, as a good soldier of Jesus Christ

2 Tim 4:3 they will not ***e*** sound doctrine...having itching ears

2 Tim 4:5 watch thou in all things, ***e*** afflictions

Heb 6:15 after he [Abraham] had patiently ***e'd***

Heb 12:2 who [Jesus] for the joy...set before him ***e'd*** the cross

Jas 1:12 Blessed is the man that ***e'th*** temptation

Jas 5:11 Behold, we count them happy which ***e***

ENEMY [IES]

Deut 20:4 LORD...goeth...to fight...against your ***e'ies***

1 Sam 18:29 Saul became David's ***e*** continually

Job 19:11 he [God] counteth me...as one of his ***e'ies***

Ps 6:7 Mine eye...waxeth old because of all mine ***e'ies***

Ps 9:3 ***e'ies*** are turned back, they shall fall

Ps 18:17 He [God] delivered me from my strong ***e***

Ps 23:5 Thou [God] preparest a table...presence of mine ***e'ies***

Ps 27:11 lead me in a plain path, because of mine ***e'ies***

Ps 61:3 thou [God] hast been... a strong tower from the ***e***

Ps 97:3 A fire...burneth up his [God's] ***e'ies*** round about

Ps 110:1 until I [God] make thine ***e'ies*** thy footstool

Prov 25:21 If thine ***e*** be hungry, give him bread

Matt 5:44 I [Jesus] say unto you, Love your ***e'ies***

Rom 12:20 Therefore if thine ***e*** hunger, feed him

1 Cor 15:25 For he [Jesus] must reign, till he hath put all ***e'ies*** under his feet

1 Cor 15:26 The last ***e*** that shall be destroyed is death

Gal 4:16 Am I [Paul]...your ***e,*** because I tell you the truth

2 Thes 3:15 count him not as an ***e,*** but admonish him

Jas 4:4 a friend of the world is the ***e*** of God

EN-GEDI (an oasis near the Dead Sea where David hid from King Saul). Josh 15:62 • **1 Sam 23:29–24:1** • 2 Chr 20:2 • Song 1:14 • Ezek 47:10.

ENMITY

Gen 3:15 I [God] will put ***e*** between thee [the serpent] and the woman

Rom 8:7 Because the carnal mind is ***e*** against God

Jas 4:4 the friendship of the world is ***e*** with God

ENOCH

1. The firstborn son of Cain and a city named for him. Gen 4:17–18.

2. The father of Methuselah, who was taken into God's presence without experiencing physical death. Gen 5:18–24 • Luke 3:37 • Heb 11:5 • Jude 14. *Henoch:* 1 Chr 1:3.

ENTER [ED, ETH, ING]

Ps 100:4 ***E*** into his [God's] gates with thanksgiving

Prov 17:10 A reproof ***e'eth*** more into a wise man than an hundred stripes into a fool

Ezek 3:24 the spirit ***e'ed*** into me [Ezekiel]

Matt 6:6 when thou prayest, ***e*** into thy closet

Matt 7:21 Not every one that saith...Lord, Lord, shall ***e*** into the kingdom of heaven

Mark 7:18 thing from without ***e'eth*** into the man, it cannot defile him

Mark 14:38 pray, lest ye ***e*** into temptation

Luke 11:52 them that were ***e'ing*** in ye hindered

Luke 13:24 Strive to ***e*** in at the strait gate

Luke 18:25 easier for a camel... than for a rich man to ***e*** into the kingdom

Luke 22:3 Then ***e'ed*** Satan into Judas surnamed Iscariot

John 3:4 can he ***e*** the second time into his mother's womb, and be born

John 10:2 he that ***e'eth*** in by the door is the shepherd

Acts 11:8 nothing...unclean hath at any time ***e'ed*** into my [Peter's] mouth

Rom 5:12 by one man sin ***e'ed*** into the world

1 Cor 2:9 ***e'ed*** into the heart of man, the things which God hath prepared

Heb 9:12 he [Jesus] ***e'ed*** in once into the holy place

ENVY [IETH, ING]

Prov 3:31 ***E*** thou not the oppressor

Prov 27:4 but who is able to stand before ***e***

Mark 15:10 chief priests had delivered him [Jesus] for ***e***

Rom 13:13 Let us walk honestly ...not in strife and ***e'ing***

1 Cor 13:4 charity ***e'ieth*** not... vaunteth not itself
Gal 5:26 not be desirous of... glory,...***e'ing*** one another
Phil 1:15 Some...preach Christ even of ***e*** and strife
Titus 3:3 living in malice and ***e***...hating one another
Jas 3:16 where ***e'ing*** and strife is, there is confusion

EPAPHRAS (a church leader who was called a "fellowprisoner" by the apostle Paul). Col 1:7–8; 4:12 • **Phlm 23.**

EPAPHRODITUS (a believer who visited Paul while he was imprisoned in Rome). Phil 2:25; **4:18.**

EPHESIANS, EPISTLE TO THE. A letter of the apostle Paul to the church at Ephesus on the theme of the risen Christ as Lord of creation and head of His body, the church.

EPHESUS (a major city of Asia Minor where Paul spent two to three years and established a church). **Acts 18:19–21; 19:1–10;** 20:16–17 • 1 Cor 15:32; 16:8 • Eph 1:1 • 1 Tim 1:3 • 2 Tim 1:18; 4:12 • Rev 1:11; 2:1.

EPHRAIM

1. A son of Joseph and ancestor of one of the twelve tribes of Israel. Gen 41:52; **48:1–20** • Num 26:28 • 1 Chr 7:20–22. The tribe of Ephraim settled in central Canaan. Josh 16:1–10.

2. A symbolic name for the nation of Israel, meaning "fruitful," used especially in the books of Isaiah, Jeremiah, and Hosea. Isa 7:2–17 • Jer 31:9–20 • Hos 5:3–14.

3. A city in the wilderness to which Jesus and His disciples retreated. John 11:54.

4. A forest where Absalom's forces were defeated by David's army. 2 Sam 18:6–18.

EPHRATAH. See *Bethlehem.*

EPHRATH. See *Bethlehem.*

EPHRON (a Hittite who sold a cave to Abraham). **Gen 23: 8–20;** 25:9; 49:29–30; 50:13.

EPICUREANS (followers of the Greek philosopher Epicurus whom Paul addressed in Athens). Acts 17:18.

EQUAL

Prov 26:7 The legs of the lame are not ***e***
Ezek 18:25 Is not my [God's] way ***e***...your ways unequal
John 5:18 he [Jesus]...said also that God was his Father, making himself ***e*** with God

Phil 2:6 Who [Jesus]...thought it not robbery to be ***e*** with God
Col 4:1 give unto your servants that which is just and ***e***

ERASTUS (a believer whom Paul sent into Macedonia). Acts 19:22 • 2 Tim 4:20.

ERR [ED]
Job 6:24 understand wherein I [Job] have ***e'ed***
Isa 9:16 leaders of this people cause them to ***e***
Isa 63:17 why hast thou [God] made us to ***e*** from thy ways
Matt 22:29 Ye do ***e,*** not knowing the scriptures
1 Tim 6:10 they have ***e'ed*** from the faith
Jas 5:19 if any of you do ***e*** from the truth

ERROR
2 Sam 6:7 God smote him [Uzzah] there for his ***e***
Matt 27:64 the last ***e*** shall be worse than the first
2 Pet 3:17 being led away with the ***e*** of the wicked

ESAIAS. See *Isaiah.*

ESAR-HADDON (a king of Assyria who succeeded his father, Sennacherib). **2 Kgs 19:37** • Ezra 4:2 • Isa 37:38.

ESAU (the oldest son of Isaac who traded his birthright for a bowl of stew). Esau was the ancestor of the Edomites. **Gen 25:26–34;** 26:34; 27:1–42; 28:6–9; 32:3–19; 33:1–16; 35:1,29; 36:1–43 • Josh 24:4 • 1 Chr 1:34–35 • Mal 1:2–3 • Rom 9:13 • Heb 12:16. *Edom:* Gen 36:8. See also *Edom.*

ESCAPE [D]
1 Sam 22:1 David...***e'd*** to the cave Adullam
Job 19:20 I [Job] am ***e'd*** with the skin of my teeth
Ps 71:2 cause me to ***e:*** incline thine [God's] ear unto me
Isa 37:31 remnant that is ***e'd*** of the house of Judah
Jer 25:35 no way to flee, nor the principal of the flock to ***e***
John 10:39 but he [Jesus] ***e'd*** out of their hand
1 Cor 10:13 God...will with the temptation also make a way to ***e***
Heb 2:3 How shall we ***e,*** if we neglect so great salvation

ESEK (a well that the servants of Isaac and Abimelech quarreled over). Gen 26:20.

ESH-BAAL. See *Ish-bosheth.*

ESH-COL (a brook explored by the spies sent into Canaan). **Num 13:22–27;** 32:9 • Deut 1:24.

ESTABLISH [ED]
Gen 9:9 I [God] ***e*** my covenant with you [Noah]
Ps 7:9 ***e*** the just: for the righteous God trieth the hearts
Ps 78:5 he [God] ***e'ed*** a testimony in Jacob
Ps 90:17 ***e*** thou [God] the work of our hands
Prov 3:19 The LORD...by understanding hath...***e'ed*** the heavens
Prov 12:19 The lip of truth shall be ***e'ed*** for ever
Prov 16:3 Commit...unto the LORD...thy thoughts shall be ***e'ed***
Ezek 16:62 I [God] will ***e*** my covenant with thee
Matt 18:16 mouth of...witnesses every word...be ***e'ed***
Acts 16:5 so were the churches ***e'ed*** in the faith
Rom 10:3 going about to ***e*** their own righteousness
Heb 8:6 he [Jesus] is the mediator of a better covenant... ***e'ed*** upon better promises

ESTHER (a young Jewish woman who became queen under King Ahasuerus of Persia and used her influence to save her countrymen). Esth 2–9.

ESTHER, BOOK OF. A historical book of the Old Testament named for its major personality, Queen Esther of Persia. This book shows that God protects and sustains His people.

ETERNAL
Deut 33:27 The ***e*** God is thy refuge
Mark 3:29 he that shall blaspheme against the Holy Ghost...is in danger of ***e*** damnation
John 17:3 life ***e,*** that they might know...God
2 Cor 4:18 things which are not seen are ***e***
2 Cor 5:1 an house not made with hands, ***e*** in the heavens
1 Tim 1:17 unto the King ***e,*** immortal, invisible
Heb 5:9 he [Jesus] became the author of ***e*** salvation
Heb 9:12 by his [Jesus'] own blood he...obtained ***e*** redemption for us

ETERNAL LIFE
Mark 10:17 what shall I do that I may inherit ***e-l***
John 3:15 whosoever believeth in him [Jesus] should not perish, but have ***e-l***
John 6:54 Whoso eateth my [Jesus'] flesh...hath ***e-l***
John 6:68 thou [Jesus] hast the words of ***e-l***
John 10:28 I [Jesus] give unto them ***e-l***
Rom 6:23 the gift of God is ***e-l*** through Jesus Christ

1 Tim 6:12 Fight the good fight of faith, lay hold on ***e-l***

1 John 2:25 promise that he [Jesus] hath promised...***e-l***

1 John 3:15 no murderer hath ***e-l*** abiding in him

1 John 5:11 God hath given to us ***e-l***...in his Son

Jude 21 mercy of our Lord Jesus Christ unto ***e-l***

ETHIOPIA (an ancient nation south of Egypt). Gen 2:13 • 2 Chr 12:3 • Job 28:19 • Ps 68:31 • Isa 45:14 • Dan 11:43 • Amos 9:7 • Acts 8:27.

EUNICE (mother of Timothy who was commended for her faith by the apostle Paul). 2 Tim 1:5.

EUPHRATES (a major river in Mesopotamia). Gen 2:14; 15:18 • Josh 1:4 • 2 Sam 8:3 • 2 Kgs 23:29 • 2 Chr 35:20 • Jer 13:4–7 • Rev 9:14; 16:12.

EUTYCHUS (a young man who fell from a window during Paul's sermon at Troas). Acts 20:9–12.

EVANGELIST [S]

Acts 21:8 entered into the house of Philip the ***e***

Eph 4:11 he [God] gave some... prophets; and some, ***e's***

2 Tim 4:5 do the work of an ***e***

EVE (first woman and mother of the human race). Gen 3:20; 4:1 • 2 Cor 11:3 • 1 Tim 2:13.

EVERLASTING

Deut 33:27 and underneath are the ***e*** arms

Ps 24:7 and be ye lift up, ye ***e*** doors

Ps 90:2 even from ***e*** to ***e,*** thou art God

Ps 100:5 For the LORD is good; his mercy is ***e***

Ps 119:144 righteousness of thy [God's] testimonies is ***e***

Isa 9:6 his [Jesus'] name shall be called...The ***e*** Father

Isa 26:4 in the LORD JEHOVAH is ***e*** strength

Isa 40:28 the ***e*** God...fainteth not, neither is weary

Isa 60:19 the LORD shall be unto thee an ***e*** light

Jer 31:3 I [God] have loved thee with an ***e*** love

Dan 7:14 his [God's] dominion is an ***e*** dominion

Matt 25:41 Depart from me [Jesus], ye cursed, into ***e*** fire

EVERLASTING COVENANT

Gen 9:16 the ***e-c*** between God and every living creature

Heb 13:20 Jesus, that great shepherd of the sheep, through the blood of the ***e-c***

EVERLASTING LIFE

John 3:16 whosoever believeth in him [Jesus] should not perish, but have ***e-l***

John 4:14 a well of water springing up into ***e-l***

John 5:24 He that...believeth on him [God] that sent me [Jesus], hath ***e-l***

John 6:47 He that believeth on me [Jesus] hath ***e-l***

EVIL [S]

Gen 50:20 ye thought ***e*** against me [Joseph]; but God meant it unto good

Deut 30:15 I [Moses] have set before thee...death and ***e***

Josh 24:15 if it seem ***e*** unto you to serve the LORD

1 Sam 16:14 an ***e*** spirit from the LORD troubled him [Saul]

Job 2:10 shall we receive good at the hand of God, and... not receive ***e***

Job 28:28 to depart from ***e*** is understanding

Ps 23:4 valley of the shadow of death, I will fear no ***e***

Ps 34:13 Keep thy tongue from ***e,*** and thy lips from...guile

Ps 38:20 They...that render ***e*** for good are...adversaries

Ps 51:4 Against thee [God]... have I...done this ***e***

Ps 119:101 I have refrained my feet from every ***e*** way

Prov 3:7 fear the LORD, and depart from ***e***

Prov 15:3 eyes of the LORD are in every place, beholding the ***e*** and the good

Prov 31:12 She will do him good and not ***e***

Isa 5:20 Woe unto them that call ***e*** good, and good ***e***

Jer 1:14 Out of the north an ***e*** shall break forth

Jer 2:13 my [God's] people have committed two ***e's***

Matt 5:11 men...shall say all manner of ***e*** against you

Matt 6:13 lead us not into temptation...deliver us from ***e***

Mark 3:4 lawful to do good on the sabbath...or to do ***e***

Luke 11:13 ye then, being ***e,*** know how to give good gifts

John 3:19 men loved darkness... because their deeds were ***e***

Rom 7:19 the ***e*** which I [Paul] would not, that I do

Rom 12:9 Abhor that which is ***e;*** cleave to...good

Rom 12:21 Be not overcome of ***e***...overcome ***e*** with good

Eph 5:16 Redeeming the time, because the days are ***e***

Eph 6:13 ye may be able to withstand in the ***e*** day

1 Thes 5:22 Abstain from all appearance of ***e***

1 Tim 6:10 love of money is the root of all ***e***

Heb 3:12 lest there be in any of you an ***e*** heart of unbelief

Jas 3:8 the tongue...is an unruly ***e,*** full of deadly poison

Jas 3:16 where envying...is, there is...every ***e*** work

3 John 11 Beloved, follow not that which is ***e***

EVILDOER [S]

Ps 26:5 I have hated the congregation of ***e's***

Ps 119:115 Depart from me, ye ***e's***

1 Pet 4:15 let none of you suffer ...as an ***e,*** or...busybody

EVIL-MERODACH (a king of Babylonia who released King Jehoiachin of Judah from prison). **2 Kgs 25:27–30** • Jer 52:31.

EXALT [ED, ETH]

1 Chr 29:11 thou [God] art ***e'ed*** as head above all

Ps 34:3 let us ***e*** his [God's] name together

Ps 46:10 I [God] will be ***e'ed*** among the heathen

Ps 57:11 Be thou ***e'ed,*** O God, above the heavens

Ps 97:9 thou [God] art ***e'ed*** far above all gods

Ps 99:5 ***E*** ye the LORD...and worship at his footstool

Prov 14:34 Righteousness ***e'eth*** a nation

Isa 25:1 O LORD, thou art my God; I will ***e*** thee

Isa 40:4 Every valley shall be ***e'ed***...hill...made low

Luke 14:11 he that humbleth himself shall be ***e'ed***

Phil 2:9 God also hath highly ***e'ed*** him [Jesus]

1 Pet 5:6 that he [God] may ***e*** you in due time

EXAMPLE

Matt 1:19 Then Joseph her [Mary's] husband...not willing to make her a publick ***e***

John 13:15 I [Jesus] have given you an ***e***

1 Tim 4:12 be thou an ***e*** of the believers, in word

EXCEEDING [LY]

Gen 17:2 I [God]...will multiply thee [Abraham] ***e'ly***

Ps 68:3 rejoice before God: yea, let them ***e'ly*** rejoice

Jon 3:3 Now Nineveh was an ***e*** great city

Jon 4:1 it displeased Jonah ***e'ly,*** and he was very angry

Matt 2:10 they [the wise men] rejoiced with ***e*** great joy

Matt 5:12 be ***e*** glad: for great is your reward in heaven

Matt 26:38 My [Jesus'] soul is ***e*** sorrowful, even unto death

Mark 15:14 cried out the more ***e'ly,*** Crucify him [Jesus]

2 Cor 4:17 our light affliction... worketh for us a far more ***e***...weight of glory

Eph 2:7 he [God] might show the ***e*** riches of his grace

Eph 3:20 unto him [Jesus] that is able to do ***e*** abundantly above all...we ask

Jude 24 him [Jesus] that is able to...present you faultless before...his glory with ***e*** joy

EXCELLENT

Ps 8:9 how ***e*** is thy [God's] name in all the earth

Ps 150:2 praise him [God] according to his ***e*** greatness

Isa 12:5 for he [God] hath done ***e*** things

Dan 6:3 because an ***e*** spirit was in him [Daniel]

1 Cor 12:31 yet show I [Paul] unto you a more ***e*** way

Heb 8:6 hath he [Jesus] obtained a more ***e*** ministry

Heb 11:4 Abel offered...a more ***e*** sacrifice than Cain

EXCUSE

Luke 14:18 they all with one consent began to make ***e***

Rom 1:20 they are without ***e***

EXHORT [ED, ING]

1 Thes 2:11 we ***e'ed*** and comforted...every one of you

2 Tim 4:2 ***e*** with all longsuffering and doctrine

Titus 2:9 ***E*** servants to be obedient unto their own masters

Heb 10:25 Not forsaking the assembling of ourselves... but ***e'ing*** one another

EXODUS, BOOK OF. An Old Testament book which recounts the release of the Hebrew people from Egyptian enslavement and the early years of their history as a nation. It describes God's miraculous provision for His people in the wilderness (16:1–17:7); Moses' reception of the Ten Commandments (chap. 20); and the building of the tabernacle in the wilderness (chaps. 36–40).

EXPEDIENT

John 11:50 ***e***...that one man should die for the people

John 16:7 ***e*** for you that I [Jesus] go away

1 Cor 6:12 All things are lawful ...but all things are not ***e***

EYE

Ex 21:24 ***E*** for ***e***, tooth for tooth, hand for hand

Deut 34:7 when he [Moses] died...***e*** was not dim, nor... natural force abated

Job 42:5 now mine [Job's] ***e*** seeth thee [God]

Ps 6:7 Mine ***e*** is consumed because of grief

Ps 17:8 Keep me as the apple of the ***e***

Prov 28:22 He that hasteth to be rich hath an evil ***e***

Matt 5:38 it hath been said...***e*** for an ***e***...tooth for a tooth

Matt 6:23 if thine ***e*** be evil, thy whole body...full of darkness

Mark 9:47 if thine ***e*** offend thee, pluck it out

Luke 6:41 the mote that is in thy brother's ***e***
1 Cor 2:9 ***E*** hath not seen, nor ear heard
1 Cor 12:17 If the whole body were an ***e,*** where...hearing
1 Cor 12:21 the ***e*** cannot say unto the hand
1 Cor 15:52 in the twinkling of an ***e,*** at the last trump
Rev 1:7 he [Jesus] cometh with clouds...every ***e*** shall see him

EYE [S] OF THE LORD
Gen 6:8 Noah found grace in the ***e's-o-t-L***
1 Kgs 15:5 David did...right in the ***e's-o-t-L***
2 Chr 16:9 ***e's-o-t-L*** run to and fro throughout the...earth
Ps 33:18 the ***e-o-t-L*** is upon them that fear him
Prov 15:3 The ***e's-o-t-L*** are in every place, beholding the evil and the good
1 Pet 3:12 the ***e's-o-t-L*** are over the righteous

EYEWITNESSES
Luke 1:2 which...were ***e,*** and ministers of the word
2 Pet 1:16 we...were ***e*** of his [Jesus'] majesty

EZEKIAS. See *Hezekiah.*

EZEKIEL (a prophet of Judah carried into exile by the Babylonians and author of the book that bears his name). Ezek 1:3. He is not mentioned outside the Book of Ezekiel.

EZEKIEL, BOOK OF. A prophetic book of the Old Testament addressed to the Jewish captives in Babylon about 585 B.C., offering God's promise that His people would be restored to their homeland after their period of suffering and exile was over.

EZION-GABER. See *Ezion-geber.*

EZION-GEBER (a town with a harbor for King Solomon's trading ships). **1 Kgs 9:26–28;** 22:48 • 2 Chr 8:17–18. *Ezion-gaber:* Num 33:35–36 • Deut 2:8 • 2 Chr 20:36.

EZRA (a scribe and priest who led a reform movement among the Jews after the Exile and author of the book that bears his name). Ezra 7:1–25; 10:1–16 • Neh 8:1–13; 12:13–36.

EZRA, BOOK OF. A historical book of the Old Testament that describes events in Jerusalem after the Jewish captives began returning to their homeland about 500 B.C.

-F-

FABLES

1 Tim 1:4 Neither give heed to ***f*** and endless genealogies

1 Tim 4:7 refuse profane and old wives' ***f***

FACE OF THE LORD

Ps 34:16 The ***f-o-t-L*** is against them that do evil

Luke 1:76 go before the ***f-o-t-L*** to prepare his ways

1 Pet 3:12 the ***f-o-t-L*** is against them that do evil

FAIR HAVENS (a harbor on the island of Crete where Paul stopped during his voyage to Rome). Acts 27:8.

FAITH

Hab 2:4 but the just shall live by his ***f***

Matt 17:20 ***f*** as a grain of mustard seed

Acts 6:8 Stephen, full of ***f*** and power, did great wonders

Rom 1:17 righteousness of God revealed from ***f*** to ***f***

Rom 3:28 justified by ***f*** without the deeds of the law

Rom 5:1 justified by ***f,*** we have peace with God

Rom 10:17 So then ***f*** cometh by hearing

1 Cor 13:13 abideth ***f,*** hope, charity, these three

Gal 2:20 I [Paul] live by the ***f*** of the Son of God

Gal 3:24 unto Christ, that we might be justified by ***f***

Gal 5:22 fruit of the Spirit is love...goodness, ***f***

Eph 2:8 by grace are ye saved through ***f***

Eph 6:16 Above all, taking the shield of ***f***

1 Tim 5:8 denied the ***f,*** and is worse than an infidel

1 Tim 6:12 Fight the good fight of ***f***

2 Tim 4:7 finished my course, I [Paul] have kept the ***f***

Heb 10:23 hold fast the profession of our ***f***

Heb 11:1 Now ***f*** is the substance of things hoped for

Heb 12:2 Jesus the author and finisher of our ***f***

Jas 2:17 ***f,*** if it hath not works, is dead, being alone

1 John 5:4 victory that overcometh the world, even our ***f***

Jude 3 contend for the ***f***... delivered unto the saints

FAITH CHAPTER OF THE BIBLE. Heb 11.

FAITHFUL [NESS]

Ps 31:23 for the LORD preserveth the ***f***

Ps 119:90 Thy [God's] ***f'ness*** is unto all generations

Prov 27:6 ***F*** are the wounds of a friend

Lam 3:23 new every morning: great is thy [God's] ***f'ness***
Matt 25:21 Well done, thou good and ***f*** servant
Luke 16:10 ***f*** in that which is least is ***f*** also in much
1 Cor 4:2 required in stewards, that a man be found ***f***
1 Cor 10:13 God is ***f,*** who will not suffer you to be tempted
2 Thes 3:3 the Lord is ***f,*** who shall stablish you
1 John 1:9 he [Jesus] is ***f*** and just to forgive us our sins
Rev 2:10 be thou ***f*** unto death

FAITHLESS
Luke 9:41 O ***f*** and perverse generation
John 20:27 Thomas...be not ***f***

FALL [EN, ETH, ING]
Ps 116:8 thou [God] hast delivered...my feet from ***f'ing***
Ps 145:14 The LORD upholdeth all that ***f***
Prov 16:18 Pride goeth before destruction...haughty spirit before a ***f***
Eccl 4:10 woe to him that is alone when he ***f'eth***
Dan 3:6 whoso ***f'eth*** not down and worshippeth shall...be cast into the...furnace
Hos 14:1 thou [Israel] hast ***f'en*** by thine iniquity
Luke 2:34 this child [Jesus] is set for the ***f***...of many
Luke 6:39 shall they not both ***f*** into the ditch
John 12:24 corn of wheat ***f*** into the ground and die
1 Cor 10:12 thinketh he standeth take heed lest he ***f***
Heb 10:31 It is a fearful thing to ***f*** into the hands of the living God
Jas 1:2 joy when ye ***f*** into divers temptations
Jude 24 Now unto him [Jesus] that is able to keep you from ***f'ing***
Rev 14:8 Babylon is ***f'en,*** is ***f'en,*** that great city

FALL OF MAN. Gen 3:1–24.

FALSE [LY]
Ex 20:16 shalt not bear ***f*** witness against thy neighbour
Lev 19:11 Ye shall not steal, neither deal ***f'ly***
Prov 11:1 A ***f*** balance is abomination to the LORD
Jer 29:9 prophesy ***f'ly*** unto you in my [God's] name
Matt 5:11 say all manner of evil against you ***f'ly,*** for my [Jesus'] sake

FALSE PROPHET [S]
Matt 7:15 Beware of ***f-p's***...in sheep's clothing
Matt 24:11 many ***f-p's*** shall rise, and shall deceive many
Mark 13:22 ***f-p's*** shall rise...show signs and wonders
Acts 13:6 a ***f-p,*** a Jew, whose name was Bar-jesus

2 Pet 2:1 there were ***f-p's*** also among the people
1 John 4:1 many ***f-p's*** are gone out into the world
Rev 19:20 the beast was taken, and with him the ***f-p***

FALSE WITNESS [ES]

Deut 5:20 Neither shalt...bear ***f-w*** against thy neighbour
Ps 35:11 ***F-w'es***...laid to my charge things that I knew not
Prov 6:19 A ***f-w*** that speaketh lies
Prov 14:5 a ***f-w*** will utter lies
Mark 14:56 many bare ***f-w*** against him [Jesus]

FAST [ING]

Ps 109:24 knees are weak through ***f'ing***
Matt 17:21 this kind goeth not out but by prayer and ***f'ing***
Mark 2:20 bridegroom [Jesus] shall be taken away...then shall they ***f***
1 Cor 16:13 Watch ye, stand ***f*** in the faith
Gal 5:1 Stand ***f***...wherewith Christ hath made us free
1 Thes 5:21 Prove all things; hold ***f*** that which is good
Heb 10:23 hold ***f*** the profession of our faith

FATHER

Gen 2:24 shall a man leave his ***f*** and his mother
Gen 17:5 a ***f*** of many nations have I [God] made thee [Abraham]
Ex 20:12 Honour thy ***f*** and thy mother
Lev 20:9 one that curseth his ***f***...shall be surely put to death
Ps 27:10 When my ***f***...forsake me...LORD will take me up
Ps 103:13 Like as a ***f*** pitieth his children
Prov 4:1 Hear...the instruction of a ***f***
Prov 15:20 A wise son maketh a glad ***f***
Isa 9:6 his [Jesus'] name shall be...The everlasting ***F***
Isa 64:8 LORD, thou art our ***f;*** we are the clay
Ezek 18:20 neither shall the ***f*** bear the iniquity of the son
Mal 2:10 Have we not all one ***f***
Matt 5:48 even as your ***F***...in heaven is perfect
Matt 6:9 Our ***F***...in heaven
Matt 10:37 loveth ***f*** or mother more than me [Jesus] is not worthy of me
Matt 23:9 one is your ***F,*** which is in heaven
Matt 28:19 baptizing them in the name of the ***F***
Mark 14:36 Abba, ***F,*** all things are possible unto thee
Luke 9:59 suffer me first to go and bury my ***f***
Luke 15:22 the ***f*** said to his servants, Bring...the best robe

Luke 23:34 ***F,*** forgive them... they know not what they do
Luke 24:49 I [Jesus] send the promise of my ***F***
John 6:44 No man can come to me [Jesus], except the ***F*** which...sent me draw him
John 10:30 I [Jesus] and my ***F*** are one
John 14:6 no man cometh unto the ***F,*** but by me [Jesus]
John 14:16 I [Jesus] will pray the ***F,*** and he shall give you another Comforter
John 15:8 Herein is my [Jesus'] ***F*** glorified...bear much fruit
John 16:23 ask the ***F*** in my [Jesus'] name, he will give it
John 20:21 my ***F*** hath sent me [Jesus], even so send I you
Acts 1:7 not for you to know the...seasons, which the ***F*** hath put in his own power
Eph 4:6 One God and ***F*** of all
Phil 2:11 confess that Jesus Christ is Lord, to the glory of God the ***F***
Col 1:19 For it pleased the ***F*** that in him [Jesus] should all fulness dwell
Jas 1:17 good gift...cometh down from the ***F*** of lights
Jas 2:21 Abraham our ***f*** justified by works
1 John 1:3 our fellowship is with the ***F,*** and with his Son
1 John 2:1 we have an advocate with the ***F,*** Jesus Christ
1 John 3:1 manner of love the ***F*** hath bestowed upon us

FAULT [LESS, S]
Luke 23:4 I [Pilate] find no ***f*** in this man [Jesus]
Gal 6:1 Brethren, if a man be overtaken in a ***f***
Jas 5:16 Confess your ***f's*** one to another
Jude 24 present you ***f'less*** before...presence of his [Jesus'] glory
Rev 14:5 without ***f*** before the throne of God

FEAR [ED, EST, ETH]
Gen 22:12 I [God] know that thou [Abraham] ***f'est*** God
Deut 6:13 ***f*** the LORD thy God, and serve him
Josh 4:14 ***f'ed*** him [Joshua], as they ***f'ed*** Moses
1 Chr 16:25 he [God] also is to be ***f'ed*** above all gods
Job 1:1 Job...was perfect... and one that ***f'ed*** God
Job 1:9 Satan answered...Doth Job ***f*** God for nought
Job 28:28 Behold, the ***f*** of the Lord, that is wisdom
Ps 19:9 ***f*** of the LORD is clean, enduring for ever
Ps 23:4 ***f*** no evil: for thou [God] art with me
Ps 27:1 The LORD is my...salvation; whom shall I ***f***
Ps 34:11 I will teach you the ***f*** of the LORD
Ps 46:2 will not we ***f,*** though the earth be removed
Ps 103:13 the LORD pitieth them that ***f*** him

Ps 111:10 ***f*** of the LORD is the beginning of wisdom

Ps 112:1 Blessed is the man that ***f'eth*** the LORD

Ps 118:6 I will not ***f***: what can man do unto me

Prov 15:16 Better is little with the ***f*** of the LORD than great treasure and trouble

Eccl 12:13 ***F*** God, and keep his commandments

Mal 4:2 that ***f*** my name shall... Sun of righteousness arise

Matt 28:8 they [the women] departed quickly from the sepulchre with ***f***

Mark 4:41 ***f'ed*** exceedingly... What manner of man is this

Luke 22:2 they [chief priests and scribes] ***f'ed*** the people

Acts 2:43 And ***f*** came upon every soul

Phil 2:12 work out your own salvation with ***f***

2 Tim 1:7 God hath not given us the spirit of ***f***

Heb 13:6 I will not ***f*** what man shall do unto me

1 John 4:18 perfect love casteth out ***f***

Rev 15:4 Who shall not ***f*** thee, O Lord...glorify thy name

FEAR NOT

Gen 15:1 ***F-n,*** Abram: I [God] am thy shield

Gen 21:17 What aileth thee, Hagar? ***f-n***

Dan 10:12 ***F-n,*** Daniel...thy words were heard

Joel 2:21 ***F-n,*** O land; be glad and rejoice

Matt 1:20 Joseph...***f-n*** to take unto thee Mary

Matt 28:5 ***F-n*** ye [women at the tomb]: for I know that ye seek Jesus

Luke 1:13 ***F-n,*** Zacharias: for thy prayer is heard

Luke 1:30 ***F-n,*** Mary: for thou hast found favour with God

Luke 2:10 ***F-n***...I [angel] bring you [shepherds] good tidings of great joy

Luke 12:32 ***F-n***...it is your Father's good pleasure to give you the kingdom

Acts 27:24 Saying, ***F-n,*** Paul; thou must be brought before Caesar

Rev 1:17 ***F-n;*** I [Jesus] am the first and the last

FEARFUL [LY, NESS]

Ps 55:5 ***F'ness*** and trembling are come upon me

Ps 139:14 I am ***f'ly*** and wonderfully made

Matt 8:26 Why are ye ***f,*** O ye of little faith

Heb 10:31 a ***f*** thing to fall into the hands of the living God

FEAST OF HARVEST OR INGATHERING. See *Pentecost.*

FEAST OF WEEKS. See *Pentecost.*

FELIX (governor of Judea who heard Paul's defense at Caesarea). Acts 23:24–26; **24:3, 10–27;** 25:14.

FELLOWSHIP

Acts 2:42 continued stedfastly in the apostles' doctrine and ***f***

2 Cor 6:14 what ***f*** hath righteousness...unrighteousness

Eph 5:11 have no ***f*** with the unfruitful works of darkness

Phil 3:10 That I [Paul] may know him [Jesus]...and the ***f*** of his sufferings

1 John 1:7 we have ***f*** one with another

FESTUS (successor of Felix as Roman governor of Judea before whom Paul made his defense). Acts 24:27; **25:1–24; 26:24–32.**

FIERY SERPENTS IN THE WILDERNESS. Num 21:4–9.

FILTHY

Ps 14:3 they are all together become ***f***

Isa 64:6 all our righteousnesses are as ***f*** rags

1 Tim 3:8 must the deacons be grave...not greedy of ***f*** lucre

FINGER OF GOD

Ex 8:19 the magicians said... This is the ***f-o-G***

Ex 31:18 gave unto Moses... two...tables of stone, written with the ***f-o-G***

Luke 11:20 if I [Jesus] with the ***f-o-G*** cast out devils

FINISH [ED]

Gen 2:1 heavens and the earth were ***f'ed***

Neh 6:15 wall was ***f'ed*** in the twenty and fifth day

Luke 14:28 counteth the cost, whether...sufficient to ***f*** it

John 4:34 My [Jesus'] meat is to...***f*** his [God's] work

John 17:4 ***f'ed*** the work which thou [God] gavest me [Jesus]

John 19:30 It is ***f'ed:*** and he [Jesus]...gave up the ghost

2 Tim 4:7 I [Paul] have ***f'ed*** my course...kept the faith

FIRE AND BRIMSTONE

Ps 11:6 Upon the wicked he [God] shall rain snares, ***f-a-b***

Luke 17:29 the same day that Lot went out of Sodom it rained ***f-a-b***

Rev 14:10 he [worshiper of beast] shall be tormented with ***f-a-b***

FIRSTFRUITS

Ex 23:19 first of the ***f***...bring into...house of...God

Prov 3:9 Honour the LORD... with the ***f*** of...thine increase

1 Cor 15:20 now is Christ risen...***f*** of them that slept

FLESH AND BLOOD

Matt 16:17 ***f-a-b*** hath not revealed it unto thee [Peter]

1 Cor 15:50 ***f-a-b*** cannot inherit the kingdom of God

Eph 6:12 wrestle not against ***f-a-b,*** but...principalities

FOOLISH [LY, NESS]

Ps 5:5 The ***f*** shall not stand in thy [God's] sight

Ps 69:5 O God, thou knowest my ***f'ness***

Prov 10:1 a ***f*** son is the heaviness of his mother

Prov 12:23 the heart of fools proclaimeth ***f'ness***

Prov 14:17 He that is soon angry dealeth ***f'ly***

Prov 15:20 a ***f*** man despiseth his mother

Eccl 4:13 Better is...a wise child than an old and ***f*** king

Matt 7:26 likened unto a ***f*** man, which built his house upon the sand

Matt 25:3 They that were ***f***... took no oil with them

1 Cor 1:23 Christ crucified... unto the Greeks ***f'ness***

1 Cor 1:27 chosen the ***f*** things... to confound the wise

1 Cor 3:19 wisdom of this world is ***f'ness*** with God

Gal 3:1 ***f*** Galatians, who hath bewitched you

Titus 3:9 avoid ***f*** questions, and genealogies

FORGIVE [ING, TH]

Num 14:18 The LORD is longsuffering...***f'ing*** iniquity

2 Chr 7:14 then will I [God] hear...and will ***f*** their sin

Ps 86:5 thou, Lord, art good, and ready to ***f***

Ps 103:3 Who [God] ***f'th*** all thine iniquities

Matt 6:14 your heavenly Father will also ***f*** you

Matt 18:21 how oft shall my brother sin...and I [Peter] ***f***

Mark 11:26 neither will your Father...***f*** your trespasses

Luke 5:21 Who can ***f*** sins, but God alone

Luke 6:37 ***f,*** and ye shall be forgiven

Luke 23:34 ***f*** them; for they know not what they do

Eph 4:32 be ye kind...***f'ing*** one another

1 John 1:9 he [Jesus] is faithful and just to ***f*** us our sins

FORGIVEN

Ps 32:1 Blessed is he whose transgression is ***f***

Matt 12:31 blasphemy against the Holy Ghost shall not be ***f***

Luke 6:37 forgive, and ye shall be ***f***

Rom 4:7 Blessed are they whose iniquities are ***f***

1 John 2:12 your sins are ***f*** you for his [Jesus'] name's sake

FORGIVENESS

Acts 26:18 that they may receive ***f*** of sins

Col 1:14 In [Jesus] we have redemption...the ***f*** of sins

FORNICATION

Matt 19:9 put away his wife, except it be for ***f***

1 Cor 5:1 reported...that there is ***f*** among you

1 Cor 6:18 committeth ***f*** sinneth against his own body

Gal 5:19 Now the works of the flesh are...Adultery, ***f***

1 Thes 4:3 this is the will of God...abstain from ***f***

Rev 17:4 a golden cup in her [woman on scarlet beast] hand full...of her ***f***

FOUNDATION [S]

Job 38:4 Where wast thou [Job] when I [God] laid the ***f's*** of the earth

Isa 28:16 I [God] lay in Zion for a ***f*** a stone

Matt 25:34 inherit the kingdom prepared for you from the ***f*** of the world

1 Cor 3:11 other ***f*** can no man lay than...Jesus Christ

Eph 2:20 built upon the ***f*** of the apostles

Heb 1:10 Thou, Lord...hast laid the ***f*** of the earth

Heb 11:10 city which hath ***f's***...builder and maker is God

Rev 21:14 And the wall of the city had twelve ***f's***

FREE [LY]

Gen 2:16 every tree of the garden thou mayest ***f'ly*** eat

Ps 51:12 uphold me with thy [God's] ***f*** spirit

Matt 10:8 ***f'ly*** ye have received, ***f'ly*** give

John 8:32 and the truth shall make you ***f***

Rom 3:24 justified ***f'ly*** by his [God's] grace through... Christ Jesus

Rom 6:18 ***f*** from sin, ye became the servants of righteousness

Rom 8:2 Jesus hath made me ***f*** from the law of sin

1 Cor 9:19 though I [Paul] be ***f*** from all men

Gal 3:28 there is neither bond nor ***f***

Gal 5:1 in the liberty wherewith Christ hath made us ***f***

Col 3:11 neither Greek nor Jew...bond nor ***f***

Rev 22:17 let him take the water of life ***f'ly***

FRUIT OF THE SPIRIT. Gal 5:22–26.

-G-

GAASH, MOUNT (a mountain where Joshua was buried). **Josh 24:29–30** • Judg 2:9 • 2 Sam 23:30 • 1 Chr 11:32.

GABRIEL (an archangel who appeared to Daniel, Zacharias, and the Virgin Mary). Dan 8:16; 9:21 • Luke 1:19,26.

GAD (a son of Jacob and ancestor of one of the twelve tribes of Israel). Gen 30:11; 35:26; 46:16; 49:19 • Ex 1:4 • 1 Chr 5:11. The tribe of Gad settled east of the Jordan River. **Num 32:1–33** • Josh 13:24,28; 22:9–34.

GADARENES (people from the area of Gadara in Perea where Jesus healed a demon-possessed man). Mark 5:1–20 • Luke 8:26,37. *Gergesenes:* Matt 8:28.

GAIN [ED]

Matt 18:15 if he shall hear thee...hast ***g'ed*** thy brother

Mark 8:36 profit a man, if he shall ***g*** the whole world

Luke 19:16 thy pound hath ***g'ed*** ten pounds

1 Cor 9:20 I [Paul] became as a Jew, that I might ***g*** the Jews

Phil 1:21 to me [Paul] to live is Christ, and to die is ***g***

1 Tim 6:6 godliness with contentment is great ***g***

GALATIA (a territory of central Asia Minor visited by Paul during the first missionary journey). **Acts 16:6; 18:23** • 1 Cor 16:1 • Gal 1:2 • 2 Tim 4:10 • 1 Pet 1:1.

GALATIANS, EPISTLE TO THE. A short epistle of the apostle Paul to the churches at Galatia on the themes of Christian liberty and justification by faith alone.

GALILEE (a Roman province in northern Palestine where Jesus spent most of His earthly ministry). Mark 1:9–28; 3:7 • Luke 23:6–55 • John 4:3–54.

GALILEE, SEA OF. A freshwater lake in northern Palestine associated with the ministry of Jesus. Mark 1:16–20; 4:35–41; 7:31. *Lake of Gennesaret:* Luke 5:1. *Sea of Chinneroth:* Josh 12:3. *Sea of Tiberias:* John 21:1.

GALLIO (a Roman ruler of Achaia who refused to get involved in the dispute between Paul and the Jewish leaders in Corinth). Acts 18:12–17.

GAMALIEL (a teacher of the law under whom Paul studied). Acts 5:33–39; **22:3.**

GARDEN OF EDEN. Gen 2:8–3:24.

GASHMU (a Samaritan leader who opposed the rebuilding of Jerusalem's walls under Nehemiah). Neh 6:6.

GATH (a major Philistine city captured by David). Josh 11:22 • 1 Sam 5:8; 6:17; 17:4; 21:10–15; 27:3–12 • 2 Kgs 12:17 • **1 Chr 18:1** • 2 Chr 11:5–8 • Amos 6:1–3 • Mic 1:10.

GAZA (a major Philistine city where Samson was killed). Josh 10:41; 11:22; 15:47 • **Judg 16:21–30** • Amos 1:6–7 • Acts 8:26. *Azzah:* Jer 25:20.

GAZER. See *Gezer.*

GEDALIAH (a friend and supporter of the prophet Jeremiah). 2 Kgs 25:22–25 • Jer 39:14; **40:5–16;** 41:1–18; 43:6.

GEDEON. See *Gideon.*

GEHAZI (Elisha's servant who was struck with leprosy because of his greed). 2 Kgs 4:12–36; **5:20–27;** 8:4–6.

GENEALOGIES OF JESUS. See *Jesus, Life and Ministry of.*

GENERATION [S]

Gen 2:4 the ***g's*** of the heavens and of the earth

Num 32:13 all the ***g,*** that had done evil...was consumed

Ps 24:6 This is the ***g*** of them that seek him [God]

Ps 33:11 thoughts of his [God's] heart to all ***g's***

Ps 71:18 I have showed thy [God's] strength unto this ***g***

Ps 85:5 draw out thine [God's] anger to all ***g's***

Ps 90:1 thou [God] hast been our dwelling place in all ***g's***

Ps 100:5 his [God's] truth endureth to all ***g's***

Prov 27:24 doth the crown endure to every ***g***

Eccl 1:4 One ***g*** passeth away, and another ***g*** cometh

Dan 4:3 and his [God's] dominion is from ***g*** to ***g***

Matt 24:34 ***g*** shall not pass, till...these things be fulfilled

Luke 3:7 ***g*** of vipers, who hath warned you

Luke 16:8 in their ***g*** wiser than the children of light

Col 1:26 mystery...hath been hid from ages and from ***g's***

1 Pet 2:9 But ye are a chosen ***g,*** a royal priesthood

GENESIS, BOOK OF. The first book of the Old Testament

that describes the creation of the universe and recounts the early history of the people of Israel, including the patriarchs Abraham, Isaac, Jacob, and Joseph.

GENNESARET, LAKE OF.
See *Galilee, Sea of.*

GENTILE [S]
Isa 42:6 a covenant of the people, for a light of the ***G's***
Isa 60:3 ***G's*** shall come to thy [God's] light
Jer 16:19 ***G's*** shall come unto thee [God] from the ends of the earth
Mal 1:11 my [God's] name shall be great among the ***G's***
Matt 12:18 Behold my [God's] servant...he shall show judgment to the ***G's***
Mark 10:42 to rule over the ***G's*** exercise lordship
Luke 2:32 A light to lighten the ***G's***...glory of...Israel
Acts 9:15 for he [Paul] is a chosen vessel...to bear my [God's] name before the ***G's***
Acts 13:46 we [Paul and Barnabas] turn to the ***G's***
Acts 14:27 he [God]...opened the door of faith unto the ***G's***
Acts 18:6 from henceforth I [Paul] will go unto the ***G's***
Rom 2:9 of the Jew first, and also of the ***G***
Rom 3:29 God of the Jews only...not also of the ***G's***
1 Cor 12:13 baptized into one body, whether...Jews or ***G's***
Eph 3:6 ***G's*** should be...partakers of his [God's] promise

GERGESENES.
See *Gadarenes.*

GERIZIM, MOUNT (a mountain considered a sacred worship place by the Samaritans). Deut 11:29; 27:12 • Josh 8:33 • Judg 9:7 • **John 4:5,20–21.**

GESHEM (an Arabian who opposed the rebuilding of Jerusalem's walls under Nehemiah). Neh 2:19; 6:1–2.

GETHSEMANE (a garden outside Jerusalem where Jesus agonized in prayer on the night before He was arrested). Matt 26:30–56 • Mark 14:32.

GEZER (a major Canaanite city captured by Joshua and settled by the Levites). **Josh 10:33;** 12:12; 16:3,10; **21:21** • Judg 1:29 • 1 Kgs 9:15–17 • 1 Chr 6:67; 7:28; 20:4. *Gazer:* 2 Sam 5:25 • 1 Chr 14:16.

GIBEAH (hometown and capital city of King Saul). **1 Sam 10:26; 15:34** • Judg 19:12–16; 20:4–43 • Hos 9:9; 10:9. *Gibeath:* Josh 18:28.

GIBEON (a Canaanite city whose inhabitants surrendered to avoid destruction by Joshua). **Josh 9:3–21;** 10:1–41 • 2 Sam 21:1–9.

GIDEON (a judge of Israel who defeated the Midianite army with a force of only three hundred warriors). Judg 6–8. *Gedeon:* Heb 11:32. *Jerubbaal:* Judg 6:25–32.

GIFT [S]
2 Chr 19:7 there is no iniquity... nor respect of persons, nor taking of ***g's***
Prov 19:6 every man is a friend to him that giveth ***g's***
Matt 2:11 they [wise men] presented...him [Jesus] ***g's***
Matt 5:24 reconciled to thy brother, and then come and offer thy ***g***
Luke 11:13 If ye then, being evil, know how to give good ***g's*** unto your children
John 4:10 If thou knewest the ***g*** of God
Rom 1:11 I [Paul] may impart unto you some spiritual ***g***
Rom 12:6 ***g's*** differing according to the grace that is given to us
1 Cor 12:4 diversities of ***g's,*** but the same Spirit
1 Cor 12:31 But covet earnestly the best ***g's***
1 Cor 13:2 though I [Paul] have the ***g*** of prophecy
2 Cor 9:15 Thanks be unto God for his unspeakable ***g***
1 Tim 4:14 Neglect not the ***g*** that is in thee
Jas 1:17 Every good ***g*** and every perfect ***g*** is from above

GIFT OF GOD
Eccl 3:13 enjoy the good of all his labour, it is the ***g-o-G***
Acts 8:20 thou [Simon the magician]...thought...the ***g-o-G*** may be purchased
Rom 6:23 ***g-o-G*** is eternal life through Jesus Christ
Eph 2:8 saved through faith... not of yourselves: it is the ***g-o-G***
2 Tim 1:6 stir up the ***g-o-G***

GIHON
1. One of the four rivers of the Garden of Eden, associated with Ethiopia. Gen 2:13.
2. A place near Jerusalem where Solomon was proclaimed king. 1 Kgs 1:33–45.

GILBOA, MOUNT (a mountain range where King Saul died). 1 Sam 31:1–8 • 2 Sam 1:6,21 • **1 Chr 10:1–8.**

GILEAD
1. A fertile, flat tableland east of the Jordan River settled by the tribes of Gad, Reuben, and Manasseh. **Deut 3:12–17** • 2 Sam 17:26 • 1 Kgs 17:1.

2. A hill where Gideon divided his army for battle against the Midianites. Judg 7:1–7.

GILGAL (a memorial site near the city of Jericho). **Josh 4:19–24;** 10:1–43 • 1 Sam 13:4–15 • Amos 4:4–5.

GIRGASHITES. See *Girgasites.*

GIRGASITES (an ancient tribe which inhabited Canaan). Gen 10:15–16. *Girgashites:* Deut 7:1.

GIVE [TH]

Gen 12:7 Unto thy [Abraham's] seed will I [God] ***g*** this land

Ex 20:12 that thy days may be long upon the land which the LORD...***g'th*** thee

Num 6:26 The LORD lift up his countenance...***g*** thee peace

Deut 16:17 Every man shall ***g*** as he is able

Josh 21:43 the LORD gave...all the land which he sware to ***g*** unto their fathers

1 Kgs 3:9 ***G*** therefore thy servant [Solomon] an understanding heart

1 Chr 16:34 ***g*** thanks unto the LORD; for he is good

Ps 5:1 ***G*** ear to my words, O LORD...my meditation

Ps 29:2 ***G*** unto the LORD the glory due unto his name

Ps 29:11 LORD will ***g*** strength unto his people

Ps 37:4 he [God] shall ***g*** thee the desires of thine heart

Ps 85:12 LORD shall ***g*** that which is good

Ps 91:11 he [God] shall ***g*** his angels charge over thee

Ps 107:1 ***g*** thanks unto the LORD, for he is good

Ps 119:125 I am thy [God's] servant; ***g*** me understanding

Ps 119:130 The entrance of thy [God's] words ***g'th*** light

Prov 2:6 For the LORD ***g'th*** wisdom

Prov 22:9 he ***g'th*** of his bread to the poor

Prov 25:21 If thine enemy be hungry, ***g*** him bread

Isa 7:14 the Lord...shall ***g*** you a sign...a virgin shall conceive...bear a son

Isa 49:6 I [God] will also ***g*** thee for a light to the Gentiles

Mic 6:7 shall I ***g*** my firstborn for my transgression

Matt 5:15 a candle...***g'th*** light unto all...in the house

Matt 6:11 ***G*** us this day our daily bread

Matt 10:8 freely ye have received, freely ***g***

Matt 11:28 Come unto me [Jesus]...I will ***g*** you rest

Matt 16:19 ***g*** unto thee the keys of the kingdom

Matt 20:28 Even as the Son of man came...to ***g*** his life a ransom for many

Mark 8:37 what shall a man ***g*** in exchange for his soul
Mark 10:40 sit on my [Jesus'] right hand...is not mine to ***g***
Luke 12:32 for it is your Father's good pleasure to ***g*** you the kingdom
Luke 15:12 ***g*** me the portion of goods that falleth to me
Luke 20:22 Is it lawful for us to ***g*** tribute unto Caesar
John 4:14 water that I [Jesus] shall ***g*** him shall never thirst
John 10:11 good shepherd ***g'th*** his life for the sheep
John 13:34 new commandment I [Jesus] ***g*** unto you
John 14:16 and he [God] shall ***g*** you another Comforter
John 16:23 Whatsoever ye shall ask...in my [Jesus'] name, he [God] will ***g*** it you
Acts 6:4 ***g*** ourselves continually to prayer
Rom 14:12 every one...shall ***g*** account...to God
1 Cor 3:7 neither he that watereth; but God that ***g'th*** the increase
1 Cor 13:3 though I [Paul] ***g*** my body to be burned
1 Cor 15:57 thanks be to God, which ***g'th*** us the victory
2 Cor 3:6 the spirit ***g'th*** life
2 Cor 9:7 let him ***g;*** not grudgingly, or of necessity
1 Thes 5:18 In every thing ***g*** thanks...this is...will of God
Jas 4:6 God...***g'th*** grace unto the humble
1 Pet 3:15 be ready always to ***g*** an answer
Rev 2:10 and I [Jesus] will ***g*** thee a crown of life

GIVING, PRINCIPLES OF.
2 Cor 8:1–24; 9:6–8.

GLAD [LY, NESS]
1 Chr 16:31 heavens be ***g,*** and let the earth rejoice
Ps 9:2 I will be ***g*** and rejoice in thee [God]
Ps 30:11 Thou [God] hast... girded me with ***g'ness***
Ps 46:4 the streams...make ***g*** the city of God
Ps 68:3 let the righteous be ***g***
Ps 100:2 Serve the LORD with ***g'ness***
Ps 118:24 the day...the LORD hath made...rejoice and be ***g*** in it
Ps 122:1 ***g*** when they said unto me, Let us go into the house of the LORD
Prov 15:20 A wise son maketh a ***g*** father
Joel 2:21 be ***g*** and rejoice: for the LORD will do great things
Matt 5:12 be exceeding ***g:*** for great is your reward
Mark 12:37 common people heard him [Jesus] ***g'ly***
Luke 15:32 meet that we should make merry, and be ***g***
John 20:20 were the disciples ***g,*** when they saw the Lord
Acts 13:48 when the Gentiles heard this, they were ***g***

Rom 10:15 beautiful are the feet...that...bring ***g*** tidings

2 Cor 12:15 I [Paul] will very ***g'ly*** spend and be spent

GLORIFY [IED, ING]

Ps 86:12 ***g*** thy [God's] name for evermore

Isa 49:3 art my [God's] servant...in whom I will be ***g'ied***

Matt 5:16 see your good works, and ***g*** your Father

Matt 9:8 multitudes...marvelled, and ***g'ied*** God

Luke 2:20 shepherds returned, ***g'ing*** and praising God

Luke 7:16 came a fear on all: and they [crowd] ***g'ied*** God

Luke 23:47 centurion saw what was done, he ***g'ied*** God

John 12:23 hour is come...Son of man should be ***g'ied***

John 14:13 that the Father may be ***g'ied*** in the Son

John 17:1 that thy Son also may ***g*** thee [God]

John 17:4 I [Jesus] have ***g'ied*** thee [God] on the earth

Rom 8:30 whom he [Jesus] justified, them he also ***g'ied***

Rom 15:6 may with one mind and one mouth ***g*** God

1 Cor 6:20 ***g*** God in your body

2 Thes 1:12 name of our Lord... may be ***g'ied*** in you

1 Pet 4:16 but let him ***g*** God on this behalf

GLORY

1 Sam 4:21 named the child Ichabod...The ***g*** is departed

1 Chr 16:24 Declare his [God's] ***g*** among the heathen

1 Chr 29:11 Thine, O LORD, is the greatness...and the ***g***

Ps 24:7 and the King of ***g*** shall come in

Ps 29:2 Give unto the LORD the ***g*** due unto his name

Ps 57:5 let thy [God's] ***g*** be above all the earth

Ps 72:19 let the whole earth be filled with his [God's] ***g***

Ps 84:11 the LORD will give grace and ***g***

Ps 96:3 Declare his [God's] ***g*** among the heathen

Ps 113:4 LORD is high above all nations, and his ***g*** above the heavens

Prov 17:6 the ***g*** of children are their fathers

Isa 6:3 the whole earth is full of his [God's] ***g***

Isa 66:18 all nations and tongues...shall come, and see my [God's] ***g***

Jer 13:16 Give ***g*** to the LORD your God

Hag 2:9 ***g*** of this latter house shall be greater

Matt 6:13 kingdom, and the power, and the ***g***

Matt 6:29 Solomon in all his ***g*** was not arrayed

Mark 10:37 sit, one on thy [Jesus'] right hand...in thy ***g***

Luke 21:27 the Son of man coming in a cloud with power and great ***g***
John 1:14 we beheld his [Jesus'] ***g***...full of grace
Rom 5:3 we ***g*** in tribulations
Rom 8:18 sufferings...are not worthy to be compared with the ***g***...revealed
2 Cor 10:17 he that glorieth, let him ***g*** in the Lord
Gal 5:26 Let us not be desirous of vain ***g***
Gal 6:14 forbid that I [Paul] should ***g***, save in the cross
1 Tim 1:17 unto the King eternal...be...***g*** for ever
Heb 2:7 thou [God] crownedst him [Jesus]with ***g***...honour
1 Pet 4:13 when his [Jesus'] ***g*** shall be revealed
1 Pet 5:4 ye shall receive a crown of ***g*** that fadeth not
Rev 4:11 Thou art worthy, O Lord, to receive ***g***

GLORY OF GOD

Ps 19:1 The heavens declare the ***g-o-G***
John 11:4 sickness is not unto death, but for the ***g-o-G***
Rom 3:23 all have sinned... come short of the ***g-o-G***
1 Cor 10:31 whatsoever ye do, do all to the ***g-o-G***
Phil 2:11 Jesus Christ is Lord, to the ***g-o-G*** the Father

GLORY OF THE LORD

Ex 24:16 the ***g-o-t-L*** abode upon mount Sinai
Ps 104:31 The ***g-o-t-L*** shall endure for ever
Isa 40:5 the ***g-o-t-L*** shall be revealed...all flesh...see it
Isa 60:1 the ***g-o-t-L*** is risen upon thee
Ezek 11:23 the ***g-o-t-L*** went up from the midst of the city
Hab 2:14 knowledge of the ***g-o-t-L***, as the waters cover the sea
Luke 2:9 ***g-o-t-L*** shone round about them [shepherds]

GNASHING OF TEETH

Matt 8:12 there shall be weeping and ***g-o-t***
Matt 22:13 cast him into outer darkness; there shall be weeping and ***g-o-t***
Luke 13:28 weeping and ***g-o-t***, when ye shall see...yourselves thrust out

GODLY [INESS]

2 Cor 7:10 ***g*** sorrow worketh repentance
1 Tim 4:8 ***g'iness*** is profitable unto all things
1 Tim 6:6 ***g'iness*** with contentment is great gain
2 Tim 3:5 a form of ***g'iness***, but denying the power
2 Tim 3:12 all that will live ***g*** in Christ Jesus shall suffer persecution

Titus 2:12 live soberly, righteously, and ***g***

GOG, PRINCE OF MAGOG (a tribal leader condemned by the prophet Ezekiel and a representative of the forces of evil which oppose God and His people). Ezek 38:2–18; 39:1–11 • Rev 20:8–15.

GOLAN (one of the six cities of refuge). Deut 4:43 • **Josh 20:8–9;** 21:27.

GOLGOTHA. See *Calvary*.

GOLIATH (a Philistine giant killed by David). **1 Sam 17:4–54;** 21:9; 22:10 • 2 Sam 21:19 • 1 Chr 20:5.

GOMER (unfaithful wife of the prophet Hosea). Hos 1:1–11; 3:1–5.

GOMORRAH (a city destroyed by God because of its wickedness). **Gen 19:23–29.** Referred to as an example of God's punishment in Deut 29:23; 32:32 • Isa 1:9–10; 13:19 • Jer 23:14; 49:18; 50:40 • Amos 4:11 • Zeph 2:9. *Gomorrha:* Matt 10:15 • 2 Pet 2:6.

GOOD SHEPHERD, JESUS AS. See *"I Am" Statements of Jesus*.

GOOD WORKS

Matt 5:16 see your ***g-w***, and glorify your Father

Acts 9:36 Dorcas...was full of ***g-w*** and almsdeeds

Eph 2:10 we are his [God's] workmanship...unto ***g-w***

2 Tim 3:17 man of God may be...furnished unto all ***g-w***

GOODNESS

Ps 23:6 Surely ***g*** and mercy shall follow me

Ps 33:5 the earth is full of the ***g*** of the LORD

Ps 107:8 that men would praise the LORD for his ***g***

Prov 20:6 Most men will proclaim every one his own ***g***

Gal 5:22 fruit of the Spirit is... gentleness, ***g***, faith

GOSHEN (an Egyptian district where the Israelites lived). Gen 45:10; 46:28–29,34; 47:1–27; 50:8 • Ex 8:22; 9:26.

GOSPEL

Matt 24:14 ***g*** of the kingdom... preached in all the world

Mark 16:15 preach the ***g*** to every creature

Luke 4:18 he [God] hath anointed me [Jesus] to preach the ***g*** to the poor

Rom 1:16 I [Paul] am not ashamed of the ***g*** of Christ

Rom 10:15 beautiful are the feet...preach the ***g*** of peace

1 Cor 9:14 they which preach the ***g*** should live of the ***g***
Gal 1:7 some that...would pervert the ***g*** of Christ
Gal 4:13 I [Paul] preached the ***g*** unto you at the first
Eph 6:15 feet shod with the preparation of the ***g*** of peace
Phil 1:12 things...have fallen out rather unto the furtherance of the ***g***
Phil 1:27 conversation be as it becometh the ***g*** of Christ
2 Tim 1:8 partaker of the afflictions of the ***g***
2 Tim 2:8 Jesus...raised from the dead according to my [Paul's] ***g***
1 Pet 4:17 end be of them that obey not the ***g*** of God

GOZAN (a place to which the people of the Northern Kingdom were deported after their defeat by the Assyrians). 2 Kgs 18:11.

GRACE
Gen 6:8 Noah found ***g*** in the eyes of the LORD
Ps 84:11 the LORD will give ***g*** and glory
John 1:14 beheld his [Jesus'] glory...full of ***g*** and truth
John 1:17 ***g*** and truth came by Jesus Christ
Rom 3:24 justified freely by his [God's] ***g***
Rom 5:20 sin abounded, ***g*** did much more abound
Rom 6:1 Shall we continue in sin, that ***g*** may abound
2 Cor 8:9 ye know the ***g*** of our Lord Jesus Christ
2 Cor 9:8 God is able to make all ***g*** abound
2 Cor 12:9 My [God's] ***g*** is sufficient for thee
Eph 1:7 forgiveness of sins, according to the riches of his [Jesus'] ***g***
Eph 2:8 by ***g*** are ye saved through faith
Eph 4:7 ***g*** according to the measure of the gift of Christ
Col 4:6 speech be alway with ***g,*** seasoned with salt
1 Tim 1:14 ***g*** of our Lord was exceeding abundant
Titus 3:7 being justified by his [Jesus'] ***g,*** we should be made heirs...of eternal life
Heb 4:16 Let us...come boldly unto the throne of ***g***
Jas 4:6 God...giveth ***g*** unto the humble
2 Pet 3:18 grow in ***g,*** and in the knowledge of...Jesus
Rev 22:21 ***g*** of our Lord Jesus Christ be with you all

GRACE OF GOD
Luke 2:40 child [Jesus] grew... ***g-o-G*** was upon him
1 Cor 15:10 by the ***g-o-G*** I [Paul] am what I am
Eph 3:7 I [Paul] was made a minister, according to the gift of the ***g-o-G***

Titus 2:11 the ***g-o-G*** that bringeth salvation

Heb 2:9 that he [Jesus] by the ***g-o-G*** should taste death for every man

1 Pet 4:10 as good stewards of the manifold ***g-o-G***

GRACIOUS [LY]

Num 6:25 The LORD...be ***g*** unto thee

Ps 77:9 Hath God forgotten to be ***g***

Ps 103:8 LORD is merciful and ***g***, slow to anger

Ps 119:29 grant me thy [God's] law ***g'ly***

Isa 33:2 O LORD, be ***g*** unto us

Amos 5:15 God...will be ***g*** unto the remnant of Joseph

Luke 4:22 bare him [Jesus] witness, and wondered at the ***g*** words

GRAVE [S]

Job 17:1 the ***g's*** are ready for me [Job]

Job 21:13 in a moment [the wicked] go down to the ***g***

Ps 30:3 thou [God] hast brought up my soul from the ***g***

Ps 88:3 my life draweth nigh unto the ***g***

Eccl 9:10 no work...nor wisdom, in the ***g***

Isa 53:9 he [God's servant] made his ***g*** with the wicked

Matt 27:52 ***g's*** were opened... bodies of the saints...arose

John 5:28 all that are in the ***g's*** shall hear his [Jesus'] voice

John 11:17 he [Lazarus] had lain in the ***g*** four days

1 Cor 15:55 O ***g***, where is thy victory

1 Tim 3:8 must the deacons be ***g***, not doubletongued

GREAT [ER]

Gen 1:16 two ***g*** lights; the ***g'er*** light to rule the day

Gen 12:2 I [God] will make of thee [Abraham] a ***g*** nation

1 Sam 12:24 how ***g*** things he [God] hath done for you

1 Chr 11:9 So David waxed ***g'er*** and ***g'er***

1 Chr 16:25 ***g*** is the LORD, and greatly to be praised

Job 32:9 ***G*** men are not always wise

Ps 31:19 Oh how ***g*** is thy [God's] goodness

Ps 47:2 the LORD...is a ***g*** King over all the earth

Ps 48:1 ***G*** is the LORD, and greatly to be praised

Ps 77:13 who is so ***g*** a God as our God

Ps 95:3 LORD is...a ***g*** King above all gods

Ps 119:156 ***G*** are thy tender mercies, O LORD

Ps 126:3 The LORD hath done ***g*** things for us

Prov 22:1 good name is rather to be chosen than ***g*** riches

Isa 9:2 people that walked in darkness have seen a ***g*** light

Jer 10:6 thy [God's] name is ***g*** in might
Jer 32:17 thou [God]...made the...earth by thy ***g*** power
Dan 7:17 These ***g*** beasts, which are four, are four kings
Joel 2:31 sun shall be turned into darkness...before the ***g***...day of the LORD
Jon 1:2 go to Nineveh, that ***g*** city, and cry against it
Hag 2:9 The glory of this latter house shall be ***g'er***
Matt 4:16 people...in darkness saw ***g*** light
Matt 5:12 Rejoice...for ***g*** is your reward in heaven
Matt 11:11 least...is ***g'er*** than he [John the Baptist]
Matt 19:22 he [rich young ruler] went away sorrowful: for he had ***g*** possessions
Matt 20:26 ***g*** among you, let him be your minister
Mark 12:31 none other commandment ***g'er*** than these
Mark 13:26 Son of man coming...with ***g*** power
Luke 1:32 He [Jesus] shall be ***g***...the Son of the Highest
Luke 2:5 Mary his [Joseph's] espoused wife, being ***g*** with child
Luke 10:2 harvest truly is ***g***, but the labourers are few
Luke 22:44 his [Jesus'] sweat was as...***g*** drops of blood
John 13:16 servant is not ***g'er*** than his lord
John 15:13 ***G'er*** love hath no man than this
Acts 16:26 a ***g*** earthquake...the foundations of the prison were shaken
Eph 5:32 a ***g*** mystery...concerning Christ and the church
Heb 2:3 escape, if we neglect so ***g*** salvation
Heb 4:14 Seeing then...we have a ***g*** high priest [Jesus]
Heb 12:1 compassed about...***g*** a cloud of witnesses
Jas 3:5 Even so the tongue...boasteth ***g*** things
1 John 4:4 ***g'er*** is he...in you
3 John 4 no ***g'er*** joy than to hear...my [John's] children walk in truth
Rev 6:17 the ***g*** day of his [God's] wrath is come

GREAT COMMISSION. See *Jesus, Life and Ministry of.*

GREAT FLOOD. Gen 7:1–8:22.

GREAT SEA (the sea on Israel's western border, known today as the *Mediterranean Sea*). Josh 1:4; 9:1. *Sea of the Philistines:* Ex 23:31.

GREECE. See *Javan.*

GRIEF

Job 2:13 they saw that his [Job's] ***g*** was very great
Ps 6:7 Mine eye is consumed because of ***g***

Prov 17:25 A foolish son is a ***g*** to his father

Isa 53:3 a man of sorrows [God's servant], and acquainted with ***g***

Jer 45:3 LORD hath added ***g*** to my [Jeremiah's] sorrow

GRIEVE [D]

Gen 6:6 repented...he [God] had made man...it ***g'd*** him

Ps 78:40 oft did they...***g*** him [God] in the desert

Ps 95:10 Forty years...was I [God] ***g'd*** with...generation

Mark 3:5 he [Jesus]...***g'd*** for the hardness of their hearts

Mark 10:22 he [rich young ruler]...went away ***g'd:*** for he had great possessions

John 21:17 Peter was ***g'd*** because he [Jesus] said...the third time, Lovest thou me

Eph 4:30 ***g*** not the holy Spirit

GROW [ETH]

Ps 104:14 He [God] causeth the grass to ***g*** for the cattle

Matt 6:28 Consider the lilies of the field, how they ***g***

Eph 2:21 the building...***g'eth*** unto an holy temple

1 Pet 2:2 sincere milk of the word, that ye may ***g*** thereby

2 Pet 3:18 ***g*** in grace, and in... our Lord and Saviour

GUIDE [S]

Ps 48:14 this God...will be our ***g*** even unto death

Isa 58:11 the LORD shall ***g*** thee continually

Matt 23:24 Ye blind ***g's,*** which strain at a gnat

John 16:13 he [Holy Spirit] will ***g*** you into all truth

Acts 8:31 How can I [Ethiopian eunuch], except some man should ***g*** me

GUILT [Y]

Deut 19:13 put away the ***g*** of innocent blood from Israel

Matt 26:66 They...said, He [Jesus] is ***g'y*** of death

1 Cor 11:27 eat...drink... unworthily, shall be ***g'y*** of the...blood of the Lord

Jas 2:10 yet offend in one point, he is ***g'y*** of all

-H-

HABAKKUK (a prophet of Judah and author of the book that bears his name). Hab 1:1; 3:1.

HABAKKUK, BOOK OF. A short prophetic book of the Old Testament that struggles with the problem of the suffering of God's people at the hands of the pagan Babylonians.

HAGAR (Sarah's Egyptian slave who became the mother of Ishmael by Abraham). **Gen 16:1–16;** 21:9–17. *Agar:* Gal 4:24.

HAGGAI (a prophet after the Exile and author of the book that bears his name). Ezra 5:1; 6:14 • Hag 1–2.

HAGGAI, BOOK OF. A short prophetic book of the Old Testament written to encourage the Jewish captives who had returned to their homeland after three generations under the Babylonians and Persians.

HAI. See *Ai.*

HALAH (a region in Assyria where captives from the Northern Kingdom were settled). 2 Kgs 17:6; 18:11 • 1 Chr 5:26.

HALF TRIBE OF MANASSEH (a phrase referring to two distinct settlements of the tribe of Manasseh—one in central Palestine and the other east of the Jordan River). Num 32:33 • Deut 29:8 • Josh 22:10 • 1 Chr 6:61,71.

HAM (youngest son of Noah and ancestor of the people of several nations). Gen 5:32; 6:10; 7:13; 9:18,22; 10:1–20; 14:5 • 1 Chr 1:4,8.

HAMAN (an aide to King Ahasuerus of Persia who plotted to kill the Jews). Esth 3:1–9:25.

HAMATH-ZOBAH. See *Zobah.*

HANAMEEL (a cousin of Jeremiah from whom the prophet bought a field). Jer 32:7–12.

HANANI (Nehemiah's brother who brought news about the suffering citizens of Jerusalem). **Neh 1:2–3;** 7:2.

HAND OF GOD

Job 2:10 receive good at the ***h-o-G,*** and...not receive evil

Eccl 9:1 the wise, and their works, are in the ***h-o-G***

Acts 7:56 I [Stephen] see...the Son of man standing on the right ***h-o-G***

Col 3:1 things which are above, where Christ sitteth on the right ***h-o-G***
1 Pet 3:22 Who [Jesus] is...on the right ***h-o-G***

HANDWRITING ON A WALL. Dan 5:5–9.

HANNAH (mother of Samuel the prophet who prayed earnestly for Samuel to be born and devoted him to God's service). **1 Sam 1:5–28;** 2:1–10.

HARAN (a pagan city of Mesopotamia where Abraham lived for a time). **Gen 11:31–32; 12:4–5;** 27:43; 28:10; 29:4 • 2 Kgs 19:12 • Isa 37:12 • Ezek 27:23. *Charran:* Acts 7:2,4.

HATE [D, ST, TH]
Lev 19:17 Thou shalt not ***h*** thy brother in thine heart
Ps 5:5 thou [God] ***h'st*** all workers of iniquity
Ps 41:7 All that ***h*** me whisper... against me
Ps 69:4 They that ***h*** me without a cause are more than the hairs of mine head
Ps 119:163 I ***h***...lying: but thy [God's] law do I love
Prov 8:13 The fear of the LORD is to ***h*** evil
Prov 13:24 He that spareth his rod ***h'th*** his son
Prov 14:20 poor is ***h'd*** even of his own neighbour
Eccl 3:8 A time to love, and a time to ***h***
Isa 1:14 your appointed feasts my [God's] soul ***h'th***
Amos 5:21 I [God] ***h,*** I despise your feast days
Matt 5:44 I [Jesus] say unto you...do good to them that ***h*** you
Matt 6:24 he will ***h*** the one, and love the other
Mark 13:13 ***h'd*** of all men for my [Jesus'] name's sake
Luke 14:26 and ***h*** not his father, and mother
John 12:25 he that ***h'th*** his life...shall keep it
John 15:18 it [the world] ***h'd*** me [Jesus] before it ***h'd*** you
John 15:23 He that ***h'th*** me [Jesus] ***h'th*** my Father also
1 John 2:9 He that saith he is in the light, and ***h'th*** his brother, is in darkness
1 John 4:20 If a man say, I love God, and ***h'th*** his brother, he is a liar

HAZAEL (a leader anointed king of Syria at God's command by the prophet Elijah). **1 Kgs 19:15–17** • 2 Kgs 8:8–29; 9:14–15; 10:32; 12:17–18; 13:3, 22–25 • 2 Chr 22:5–6 • Amos 1:4.

HAZOR (a royal Canaanite city destroyed by Joshua). **Josh 11:1–13;** 12:19; 19:36 • Judg

4:2,17 • 1 Sam 12:9 • 1 Kgs 9:15 • 2 Kgs 15:29.

HEAD [S]

Gen 3:15 it shall bruise thy [the serpent's] ***h***

1 Sam 17:51 David...slew him [Goliath]...cut off his ***h***

2 Sam 14:25 to the crown of his ***h*** there was no blemish in him [Absalom]

1 Chr 29:11 thou [God] art exalted as ***h*** above all

Job 1:20 Job arose...and shaved his ***h***

Ps 3:3 thou, O LORD, art...the lifter up of mine ***h***

Ps 23:5 thou [God] anointest my ***h*** with oil

Ps 24:7 Lift up your ***h's,*** O ye gates

Ps 118:22 The stone...is become the ***h*** stone

Ps 140:7 God...hast covered my ***h*** in the day of battle

Jer 9:1 Oh that my [Jeremiah's] ***h*** were waters

Dan 7:6 beast had also four ***h's***

Matt 10:30 hairs of your ***h*** are all numbered

Matt 21:42 The stone which the builders rejected...is become the ***h*** of the corner

Matt 27:39 they...reviled him [Jesus], wagging their ***h's***

Mark 6:28 brought his [John the Baptist's] ***h*** in a charger

Mark 14:3 a woman... brake the box, and poured it [ointment] on his [Jesus'] ***h***

Mark 15:17 a crown of thorns, and put it about his [Jesus'] ***h***

Luke 9:58 Son of man hath not where to lay his ***h***

John 19:30 he [Jesus] bowed his ***h,*** and gave up the ghost

Acts 18:6 Your blood be upon your own ***h's***

Rom 12:20 heap coals of fire on his [your enemy's] ***h***

1 Cor 11:3 and the ***h*** of the woman is the man

1 Cor 12:21 eye cannot say... nor...the ***h*** to the feet, I have no need of you

Col 1:18 he [Jesus] is the ***h*** of the body, the church

Rev 1:14 His ***h*** and his hairs were white like wool

Rev 17:3 I [John] saw a woman...having seven ***h's*** and ten horns

HEAL [ING]

2 Chr 7:14 I [God will] hear from heaven...forgive their sin...***h*** their land

Ps 41:4 LORD, be merciful unto me: ***h*** my soul

Eccl 3:3 A time to kill, and a time to ***h***

Jer 3:22 I [God] will ***h*** your backslidings

Mal 4:2 Sun of righteousness arise with ***h'ing*** in his wings

Matt 4:23 Jesus went about... ***h'ing*** all manner of sickness

Matt 10:8 ***H*** the sick, cleanse the lepers, raise the dead

Luke 4:18 he [God] hath sent me [Jesus] to ***h*** the broken-hearted

Luke 9:2 he [Jesus] sent them [disciples]...to ***h*** the sick

1 Cor 12:30 Have all the gifts of ***h'ing***...do all interpret

HEAR [EST, ETH, ING]

Deut 6:4 ***H,*** O Israel: The LORD our God is one

1 Sam 3:9 Speak, LORD, for thy servant [Samuel] ***h'eth***

Job 35:13 Surely God will not ***h*** vanity

Job 42:5 I [Job] have heard of thee by the ***h'ing*** of the ear

Ps 4:3 the LORD will ***h*** when I call unto him

Ps 17:6 incline thine [God's] ear...and ***h*** my speech

Ps 55:17 and he [God] shall ***h*** my voice

Ps 65:2 O thou [God] that ***h'est*** prayer

Ps 69:33 For the LORD ***h'eth*** the poor

Ps 86:1 Bow down thine ear, O LORD, ***h*** me

Ps 115:6 They have ears, but they ***h*** not

Prov 4:1 ***H,*** ye children, the instruction of a father

Prov 13:1 wise son ***h'eth*** his father's instruction

Prov 18:13 answereth a matter before he ***h'eth*** it, it is folly

Prov 19:20 ***H*** counsel, and receive instruction

Eccl 7:5 better to ***h*** the rebuke of the wise, than...to ***h*** the song of fools

Isa 1:2 ***H,*** O heavens, and give ear, O earth

Isa 59:1 LORD's hand is not shortened...neither his ear heavy, that it cannot ***h***

Isa 65:24 while they are yet speaking, I [God] will ***h***

Jer 22:29 O earth...***h*** the word of the LORD

Ezek 37:4 dry bones, ***h*** the word of the LORD

Matt 7:24 ***h'eth*** these sayings of mine [Jesus]...doeth them

Matt 13:9 Who hath ears to ***h,*** let him ***h***

Matt 13:13 ***h'ing*** they ***h*** not, neither do they understand

Matt 13:16 blessed are your... ears, for they ***h***

Matt 17:5 This is my [God's] beloved Son...***h*** ye him

Mark 7:37 he [Jesus] maketh... the deaf to ***h***

Luke 2:46 found him [Jesus]... sitting in the midst of the doctors...***h'ing*** them

Luke 8:21 my [Jesus'] brethren are these which ***h*** the word of God, and do it

Luke 11:28 Yea...blessed are they that ***h*** the word of God, and keep it

John 3:8 wind bloweth...thou ***h'est*** the sound thereof

John 10:27 My [Jesus'] sheep ***h*** my voice...I know them

Acts 2:8 how ***h*** we every man in our own tongue

Acts 9:7 the men...stood speechless, ***h'ing*** a voice, but seeing no man

Acts 17:21 Athenians...spent their time...but...to ***h*** some new thing

Acts 28:28 salvation...is sent unto the Gentiles...that they will ***h*** it

Rom 10:14 how shall they ***h*** without a preacher

1 Cor 12:17 whole body were an eye, where were the ***h'ing***

Jas 1:19 let every man be swift to ***h,*** slow to speak

1 John 5:14 if we ask any thing according to his [God's] will, he ***h'eth*** us

Rev 2:7 ***h*** what the Spirit saith unto the churches

Rev 3:20 any man ***h*** my [Jesus'] voice...open the door

Rev 22:17 let him that ***h'eth*** say, Come

HEARD [EST]

Gen 3:8 they [Adam and Eve] ***h*** the voice of the LORD God

Ex 3:7 I [God] have surely...***h*** their [Israel's] cry

Job 42:5 I [Job] have ***h***...by the hearing of the ear

Ps 28:6 the LORD...hath ***h*** the voice of my supplications

Ps 34:4 I sought the LORD, and he ***h*** me...delivered me

Ps 40:1 he [God] inclined unto me, and ***h*** my cry

Ps 116:1 I love the LORD, because he hath ***h*** my voice

Ps 119:26 I have declared my ways...thou [God] ***h'est*** me

Isa 6:8 ***h*** the voice of the Lord, saying, Whom shall I send

Isa 40:28 hast thou not ***h***... God...fainteth not

Isa 42:2 He [God's servant] shall not...cause his voice to be ***h*** in the street

Jer 31:15 A voice was ***h*** in Ramah...bitter weeping

Matt 6:7 the heathen...think that they shall be ***h*** for their much speaking

Mark 12:37 common people ***h*** him [Jesus] gladly

Luke 2:20 shepherds returned... praising God for all...they had ***h*** and seen

Luke 12:3 spoken in darkness shall be ***h*** in the light

Acts 4:20 speak the things which we have seen and ***h***

Acts 9:4 ***h*** a voice saying... Saul, Saul

Acts 11:1 apostles...***h*** that the Gentiles had also received the word of God

Acts 17:32 ***h*** of the resurrection...some mocked

Rom 10:14 how shall they believe in him [Jesus] of whom they have not ***h***

1 Cor 2:9 Eye hath not seen, nor ear ***h***

Phil 4:9 things, which ye have... ***h,*** and seen...do

1 John 1:3 which we have seen and ***h*** declare we unto you

1 John 3:11 the message that ye ***h*** from the beginning

Rev 1:10 I [John] was in the Spirit on the Lord's day, and ***h*** behind me a great voice

HEART [S]

Ex 7:14 the LORD said...Pharaoh's ***h*** is hardened

Deut 6:5 love the LORD thy God with all thine ***h***

Deut 10:16 Circumcise therefore the foreskin of your ***h***

1 Sam 12:24 serve him [God] in truth with all your ***h***

Ps 7:10 God...saveth the upright in ***h***

Ps 13:5 my ***h*** shall rejoice in thy [God's] salvation

Ps 19:8 statutes of the LORD are right, rejoicing the ***h***

Ps 19:14 Let the...meditation of my ***h,*** be acceptable

Ps 24:4 He that hath clean hands, and a pure ***h***

Ps 37:4 he [God] shall give thee the desires of thine ***h***

Ps 40:8 thy [God's] law is within my ***h***

Ps 51:10 Create in me a clean ***h,*** O God

Ps 53:1 fool hath said in his ***h,*** There is no God

Ps 66:18 regard iniquity in my ***h,*** the Lord will not hear me

Ps 90:12 teach us to number our days, that we may apply our ***h's*** unto wisdom

Ps 119:11 Thy [God's] word have I hid in mine ***h***

Ps 139:23 Search me, O God, and know my ***h***

Ps 147:3 He [God] healeth the broken in ***h***

Prov 2:2 apply thine ***h*** to understanding

Prov 3:5 Trust in the LORD with all thine ***h***

Prov 15:13 merry ***h*** maketh a cheerful countenance

Prov 16:5 Every one that is proud in ***h*** is an abomination

Prov 17:22 A merry ***h*** doeth good like a medicine

Prov 21:2 but the LORD pondereth the ***h's***

Eccl 9:7 and drink thy wine with a merry ***h***

Jer 17:9 The ***h*** is deceitful above all things

Jer 29:13 ye shall...find me [God], when ye shall search...with all your ***h***

Jer 31:33 I [God] will...write it [God's law] in their ***h's***

Ezek 11:19 one ***h,*** and I will put a new spirit within you

Ezek 36:26 new ***h*** also will I [God] give you

Matt 5:8 Blessed are the pure in ***h***...they shall see God

Matt 6:21 where your treasure is, there will your ***h*** be also

Matt 11:29 I [Jesus] am meek and lowly in ***h***

Matt 15:8 honoureth me [Jesus] with their lips; but their ***h*** is far from me

Mark 12:30 love the Lord thy God with all thy ***h***

Luke 2:19 Mary kept all these things...pondered...in her ***h***

John 14:1 Let not your ***h*** be troubled

Acts 4:32 them that believed were of one ***h***

Rom 1:24 God also gave them up...through the lusts of their own ***h's***

Rom 5:5 love of God is shed abroad in our ***h's***

Rom 10:9 believe in thine ***h*** that God hath raised him [Jesus] from the dead

2 Cor 3:2 Ye are our epistle written in our ***h's***

2 Cor 4:6 God...hath shined in our ***h's***

2 Cor 9:7 as he purposeth in his ***h,*** so let him give

Phil 4:7 peace of God...shall keep your ***h's*** and minds through Christ

2 Thes 3:5 Lord direct your ***h's*** into the love of God

Heb 3:12 lest there be in any of you an evil ***h*** of unbelief

Heb 3:15 harden not your ***h's,*** as in the provocation

Heb 4:12 word of God is quick... a discerner...of the ***h***

Jas 4:8 purify your ***h's,*** ye double minded

HEAVEN [S]

Gen 1:1 God created the ***h*** and the earth

Deut 1:10 ye are this day as the stars of ***h***

Deut 4:39 that the LORD he is God in ***h*** above

2 Sam 22:14 The LORD thundered from ***h***

1 Kgs 8:23 no God like thee, in ***h*** above, or on earth beneath

2 Kgs 2:11 Elijah went up by a whirlwind into ***h***

1 Chr 16:26 gods of the people are idols...LORD made the ***h's***

2 Chr 7:14 will I [God] hear from ***h***...forgive their sin

Job 28:24 For he [God]...seeth under the whole ***h***

Ps 8:3 consider thy [God's] ***h's,*** the work of thy fingers

Ps 11:4 LORD's throne is in ***h***

Ps 19:1 The ***h's*** declare the glory of God

Ps 57:5 Be thou exalted, O God, above the ***h's***

Ps 89:6 who in the ***h*** can be compared unto the LORD

Ps 103:11 For as the ***h*** is high above the earth, so great is his [God's] mercy

Ps 108:5 Be thou exalted, O God, above the ***h's***

Ps 121:2 help cometh from the LORD...made ***h*** and earth

Ps 136:26 thanks unto the God of ***h***...mercy endureth for ever

Ps 139:8 If I ascend up into ***h,*** thou [God] art there

Eccl 3:1 a time to every purpose under the ***h***

Isa 55:9 ***h's*** are higher than the earth, so are my [God's] ways higher than your ways

Jer 23:24 Do not I fill ***h*** and earth? saith the LORD

Jer 32:17 thou [God] hast made the ***h*** and the earth by thy great power

Jer 51:15 He [God]...hath stretched out the ***h*** by his understanding

Mal 3:10 prove me...if I [God] will not open you the windows of ***h***

Matt 4:17 Jesus began to preach...Repent: for the kingdom of ***h*** is at hand

Matt 5:3 poor in spirit: for theirs is the kingdom of ***h***

Matt 5:12 great is your reward in ***h:*** for so persecuted they the prophets...before you

Matt 5:34 Swear not at all; neither by ***h***

Matt 5:48 even as your Father which is in ***h*** is perfect

Matt 6:9 Father which art in ***h,*** Hallowed be thy name

Matt 6:20 lay up for yourselves treasures in ***h***

Matt 7:21 Not every one...shall enter...kingdom of ***h***

Matt 16:19 give unto thee [Peter] the keys of the kingdom of ***h***

Matt 18:3 become as little children, ye shall not enter into the kingdom of ***h***

Matt 19:14 of such [little children] is the kingdom of ***h***

Matt 26:64 shall ye see the Son of man...coming in the clouds of ***h***

Matt 28:18 All power is given unto me [Jesus] in ***h*** and in earth

Mark 1:10 he [Jesus] saw the ***h's*** opened, and the Spirit... descending upon him

Mark 13:32 But of that hour knoweth no man, no, not the angels which are in ***h***

Luke 3:22 voice came from ***h,*** which said...in thee [Jesus] I [God] am well pleased

Luke 16:17 easier for ***h*** and earth to pass, than one tittle of the law to fail

Luke 24:51 he [Jesus] was parted...carried up into ***h***

John 3:27 receive nothing, except it be given him from ***h***

John 6:38 I [Jesus] came down from ***h,*** not to do mine own will, but...him that sent me

Acts 1:11 men of Galilee, why stand ye gazing up into ***h***

Acts 4:12 none other name under ***h*** given among men, whereby we must be saved

2 Cor 5:1 house not made with hands, eternal in the ***h's***

Phil 2:10 every knee should bow, of things in ***h***

1 Thes 4:16 Lord himself shall descend from ***h*** with a shout
Jas 5:12 swear not, neither by ***h***...let your yea be yea
2 Pet 3:13 we...look for new ***h's*** and a new earth
Rev 5:3 no man in ***h***...was able to open the book
Rev 20:1 angel come down from ***h***, having the key of the bottomless pit
Rev 21:1 And I [John] saw a new ***h*** and a new earth

HEAVEN AND EARTH
Gen 14:19 Blessed be Abram... possessor of ***h-a-e***
Ex 20:11 in six days the LORD made ***h-a-e***
Ps 69:34 Let the ***h-a-e*** praise him [God], the seas
Ps 124:8 Our help is in...the LORD, who made ***h-a-e***
Matt 5:18 Till ***h-a-e*** pass, one jot...shall in no wise pass
Matt 24:35 ***H-a-e*** shall pass away, but my [Jesus'] words shall not pass away
Acts 17:24 Lord of ***h-a-e***, dwelleth not in temples made with hands

HEAVENLY
Matt 6:14 your ***h*** Father will also forgive you
Luke 2:13 with the angel a multitude of the ***h*** host
John 3:12 how shall ye believe, if I [Jesus] tell you of ***h*** things
Acts 26:19 I [Paul] was not disobedient unto the ***h*** vision

HEBREWS, EPISTLE TO THE. An epistle, author unknown, written to believers of Jewish background to show that Jesus had replaced the Old Testament ceremonial law and sacrificial system.

HEBRON (an ancient town in Canaan where Sarah died and that later became one of the six cities of refuge). Gen 13:18; **23:2–20;** 35:27; 37:14 • Josh 10:3–39 • Judg 1:10,20 • 2 Sam 3:2–32; 5:1–13 • 1 Chr 11:1–3 • 2 Chr 11:10. *Kirjath-arba:* Gen 23:2 • Josh 14:15.

HEED
Josh 23:11 Take good ***h***...that ye love the LORD
Prov 17:4 A wicked doer giveth ***h*** to false lips
Matt 6:1 Take ***h*** that ye do not your alms before men
Mark 8:15 Take ***h***, beware of the...Pharisees
Luke 12:15 Take ***h***, and beware of covetousness
Luke 21:8 Take ***h***...be not deceived: for many shall come in my [Jesus'] name
1 Cor 3:10 every man take ***h*** how he buildeth thereupon
1 Cor 10:12 thinketh he standeth take ***h*** lest he fall

Heb 3:12 Take ***h***...lest there be in...you an evil heart

HEIR [S]

Mark 12:7 This is the ***h;*** come, let us kill him
Gal 3:29 Abraham's seed, and ***h's*** according to the promise
Gal 4:7 if a son, then an ***h*** of God through Christ
Titus 3:7 justified by his [Jesus'] grace...be made ***h's***
Heb 1:2 whom he [God] hath appointed ***h*** [Jesus] of all things
Heb 11:9 Isaac and Jacob, the ***h's*** with him [Abraham] of the same promise

HELL

Job 26:6 ***H*** is naked before him, and destruction hath no covering
Ps 18:5 sorrows of ***h*** compassed me about
Ps 139:8 make my bed in ***h,*** behold, thou [God] art there
Prov 27:20 ***H*** and destruction are never full
Jon 2:2 out of the belly of ***h*** cried I [Jonah]
Matt 5:22 say, Thou fool, shall be in danger of ***h*** fire
Matt 10:28 fear him...able to destroy...soul and body in ***h***
Matt 16:18 gates of ***h*** shall not prevail against it [the church]
Luke 10:15 Capernaum...shalt be thrust down to ***h***
Rev 1:18 I [Jesus]...have the keys of ***h*** and of death
Rev 20:14 death and ***h*** were cast into the lake of fire

HENOCH. See *Enoch,* No. 2.

HERMOGENES (a believer who deserted Paul). 2 Tim 1:15.

HERMON, MOUNT (a mountain in Syria that marked the northern limit of Joshua's conquest). **Josh 11:3,17;** 12:1,5 • Pss 89:12; 133:3. *Senir:* Ezek 27:5. *Shenir, Sirion:* Deut 3:9.

HEROD (the name of several Roman rulers in Palestine during New Testament times).

1. Herod the Great, who ordered the slaughter of innocent children after Jesus was born. **Matt 2:1–22** • Luke 1:5.

2. Herod Archelaus, son and successor of Herod the Great. Matt 2:22.

3. Herod Philip, ruler in northern Galilee when Jesus began His public ministry. Luke 3:1,19–20.

4. Herod Antipas, who executed John the Baptist. **Matt 14:1–12** • Mark 6:14–22; 8:15 • Luke 3:1,19; 9:7,9; 13:31; 23:7–12 • Acts 4:27; 13:1.

5. Herod Agrippa I, who executed James, leader of the Jerusalem church. Acts 12:1–19.

6. Herod Agrippa II, before whom Paul made his defense at Caesarea. Acts 25:13–26:32.

HERODIANS (an influential Jewish group that joined forces with the Pharisees against Jesus). Matt 22:16 • **Mark 3:6;** 12:13.

HERODIAS (wife of Herod Antipas who had John the Baptist executed). **Matt 14:1–11** • Mark 6:17.

HEZEKIAH (a godly king of Judah who implemented religious reforms). 2 Kgs 18:1–8; 19:1–37; 20:1–21 • **2 Chr 29:1–36; 31:1–21** • Isa 38:9–22. *Ezekias:* Matt 1:9.

HID [DEN]

Gen 3:8 Adam and his wife ***h*** themselves from...the LORD

Ex 3:6 Moses ***h*** his face; for he was afraid to look upon God

Ps 38:9 my groaning is not ***h*** from thee [God]

Ps 51:6 in the ***h'den*** part thou [God] shalt make me to know wisdom

Ps 119:11 Thy [God's] word have I ***h*** in mine heart

Isa 53:3 we ***h***...our faces from him [God's servant]

Matt 5:14 A city that is set on an hill cannot be ***h***

Matt 11:25 thou [God] hast ***h*** these things from the wise

Luke 13:21 It [kingdom of God] is like leaven, which a woman took and ***h***

1 Cor 2:7 the ***h'den*** wisdom, which God ordained before the world unto our glory

Heb 11:23 Moses...was ***h*** three months of his parents

HIDE [ING, ST, TH]

Job 14:13 thou [God] wouldest ***h*** me in the grave

Ps 10:1 why ***h'st*** thou [God] thyself in times of trouble

Ps 13:1 how long wilt thou [God] ***h*** thy face from me

Ps 17:8 ***h*** me under the shadow of thy [God's] wings

Ps 51:9 ***H*** thy [God's] face from my sins

Ps 69:17 ***h*** not thy [God's] face from thy servant

Ps 119:114 Thou [God] art my ***h'ing*** place and my shield

Prov 19:24 A slothful man ***h'th*** his hand in his bosom

Isa 45:15 thou art a God that ***h'st*** thyself

Jer 23:24 Can any ***h*** himself in secret places that I [God] shall not see him

Rev 6:16 ***h*** us from the face of him that sitteth on the throne

HIERAPOLIS (a city in Asia Minor mentioned by Paul). Col 4:13.

HIGH [ER, EST, LY]

Gen 14:18 Melchizedek...was the priest of the most ***h*** God

Deut 28:1 God will set thee on ***h*** above all nations
Job 41:34 He [God] beholdeth all ***h*** things
Ps 7:17 I will...sing praise to the name of the LORD most ***h***
Ps 47:2 the LORD most ***h*** is terrible...a great King
Ps 61:2 lead me to the rock that is ***h'er*** than I
Ps 69:29 let thy salvation, O God, set me up on ***h***
Ps 91:1 He that dwelleth in the secret place of the most ***H***
Ps 93:4 LORD on ***h*** is mightier than...many waters
Ps 97:9 thou, LORD, art ***h*** above all the earth
Ps 99:2 The LORD...is ***h*** above all the people
Ps 103:11 as the heaven is ***h*** above the earth, so great is his [God's] mercy
Ps 113:4 The LORD is ***h*** above all nations
Isa 6:1 I [Isaiah] saw also the Lord...***h*** and lifted up
Isa 33:5 The LORD is exalted; for he dwelleth on ***h***
Isa 52:13 my [God's] servant shall be exalted...be very ***h***
Isa 55:9 heavens are ***h'er*** than the earth, so are my [God's] ways ***h'er*** than your ways
Matt 4:8 the devil taketh him [Jesus] up into an exceeding ***h*** mountain
Luke 1:28 Hail, thou [Mary] that art ***h'ly*** favoured
Luke 1:32 He [Jesus]...shall be called the Son of the ***H'est***
Luke 2:14 Glory to God in the ***h'est***...on earth peace
Luke 20:46 Beware of the scribes, which...love...the ***h'est*** seats in the synagogues
Luke 24:49 tarry...until... endued with power from on ***h***
Rom 13:1 be subject unto the ***h'er*** powers
Eph 4:8 ascended up on ***h,*** he [Jesus] led captivity captive
Eph 6:12 wrestle...against spiritual wickedness in ***h*** places
Phil 2:9 God also hath ***h'ly*** exalted him [Jesus]
Phil 3:14 the prize of the ***h*** calling of God in Christ Jesus

HIGH PRIEST [S]

Matt 26:65 ***h-p*** rent his clothes, saying, He [Jesus] hath spoken blasphemy
John 18:19 ***h-p*** then asked Jesus of his...doctrine
Heb 3:1 Apostle and ***H-P*** of our profession, Christ Jesus
Heb 4:15 we have not an ***h-p*** which cannot be touched with...our infirmities
Heb 6:20 even Jesus, made an ***h-p*** for ever
Heb 7:27 Who [Jesus] needeth not daily, as those ***h-p's,*** to offer up sacrifice

HIGH PRIESTLY PRAYER OF JESUS. John 17:1–26.

HILKIAH (a high priest during King Josiah's reign who found the lost book of the Law). **2 Kgs 22:4–23:4** • 2 Chr 34:9–22.

HINNOM, VALLEY OF (a narrow ravine outside Jerusalem where pagan worship involving child sacrifice was conducted). Josh 15:8; 18:16 • 2 Kgs 23:10 • **2 Chr 28:3;** 33:6 • Neh 11:30 • Jer 7:31–32; **19:2–6.**

HIRAM (a king of Tyre who assisted David and Solomon with their building projects in Jerusalem). **2 Sam 5:11** • **1 Kgs 5:1–12;** 9:11–27; 10:11,22 • 1 Chr 14:1. *Huram:* 2 Chr 2:3–12.

HITTITES (an ancient people who lived in Canaan). Gen 23:10–20 • 2 Sam 11:15–17 • 1 Kgs 15:5.

HOBAB. See *Jethro.*

HOLD [ING]

Ex 20:7 the LORD will not ***h*** him guiltless that taketh his name in vain

Job 6:24 Teach me, and I will ***h*** my tongue

Ps 83:1 Keep not thou silence, O God: ***h*** not thy peace

Ps 139:10 thy [God's] right hand shall ***h*** me

Jer 2:13 they have...hewed them out...cisterns, that can ***h*** no water

Luke 16:13 he will ***h*** to the one, and despise the other

Phil 2:16 ***H'ing*** forth the word of life...I [Paul] may rejoice

1 Thes 5:21 Prove all things; ***h*** fast that which is good

1 Tim 3:9 ***H'ing*** the mystery of the faith

Heb 4:14 we have a great high priest...Jesus...let us ***h*** fast our profession

Heb 10:23 ***h*** fast the profession of our faith

Rev 3:11 ***h*** that fast...that no man take thy crown

HOLY [INESS]

Ex 3:5 place whereon thou [Moses] standest is ***h*** ground

Ex 15:11 who is like thee [God], glorious in ***h'iness***

Ex 20:8 Remember the sabbath day, to keep it ***h***

Lev 11:44 ye shall be ***h;*** for I [God] am ***h***

Lev 20:7 be ye ***h:*** for I am the LORD your God

Ps 11:4 The LORD is in his ***h*** temple

Ps 24:3 who shall stand in his [God's] ***h*** place

Ps 29:2 worship the LORD in the beauty of ***h'iness***

Ps 51:11 take not thy [God's] ***h*** spirit from me

Ps 89:18 and the ***H*** One of Israel is our king
Ps 96:9 worship the LORD in the beauty of ***h'iness***
Ps 99:5 worship at his [God's] footstool; for he is ***h***
Ps 103:1 all that is within me, bless his [God's] ***h*** name
Ps 145:21 let all flesh bless his [God's] ***h*** name for ever
Isa 6:3 one [seraphim] cried... ***H, h, h,*** is the LORD of hosts
Hab 2:20 the LORD is in his ***h*** temple...earth keep silence
Rom 12:1 bodies a living sacrifice, ***h,*** acceptable unto God
Rom 16:16 Salute one another with an ***h*** kiss
1 Cor 3:17 temple of God is ***h,*** which temple ye are
Eph 5:27 it [the church] should be ***h*** and without blemish
1 Thes 4:7 God hath...called us unto...***h'iness***
1 Tim 2:8 men pray every where, lifting up ***h*** hands
2 Tim 3:15 And that from a child thou [Timothy] hast known the ***h*** scriptures
1 Pet 1:16 it is written, Be ye ***h;*** for I [God] am ***h***
1 Pet 2:5 Ye also...are built up...an ***h*** priesthood
1 Pet 2:9 ye are a chosen generation...an ***h*** nation
Rev 21:2 I John saw the ***h*** city, new Jerusalem

HOLY GHOST
Matt 1:18 she [Mary] was found with child of the ***H-G***
Matt 3:11 he [Jesus] shall baptize you with the ***H-G***
Matt 12:31 blasphemy against the ***H-G*** shall not be forgiven
Matt 28:19 baptizing them in the name of the...***H-G***
Luke 1:35 The ***H-G*** shall come upon thee [Mary]
Luke 1:67 Zacharias was filled with the ***H-G***
Luke 2:25 the ***H-G*** was upon him [Simeon]
Luke 3:22 ***H-G*** descended... like a dove upon him [Jesus]
John 14:26 the ***H-G***...shall teach you all things
Acts 1:8 receive power, after that...***H-G*** is come upon you
Acts 6:3 look ye out...seven men...full of the ***H-G***
Acts 13:2 ***H-G*** said, Separate me Barnabas and Saul
Rom 14:17 kingdom of God is... joy in the ***H-G***
1 Cor 12:3 and that no man can say that Jesus is the Lord, but by the ***H-G***
2 Pet 1:21 holy men of God spake...by the ***H-G***

HONEST [LY, Y]
Acts 6:3 seven men of ***h*** report
Rom 13:13 Let us walk ***h'ly***... not in rioting
Phil 4:8 things are ***h,*** whatsoever things are just

1 Tim 2:2 lead a quiet...life in all godliness and ***h'y***

HONOUR [ED, ETH]

Ex 20:12 ***H*** thy father and thy mother

1 Chr 16:27 Glory and ***h*** are in his [God's] presence

Ps 8:5 thou [God]...hast crowned him [man] with glory and ***h***

Prov 3:9 ***H*** the LORD with thy substance...and...firstfruits

Prov 22:4 By...the fear of the LORD are riches, and ***h***

Matt 13:57 Jesus said...A prophet is not without ***h,*** save in his own country

Mark 7:6 people ***h'eth*** me [Jesus] with their lips, but their heart is far from me

John 5:23 ***h'eth*** not the Son ***h'eth*** not the Father

John 12:26 if any man serve me [Jesus], him will my Father ***h***

Rom 12:10 Be kindly affectioned one to another...in ***h*** preferring one another

1 Cor 12:26 one member be ***h'ed,*** all the members rejoice

Rev 4:11 Thou art worthy, O Lord, to receive glory and ***h***

HOPE [D]

Job 7:6 My [Job's] days...are spent without ***h***

Ps 38:15 in thee, O LORD, do I ***h***...thou wilt hear

Ps 71:5 thou art my ***h,*** O Lord

Ps 119:114 Thou [God] art my... shield: I ***h*** in thy word

Ps 146:5 Happy is he...whose ***h*** is in the LORD

Jer 17:7 Blessed is the man... whose ***h*** the LORD is

Lam 3:24 LORD is my portion... therefore...I ***h*** in him

Rom 12:12 Rejoicing in ***h;*** patient in tribulation

Rom 15:13 the God of ***h*** fill you with all joy

1 Cor 13:13 now abideth faith, ***h,*** charity, these three

Col 1:27 which is Christ in you, the ***h*** of glory

1 Thes 4:13 that ye sorrow not... as others which have no ***h***

Heb 11:1 faith is the substance of things ***h'd*** for

1 Pet 3:15 every man that asketh you a reason of the ***h*** that is in you

HOPHNI (an immoral son of Eli the high priest who was killed by the Philistines). 1 Sam 1:3; 2:12–17; **4:1–11.**

HOR, MOUNT (a mountain in Moab where Aaron died). **Num 20:22–29;** 21:4; 33:37–41 • Deut 32:50.

HOSEA (a prophet to the Northern Kingdom and author of the book that bears his name). Hos 1:1–2. *Osee:* Rom 9:25.

HOSEA, BOOK OF. A prophetic book of the Old Testament that compares the idolatry of God's people with the physical adultery of the prophet's wife, Gomer (1:2–5; 2:2–5). Just as Hosea redeemed her from slavery and restored her as his mate, God promised that He would eventually restore His people after a period of punishment by their enemies (4:1–14:9).

HOSHEA

1. The last king of Israel who was taken to Assyria as a captive. 2 Kgs 15:30; **17:1–6;** 18:1–10.

2. Another name for Joshua. See *Joshua.*

HOSPITALITY

1 Tim 3:2 A bishop then must be...given to ***h,*** apt to teach

1 Pet 4:9 Use ***h*** one to another without grudging

HOUR [S]

Matt 10:19 given you in that same ***h*** what ye shall speak

Matt 24:42 know not what ***h*** your Lord doth come

Matt 26:40 ye [Peter] not watch with me [Jesus] one ***h***

Mark 13:32 of that day and that ***h*** knoweth no man

Luke 12:40 Son of man cometh at an ***h*** when ye think not

John 11:9 Are there not twelve ***h's*** in the day

John 12:23 ***h*** is come...Son of man should be glorified

HOUSE [S]

Gen 12:1 Get thee [Abraham]... from thy father's ***h***

Gen 28:17 he [Jacob]...said... this is none other but the ***h*** of God

Gen 39:4 he [Potiphar] made him [Joseph] overseer over his ***h***

Ex 12:7 blood...strike it...on the upper door post of the ***h's***

Ex 20:2 I am...God, which have brought thee...out of the ***h*** of bondage

Ex 20:17 Thou shalt not covet thy neighbour's ***h***

Deut 6:7 talk of them when thou sittest in thine ***h***

Deut 25:14 not have in thine ***h*** divers measures

Josh 24:15 but as for me [Joshua] and my ***h,*** we will serve the LORD

2 Sam 12:10 sword shall never depart from thine [David's] ***h***

1 Kgs 12:19 Israel rebelled against the ***h*** of David

1 Chr 17:1 I [David] dwell in an ***h*** of cedars

1 Chr 22:6 Then he [David]... charged him [Solomon] to build an ***h*** for the LORD

2 Chr 2:1 Solomon determined to build an ***h*** for the...LORD

2 Chr 7:16 sanctified this ***h,*** that my [God's] name may be there for ever

2 Chr 21:7 Lord would not destroy the ***h*** of David

Job 17:13 If I [Job] wait, the grave is mine ***h***

Job 22:18 Yet he [God] filled their ***h's*** with good things

Ps 66:13 I will go into thy [God's] ***h*** with...offerings

Ps 69:9 the zeal of thine ***h*** hath eaten me up

Ps 84:4 Blessed are they that dwell in thy [God's] ***h***

Ps 84:10 rather be a doorkeeper in the ***h*** of my God

Ps 127:1 Except the Lord build the ***h***

Prov 12:7 the ***h*** of the righteous shall stand

Prov 15:25 The Lord will destroy the ***h*** of the proud

Isa 2:5 ***h*** of Jacob...let us walk in the light of the Lord

Jer 18:3 Then I [Jeremiah] went down to the potter's ***h***

Jer 29:28 build ye ***h's,*** and dwell in them

Ezek 43:5 the glory of the Lord filled the ***h***

Amos 3:15 great ***h's*** shall have an end, saith the Lord

Hag 2:9 glory of this latter ***h***... greater than of the former

Mal 3:10 that there may be meat in mine [God's] ***h***

Matt 2:11 they [wise men] were come into the ***h,*** they saw the young child [Jesus]

Matt 7:24 a wise man, which built his ***h*** upon a rock

Matt 10:6 go rather to the lost sheep of the ***h*** of Israel

Matt 13:57 Jesus said...A prophet is not without honour, save...in his own ***h***

Matt 15:24 I [Jesus] am not sent but unto the lost sheep of the ***h*** of Israel

Matt 23:14 ye [scribes and Pharisees] devour widows' ***h's***

Mark 3:25 if a ***h*** be divided against itself

Mark 11:17 My [God's] ***h*** shall be called...the ***h*** of prayer

Luke 14:23 compel them to come in...my ***h*** may be filled

Luke 19:9 This day is salvation come to this ***h***

John 14:2 In my Father's ***h*** are many mansions

Acts 16:31 and thou shalt be saved, and thy ***h***

Acts 28:30 Paul dwelt two... years in his own hired ***h***

1 Cor 16:19 Aquila and Priscilla salute you...with the church...in their ***h***

2 Cor 5:1 a building of God, an ***h*** not made with hands

1 Tim 3:5 if a man know not how to rule his own ***h***

1 Tim 3:12 deacons...ruling... their own ***h's*** well

1 Tim 5:8 for those of his own ***h,*** he hath denied the faith

1 Pet 2:5 Ye also...are built up a spiritual ***h***

1 Pet 4:17 judgment must begin at the ***h*** of God

Eph 2:19 fellowcitizens with the saints, and of the ***h*** of God

HOUSE OF THE LORD

Deut 23:18 Thou shalt not bring...the price of a dog, into the ***h-o-t-L***

1 Sam 3:15 Samuel...opened the doors of the ***h-o-t-L***

1 Kgs 6:1 he [Solomon] began to build the ***h-o-t-L***

1 Kgs 8:11 glory of the LORD had filled the ***h-o-t-L***

1 Kgs 8:63 the king [Solomon] and all the children of Israel dedicated the ***h-o-t-L***

1 Kgs 14:26 And he [Shishak] took away the treasures of the ***h-o-t-L***

2 Kgs 22:8 I [Hilkiah] have found the book of the law in the ***h-o-t-L***

2 Kgs 25:9 he [Nebuzar-adan] burnt the ***h-o-t-L***

2 Chr 36:7 Nebuchadnezzar also carried of the vessels of the ***h-o-t-L*** to Babylon

Ps 23:6 I will dwell in the ***h-o-t-L*** for ever

Ps 27:4 I may dwell in the ***h-o-t-L*** all the days

Ps 122:1 glad when they said... Let us go into the ***h-o-t-L***

HOUSEHOLD

Matt 10:36 a man's foes shall be they of his own ***h***

Gal 6:10 do good unto...them who are of the ***h*** of faith

HULDAH (a prophetess who foretold the collapse of Jerusalem). 2 Kgs 22:14–20 • 2 Chr 34:22–28.

HUMBLE [D, TH]

Ps 10:12 O God, lift up thine hand: forget not the ***h***

Ps 35:13 clothing was sackcloth: I ***h'd*** my soul

Isa 5:15 and the mighty man shall be ***h'd***

Matt 18:4 shall ***h*** himself as this little child...is greatest

Luke 18:14 he that ***h'th*** himself shall be exalted

Phil 2:8 he [Jesus] ***h'd*** himself... became obedient unto death

Jas 4:10 ***H*** yourselves...and he [God] shall lift you up

HUMILITY

Acts 20:19 Serving the Lord with all ***h*** of mind

1 Pet 5:5 be clothed with ***h:*** for God resisteth the proud

HUR (a man who held up the arms of Moses to give the Israelites victory over the Amalekites). **Ex 17:8–13;** 24:14.

HURAM. See *Hiram.*

HUSBAND [S]

Gen 3:16 thy [Eve's] desire shall be to thy ***h***

Prov 12:4 A virtuous woman is a crown to her ***h***

Isa 54:5 For thy Maker is thine ***h;*** the LORD of hosts is his name

Matt 1:19 Joseph her [Mary's] ***h,*** being a just man

Mark 10:12 if a woman shall put away her ***h***...she committeth adultery

1 Cor 7:3 the ***h*** render unto the wife due benevolence

1 Cor 7:14 unbelieving ***h*** is sanctified by the wife

Eph 5:25 ***H's,*** love your wives... as Christ...loved the church

Col 3:19 ***H's,*** love your wives, and be not bitter against them

1 Tim 3:2 A bishop...must be blameless, the ***h*** of one wife

1 Tim 3:12 let the deacons be the ***h's*** of one wife

1 Pet 3:1 wives, be in subjection to your own ***h's***

Rev 21:2 I John saw...new Jerusalem...prepared as a bride adorned for her ***h***

HUSHAI (a friend of King David who remained loyal to the king during Absalom's rebellion). 2 Sam 15:32–37; 16:16–18; 17:5–15 • 1 Kgs 4:16 • 1 Chr 27:33.

HYMENAEUS (an early believer who denied the faith and was excommunicated by Paul). 1 Tim 1:19–20 • 2 Tim 2:16–18.

HYPOCRISY

Matt 23:28 within ye [Pharisees] are full of ***h***

Mark 12:15 But he [Jesus], knowing their [Pharisees'] ***h,*** said...bring me a penny

HYPOCRITE [S]

Job 20:5 and the joy of the ***h*** but for a moment

Matt 6:2 do not sound a trumpet...as the ***h's*** do

Matt 6:16 be not, as the ***h's,*** of a sad countenance

Matt 7:5 ***h,*** first cast out the beam out of thine own eye

Matt 23:13 woe unto you, scribes and Pharisees, ***h's***

Luke 13:15 ***h,*** doth not...you on the sabbath...lead him [ox] away to watering

-I-

I AM GOD

Ps 46:10 Be still, and know that ***I-a-G***

Isa 45:22 be ye saved, all the ends of the earth: for ***I-a-G***

Hos 11:9 ***I-a-G,*** and not man

"I AM" STATEMENTS OF JESUS IN JOHN'S GOSPEL

1. Bread of life (John 6:35)
2. Light of the world (John 8:12)
3. Door of the sheep (John 10:7)
4. Good shepherd (John 10:11,14)
5. Resurrection and the life (John 11:25)
6. Way, the truth, and the life (John 14:6)
7. True vine (John 15:1)

IBZAN (a minor judge of Israel). Judg 12:8–10.

ICHABOD (a grandson of Eli who was given this symbolic name, meaning "inglorious," when his mother learned that Eli and Phinehas were dead). 1 Sam 4:19–22.

ICONIUM (a city in Asia Minor visited by Paul and Barnabas). **Acts 13:51; 14:1, 19–22;** 16:1–7 • 2 Tim 3:11.

IDLE [NESS]

Prov 19:15 and an ***i*** soul shall suffer hunger

Prov 31:27 She...eateth not the bread of ***i'ness***

Eccl 10:18 and through ***i'ness*** of the hands the house droppeth through

Matt 12:36 every ***i*** word that men shall speak, they shall give account

Luke 24:11 words seemed to them [the disciples] as ***i*** tales

IDOL [S]

Lev 19:4 Turn ye not unto ***i's***

1 Chr 16:26 all the gods of the people are ***i's***

Ps 135:15 The ***i's*** of the heathen are silver and gold

Ezek 14:6 Repent, and turn... from your ***i's***

Acts 7:41 they made a calf... offered sacrifice unto the ***i***

1 Cor 8:4 we know that an ***i*** is nothing in the world

2 Cor 6:16 what agreement hath...temple of God with ***i's***

1 John 5:21 Little children, keep yourselves from ***i's***

IDUMEA. See *Edom,* No. 2.

IGNORANCE

Num 15:27 And if any soul sin through ***i***

Acts 17:30 And the times of this ***i*** God winked at

1 Pet 2:15 ye may put to silence the ***i*** of foolish men

IGNORANT [LY]

Acts 4:13 they [the Sanhedrin]... perceived that they [Peter and John] were...***i*** men

Acts 17:23 Whom...ye ***i'ly*** worship, him [Jesus] declare I [Paul] unto you

1 Cor 12:1 concerning spiritual gifts...I [Paul] would not have you ***i***

1 Thes 4:13 not have you to be ***i*,** brethren, concerning them which are asleep

2 Pet 3:8 be not ***i*** of this...one day is with the Lord as a thousand years

IMAGE [S]

Gen 31:19 Rachel had stolen the ***i's*** that were her father's

Ex 20:4 Thou shalt not make unto thee any graven ***i***

Deut 7:25 graven ***i's*** of their gods shall ye burn with fire

2 Kgs 17:10 they set them up ***i's*** and groves

Ps 97:7 Confounded be all they that serve graven ***i's***

Ps 106:19 They made a calf... and worshipped the molten ***i***

Isa 21:9 all the graven ***i's*** of her [Babylon's] gods he [God] hath broken

Isa 42:8 my glory will I [God] not give...neither my praise to graven ***i's***

Dan 3:18 we [Daniel's three friends] will not...worship the golden ***i***

Mic 1:7 all the graven ***i's***... shall be beaten to pieces

Mark 12:16 And he [Jesus] saith...Whose is this ***i*** and superscription

Rom 1:23 changed the glory of...God into an ***i*** made like to corruptible man

Rom 8:29 to be conformed to the ***i*** of his [God's] Son

1 Cor 15:49 we shall also bear the ***i*** of the heavenly

2 Cor 3:18 But we all...are changed into the same ***i*** from glory to glory

Col 1:15 Who [Jesus] is the ***i*** of the invisible God

IMAGE OF GOD

Gen 1:27 God created man...in the ***i-o-G***

Gen 9:6 for in the ***i-o-G*** made he [God] man

2 Cor 4:4 the glorious gospel of Christ, who is the ***i-o-G***

IMAGINATION [S]

Gen 6:5 God saw that...every ***i*** of the thoughts of his [man's] heart was only evil

Jer 16:12 ye walk every one after the ***i*** of his evil heart

Lam 3:61 Thou [God] hast heard...their ***i's*** against me

Luke 1:51 he [God]...scattered the proud in the ***i*** of their hearts

Rom 1:21 they glorified him not as God...but became vain in their ***i's***

IMMORTALITY

1 Cor 15:53 For...this mortal must put on ***i***

2 Tim 1:10 Jesus...hath brought life and ***i*** to light through the gospel

IMPOSSIBLE

Matt 17:20 and nothing shall be ***i*** unto you

Mark 10:27 With men it is ***i,*** but not with God

Luke 18:27 things...***i*** with men are possible with God

Heb 11:6 without faith it is ***i*** to please him [God]

IMPUTE [D, ING, TH]

Ps 32:2 Blessed is the man unto whom the LORD ***i'th*** not iniquity

Rom 4:8 Blessed is the man to whom the Lord will not ***i*** sin

Rom 4:22 it was ***i'd*** to him [Abraham] for righteousness

2 Cor 5:19 To wit...God was in Christ...not ***i'ing*** their trespasses unto them

Jas 2:23 it was ***i'd*** unto him [Abraham] for righteousness

IN CHRIST

Rom 8:1 no condemnation to them which are ***i-C***

Rom 12:5 we, being many, are one body ***i-C***

1 Cor 4:10 fools for Christ's sake, but ye are wise ***i-C***

1 Cor 15:19 in this life only we have hope ***i-C***

1 Cor 15:22 as in Adam all die, even so ***i-C*** shall all be made alive

2 Cor 2:14 unto God, which... causeth us to triumph ***i-C***

2 Cor 5:17 if any man be ***i-C,*** he is a new creature

2 Cor 5:19 To wit, that God was ***i-C,*** reconciling the world unto himself

Eph 1:10 he [God] might gather...in one all things ***i-C***

Phil 2:1 If there be therefore any consolation ***i-C***

Phil 2:5 Let this mind be in you, which was also ***i-C***

Phil 3:14 the prize of the high calling of God ***i-C***

1 Thes 4:16 the dead ***i-C*** shall rise first

IN THE BEGINNING

Gen 1:1 ***I-t-b*** God created the heaven and the earth

John 1:1 ***I-t-b*** was the Word, and the Word was with God

Heb 1:10 Thou, Lord, ***i-t-b*** hast laid the foundation of the earth

IN THE SIGHT OF GOD

Prov 3:4 find favour and good understanding ***i-t-s-o-G***

Luke 16:15 that which is highly esteemed among men is abomination ***i-t-s-o-G***

Gal 3:11 no man is justified by the law ***i-t-s-o-G***

IN THE SPIRIT

Ezek 37:1 The hand of the LORD...carried me [Ezekiel] out ***i-t-s*** of the LORD

John 11:33 When Jesus...saw her [Mary] weeping...he groaned ***i-t-s***

Acts 19:21 Paul purposed ***i-t-s***... to go to Jerusalem

Acts 20:22 I [Paul] go bound ***i-t-s*** unto Jerusalem

Rom 8:9 But ye are not in the flesh, but ***i-t-S***

Gal 5:16 Walk ***i-t-S***...not fulfil the lust of the flesh

Gal 5:25 If we live ***i-t-S,*** let us also walk ***i-t-S***

Rev 1:10 I [John] was ***i-t-S*** on the Lord's day

Rev 21:10 he [an angel] carried me [John] away ***i-t-s*** to a great...mountain

INCLINE [D, TH]

Ps 17:6 ***i*** thine [God's] ear unto me...hear my speech

Ps 40:1 I waited patiently... and he [God] ***i'd*** unto me, and heard my cry

Prov 2:18 her [the strange woman's] house ***i'th*** unto death

Prov 4:20 My son...***i*** thine ear unto my sayings

INCORRUPTIBLE

1 Cor 9:25 they do it to obtain a corruptible crown...we an ***i***

1 Cor 15:52 dead shall be raised ***i,*** and we shall all be changed

INCREASE [D, ING, TH]

Gen 7:18 the waters...were ***i'd*** greatly upon the earth

Ex 1:7 the children of Israel... ***i'd*** abundantly

Lev 26:4 and the land shall yield her ***i***

Job 1:10 his [Job's] substance is ***i'd*** in the land

Ps 3:1 how are they ***i'd*** that trouble me [David]

Ps 67:6 Then shall the earth yield her ***i***

Ps 73:12 these are the ungodly...they ***i*** in riches

Ps 105:24 And he [God] ***i'd*** his people greatly

Prov 1:5 A wise man will hear, and will ***i*** learning

Prov 24:5 a man of knowledge ***i'th*** strength

Eccl 1:18 he that ***i'th*** knowledge ***i'th*** sorrow

Eccl 5:10 not be satisfied with silver; nor he that loveth abundance with ***i***

Isa 9:7 Of the ***i*** of his [Messiah's] government and peace there shall be no end

Luke 2:52 Jesus ***i'd*** in wisdom and stature

Luke 17:5 apostles said unto the Lord, ***I*** our faith

John 3:30 He [Jesus] must ***i,*** but I [John the Baptist] must decrease

Acts 6:7 word of God ***i'd;*** and the...disciples multiplied

1 Cor 3:7 neither is he that planteth any thing...but God that giveth the ***i***
Col 1:10 being fruitful in every good work, and ***i'ing*** in the knowledge of God
1 Thes 3:12 the Lord make you to ***i*** and abound in love

INDIA (a region that served as the eastern limit of the Persian Empire). Esth 1:1; 8:9.

INFIRMITY [IES]
Ps 77:10 my ***i:*** but I will remember...the most High
Prov 18:14 The spirit of a man will sustain his ***i***
Matt 8:17 might be fulfilled... Himself [Jesus] took our ***i'ies***...bare our sicknesses
Rom 8:26 the Spirit also helpeth our ***i'ies***
Rom 15:1 We...strong ought to bear the ***i'ies*** of the weak
2 Cor 12:9 gladly...will I [Paul] ...glory in my ***i'ies***
Gal 4:13 through ***i*** of the flesh I [Paul] preached the gospel
Heb 4:15 not an high priest [Jesus] which cannot be touched with...our ***i'ies***

INHERIT [ED]
Josh 14:1 countries which the children of Israel ***i'ed***
Ps 37:9 those that wait upon the LORD...shall ***i*** the earth
Ps 37:29 The righteous shall ***i*** the land
Prov 11:29 He that troubleth his own house...***i*** the wind
Matt 5:5 Blessed are the meek: for they shall ***i*** the earth
Matt 25:34 Come...***i*** the kingdom prepared for you
Luke 18:18 Good Master, what shall I [rich young ruler] do to ***i*** eternal life
1 Cor 6:10 nor extortioners, shall ***i*** the kingdom of God
Gal 5:21 they which do such things shall not ***i*** the kingdom of God
Rev 21:7 He that overcometh shall ***i*** all things

INHERITANCE
Num 18:23 among...Israel they [Levites] have no ***i***
Num 27:8 a man die, and have no son...cause his ***i*** to pass unto his daughter
Deut 32:9 Jacob is the lot of his [God's] ***i***
Josh 11:23 Joshua gave it [Canaan] for an ***i*** unto Israel
Ps 2:8 I [God] shall give thee the heathen for thine ***i***
Ps 33:12 Blessed is...the people whom he [God] hath chosen for his own ***i***
Ps 94:14 neither will he [God] forsake his ***i***
Prov 20:21 An ***i*** may be gotten hastily at the beginning
Mark 12:7 kill him [the heir], and the ***i*** shall be ours
Eph 1:11 In whom [Jesus] also we have obtained an ***i***

Eph 5:5 no...idolater, hath...***i*** in the kingdom of Christ
Heb 11:8 Abraham...called... into a place which he should after receive for an ***i,*** obeyed

INIQUITY [IES]
Ex 20:5 I the LORD...am a jealous God, visiting the ***i*** of the fathers upon the children
Num 14:18 The LORD is longsuffering...forgiving ***i***
Job 13:23 How many are mine ***i'ies*** and sins
Job 15:16 filthy is man, which drinketh ***i*** like water
Job 34:22 There is no darkness...where the workers of ***i*** may hide
Ps 5:5 thou [God] hatest all workers of ***i***
Ps 25:11 O LORD, pardon mine ***i;*** for it is great
Ps 31:10 my strength faileth because of mine ***i***
Ps 51:2 Wash me throughly from mine ***i***
Ps 51:5 I was shapen in ***i;*** and in sin did my mother conceive me
Ps 51:9 blot out all mine ***i'ies***
Ps 85:2 Thou [God] hast forgiven the ***i*** of thy people
Ps 103:10 He [God] hath not dealt with us...nor rewarded us according to our ***i'ies***
Prov 10:29 destruction shall be to the workers of ***i***
Isa 6:7 thine [Isaiah's] ***i*** is taken away
Isa 40:2 her [Israel's] ***i*** is pardoned: for she hath received...double for all her sins
Isa 53:5 he [God's servant] was bruised for our ***i'ies***
Isa 53:6 LORD...laid on him [God's servant]...***i*** of us all
Isa 59:2 ***i'ies*** have separated... you and your God
Isa 64:6 our ***i'ies,*** like the wind, have taken us away
Jer 14:20 We acknowledge, O LORD...the ***i*** of our fathers
Jer 31:30 every one shall die for his own ***i***
Lam 5:7 we have borne their [our fathers'] ***i'ies***
Matt 23:28 ye [Pharisees] are full of hypocrisy and ***i***
Luke 13:27 depart from me [Jesus], all ye workers of ***i***
Rom 4:7 Blessed are they whose ***i'ies*** are forgiven
1 Cor 13:6 [charity] rejoiceth not in ***i,*** but...in the truth
2 Tim 2:19 every one that nameth the name of Christ depart from ***i***
Heb 10:17 sins and ***i'ies*** will I [God] remember no more
Jas 3:6 the tongue is a fire, a world of ***i***

INSTRUCT [ED]
Job 40:2 Shall he that contendeth with the Almighty ***i*** him
Ps 32:8 I [God] will ***i*** thee and teach thee...guide thee

Prov 21:11 when the wise is ***i'ed,*** he receiveth knowledge
Luke 1:4 certainty of those things, wherein thou hast been ***i'ed***
1 Cor 2:16 who hath known the mind of the Lord, that he may ***i*** him
Phil 4:12 I [Paul] am ***i'ed*** both to be full and to be hungry

INTEGRITY
Job 2:9 Dost thou [Job] still retain thine ***i***
Job 31:6 Let me [Job] be weighed...that God may know mine ***i***
Ps 25:21 Let ***i*** and uprightness preserve me
Prov 19:1 Better is the poor that walketh in his ***i,*** than he that is perverse
Prov 20:7 The just man walketh in his ***i***

INTERCESSION [S]
Rom 8:26 the Spirit itself maketh ***i***...with groanings
Rom 8:34 who [Jesus]... maketh ***i*** for us
1 Tim 2:1 that...prayers, ***i's,*** and giving of thanks, be made for all men
Heb 7:25 he [Jesus] ever liveth to make ***i*** for them

INVISIBLE
Rom 1:20 ***i*** things of him [God]...are clearly seen
Col 1:15 Who [Jesus] is the image of the ***i*** God
1 Tim 1:17 unto the King eternal, immortal, ***i***...be honour and glory

ISAAC (a son born to Abraham and Sarah in their old age and father of Jacob and Esau). Gen 17:19,21; **21:3–12;** 22:2–14; 24:4–67; **25:5–28;** 26:1–35; 27:1–46 • Heb 11:9,20.

ISAIAH (a major prophet of Judah and author of the book that bears his name; he warned that the nation would be destroyed by Assyria, but a righteous remnant would be saved). 2 Kgs 19:2–20; 20:1–19 • 2 Chr 26:22; 32:20,32 • **Isa 1:2–9; 11:11.** *Esaias:* Matt 4:14.

ISAIAH, BOOK OF. A major Old Testament prophetic book noted for its prediction of the coming Messiah (7:14; 9:7) and particularly its emphasis on the Messiah as God's "suffering servant" (42:1–9; 49:1–6; 50:4–9; 52:13–53:12). Many Bible students call Isaiah the "fifth Gospel" because it echoes the New Testament themes of salvation and redemption.

ISCARIOT, JUDAS (the disciple who betrayed Jesus). Matt 10:4; 26:14,25,47; 27:3 • Mark 3:19; 14:10,43 • Luke 22:3,

47–48 • John 6:71; 12:4; 13:2, 26,29; 18:2–5 • Acts 1:16,25.

ISH-BOSHETH (a son of King Saul who succeeded his father as king of Israel and served briefly until defeated by David). 2 Sam 2:8–15; 3:7–15; 4:5–12. *Esh-baal:* 1 Chr 8:33.

ISHMAEL (Abraham's son born to Sarah's maid Hagar; known as the father of the Arab peoples). **Gen 16:1–16;** 17:25; 21:8–21; 25:9–18 • 1 Chr 1:28–31.

ISRAEL

1. Another name for Jacob. Gen 32:28; 35:10. See *Jacob.*

2. The Northern Kingdom, formed when the ten northern tribes rebelled against the two southern tribes and established its own kingship under Rehoboam. 1 Kgs 12:1–33.

3. A general name for the entire nation of the Jewish people. Num 1:2.

ISSACHAR (a son of Jacob and ancestor of one of the twelve tribes of Israel). Gen 30:17–18; 35:23; 46:13; 49:14 • Ex 1:3 • Num 1:8,28–29 • Josh 17:10–11 • Judg 5:15 • 1 Chr 2:1; 7:1; 12:32,40 • Ezek 48:25–26,33. The tribe of Issachar settled in northern Canaan. Josh 19:17–23.

ITHAMAR (youngest son of Aaron who oversaw the tabernacle during the wilderness wanderings). Ex 6:23; 28:1; **38:21** • Lev 10:6–16 • 1 Chr 24:1–6.

ITUREA (a small province ruled by Herod Philip when John the Baptist began his ministry). Luke 3:1.

-J-

JABBOK (a small stream beside which Jacob wrestled with an angel). **Gen 32:22–31** • Num 21:24 • Deut 2:37; 3:16 • Josh 12:2 • Judg 11:13,22.

JACHIN AND BOAZ (two bronze pillars which stood in front of Solomon's temple at Jerusalem). 1 Kgs 7:13–22 • 2 Chr 3:17.

JACOB (father of several sons who became the ancestors of the twelve tribes of Israel). See **Gen 25:19–34; 27:1–35:29; 48:1–49:33** for a sketch of Jacob.

1. Born with twin brother Esau (Gen 25:21–26)
2. Secured Esau's birthright (Gen 25:28–34)
3. Secured his father's blessing (Gen 27:1–41)
4. Fled to Haran (Gen 27:42–28:10)
5. Saw vision of angels at Bethel (Gen 28:11–22)
6. Worked seven years for Leah (Gen 29:16–25)
7. Worked seven years for Rachel (Gen 29:26–30)
8. Birth of his sons (Gen 29:31–30:24)
9. Wrestled with an angel at Peniel (Gen 32:24–30)
10. Name changed from Jacob to *Israel* (Gen 32:28; 35:10)
11. Reconciled with Esau (Gen 33:1–16)
12. Blessed Joseph and Joseph's sons (Gen 48:1–22)
13. Blessed his other sons (Gen 49:1–28)
14. Died in Egypt (Gen 49: 29–33)
15. Buried in Canaan (Gen 50:1–14)

Jacob is also mentioned in Ex 1:1,5 • Lev 26:42 • Josh 24:4 • 1 Sam 12:8 • Mal 1:2 • Matt 1:2; 8:11 • Luke 1:33; 13:28 • John 4:5,12 • Acts 3:13; 7:8–46 • Rom 9:13; 11:26 • Heb 11:9,20–21.

JAEL (a woman who killed Sisera, a commander of the forces of King Jabin of Hazor). **Judg 4:17–22;** 5:6,24.

JAH. See *Jehovah.*

JAIR (a minor judge of Israel). Judg 10:3–5.

JAIRUS (a ruler of a synagogue whose daughter was raised from the dead by Jesus). Mark 5:22–23,36–43 • Luke 8:41–42,49–56.

JAMBRES (an Egyptian magician who opposed Moses). 2 Tim 3:8.

JAMES

1. A son of Zebedee and a disciple of Jesus. Matt 4:21; 10:2; 17:1 • Mark 1:19,29; 3:17; 5:37; 9:2; 10:35,41; 13:3; 14:33 • Luke 5:10; 6:14; 8:51; 9:28,54 • Acts 1:13; 12:2.

2. A son of Alphaeus and a disciple of Jesus. Matt 10:3 • Mark 3:18 • Luke 6:15 • Acts 1:13.

3. A half brother of Jesus who became a leader in the church at Jerusalem and probable author of the New Testament book that bears his name. Matt 13:55; 27:56 • Mark 6:3; 15:40; 16:1 • Acts 12:17; 15:13; 21:18 • 1 Cor 15:7 • Gal 1:19; 2:9,12 • Jas 1:1 • Jude 1.

JAMES, EPISTLE OF. A short epistle written probably by James, the half brother of Jesus, and known for its plain language and practical application of the gospel to the believer's daily life.

JANNES (an Egyptian magician who opposed Moses). 2 Tim 3:8.

JAPHETH (a son of Noah considered the father of the Indo-European races). Gen 5:32; 6:10; 7:13; **9:18–27; 10:1–5** • 1 Chr 1:4–5.

JAPHO. See *Joppa.*

JASHOBEAM (chief of David's mighty men, or brave warriors). 1 Chr 11:10–11; 27:2.

JASON (a citizen of Thessalonica who provided lodging for Paul and Silas). Acts 17:5–9.

JAVAN (a son of Japheth considered the father of the Ionians, or Greeks). Gen 10:2,4 • 1 Chr 1:5–7 • Isa 66:19.

JEBUS. See *Jerusalem.*

JEBUSITES (tribal enemies of the Israelites from whom David took the city of Jebus, or Jerusalem). Gen 15:21 • Josh 15:63 • Judg 1:21; 3:5; 19:11 • **2 Sam 5:6–9** • 1 Kgs 9:20 • 1 Chr 11:4–6 • 2 Chr 8:7 • Ezra 9:1 • Neh 9:8.

JECONIAH. See *Jehoiachin.*

JEHOAHAZ

1. A king of the Northern Kingdom who led the nation into sin and idolatry. 2 Kgs 10:35; **13:1–8** • 2 Chr 25:17,25.

2. Son and successor of Josiah as king of Judah. Jehoahaz reigned only three months. 2 Kgs 23:31–34 • 2 Chr 36:2,4. *Shallum:* 1 Chr 3:15.

JEHOASH. See *Joash,* No. 1.

JEHOIACHIN (son and successor of Jehoiakim as king of Judah. Jehoiachin reigned only three months). **2 Kgs 24:8–16;** 25:27 • 2 Chr 36:8–9 • Jer 52:31. *Coniah:* Jer 22:24. *Jeconiah:* 1 Chr 3:16–17.

JEHOIAKIM (a king of Judah who was defeated and carried away as a captive by the Babylonians). 2 Kgs 24:1–6 • 1 Chr 3:15–16 • **2 Chr 36:4–8** • Jer 26:1–23; 36:1–32 • Dan 1:1–2. *Eliakim:* 2 Kgs 23:34.

JEHORAM

1. A king of Judah who murdered his own brothers in order to succeed his father Jehoshaphat. 1 Kgs 22:50 • **2 Chr 21:1–20.** *Joram:* 2 Kgs 8:21.

2. A king of Israel who was assassinated by Jehu. 2 Kgs 1:17; 3:1,6; **9:24.** *Joram:* 2 Kgs 8:16.

JEHOSHAPHAT (a king of Judah who implemented religious reforms). 1 Kgs 22:2–50 • **2 Chr 17:1–12;** 18:1–21:1. *Josaphat:* Matt 1:8.

JEHOSHUAH. See *Joshua.*

JEHOVAH (a name for God, rendered "LORD" in most translations of the Bible, which comes from a Hebrew verb meaning "to be," indicating His eternity and self-existence). Ex 6:3 • Ps 83:18 • Isa 12:2; 26:4. *JAH:* Ps 68:4.

JEHOVAH-JIREH (a name for God meaning "the LORD will provide"). Gen 22:14.

JEHOVAH-NISSI (a name for God meaning "the LORD is my banner"). Ex 17:15–16.

JEHOVAH-SHALOM (name of an altar built by Gideon, meaning "the LORD is peace"). Judg 6:24.

JEHU (a king of Israel who gained the throne by killing King Ahab's descendants). 2 Kgs 9:2–10:36.

JEMIMA (a daughter of Job born after his recovery from affliction). Job 42:14.

JEPHTHAE. See *Jephthah.*

JEPHTHAH (a judge of Israel who made a rash vow to sacrifice his only child as an offering to God). **Judg 11:1–40;** 12:1–7. *Jephthae:* Heb 11:32.

JEREMIAH (a major prophet who preached God's message of doom to the nation of Judah before it fell to the Babylonians and author of the book that bears his name). He is mentioned outside the Book of Jeremiah in 2 Chr 35:25; 36:12, 21–22 • Ezra 1:1 • Dan 9:2. *Jeremias:* Matt 16:14. *Jeremy:* Matt 2:17; 27:9.

JEREMIAH, BOOK OF. A major Old Testament prophetic book noted for its warnings that the nation of Judah would fall to the Babylonians unless the people repented and turned back to God. Jeremiah also expounded the concept of a new covenant (Jer 31). This new agreement between God and His people, based on grace and forgiveness, was needed because the old covenant of law had failed to keep the people on the path of righteousness.

JEREMIAS. See *Jeremiah.*

JEREMY. See *Jeremiah.*

JERICHO (a Canaanite city captured by Joshua and regarded as one of the world's oldest cities). Num 22:1; 31:12 • Deut 34:3 • **Josh 6:1–27** • 2 Kgs 2:4–18. The Jericho of the New Testament was built on a site near Old Testament Jericho. Matt 20:29 • Mark 10:46 • Luke 19:1.

JEROBOAM

1. Jeroboam I, first king of the Northern Kingdom after the kingdom of Solomon split into two separate nations following the death of Solomon. 1 Kgs 12:17–30 • 2 Chr 13:19–20.

2. Jeroboam II, king of Israel who was denounced for his encouragement of idol worship. 2 Kgs 14:16–29 • **Amos 7:7–9.**

JERUBBAAL. See *Gideon.*

JERUSALEM (the religious and political capital of the Jewish people and the city where Jesus was crucified).

1. Called *Salem* in Abraham's time (Gen 14:18)

2. Then known as *Jebus,* captured by David and made his capital (2 Sam 5:6–8 • 1 Chr 11:4)

3. Site of first temple built by Solomon (1 Kgs 5:5–8)

4. Captured by Babylonia (Jer 39:1–8)

5. Temple rebuilt under Zerubbabel (Ezra 1:1–4)

6. Walls rebuilt under Nehemiah (Neh 12:27–47)

7. Jesus predicted its destruction (Luke 19:41–44)

8. Jesus enters as the triumphant Messiah (Matt 21:9–10)

9. Jesus crucified outside the city (Luke 9:31; 23:33)

10. Church begins at Jerusalem (Acts 2:1–47)

11. Future heavenly city described as "new Jerusalem" (Rev 21:1–3)

JESHUA. See *Joshua.*

JESSE (father of David and an ancestor of Christ). **Ruth 4:17,22** • 1 Sam 16:1–22 • 1 Chr 2:13–15 • Isa 11:1–10 • **Matt 1:5–6** • Luke 3:32 • Acts 13:22 • Rom 15:12.

JESUS, APPEARANCES OF, AFTER HIS RESURRECTION

1. To Mary Magdalene at the empty tomb (Mark 16:9 • John 20:11–18)

2. To other women at the empty tomb (Matt 28:1–10)

3. To two followers on their way to Emmaus (Mark 16:12–13 • Luke 24:13–32)

4. To Peter, apparently in Jerusalem (Luke 24:33–35)

5. To ten of His disciples in Jerusalem, Thomas absent (Luke 24:36–43 • John 20:19–25)

6. To the eleven disciples in Jerusalem, Thomas present (John 20:26–29)

7. To His disciples at the Sea of Galilee (John 21:1–14)

8. To His disciples at His ascension near Jerusalem (Mark 16:19–20 • Luke 24:44–53)

9. To five hundred followers (1 Cor 15:6)

10. To James and all the apostles (1 Cor 15:7)

11. To the apostle Paul (1 Cor 15:8)

JESUS, LIFE AND MINISTRY OF

1. Genealogies of (Matt 1:1–17 • Luke 3:23–38)

2. Birth in Bethlehem (Luke 2:1–20)

3. Flight into Egypt and settlement in Nazareth (Matt 2:13–23 • Luke 2:39–40)

4. Found among esteemed teachers in Jerusalem (Luke 2:41–52)

5. Baptized by John the Baptist (Matt 3:13–17 • Mark 1:9–11)

6. Tempted in the wilderness (Matt 4:1–11 • Mark 1:12–13 • Luke 4:1–13)

7. Centered His early ministry around Capernaum in Galilee (Matt 4:13–16 • Luke 4:22–31)

8. Selected twelve disciples for special training (Matt 10:2–4 • Mark 3:13–19 • Luke 6:12–16)

9. Sermon on the Mount (Matt 5:1–7:29 • Luke 6:17–49)

10. Sent disciples out to preach and heal (Matt 10:1, 5–42 • Mark 6:7–13 • Luke 9:1–6)

11. Predicted His death, resurrection, and return (Luke 12:35–59)

12. Transfiguration (Matt 17:1–8 • Mark 9:2–8 • Luke 9:28–36)

13. Triumphal entry into Jerusalem (Matt 21:1–11 • Mark 11:1–11 • Luke 19:28–40 • John 12:12–19)

14. Instituted the Memorial Supper (Matt 26:26–30 • Mark 14:22–26 • Luke 22:14–20)

15. Agonized in prayer in Gethsemane (Matt 26:36–46 • Mark 14:26,32–42 • Luke 22:39–46)

16. Betrayed by Judas and arrested (Matt 26:47–56 • Mark 14:43–52 • Luke 22:47–53 • John 18:1–12)

17. Trial before the Jewish authorities (Matt 26:57–68; 27:1–2 • Mark 14:53–65; 15:1 • Luke 22:54–23:1 • John 18:24)

18. Trial before Pilate (Matt 27:2–26 • Mark 15:1–15 • Luke 23:2–25 • John 18:28–19:16)

19. Crucifixion by Roman soldiers (Matt 27:33–37 • Mark 15:22–26 • Luke 23:32–34 • John 19:17–24)

20. Death (Matt 27:45–54 • Mark 15:33–39 • Luke 23:44–48 • John 19:28–30)

21. Burial in Joseph's tomb (Matt 27:57–60 • Mark 15:42–46 • Luke 23:50–54 • John 19:38–42)

22. Resurrection (Matt 28:2–4 • 1 Cor 15:1–19)

23. Appearances to His followers. See *Jesus, Appearances of, After His Resurrection.*

24. Great Commission to His followers (Matt 28:16–20 • Mark 16:15–18 • Acts 1:7–8)

25. Ascension to His Father (Mark 16:19 • Luke 24:50–51 • Acts 1:9–11)

JESUS, MIRACLES OF

1. Blind Bartimaeus healed (Matt 20:29–34 • Mark 10:46–52 • Luke 18:35–43)

2. Blind man at Bethsaida healed (Mark 8:22–26)

3. Centurion's servant healed (Matt 8:5–13 • Luke 7:1–10)

4. Daughter of a Canaanite woman healed (Matt 15:21–28 • Mark 7:24–30)

5. Deaf man healed (Mark 7:31–37)

6. Demon-possessed blind man healed (Matt 12:22–24)

7. Demon-possessed boy healed (Matt 17:14–21 • Mark 9:14–29 • Luke 9:37–42)

8. Demon-possessed deaf man healed (Matt 9:32–34)

9. Demon-possessed man healed at Capernaum (Mark 1:21–26 • Luke 4:31–35)

10. Ear of Malchus healed (Luke 22:50–51 • John 18:10)

11. Feeding of the five thousand (Matt 14:13–23 • Mark 6:30–44 • Luke 9:10–17 • John 6:1–15)

12. Feeding of the four thousand (Matt 15:29–38 • Mark 8:1–10)

13. First miraculous catch of fish on the Sea of Galilee (Luke 5:4–10)

14. Jairus's daughter healed (Matt 9:23–26 • Mark 5:35–42 • Luke 8:49–56)

15. Lame man healed on the sabbath (John 5:1–15)

16. Lazarus raised from the dead (John 11:1–44)

17. A leper healed (Matt 8:1–4 • Mark 1:40–45 • Luke 5:12–16)

18. Man blind from birth healed (John 9:1–41)

19. Man with a paralyzed hand healed on the Sabbath (Matt 12:9–14 • Mark 3:1–6 • Luke 6:6–11)

20. Man with the dropsy healed (Luke 14:1–6)

21. Paralyzed man healed (Matt 9:1–8 • Mark 2:1–12 • Luke 5:17–26)

22. Peter's mother-in-law healed (Matt 8:14–15 • Mark 1:29–31 • Luke 4:38–39)

23. Production of a coin to pay the temple tax (Matt 17:24–27)

24. Royal official's son healed (John 4:46–54)

25. Second miraculous catch of fish at the Sea of Galilee (John 21:1–14)

26. Stilling of the storm (Matt 8:18,23–27 • Mark 4:35–41 • Luke 8:22–25)

27. Ten lepers healed (Luke 17:11–19)

28. Transfiguration before His disciples (Matt 17:1–8 • Mark 9:2–8 • Luke 9:28–36)

29. Two blind men healed (Matt 9:27–31)

30. Walking on the water (Matt 14:24–36 • Mark 6:45–56 • John 6:16–21)

31. Water turned into wine (John 2:1–11)

32. Widow's son raised from the dead (Luke 7:11–17)

33. Wild man among the tombs healed (Matt 8:28–34 • Mark 5:1–20 • Luke 8:26–39)

34. Withering of a fig tree (Matt 21:19–22 • Mark 11:20–26)

35. Woman with a crooked back healed (Luke 13:10–17)

36. Woman with a hemorrhage healed (Matt 9:20–22 • Mark 5:24–34 • Luke 8:43–48)

JESUS, PARABLES OF

1. The barren fig tree (Luke 13:1–9)

2. Building on sand and rock (Matt 7:24–27)

3. The dishonest manager (Luke 16:1–8)
4. The dragnet (Matt 13:47–51)
5. The good Samaritan (Luke 10:25–37)
6. The hidden treasure (Matt 13:44)
7. The lamp on a lampstand (Mark 4:21–25 • Luke 8:16–18)
8. The landowner (Matt 13:52)
9. The large banquet (Luke 14:15–24)
10. The lost coin (Luke 15:8–10)
11. The lost sheep (Matt 18:12–14 • Luke 15:1–7)
12. The minas (Luke 19:11–27)
13. The mustard seed (Matt 13:31–32 • Mark 4:30–32 • Luke 13:18–19)
14. The pearl of great price (Matt 13:45–46)
15. The persistent widow (Luke 18:1–8)
16. The prodigal son (Luke 15:11–32)
17. The proud Pharisee (Luke 18:9–14)
18. The rich fool (Luke 12:13–21)
19. The rich man and Lazarus (Luke 16:19–31)
20. The sower and the soils (Matt 13:1–9 • Mark 4:1–9 • Luke 8:4–8)
21. The talents (Matt 25:14–30)
22. The ten virgins (Matt 25:1–13)
23. The two vineyard workers (Matt 21:28–32)
24. The unforgiving servant (Matt 18:23–35)
25. The vineyard owner (Matt 21:33–46 • Mark 12:1–12 • Luke 20:9–19)
26. The vineyard workers (Matt 20:1–16)
27. The wedding banquet (Matt 22:1–14)
28. The wheat and the tares (Matt 13:24–30)
29. The yeast (Matt 13:33–35 • Luke 13:20–21)

JESUS, PROPHECIES ABOUT. See *Messianic Prophecies.*

JETHRO (Moses' father-in-law who advised Moses to delegate some of his leadership responsibilities). Ex 3:1; 4:18; **18:1–27.** *Hobab:* Num 10:29. *Reuel:* Ex 2:18.

JEZEBEL (a wife of King Ahab who promoted Baal worship in Israel). 1 Kgs 16:31; 18:4,13; 19:1–2; 21:5–25 • 2 Kgs 9:7–37 • Rev 2:20.

JEZREEL (a symbolic name, meaning "God scatters," given by the prophet Hosea to his son to show that King Jehu and his family would be punished). Hos 1:3–5.

JOAB (commander of King David's army during most of David's reign). 1 Sam 26:6 • 2 Sam 2:13–32; 3:22–31; 11:1–25; 14:1–33; 18:2–29; 20:9–23 • 1 Kgs 2:5–33 • 1 Chr 11:6–39; 19:8–15; 21:2–6; 27:7, 24,34.

JOANNA (a woman who prepared spices for Jesus' burial and proclaimed His resurrection). Luke 8:1–3; 23:55–56; **24:1–10.**

JOASH

1. A king of Judah who brought religious reforms to the nation but then turned to idol worship. 2 Kgs 12:4–20 • 2 Chr 24:1–22. *Jehoash:* 2 Kgs 11:21.

2. A king of Israel who led the nation into sin through his idolatry. 2 Kgs 13:10–25.

JOATHAM. See *Jotham.*

JOB (a godly man whose faith sustained him through fierce trials and sufferings). **Job 1:1–22; 42:1–17** • Ezek 14:14,20 • Jas 5:11.

JOB, BOOK OF. A wisdom book of the Old Testament that addresses the issue of human suffering. The book is written in the form of a poetic drama revolving around the discussion of this problem by Job and his three friends: Eliphaz, Bildad, and Zophar.

JOEL (a prophet of Judah in the days of King Uzziah and author of the book that bears his name). Joel 1:1 • Acts 2:16.

JOEL, BOOK OF. A brief prophetic book of the Old Testament that uses a devastating swarm of locusts (1:1–20) as an early warning sign of God's judgment in order to call His people to repentance. The prophet predicted the outpouring of God's spirit (2:28–32), an event that happened on the day of Pentecost (Acts 2:16–21).

JOHANAN (a supporter of Gedaliah, governor of Judah, who took a remnant of the Jews to Egypt). **2 Kgs 25:22–23** • Jer 40:8–16; **41:11–18**; 42:1,8; 43:2–6.

JOHN, FIRST, SECOND, AND THIRD EPISTLES OF. Three short epistles written by John, one of the twelve disciples of Jesus. First John focuses on such themes as the incarnation of Christ (1:1–5) and the meaning of love and fellowship

(2:15–5:3). Second John calls on believers to abide in the commandments of God (vv. 1–10). Third John commends two believers and condemns a third.

JOHN, GOSPEL OF. One of the four Gospels, written by the apostle John to show that "Jesus is the Christ, the Son of God" (20:31). John is unique among the Gospels in that it majors on the theological meaning of the events in Jesus' life rather than the events themselves. Also unique to John's Gospel are the "I am" sayings of Jesus, in which Jesus reveals characteristics of His divine nature.

JOHN THE APOSTLE (a fisherman from Galilee who became one of the twelve apostles of Jesus and author of the Gospel that bears his name as well as the books of 1, 2, 3 John and Revelation). Matt 4:21; 10:2; 17:1 • Mark 1:19,29; 3:17; 5:37; 9:2,38; 10:35,41; 13:3; 14:33 • Luke 5:10; 6:14; 8:51; 9:28,49,54; 22:8 • Acts 1:13; 3:1–11; 4:13,19; 8:14; 12:2 • Gal 2:9 • Rev 1:1,4,9; 21:2.

JOHN THE BAPTIST (a prophet who prepared the way for Christ). Matt 3:1–14; 4:12; 9:14; 11:2–18; 14:2–10; 16:14; 17:13; 21:25–32 • Mark 1:4–14; 2:18; 6:14–29; 8:28; 11:30–32 • Luke 1:13–63; 3:2–20; 5:33; 7:18–33; 9:7–9; 11:1; 16:16; 20:4,6 • John 1:6–40; 3:23–27; 4:1; 5:33–36; 10:40–41 • Acts 1:5,22; 10:37; 11:16; 13:24–25; 19:4.

JONAH (a prophet swallowed by a "great fish" while fleeing from God's call to preach at Nineveh in Assyria). 2 Kgs 14:25 • Jon 1:17. *Jonas:* Luke 11:30.

JONAH, BOOK OF. A short prophetic book of the Old Testament that emphasizes God's universal love. Through his experience of preaching to the pagan citizens of Nineveh, Jonah learned that God is concerned for all people, not just the citizens of his native land (4:1–11).

JONAS. See *Jonah.*

JONATHAN (a loyal friend of David). 1 Sam 13:2–22; 14:1–49; 18:1–4; 19:1–7; 20:1–42; 23:16–18; 31:2 • 2 Sam 1:4–26; 4:4; 9:3–7; 21:7–14 • 1 Chr 8:33–34; 9:39–40; 10:2.

JOPPA (a city where Peter had his vision on full acceptance of the Gentiles). 2 Chr 2:16 • Ezra 3:7 • Jon 1:3 • Acts

9:36–43; **10:5–32;** 11:5,13. *Japho:* Josh 19:46.

JORAM. See *Jehoram.*

JORDAN RIVER (the major river of Palestine in which Jesus was baptized). Gen 13:8–13; 32:10 • Num 34:12 • Deut 3:27 • Josh 3:17; 4:1–24 • 2 Sam 17:22–24 • 2 Kgs 2:5–14; 5:10–14 • **Matt 3:6–15.**

JOSAPHAT. See *Jehoshaphat.*

JOSEPH

1. A son of Jacob, sold into slavery by his brothers, who became a high official in the Egyptian government. See **Gen 37–50** for a sketch of Joseph. Ex 1:5–8; 13:19 • Num 27:1; 32:33; 34:23; 36:12 • Deut 27:12 • Josh 14:4; 16:1,4; 17:1–16; 24:32 • Ps 105:17 • John 4:5 • Acts 7:9–18 • Heb 11:21–22.

2. The husband of Mary, Jesus' mother. Matt 1:16–24; 2:13–23 • Luke 1:27; 2:4–43; 3:23 • John 1:45; 6:42.

3. A secret disciple of Jesus who buried Jesus in his own tomb. Matt 27:57–60 • **Mark 15:43–46** • **Luke 23:50–53** • John 19:38.

JOSES. See *Barnabas.*

JOSHUA (Moses' successor who led the Israelites into the Promised Land and rallied the people to victory over the Canaanites). Ex 17:9–14; 24:13; 32:17; 33:11 • Num 11:28; 14:6–38; 26:65; 27:18–23; 32:12,28; 34:17 • Deut 1:38; 3:21,28; 31:3–23; 34:9 • **Josh 1:1–24:31** • Judg 2:6–23 • 1 Kgs 16:34. *Hoshea:* Deut 32:44. *Jehoshuah:* 1 Chr 7:27. *Jeshua:* Neh 8:17. *Oshea:* Num 13:8.

JOSHUA, BOOK OF. An Old Testament book that details the conquest and settlement of the land of Canaan by the Israelites under the leadership of Joshua.

JOSIAH (a king of Judah who led a reform movement to reestablish God's Law and abolish idolatry). 2 Kgs 22:3–9; **23:3–25.** *Josias:* Matt 1:10–11.

JOTHAM (a king of Judah who failed to destroy places of pagan worship). **2 Kgs 15:5–38;** 16:1 • 1 Chr 3:12; 5:17 • 2 Chr 26:21,23; 27:1–9 • Isa 1:1; 7:1 • Hos 1:1 • Mic 1:1. *Joatham:* Matt 1:9.

JOURNEY [ED, ING, INGS]

Gen 12:9 Abram ***j'ed,*** going on still toward the south

Ex 3:18 let us [Israelites] go... three days' ***j***...that we may sacrifice to the LORD

Jon 3:3 Nineveh was...great city of three days' ***j***
Luke 9:3 Take nothing for your ***j,*** neither staves
Luke 10:33 Samaritan, as he ***j'ed,*** came where he [the wounded traveler] was
Luke 13:22 he [Jesus] went through the cities...teaching, and ***j'ing*** toward Jerusalem
Luke 15:13 younger son...took his ***j*** into a far country
Acts 9:3 as he [Paul] ***j'ed,*** he came near Damascus
2 Cor 11:26 In ***j'ings*** often, in perils of waters

JOY
Ps 16:11 in thy [God's] presence is fulness of ***j***
Ps 30:5 weeping may endure for a night, but ***j*** cometh in the morning
Ps 43:4 Then will I go...unto God my exceeding ***j***
Ps 51:12 Restore...the ***j*** of thy [God's] salvation
Ps 126:5 They that sow in tears shall reap in ***j***
Prov 15:21 Folly is ***j*** to him that is destitute of wisdom
Isa 12:3 with ***j***...draw water out of the wells of salvation
Isa 52:9 Break forth into ***j***...ye waste places of Jerusalem
Lam 5:15 ***j*** of our heart is ceased; our dance is turned into mourning
Hab 3:18 I will ***j*** in the God of my salvation
Matt 2:10 they [wise men]... rejoiced with...great ***j***
Matt 28:8 And they [the women] departed quickly... with fear and great ***j***
Luke 2:10 bring you [shepherds] good tidings of great ***j***
Luke 15:10 ***j***...over one sinner that repenteth
John 16:20 your sorrow shall be turned into ***j***
Acts 20:24 I [Paul] might finish my course with ***j***
Rom 14:17 kingdom of God is... peace, and ***j***
Gal 5:22 fruit of the Spirit is love, ***j,*** peace
Heb 12:2 who [Jesus] for the ***j*** that was set before him endured the cross
Jas 1:2 count it all ***j*** when ye fall into divers temptations
3 John 4 no greater ***j***...children walk in truth

JOYFUL [LY, NESS]
Ps 35:9 my soul shall be ***j*** in the LORD
Ps 66:1 Make a ***j*** noise unto God, all ye lands
Ps 95:1 make a ***j*** noise to the rock of our salvation
Ps 149:5 Let the saints be ***j*** in glory...sing aloud
Eccl 9:9 Live ***j'ly*** with the wife whom thou lovest
Isa 49:13 Sing, O heavens; and be ***j,*** O earth
Luke 19:6 he [Zacchaeus]... received him [Jesus] ***j'ly***

Col 1:11 Strengthened...unto all patience...with ***j'ness***

JUBAL (a musician regarded as the ancestor of those who play the harp and the flute). Gen 4:21.

JUDAEA (a district in southern Palestine in New Testament times). Matt 2:1,5,22 • Mark 1:5; 3:7 • Luke 6:17 • John 4:3,47,54 • Acts 10:37 • Rom 15:31 • 2 Cor 1:16 • Gal 1:22 • 1 Thes 2:14.

JUDAH

1. A son of Jacob and ancestor of one of the twelve tribes of Israel. Gen 29:35; 38:1–26; 43:3,8; 44:14–18; 46:12,28; 49:8–9 • Ex 1:2 • Num 26:19 • Ruth 4:12 • 1 Chr 2:1–10; 4:1,21,27; 5:2; 9:4 • Neh 11:24. The tribe of Judah settled in southern Canaan. Josh 15:1–12.

2. The Southern Kingdom, or nation of Judah, with Jerusalem as its capital that was overrun and taken into exile by the Babylonians. 2 Chr 36:4–20.

JUDAS (one of the twelve disciples of Jesus, called "brother of James" to set him apart from the disciple Judas [Iscariot] who betrayed Jesus). Luke 6:16 • John 14:22 • Acts 1:13. *Lebbaeus:* Matt 10:3. *Thaddaeus:* Mark 3:18.

JUDAS ISCARIOT. See *Iscariot, Judas.*

JUDE (half brother of Jesus and author of the New Testament epistle that bears his name). Jude 1. *Judas:* Matt 13:55.

JUDE, EPISTLE OF. A short letter written like a brief essay or tract and addressed to the problem of false teachings in the early church.

JUDGE [S, ST, TH]

Gen 18:25 Shall not the ***J*** of all the earth do right

Ex 18:13 on the morrow... Moses sat to ***j*** the people

Judg 2:16 LORD raised up ***j's***

1 Sam 2:10 the LORD shall ***j*** the ends of the earth

1 Sam 8:6 they [the people] said, Give us a king to ***j*** us

1 Kgs 3:9 Give...thy [God's] servant [Solomon] an understanding heart to ***j*** thy people

Job 22:13 can he [God] ***j*** through the dark cloud

Ps 7:8 ***j*** me, O LORD, according to my righteousness

Ps 7:11 God ***j'th*** the righteous

Ps 43:1 ***J*** me, O God, and plead my cause

Ps 72:2 He [God] shall ***j*** thy people with righteousness

Ps 75:7 God is the ***j***...putteth down one...setteth up another

Prov 31:9 ***j*** righteously, and plead the cause of the poor

Lam 3:59 thou [God] hast seen my wrong: ***j*** thou my cause

Matt 7:1 ***J*** not, that ye be not judged

John 7:24 ***J*** not according to the appearance

John 12:48 word that I [Jesus] have spoken...shall ***j*** him in the last day

Rom 14:10 But why dost thou ***j*** thy brother

2 Tim 4:1 Jesus Christ, who shall ***j*** the quick and the dead

2 Tim 4:8 the righteous ***j,*** shall give me [Paul] at that day [a crown of righteousness]

Jas 2:4 ye...are become ***j's*** of evil thoughts

Jas 4:12 one lawgiver [God]... who art thou that ***j'st*** another

Rev 19:11 in righteousness he [Jesus] doth ***j***

JUDGES, BOOK OF. A historical book of the Old Testament that records the exploits of several different judges, or military deliverers, in Israel's history.

JUDGES OF ISRAEL (popular military leaders or deliverers who led Israel between the time of Joshua's death and the beginning of the kingship). The judges of Israel were: Othniel (Judg 3:9–11), Ehud (Judg 3:15–30), Shamgar (Judg 3:31), Deborah and Barak (Judg 4:4–24), Gideon (Judg 6:11–8:32), Abimelech (Judg 9:1–54), Tola (Judg 10:1–2), Jair (Judg 10:3–5), Jephthah (Judg 11:1–12:7), Ibzan (Judg 12:8–10), Elon (Judg 12:11–12), Abdon (Judg 12:13–15), Samson (Judg 14:1–16:31), Eli (1 Sam 4:15–18), Samuel (1 Sam 7:15), and Samuel's sons (1 Sam 8:1–3).

JUDGMENT

Ex 12:12 against all the gods of Egypt I [God]...execute ***j***

1 Chr 18:14 David reigned... and executed ***j***

Job 8:3 Doth God pervert ***j***

Job 32:9 neither do the aged understand ***j***

Ps 1:5 the ungodly shall not stand in the ***j***

Ps 72:2 He [God] shall judge... thy poor with ***j***

Ps 101:1 I will sing of mercy and ***j:*** unto thee [God]

Ps 119:66 Teach me good ***j*** and knowledge

Prov 21:3 To do justice and ***j*** is more acceptable to the LORD than sacrifice

Prov 29:26 every man's ***j*** cometh from the LORD
Eccl 12:14 God shall bring every work into ***j***
Isa 42:1 he [God's servant] shall bring forth ***j*** to the Gentiles
Jer 9:24 I am the LORD which exercise ... ***j***
Jer 33:15 he [Messiah] shall execute ***j*** and righteousness
Amos 5:24 But let ***j*** run down as waters
Matt 5:22 whosoever is angry with his brother...shall be in danger of the ***j***
John 5:30 as I [Jesus] hear, I judge: and my ***j*** is just
John 9:39 For ***j*** I [Jesus] am come into this world
Rom 14:10 we shall all stand before the ***j*** seat of Christ
2 Cor 5:10 we must all appear before the ***j*** seat of Christ
Heb 9:27 appointed unto men once to die, but after this the ***j***
1 Pet 4:17 ***j*** must begin at the house of God
1 John 4:17 we may have boldness in the day of ***j***
Rev 14:7 Fear God...for the hour of his ***j*** is come

JUDGMENT OF GOD
Rom 2:3 thinkest thou...that thou shalt escape the ***j-o-G***
2 Thes 1:5 a manifest token of the righteous ***j-o-G***

JUPITER (chief god of Roman mythology and a name applied to Barnabas by the citizens of Lystra). Acts 14:12.

JUST [LY]
Gen 6:9 Noah was a ***j*** man
Job 4:17 Shall mortal man be more ***j*** than God
Ps 37:12 The wicked plotteth against the ***j***
Prov 4:18 path of the ***j*** is as the shining light
Prov 11:1 a ***j*** weight is his [God's] delight
Prov 20:7 The ***j*** man walketh in his integrity
Eccl 7:20 not a ***j*** man upon earth, that...sinneth not
Isa 45:21 no God...beside me; a ***j*** God and a Saviour
Mic 6:8 what doth the LORD require...but to do ***j'ly***
Hab 2:4 but the ***j*** shall live by his faith
Matt 1:19 Joseph her [Mary's] husband, being a ***j*** man
Luke 2:25 Simeon...was ***j*** and devout
Rom 1:17 as it is written, The ***j*** shall live by faith
Col 4:1 give unto your servants that which is ***j***
1 Pet 3:18 For Christ also hath once suffered for sins, the ***j*** for the unjust
1 John 1:9 he [Jesus] is faithful and ***j*** to forgive us our sins

JUSTICE

Job 8:3 or doth the Almighty pervert ***j***

Ps 82:3 do ***j*** to the afflicted and needy

Prov 21:3 To do ***j***...is more acceptable...than sacrifice

Jer 23:5 a King [Jesus] shall... execute judgment and ***j***

JUSTIFICATION

Rom 4:25 Who [Jesus]...was raised again for our ***j***

Rom 5:18 by the righteousness of one [Jesus] the free gift came...unto ***j*** of life

JUSTIFY [IED, IETH]

Job 9:20 If I ***j*** myself, mine own mouth...condemn me

Job 25:4 How then can man be ***j'ied*** with God

Matt 12:37 by thy words thou shalt be ***j'ied***

Rom 3:24 ***j'ied*** freely by his [God's] grace through... Christ Jesus

Rom 3:28 ***j'ied*** by faith without the deeds of the law

Rom 5:1 being ***j'ied*** by faith, we have peace with God

Rom 8:33 It is God that ***j'ieth***

1 Cor 6:11 ye are ***j'ied*** in the name of the Lord

Gal 2:16 a man is not ***j'ied*** by the works of the law

Titus 3:7 ***j'ied*** by his [God's] grace, we should be made heirs...of eternal life

Jas 2:21 Was not Abraham our father ***j'ied*** by works

-K-

KADESH (a wilderness region where the Israelites camped before entering Canaan). Gen 14:7; 16:14; 20:1 • Num 20:1,14, 16–22; **33:36–37** • Deut 1:46 • Judg 11:16–17 • Ps 29:8. *Kadesh-barnea:* **Num 32:8** • Josh 14:7.

KEDAR (a son of Ishmael and founder of an Arabic tribe). Gen 25:12–13 • Isa 21:17 • Jer 49:28–29.

KEDESH (one of the six cities of refuge, situated in the territory of Naphtali). Josh 20:1–7 • Judg 4:10–11 • 1 Chr 6:76.

KEEP [ETH, ING]

Gen 2:15 God...put him [Adam] into the garden of Eden...to ***k*** it

Ex 12:14 ***k*** it [the Passover] a feast to the LORD

Ex 19:5 ***k*** my [God's] covenant, then ye shall be a peculiar treasure

Ex 20:8 Remember the sabbath day, to ***k*** it holy

Ex 31:14 ***k*** the sabbath...it is holy unto you

Deut 5:10 showing mercy unto...them that...***k*** my [God's] commandments

Ps 17:8 ***K*** me as the apple of the eye...hide me

Ps 34:13 ***K*** thy tongue from evil...thy lips from...guile

Ps 91:11 he [God] shall...***k*** thee in all thy ways

Ps 119:4 Thou [God] hast commanded us to ***k*** thy precepts

Ps 119:34 Give me understanding, and I shall ***k*** thy [God's] law

Ps 119:146 save me...I shall ***k*** thy [God's] testimonies

Ps 121:4 he [God] that ***k'eth*** Israel...neither slumber nor sleep

Ps 127:1 except the LORD ***k*** the city, the watchman waketh but in vain

Ps 141:3 Set a watch, O LORD... ***k*** the door of my lips

Prov 3:1 let thine heart ***k*** my [God's] commandments

Prov 4:23 ***K*** thy heart with all diligence

Prov 13:3 He that ***k'eth*** his mouth ***k'eth*** his life

Prov 21:23 ***k'eth*** his...tongue ***k'eth*** his soul from troubles

Prov 29:11 fool uttereth all his mind...wise man ***k'eth*** it in

Eccl 3:7 time to ***k*** silence, and a time to speak

Isa 26:3 wilt ***k*** him...whose mind is stayed on thee [God]

Ezek 20:19 walk in my [God's] statutes, and ***k*** my judgments

Hab 2:20 let all the earth ***k*** silence before him [God]

Mark 7:9 reject the commandment...that ye [Pharisees] may ***k*** your own tradition
Luke 2:8 shepherds...***k'ing*** watch over their flock
Luke 11:28 Yea rather, blessed are they that hear the word of God, and ***k*** it
John 9:16 This man [Jesus] is not of God, because he ***k'eth*** not the sabbath
John 14:15 If ye love me [Jesus], ***k*** my commandments
John 15:10 If ye ***k*** my [Jesus'] commandments, ye shall abide in my love
1 Cor 7:19 Circumcision is nothing...but the ***k'ing*** of the commandments
1 Cor 9:27 But I [Paul] ***k*** under my body, and bring it into subjection
1 Cor 14:28 no interpreter, let him ***k*** silence in the church
Eph 4:3 ***k*** the unity of the Spirit in the bond of peace
Phil 4:7 peace of God...***k*** your hearts...through Christ
2 Thes 3:3 Lord...shall stablish you...***k*** you from evil
2 Tim 1:12 he [Jesus] is able to ***k*** that...I have committed
Jas 1:27 Pure religion...is this... to ***k*** himself unspotted
Jas 2:10 ***k*** the whole law, and yet offend in one point, he is guilty of all
1 John 5:3 this is the love of God...***k*** his commandments
1 John 5:21 Little children, ***k*** yourselves from idols
Jude 24 unto him [Jesus] that is able to ***k*** you from falling
Rev 2:26 he that...***k'eth*** my [Jesus'] works...to him will I give power

KEEP HIS COMMANDMENTS

Deut 13:4 Ye shall walk after the LORD...and ***k-h-c***
Ps 78:7 That they might...not forget the works of God, but ***k-h-c***
Eccl 12:13 ***k-h-c:*** for this is the whole duty of man
1 John 2:3 we do know that we know him, if we ***k-h-c***

KENAN (a son of Enoch and great-grandson of Adam). 1 Chr 1:1–2. *Cainan:* Gen 5:9.

KENITES (a nomadic Midianite tribe that was friendly toward the Israelites). Gen 15:19 • Num 24:20–22 • Judg 4:11,17–22 • 1 Sam 15:6; 30:29 • 1 Chr 2:55.

KENIZZITES (a Canaanite tribe whose land was promised to Abraham's descendants). Gen 15:18–19.

KEPT

Ex 3:1 Moses ***k*** the flock of Jethro

Ps 18:21 For I have ***k*** the ways of the LORD
Ps 32:3 When I ***k*** silence, my bones waxed old
Ps 78:56 they...provoked... God...***k*** not his testimonies
Ps 119:55 I have remembered thy [God's] name...and have ***k*** thy law
Matt 19:20 these things have I ***k*** from my youth
Luke 2:19 But Mary ***k*** all these things...in her heart
John 17:12 I [Jesus] ***k*** them [the disciples] in thy [God's] name...none...is lost
Gal 3:23 before faith came, we were ***k*** under the law
2 Tim 4:7 I [Paul]...have fought a good fight...***k*** the faith
1 Pet 1:5 ***k*** by the power of God through faith

KETURAH (a wife of Abraham whose sons were ancestors of Arabian tribes). Gen 25:1,4 • 1 Chr 1:32–33.

KEY [S]
Matt 16:19 give unto thee the ***k's*** of the kingdom
Rev 9:1 to him [angel] was given...***k*** of...bottomless pit

KIDRON (a valley or ravine that David crossed while fleeing from his son Absalom). **2 Sam 15:23–30** • 2 Kgs 23:4–6,12 • 2 Chr 15:16; 29:16; 30:14 • Jer 31:40. *Cedron:* John 18:1.

KILL [ED, EST, ETH]
Gen 37:31 they [Joseph's brothers]...***k'ed*** a kid of the goats
Ex 2:14 intendest thou [Moses] to ***k*** me [Hebrew slave], as thou ***k'est*** the Egyptian
Ex 20:13 Thou shalt not ***k***
Num 35:15 every one that ***k'eth*** any person unawares may flee
Deut 5:17 Thou shalt not ***k***
1 Sam 2:6 The LORD ***k'eth,*** and maketh alive
2 Sam 12:9 thou [David] hast ***k'ed*** Uriah the Hittite
Ps 44:22 for thy [God's] sake are we ***k'ed*** all the day long
Prov 21:25 The desire of the slothful ***k'eth*** him
Eccl 3:3 A time to ***k,*** and a time to heal
Matt 5:21 whosoever shall ***k***... in danger of the judgment
Matt 23:37 O Jerusalem...thou that ***k'est*** the prophets
Mark 3:4 Is it lawful...on the sabbath...save life, or to ***k***
Mark 8:31 Son of man must suffer...and be ***k'ed***
Mark 9:31 after...he [Jesus] is ***k'ed,*** he shall rise
Mark 12:7 ***k*** him [the heir]... inheritance shall be ours
Luke 12:4 Be not afraid of them that ***k*** the body
Luke 12:5 after he hath ***k'ed*** hath power to cast into hell
Luke 15:23 bring hither the fatted calf, and ***k*** it

Luke 22:2 chief priests and scribes sought how they might ***k*** him [Jesus]
John 10:10 thief cometh...to ***k,*** and to destroy
John 16:2 whosoever ***k'eth*** you will think that he doeth God service
Acts 10:13 Peter; ***k,*** and eat
Acts 12:2 he [Herod] ***k'ed*** James the brother of John
Rom 8:36 For thy sake we are ***k'ed*** all the day long
2 Cor 3:6 letter ***k'eth,*** but the spirit giveth life
Jas 4:2 ye ***k,*** and desire to have, and cannot obtain
Rev 11:7 beast...shall overcome them [two witnesses], and ***k*** them

KINGDOM [S]

Ex 19:6 unto me [God] a ***k*** of priests, and an holy nation
1 Sam 15:28 The LORD hath rent the ***k*** of Israel from thee [Saul] this day
2 Sam 7:16 thine [David's] house and thy ***k*** shall be established for ever
1 Kgs 4:21 And Solomon reigned over all ***k's***
1 Chr 29:11 thine is the ***k,*** O LORD...thou art exalted
Ps 22:28 the ***k*** is the LORD's
Ps 68:32 Sing unto God, ye ***k's*** of the earth
Ps 145:13 Thy [God's] ***k*** is an everlasting ***k***
Dan 2:39 after thee [Nebuchadnezzar] shall arise another ***k***
Dan 4:3 his [God's] ***k*** is an everlasting kingdom
Dan 4:31 The ***k*** is departed from thee [Nebuchadnezzar]
Dan 5:28 Thy [Belshazzar's] ***k*** is divided...given to...Medes
Matt 6:10 Thy [God's] ***k*** come. Thy will be done
Matt 8:12 children of the ***k***... cast...into outer darkness
Matt 24:7 nation shall rise against nation...***k*** against ***k***
Mark 3:24 ***k*** be divided against itself, that ***k*** cannot stand
Luke 1:33 of his [Jesus'] ***k*** there shall be no end
Luke 4:5 the devil...showed unto him [Jesus] all the ***k's*** of the world
Luke 12:32 your Father's good pleasure to give you the ***k***
Luke 23:42 remember me [thief] when thou [Jesus] comest into thy ***k***
John 18:36 My [Jesus'] ***k*** is not of this world
1 Thes 2:12 God, who hath called you unto his ***k***
Rev 11:15 ***k's*** of this world are become the ***k's*** of our Lord

KINGDOM OF GOD

Matt 6:33 seek ye first the ***k-o-G***, and his righteousness
Mark 1:15 time is fulfilled, and the ***k-o-G*** is at hand
Mark 9:47 better...to enter into the ***k-o-G*** with one eye

Mark 10:14 forbid them [children] not...such is the ***k-o-G***

Mark 10:25 eye of a needle, than for a rich man to enter into the ***k-o-G***

Luke 9:2 he [Jesus] sent them [the disciples]...to preach... ***k-o-G***

Luke 9:62 No man...looking back, is fit for the ***k-o-G***

John 3:3 Except a man be born again...cannot see the ***k-o-G***

Rom 14:17 ***k-o-G*** is not meat and drink; but righteousness

1 Cor 6:9 the unrighteous shall not inherit the ***k-o-G***

1 Cor 15:50 flesh and blood cannot inherit the ***k-o-G***

KINGDOM OF HEAVEN

Matt 5:10 Blessed are they which are persecuted... their's is the ***k-o-h***

Matt 5:20 ye shall in no case enter into the ***k-o-h***

Matt 7:21 Not every one that saith unto me, Lord, Lord, shall enter into the ***k-o-h***

Matt 16:19 I [Jesus] will give... thee...keys of the ***k-o-h***

Matt 18:4 humble himself as this little child, the same is greatest in the ***k-o-h***

Matt 23:13 ye [scribes and Pharisees] shut up the ***k-o-h*** against men

KINGS, BOOKS OF FIRST AND SECOND. Two historical books of the Old Testament that cover a period of roughly four centuries in Jewish history—from about 970 to 587 B.C. First Kings begins with the reign of Solomon as successor to David (1 Kgs 1:1–11:43). The closing chapters of 2 Kings cover the final years of the nation of Judah before it fell to the Babylonians.

KING'S HIGHWAY (an important road linking Damascus and Egypt that ran through Israel). Num 20:17–21.

KIRJATH-ARBA. See *Hebron.*

KIRJATH-JEARIM (a fortified city of the Gibeonites where the ark of the covenant was kept for a time). Josh 9:17; 15:60; 18:28 • **1 Chr 13–16.** *Baalah:* Josh 15:9.

KISHON (a river in northern Palestine where Elijah killed the prophets of Baal). Judg 4:13 • **1 Kgs 18:40.** *Kison:* Ps 83:9.

KISON. See *Kishon.*

KISS [ED]

Gen 50:1 Joseph...wept upon him [Jacob], and ***k'ed*** him

Ps 85:10 righteousness and peace have ***k'ed*** each other

Matt 26:49 he [Judas]...said, Hail...and ***k'ed*** him [Jesus]
Luke 15:20 his [prodigal son's] father...fell on his neck, and ***k'ed*** him
Luke 22:48 Judas, betrayest thou the Son of man with a ***k***
2 Cor 13:12 Greet one another with an holy ***k***
1 Pet 5:14 Greet ye one another with a ***k*** of charity

KITTIM. See *Cyprus.*

KNOCK [ED]
Luke 11:9 ***k,*** and it shall be opened unto you
Acts 12:13 as Peter ***k'ed*** at the door...a damsel came
Rev 3:20 I [Jesus] stand at the door, and ***k***

KNOW THAT I AM THE LORD
Ex 7:5 Egyptians shall ***k-t-I-a-t-L,*** when I stretch forth mine hand upon Egypt
Ezek 6:7 slain shall fall...and ye shall ***k-t-I-a-t-L***
Ezek 16:62 will establish my covenant with thee; and thou shalt ***k-t-I-a-t-L***
Ezek 30:19 will I execute judgments in Egypt: and they shall ***k-t-I-a-t-L***

KNOW THE LORD
Jer 31:34 they shall teach no more...***K-t-L:*** for they shall all know me
Heb 8:11 not teach...his brother, saying, ***K-t-L:*** for all shall know me

KNOWLEDGE
Gen 2:17 tree of the ***k*** of good and evil, thou shalt not eat
1 Sam 2:3 for the LORD is a God of ***k,*** and by him actions are weighed
Job 21:22 Shall any teach God ***k?*** seeing he judgeth
Job 35:16 he [Job] multiplieth words without ***k***
Ps 19:2 night unto night showeth ***k***
Ps 139:6 Such ***k*** is too wonderful for me
Ps 144:3 what is man, that thou [God] takest ***k*** of him
Prov 1:7 fear of the LORD is the beginning of ***k***
Prov 10:14 Wise men lay up ***k:*** but the mouth of the foolish is near destruction
Prov 20:15 the lips of ***k*** are a precious jewel
Prov 24:5 a man of ***k*** increaseth strength
Eccl 1:18 he that increaseth ***k*** increaseth sorrow
Hos 6:6 I [God] desired...***k*** of God more than...offerings
Hab 2:14 earth...filled with the ***k*** of the glory of the LORD
Rom 11:33 depth of the riches... wisdom and ***k*** of God

1 Cor 12:8 to one is given... word of wisdom: to another... word of ***k***

1 Cor 13:2 though I [Paul]... understand...all ***k***

Eph 3:19 know the love of Christ, which passeth ***k***

Phil 1:9 love may abound...in ***k*** and in all judgment

1 Tim 2:4 all men...to come unto the ***k*** of the truth

2 Tim 3:7 never able to come to the ***k*** of the truth

2 Pet 1:5 add to your faith virtue; and to virtue ***k***

2 Pet 3:18 grow in grace, and in the ***k*** of our Lord

KOHATH (a son of Levi and founder of the Kohathites, priests who cared for the tabernacle accessories). Gen 46:11 • Ex 6:18–19 • Num 3:30–31.

KORAH (leader of a rebellion against Moses in the wilderness). Ex 6:21,24 • Num 16:30–33. *Core:* Jude 11.

-L-

LABAN (father of Leah and Rachel, who were given in marriage to Jacob). Gen 24:29, 50; 29:5–29; 30:25–40; 31:2–55.

LABOUR [ED, ETH, S]

Ex 20:9 Six days shalt thou ***l,*** and do all thy work

Ps 104:23 Man goeth forth...to his ***l*** until the evening

Ps 127:1 Except the LORD build the house, they ***l*** in vain that build it

Prov 23:4 **L** not to be rich

Eccl 3:9 What profit hath he... wherein he ***l'eth***

Eccl 3:13 man should...enjoy the good of all his ***l***

Matt 11:28 Come unto me [Jesus], all ye that ***l*** and are heavy laden

1 Cor 3:8 his own reward according to his own ***l***

1 Cor 15:58 your ***l*** is not in vain in the Lord

2 Cor 11:23 in ***l's***...abundant, in stripes above measure

Phil 2:16 I [Paul] have not... ***l'ed*** in vain

Heb 4:11 Let us ***l*** therefore to enter into that rest

LABOURER [S]

Matt 9:37 The harvest...is plenteous, but the ***l's*** are few

Luke 10:7 for the ***l*** is worthy of his hire

1 Cor 3:9 For we are ***l's*** together with God

LACHISH (an Amorite city captured by Joshua). **Josh 10:3–35;** 12:11; 15:39 • 2 Kgs 14:19; 18:14–17 • 2 Chr 25:27 • Neh 11:30 • Isa 36:1–2 • Jer 34:1,7.

LACK [ED, EST]

Gen 18:28 wilt thou [God] destroy all the city for ***l*** of five

Hos 4:6 people are destroyed for ***l*** of knowledge

Matt 19:20 these things have I kept...what ***l*** I yet

Luke 18:22 ***l'est*** thou one thing: sell all...distribute unto the poor

Luke 22:35 When I [Jesus] sent you [the disciples] without purse...***l'ed*** ye any thing

Jas 1:5 any of you ***l*** wisdom, let him ask of God

LAISH. See *Dan,* No. 2.

LAMB OF GOD

John 1:29 the ***L-o-G***...taketh away the sin of the world

John 1:36 he [John the Baptist] saith, Behold the ***L-o-G***

LAME

Prov 26:7 The legs of the ***l*** are not equal

Luke 7:22 tell John...how that the blind see, the ***l*** walk

Luke 14:13 call the poor...the ***l,*** the blind

LAMECH (father of Noah). **Gen 5:25–31** • 1 Chr 1:3 • Luke 3:36.

LAMENTATIONS, BOOK OF. A short book of the Old Testament that expresses the prophet Jeremiah's grief at the destruction of Jerusalem and the temple by the pagan Babylonians.

LAMP [S]

Judg 7:20 brake the pitchers... held the ***l's*** in their...hands

2 Sam 22:29 For thou art my ***l,*** O LORD

Job 41:19 Out of his [God's] mouth go burning ***l's***

Ps 119:105 Thy [God's] word is a ***l*** unto my feet

Matt 25:3 foolish took their ***l's,*** and took no oil

LAODICEA (a major city in Asia Minor where one of the seven churches addressed in the Book of Revelation was located). Col 2:1; 4:13–16 • **Rev 3:14–18.**

LASCIVIOUSNESS

Gal 5:19 works of the flesh are...Adultery...***l***

Jude 4 certain men...turning the grace of our God into ***l***

LAST

Prov 23:32 At the ***l*** it [wine] biteth like a serpent

Isa 2:2 in the ***l*** days...LORD'S house shall be established

Isa 44:6 I [God] am the first, and I am the ***l***

Matt 20:8 give them [the laborers] their hire...from the ***l*** unto the first

Mark 9:35 desire to be first, the same shall be ***l***

Mark 10:31 many that are first shall be ***l***

1 Cor 15:26 The ***l*** enemy... destroyed is death

1 Cor 15:45 the ***l*** Adam was made a quickening spirit

2 Tim 3:1 in the ***l*** days perilous times shall come

Heb 1:2 Hath in these ***l*** days spoken...by his [God's] Son

Rev 1:11 I [Jesus] am Alpha and Omega, the first and the ***l***

Rev 22:13 I [Jesus] am...the first and the ***l***

LAWFUL [LY]

Matt 12:2 thy [Jesus'] disciples do that which is not ***l***... upon the sabbath day

Matt 19:3 Is it ***l*** for a man to put away his wife

Mark 3:4 Is it ***l*** to do good on the sabbath...or...evil

Mark 12:14 Is it ***l*** to give tribute to Caesar

1 Cor 6:12 All things are ***l*** unto me [Paul], but all things are not expedient

1 Tim 1:8 the law is good, if a man use it ***l'ly***

LAWLESS

1 Tim 1:9 law is...made...for the ***l*** and disobedient

LAY [ETH, ING]

Ps 71:10 they that ***l*** wait for my soul take counsel

Prov 10:14 Wise men ***l*** up knowledge

Isa 28:16 I [God] ***l*** in Zion for a foundation...a tried stone

Jer 6:21 Behold, I [God] will ***l*** stumblingblocks before this people

Ezek 25:17 know that I am the LORD, when I shall ***l*** my vengeance upon them

Matt 6:20 ***l*** up for yourselves treasures in heaven

Matt 28:6 Come, see the place where the Lord ***l***

Luke 9:58 Son of man hath not where to ***l*** his head

Luke 12:21 he that ***l'eth*** up treasure...not rich toward God

Luke 21:12 ***l*** their hands on you [the disciples], and persecute you

John 10:15 I [Jesus] ***l*** down my life for the sheep

John 13:37 Peter said...Lord... I will ***l*** down my life for thy [Jesus'] sake

John 15:13 that a man ***l*** down his life for his friends

1 Cor 3:11 can no man ***l*** than that is laid...Jesus Christ

1 Cor 16:2 ***l*** by him in store, as God hath prospered

1 Tim 4:14 with the ***l'ing*** on of the hands of the presbytery

1 Tim 5:22 **L** hands suddenly on no man

Heb 12:1 ***l*** aside...the sin which doth...beset us

1 Pet 2:1 ***l'ing*** aside all malice, and all guile

LAZARUS (the brother of Mary and Martha whom Jesus raised from the dead). **John 11:1–44;** 12:1–11.

LEAD [ETH]

Ex 13:21 LORD went before them [Israelites]...to ***l*** them

Ps 23:2 he [God] ***l'eth*** me beside the still waters

Ps 25:5 **L** me in thy [God's] truth, and teach me

Ps 61:2 ***l*** me to the rock that is higher than I

Ps 139:10 Even there shall thy [God's] hand ***l*** me

Isa 11:6 and a little child shall ***l*** them

Isa 40:11 He [God]...shall gently ***l*** those...with young

Matt 6:13 ***l*** us not into temptation...deliver us from evil

Matt 7:14 narrow is the way, which ***l'eth*** unto life

Luke 6:39 he [Jesus] spake a parable...Can...blind ***l***... blind

Rev 7:17 Lamb...shall ***l*** them unto living...waters

LEAH (a wife of Jacob who gave birth to several of his children). **Gen 29:16–35; 30:9–20;** 31:4,14; 33:1–7; 34:1; 35:23; 46:15,18; 49:31.

LEARN [ED, ING]

Ps 119:73 understanding, that I may ***l*** thy [God's] commandments

Prov 1:5 A wise man...will increase ***l'ing***

Isa 1:17 ***L*** to do well...relieve the oppressed

Jer 10:2 Thus saith the LORD, ***L*** not the way of the heathen

Dan 1:17 God gave them [Daniel and his friends]...skill in all ***l'ing*** and wisdom

Matt 11:29 Take my [Jesus'] yoke...and ***l*** of me

Phil 4:11 I [Paul] have ***l'ed,*** in whatsoever state I am, therewith to be content

2 Tim 3:7 ***l'ing,*** and never able to come to the...truth

Heb 5:8 Though he [Jesus] were a Son, yet ***l'ed*** he obedience

LEAST

Matt 2:6 Bethlehem, in the land of Juda, art not the ***l*** among the princes of Juda

Matt 25:40 as ye have done it unto one of the ***l*** of these my [Jesus'] brethren

Luke 7:28 he that is ***l*** in the kingdom...is greater than he [John the Baptist]

Luke 9:48 ***l*** among you all, the same shall be great

Eph 3:8 Unto me [Paul], who am less than the ***l*** of all saints

LEAVEN

Matt 13:33 kingdom of heaven is like unto ***l***

Luke 12:1 Beware ye of the ***l*** of the Pharisees

1 Cor 5:6 a little ***l*** leaveneth the whole lump

LEBANON (a rugged mountainous region in northern Palestine). Deut 1:7; 3:25 • Josh 11:16–17; 12:7; 13:5–7 • Judg 3:1–3 • 1 Kgs 5:5–18 • Isa 29:17; 37:24 • Ezek 17:3 • Hos 14:5–7.

LEBBAEUS. See *Judas.*

LED

Ps 68:18 Thou hast ascended on high...***l*** captivity captive

Prov 4:11 I have taught thee... ***l*** thee in right paths

Isa 55:12 go out with joy, and be ***l*** forth with peace

Luke 4:1 Jesus...was ***l*** by the Spirit into the wilderness

Luke 24:50 he [Jesus] ***l*** them out as far as to Bethany

Acts 8:32 He [Jesus] was ***l*** as a sheep to the slaughter

Acts 9:8 ***l*** him [Paul] by the hand...into Damascus
Rom 8:14 ***l*** by the Spirit of God...are the sons of God
Gal 5:18 if ye be ***l*** of the Spirit...not under the law
2 Pet 3:17 lest ye also, being ***l*** away with the error of the wicked, fall

LEHI (a site where Samson killed one thousand Philistines). Judg 15:9–15.

LEMUEL (an unknown king mentioned in the Book of Proverbs). Prov 31:1–31.

LEPER [S]
2 Kgs 5:1 Naaman...was also a mighty man...but he was a ***l***
2 Kgs 15:5 the king [Azariah]...was a ***l*** unto...his death
Matt 8:2 there came a ***l*** and worshipped him [Jesus]
Matt 11:5 ***l's*** are cleansed, and the deaf hear
Mark 14:3 in...house of Simon the ***l,*** as he [Jesus] sat at meat
Luke 17:12 there met him [Jesus] ten men that were ***l's***

LEVI

1. A son of Jacob and ancestor of the Levites. Gen 29:34; 34:25,30; 35:23; 49:5 • Ex 1:2; 6:16 • Num 3:17; 16:1; 26:59 • 1 Chr 6:38,43,47 • Ezra 8:18. The tribe of Levi, known as the Levites, were responsible for taking care of the tabernacle and temple and assisting the priests in their ceremonial duties. Num 3:5–8.

2. Another name for Matthew. See *Matthew.*

LEVITICUS, BOOK OF. An Old Testament book filled with instructions about sanctification of the priests, regulations for worship and ceremonial offerings, and personal purification and dietary laws. The theme of the book is holiness.

LIAR [S]
Ps 116:11 I said in my haste, All men are ***l's***
Prov 19:22 a poor man is better than a ***l***
Rom 3:4 let God be true, but every man a ***l***
Titus 1:12 The Cretians are alway ***l's,*** evil beasts
1 John 1:10 that we have not sinned...make him [God] a ***l***
1 John 4:20 say, I love God...hateth his brother, he is a ***l***

LIBERTY
Lev 25:10 hallow the fiftieth year, and proclaim ***l***
Ps 119:45 walk at ***l:*** for I seek thy [God's] precepts
Isa 61:1 sent me [God's servant]...to proclaim ***l*** to the captives

Luke 4:18 to set at ***l*** them that are bruised
Acts 26:32 This man [Paul] might have been set at ***l***
1 Cor 8:9 lest...this ***l*** of yours become a stumblingblock
2 Cor 3:17 where the Spirit of the Lord is, there is ***l***
Gal 5:1 Stand fast therefore in the ***l*** wherewith Christ hath made us free
2 Pet 2:19 While they promise them ***l,*** they...are the servants of corruption

LIBYA (Greek name for Africa). Jer 46:9 • Ezek 30:5; 38:5 • Dan 11:43 • Acts 2:10. *Lubim:* Nah 3:9. *Phut:* Ezek 27:10.

LIE [S, ST, TH]
Lev 19:11 not steal...neither ***l*** one to another
Num 23:19 God is not a man, that he should ***l***
Job 13:4 forgers of ***l's***...physicians of no value
Ps 23:2 He [God] maketh me to ***l*** down in green pastures
Ps 58:3 the wicked...go astray ...speaking ***l's***
Ps 62:9 men of high degree are a ***l:*** to be laid in the balance
Prov 3:24 When thou ***l'st*** down, thou shalt not be afraid... sleep shall be sweet
Prov 14:5 A faithful witness will not ***l***
Prov 14:25 but a deceitful witness speaketh ***l's***
Isa 11:6 and the leopard shall ***l*** down with the kid
Ezek 34:15 I [God] will feed my flock, and I will cause them to ***l*** down
Nah 3:1 Woe to the bloody city... full of ***l's*** and robbery
Zeph 3:13 remnant of Israel shall not...speak ***l's***
Mark 5:23 My [Jairus's]... daughter ***l'th*** at the point of death
Acts 5:3 Ananias, why hath Satan filled thine heart to ***l***
Rom 1:25 changed the truth of God into a ***l***
Rom 12:18 as much as ***l'th*** in you, live peaceably
1 John 1:6 say that we have fellowship with him [God], and walk in darkness, we ***l***

LIFE
Gen 2:7 And the LORD God... breathed into his [man's] nostrils the breath of ***l***
Deut 19:21 ***l*** shall go for ***l,*** eye for eye, tooth for tooth
Josh 1:5 not any man...stand before thee [Joshua] all the days of thy ***l***
Job 2:6 he [Job] is in thine [Satan's] hand; but save his ***l***
Job 36:6 He [God] preserveth not the ***l*** of the wicked
Ps 23:6 mercy shall follow me all the days of my ***l***

Ps 27:1 LORD is the strength of my ***l;*** of whom...be afraid
Ps 31:10 ***l*** is spent with grief, and my years with sighing
Ps 38:12 They...that seek after my ***l*** lay snares for me
Prov 4:23 Keep thy heart...for out of it are the issues of ***l***
Prov 8:35 For whoso findeth me findeth ***l***
Prov 18:21 Death and ***l*** are in the...tongue
Jer 21:8 I [God] set before you... ***l,*** and...death
Matt 6:25 no thought for your ***l,*** what ye shall eat
Matt 19:16 what good thing shall I do...have eternal ***l***
Matt 20:28 Even as the Son of man came...to give his ***l*** a ransom for many
Mark 8:35 whosoever will save his ***l*** shall lose it
Luke 12:15 man's ***l*** consisteth not in the abundance of the things...he possesseth
John 1:4 In him [Jesus] was ***l***... the light of men
John 3:15 whosoever believeth ...have eternal ***l***
John 3:36 He that believeth on the Son hath everlasting ***l***
John 6:35 I [Jesus] am the bread of ***l***
John 6:47 He that believeth on me [Jesus] hath everlasting ***l***
John 10:10 I [Jesus] am come that they might have ***l***
John 10:15 and I [Jesus] lay down my ***l*** for the sheep
John 11:25 I [Jesus] am the resurrection, and the ***l***
John 14:6 I [Jesus] am the way, the truth, and the ***l***
John 15:13 that a man lay down his ***l*** for his friends
Rom 6:23 gift of God is eternal ***l*** through Jesus Christ
Rom 8:38 death, nor ***l,*** nor angels, nor principalities
1 Cor 15:19 in this ***l*** only we have hope in Christ, we are...most miserable
Phil 2:16 Holding forth the word of ***l***
Jas 4:14 what is your ***l?*** It is even a vapour, that... vanisheth away
1 John 2:25 this is the promise ...even eternal ***l***
1 John 3:14 passed from death unto ***l***...we love the brethren
1 John 5:12 He that hath the Son hath ***l***
Rev 20:15 not found written in the book of ***l*** was cast into the lake of fire
Rev 22:17 let him take the water of ***l*** freely

LIGHT [S]

Gen 1:3 God said, Let there be ***l:*** and there was ***l***
Gen 1:16 two great ***l's;*** the greater ***l*** to rule the day
Ps 27:1 The LORD is my ***l*** and my salvation
Ps 119:105 Thy [God's] word is...a ***l*** unto my path

Prov 4:18 path of the just is as the shining ***l***
Isa 2:5 come ye, and let us walk in the ***l*** of the LORD
Isa 9:2 people...in darkness have seen a great ***l***
Isa 60:1 Arise, shine; for thy ***l*** is come
Isa 60:3 Gentiles shall come to thy [God's] ***l***
Amos 5:18 day of the LORD is darkness, and not ***l***
Matt 5:14 Ye are the ***l*** of the world
Matt 11:30 my [Jesus'] yoke is easy, and my burden is ***l***
Luke 2:32 A ***l*** to lighten the Gentiles...glory of...Israel
Luke 16:8 children of this world are...wiser than the children of ***l***
John 1:4 In him [Jesus] was life...life was the ***l*** of men
John 1:9 That was the true ***L*** [Jesus]
John 8:12 I [Jesus] am the ***l*** of the world
Acts 9:3 shined round about him [Paul] a ***l*** from heaven
Acts 13:47 set thee [Paul] to be a ***l*** of the Gentiles
Acts 26:18 turn them from darkness to ***l***
Rom 13:12 and let us put on the armour of ***l***
Phil 2:15 midst of...perverse nation...ye shine as ***l's***
Jas 1:17 Every good gift...is... from the Father of ***l's***
1 Pet 2:9 who [Jesus] hath called you...into his marvellous ***l***
1 John 1:5 God is ***l***, and in him is no darkness
1 John 2:10 He that loveth his brother abideth in the ***l***

LIGHT OF THE WORLD, JESUS AS. See *"I Am" Statements of Jesus.*

LIKENESS
Gen 1:26 make man in our image, after our ***l***
Ezek 10:10 four had one ***l***, as if a wheel had been in the midst of a wheel
Phil 2:7 took upon him [Jesus] ...form of a servant...made in the ***l*** of men

LIVE [ING, S, TH]
Gen 2:7 and man became a ***l'ing*** soul
Gen 45:7 God sent me [Joseph] ...to save your ***l's***
Deut 8:3 that man doth not ***l*** by bread only
Job 14:14 If a man die, shall he ***l*** again
Job 19:25 I [Job] know that my redeemer ***l'th***
Ps 63:4 Thus will I bless thee [God] while I ***l***
Ps 142:5 Thou [God] art my refuge and my portion in the land of the ***l'ing***
Jer 2:13 forsaken me [God] the fountain of ***l'ing*** waters

Ezek 37:3 Son of man, can these bones ***l***

Dan 6:26 men tremble and fear before the God of Daniel...the ***l'ing*** God

Jon 4:3 better for me [Jonah] to die than to ***l***

Hab 2:4 but the just shall ***l*** by his faith

Matt 4:4 Man shall not ***l*** by bread alone

Mark 12:27 not the God of the dead, but...of the ***l'ing***

Mark 12:44 she [a widow]... cast in...all her ***l'ing***

Luke 9:56 Son of man is not come to destroy men's ***l's,*** but to save them

Luke 15:13 younger son... wasted his substance with riotous ***l'ing***

Luke 24:5 Why seek...the ***l'ing*** among the dead

John 4:10 he [Jesus] would have given...***l'ing*** water

John 6:51 I [Jesus] am the ***l'ing*** bread

John 11:25 believeth in me [Jesus], though he were dead, yet shall he ***l***

John 11:26 ***l'th***...in me [Jesus] shall never die

Acts 17:28 in him [Jesus] we ***l,*** and move...have our being

Rom 12:1 present your bodies a ***l'ing*** sacrifice

Rom 12:18 If it be possible...***l*** peaceably with all men

Rom 14:7 none...***l'th*** to himself ...no man dieth to himself

Rom 14:8 whether we ***l***...or die, we are the Lord's

1 Cor 9:14 preach the gospel should ***l*** of the gospel

Gal 2:14 why compellest thou [Peter] the Gentiles to ***l*** as do the Jews

Gal 2:19 I [Paul]...am dead to the law...might ***l*** unto God

Gal 2:20 I [Paul] ***l;*** yet not I, but Christ ***l'th*** in me

Gal 5:25 ***l*** in the Spirit, let us also walk in the Spirit

Phil 1:21 to me [Paul] to ***l*** is Christ, and to die is gain

1 John 3:16 we ought to lay down our ***l's*** for the brethren

1 John 4:9 God sent his...Son... we might ***l*** through him

Rev 1:18 I am he [Jesus] that ***l'th,*** and was dead

LIVELY

Ps 38:19 mine enemies are ***l,*** and they are strong

1 Pet 1:3 a ***l*** hope by the resurrection of Jesus Christ

1 Pet 2:5 Ye also, as ***l*** stones, are built up a spiritual house

LIVING GOD

Josh 3:10 ye shall know that the ***l-G*** is among you

Ps 42:2 My soul thirsteth for God, for the ***l-G***

Jer 10:10 he [God] is the ***l-G,*** and an everlasting king

Dan 6:20 O Daniel, servant of the ***l-G***

Matt 16:16 Peter...said, Thou art the Christ...Son of the ***l-G***
John 6:69 we [the disciples] believe and are sure…thou art...the Son of the ***l-G***
2 Cor 6:16 for ye are the temple of the ***l-G***
1 Tim 3:15 church of the ***l-G,*** the...ground of the truth
Heb 10:31 a fearful thing to fall into the hands of the ***l-G***

LO-AMMI (a symbolic name for Hosea's son, meaning "not my people," and signifying God's rejection of Israel). Hos 1:8–9.

LOD. See *Lydda.*

LONGSUFFERING
Ps 86:15 But thou, O Lord, art...gracious, ***l***
Gal 5:22 fruit of the Spirit is love...***l,*** gentleness
2 Pet 3:9 Lord is...***l*** to us-ward, not willing that any should perish

LORD IS GOOD
Ps 34:8 O taste and see that the ***L-i-g***
Ps 100:5 the ***L-i-g;*** his mercy is everlasting
Lam 3:25 The ***L-i-g*** unto them that wait for him
Nah 1:7 The ***L-i-g,*** a strong hold in the day of trouble

LORD WAS WITH HIM
Gen 39:3 his [Joseph's] master saw that the ***L-w-w-h***
1 Sam 3:19 Samuel grew, and the ***L-w-w-h***
1 Sam 18:12 Saul was afraid of David, because the ***L-w-w-h***
1 Sam 18:14 David behaved himself wisely...the ***L-w-w-h***
2 Kgs 18:7 the ***L-w-w-h;*** and he [Hezekiah] prospered
1 Chr 9:20 Phinehas...was the ruler...and the ***L-w-w-h***
Luke 1:66 hand of the ***L-w-w-h*** [John the Baptist]

LORD'S PRAYER. Matt 6:9–13 • Luke 11:1–4.

LORD'S SUPPER. Matt 26: 26–30 • Mark 14:22–26 • Luke 22:14–20 • 1 Cor 11:17–34.

LO-RUHAMAH (a symbolic name for Hosea's daughter, meaning "unloved," and expressing God's displeasure with Israel). Hos 1:6.

LOSE [TH]
Eccl 3:6 A time to get, and a time to ***l***
Matt 10:39 ***l'th*** his life for my [Jesus'] sake shall find it
Mark 8:36 gain the whole world, and ***l*** his own soul
Luke 17:33 Whosoever shall... save his life shall ***l*** it

LOSS
Acts 27:22 no ***l*** of any man's life...but of the ship
1 Cor 3:15 man's work shall be burned, he shall suffer ***l***
Phil 3:7 what things were gain to me [Paul]...I counted ***l***

LOST
Ps 119:176 I have gone astray like a ***l*** sheep
Matt 15:24 I [Jesus] am not sent but unto the ***l*** sheep of the house of Israel
Luke 15:6 I have found my sheep which was ***l***
Luke 19:10 For the Son of man is come to seek and to save that which was ***l***
John 17:12 I [Jesus] have kept, and none of them [the disciples] is ***l***

LOT (Abraham's nephew who escaped the destruction of Sodom). Gen 11:27,31; 12:4–5; 13:1–14; 14:12–16; **19:1–29** • Deut 2:9,19 • Ps 83:8 • Luke 17:28–29 • 2 Pet 2:7.

LOT'S WIFE TURNED INTO A PILLAR OF SALT. Gen 19:26.

LOVE [D, ING, LY, ST, TH]
Gen 29:20 unto him [Jacob] but a few days, for the ***l*** he had to her [Rachel]
Gen 37:3 Israel ***l'd*** Joseph more than all his children
Lev 19:18 ***l*** thy neighbour as thyself: I am the LORD
Deut 6:5 ***l*** the LORD thy God with all thine heart
Josh 23:11 Take good heed... that ye ***l*** the LORD your God
Job 19:19 they whom I [Job] ***l'd*** are turned against me
Ps 87:2 The LORD ***l'th*** the gates of Zion
Ps 116:1 I ***l*** the LORD, because he hath heard my voice
Ps 119:97 O how ***l*** I thy [God's] law
Prov 3:12 whom the LORD ***l'th*** he correcteth
Prov 7:18 take our fill of ***l*** until the morning
Prov 10:12 Hatred stirreth up strifes: but ***l*** covereth all sins
Prov 17:17 A friend ***l'th*** at all times
Prov 22:1 good name...to be chosen than great riches... ***l'ing*** favour rather than silver
Eccl 3:8 A time to ***l***, and a time to hate
Eccl 9:9 Live joyfully with the wife whom thou ***l'st***
Song 2:4 his [God's] banner over me was ***l***
Song 8:7 Many waters cannot quench ***l***
Jer 31:3 I [God] have ***l'd*** thee with an everlasting ***l***
Hos 11:4 I [God] drew them with...bands of ***l***
Mic 6:8 what doth the LORD require...but to...***l*** mercy

Matt 5:44 ***L*** your enemies, bless them that curse you

Matt 10:37 ***l'th*** father or mother more than me [Jesus] is not worthy of me

Matt 22:39 Thou shalt ***l*** thy neighbour as thyself

Luke 16:13 he will hate the one, and ***l*** the other

John 3:16 God so ***l'd*** the world... gave his only...Son

John 13:34 ***l*** one another; as I [Jesus] have ***l'd*** you

John 14:15 If ye ***l*** me [Jesus], keep my commandments

John 15:9 Father hath ***l'd*** me [Jesus], so have I ***l'd*** you

John 21:15 Simon...***l'st*** thou me [Jesus] more than these

Rom 5:8 God commendeth his ***l*** toward us

Rom 8:28 we know that all things work together for good to them that ***l*** God

Rom 8:37 we are more than conquerors through him [Jesus] that ***l'd*** us

1 Cor 2:9 the things which God hath prepared for them that ***l*** him

2 Cor 5:14 the ***l*** of Christ constraineth us

2 Cor 9:7 for God ***l'th*** a cheerful giver

Gal 2:20 live by...faith of...Son of God, who ***l'd*** me [Paul]

Gal 5:22 But the fruit of the Spirit is ***l,*** joy, peace

Eph 3:19 ***l*** of Christ, which passeth knowledge

Eph 4:15 speaking the truth in ***l***...grow up into him [Jesus]

Eph 5:2 walk in ***l,*** as Christ also hath ***l'd*** us

Eph 5:25 Husbands, ***l*** your wives, even as Christ also ***l'd*** the church

Phil 1:9 that your ***l*** may abound yet more and more

Phil 4:8 whatsoever things are ***l'ly***...of good report

1 Tim 6:10 ***l*** of money is the root of all evil

2 Tim 1:7 God hath not given us the spirit of fear; but...***l***

Heb 12:6 whom the Lord ***l'th*** he chasteneth

Jas 1:12 receive the crown of life...promised to them that ***l*** him [Jesus]

1 John 2:10 He that ***l'th*** his brother abideth in the light

1 John 2:15 any man ***l*** the world, the ***l*** of the Father is not in him

1 John 3:14 He that ***l'th*** not his brother abideth in death

1 John 4:7 every one that ***l'th*** is born of God

1 John 4:10 not that we ***l'd*** God, but that he ***l'd*** us

1 John 4:16 he that dwelleth in ***l*** dwelleth in God

1 John 4:19 We ***l*** him [Jesus], because he first ***l'd*** us

1 John 4:20 how can he ***l*** God whom he hath not seen

1 John 5:3 this is the ***l*** of God ...keep his commandments
Rev 2:4 thou [the church at Ephesus] hast left thy first ***l***

LOVE CHAPTER OF THE BIBLE. 1 Cor 13.

LOVE OF GOD
Rom 5:5 the ***l-o-G*** is shed abroad in our hearts
Rom 8:39 height, nor depth... shall...separate us from the ***l-o-G***...in Christ
1 John 3:16 perceive we the ***l-o-G***, because he [Jesus] laid down his life for us
1 John 4:9 In this [God's Son] was manifested the ***l-o-G*** toward us

LOVE ONE ANOTHER
John 13:34 That ye ***l-o-a;*** as I [Jesus] have loved you
Rom 13:8 Owe no man any thing, but to ***l-o-a***
1 John 3:11 the message...ye heard...we should ***l-o-a***
1 John 4:7 Beloved, let us ***l-o-a:*** for love is of God

LOVE THY NEIGHBOUR
Matt 5:43 it hath been said, Thou shalt ***l-t-n,*** and hate thine enemy
Matt 19:19 Thou shalt ***l-t-n*** as thyself
Matt 22:39 second is like unto it, Thou shalt ***l-t-n*** as thyself
Mark 12:31 ***l-t-n*** as thyself. There is none other commandment greater
Rom 13:9 any other commandment...namely, Thou shalt ***l-t-n*** as thyself
Gal 5:14 all the law is fulfilled in one word...***l-t-n*** as thyself
Jas 2:8 fulfil the royal law... Thou shalt ***l-t-n*** as thyself

LOVINGKINDNESS
Ps 36:7 How excellent is thy ***l,*** O God
Ps 63:3 thy [God's] ***l*** is better than life, my lips...praise thee
Ps 92:2 To show forth thy [God's] ***l*** in the morning
Jer 9:24 I am the LORD which exercise ***l,*** judgment

LUBIM. See *Libya.*

LUCAS. See *Luke.*

LUCIFER. See *Satan.*

LUDIM (a people descended from Mizraim, a son of Ham). Gen 10:13 • 1 Chr 1:11.

LUKE (a believer of Gentile descent, apparently a physician, who accompanied Paul on some of his missionary journeys and author of the Gospel that bears his name, as well as the Book of Acts). Col 4:14 • 2 Tim 4:11. *Lucas:* Phlm 24.

LUKE, GOSPEL OF. One of the four Gospels which portrays Jesus as the Savior of all people, Gentiles as well as Jews. Luke shows that Jesus associated with all types of people, including sinners (5:30; 15:2), the poor and outcasts (6:20–23; 16:19–31), and the Samaritans (17:11–19).

LUST [S]

Matt 5:28 whosoever looketh on a woman to ***l*** after her

Mark 4:19 the ***l's***...entering in, choke the word

Rom 1:24 God...gave them up to uncleanness through the ***l's*** of their own hearts

Gal 5:16 Walk in the Spirit... not fulfil the ***l*** of the flesh

Jas 4:3 that ye may consume it upon your ***l's***

1 John 2:16 the ***l*** of the eyes, and the pride of life

LUZ. See *Bethel.*

LYCAONIA (a Roman province of Asia Minor visited by Paul). Acts 14:1–6,11.

LYCIA (a province of Asia Minor visited by Paul). Acts 27:5.

LYDDA (a town where Peter healed a lame man). Acts 9:32–35. *Lod:* 1 Chr 8:12 • Ezra 2:33 • Neh 7:37; 11:35.

LYDIA (a businesswoman converted under Paul's ministry at Philippi). Acts 16:14–15,40.

LYSANIAS (governor of Abilene, a region in Syria, when John the Baptist began his ministry). Luke 3:1.

LYSTRA (a city in Asia Minor where Paul was stoned by unbelieving Jews). **Acts 14: 6–20;** 16:1–2 • 2 Tim 3:11.

-M-

MACEDONIA (a mountainous country north of Greece and the first European territory visited by the apostle Paul). **Acts 16:9–12;** 18:5; 19:21–29; 20:1–3; 27:2 • Rom 15:26 • 1 Cor 16:5 • 2 Cor 1:16; 2:13; 7:5; 8:1; 9:2–4; 11:9 • Phil 4:15 • 1 Thes 1:7–8; 4:10 • 1 Tim 1:3.

MACHIR (son of Manasseh and ancestor of the Machirites). Gen 50:23 • Num 26:29; 32:39–40 • Judg 5:14.

MACHPELAH (a field with a cave that Abraham bought as a burial ground). **Gen 23:7–19;** 25:9; 49:29–31; 50:13.

MAD [NESS]

1 Sam 21:13 he [David]...feigned himself ***m*** in their hands

Luke 6:11 they [scribes and Pharisees] were filled with ***m'ness***...what they might do to Jesus

John 10:20 He [Jesus] hath a devil, and is ***m***

Acts 26:24 Paul...much learning doth make thee ***m***

MADIAN. See *Midian,* No. 2.

MAGDALA (a city near the Sea of Galilee and probably the home of Mary Magdalene). Matt 15:39; 27:56.

MAGNIFY [IED]

Josh 4:14 LORD ***m'ied*** Joshua in the sight of all Israel

Job 7:17 What is man, that thou [God] shouldest ***m*** him

Ps 34:3 ***m*** the LORD with me

Ps 40:16 The LORD be ***m'ied***

Ps 69:30 I will...***m*** him [God] with thanksgiving

Luke 1:46 Mary said, My soul doth ***m*** the Lord

Phil 1:20 Christ shall be ***m'ied*** in my [Paul's] body

MAHANAIM (a sacred site where Jacob was visited by angels). **Gen 32:1–2** • Josh 13:26–30; 21:38 • 2 Sam 2:8–29; 17:24,27 • 1 Kgs 4:14 • 1 Chr 6:80.

MAHER-SHALAL-HASH-BAZ (a symbolic name for Isaiah's son, meaning "hasten the booty," signifying that Assyria would conquer Israel and Syria). Isa 8:1–4.

MALACHI (a prophet after the Exile and author of the book that bears his name). Mal 1:1.

MALACHI, BOOK OF. A short prophetic book of the Old Testament written after the Exile and directed against the shallow worship practices of the Jewish people.

MALCHI-SHUA (a son of King Saul who was killed by the Philistines at Gilboa). 1 Chr 10:2. *Melchi-shua:* 1 Sam 14:49.

MALCHUS (a servant whose ear was cut off by Peter). John 18:10–11.

MALE

Gen 1:27 ***m*** and female created he [God] them

Mark 10:6 from the beginning of the creation God made them ***m*** and female

Luke 2:23 Every ***m***...shall be called holy to the Lord

Gal 3:28 neither ***m*** nor female... all one in Christ Jesus

MALICE

Eph 4:31 Let all bitterness, and wrath, and anger...be put away from you, with all ***m***

Titus 3:3 living in ***m*** and envy

1 Pet 2:1 Wherefore laying aside all ***m,*** and all guile

MAMRE

1. A town or district near Hebron where Abraham lived. Gen 13:18; 18:1–4; 23:17–19; 25:9; 35:27; 49:30; 50:13.

2. An Amorite supporter of Abraham. Gen 14:13,24.

MANASSEH

1. A son of Joseph and ancestor of one of the twelve tribes of Israel. Gen 41:51; 46:20; 48:1–20; 50:23 • Num 26:28–29; 27:1; 32:39–41; 36:1 • Deut 3:12–15 • Josh 13:31; 17:1–3 • 1 Kgs 4:13 • 1 Chr 7:14,17. *Manasses:* Rev 7:6. The tribe of Manasseh settled in central and northern Canaan on both sides of the Jordan River. Josh 17:1–17.

2. A king of Judah who encouraged pagan worship among the people. **2 Kgs 21:1–16** • 2 Chr 33:1–20.

MANASSES. See *Manasseh.*

MANIFEST [ED]

Mark 4:22 nothing hid, which shall not be ***m'ed***

Luke 8:17 nothing is secret, that shall not be made ***m***

John 9:3 that the works of God should be made ***m*** in him

1 Cor 3:13 Every man's work shall be made ***m***

2 Cor 4:10 life also of Jesus might be made ***m*** in our body

1 Tim 3:16 God was ***m*** in the flesh, justified in the Spirit

1 John 3:8 For this purpose the Son of God was ***m'ed***

1 John 4:9 In this [Jesus' death]...***m'ed*** the love of God

Rev 15:4 thy [God's] judgments are made ***m***

MANKIND
1 Cor 6:9 unrighteous shall not inherit...nor abusers of themselves with ***m***
Jas 3:7 every kind of beasts... hath been tamed of ***m***

MANNA PROVIDED FOR ISRAEL IN THE WILDERNESS. Ex 16:13–31.

MARA (a name, meaning "bitter," which signified Naomi's sorrow). Ruth 1:3–21.

MARAN-ATHA (an Aramaic phrase, meaning "come, O Lord," which expresses hope for the second coming of Jesus). 1 Cor 16:22.

MARCUS. See *Mark.*

MARK (a believer and author of the Gospel that bears his name who accompanied Paul and Barnabas on the first missionary journey as far as Perga and then returned to Jerusalem). Acts 12:12; **13:13;** 15:36–41 • 2 Tim 4:11. *Marcus:* 1 Pet 5:13.

MARK, GOSPEL OF. One of the four Gospels and probably the first to be written. Mark portrays Jesus as a person of action. He also emphasizes the humanity of Jesus, including incidents which reveal His disappointment (8:12), anger (11:15–17), sorrow (14:34), and fatigue (4:38).

MARRIAGE
Matt 22:2 a certain king, which made a ***m*** for his son
Mark 12:25 neither marry, nor are given in ***m***
John 2:1 there was a ***m*** in Cana of Galilee
Heb 13:4 ***M*** is honourable in all...the bed undefiled
Rev 19:9 called unto the ***m*** supper of the Lamb

MARRY [IED, IETH]
Jer 3:14 Turn...for I [God] am ***m'ied*** unto you
Matt 5:32 shall ***m*** her that is divorced committeth adultery
Mark 10:11 Whosoever...put away his wife, and ***m*** another, committeth adultery
Luke 14:20 ***m'ied*** a wife, and therefore I cannot come
Luke 16:18 putteth away his wife, and ***m'ieth*** another, committeth adultery
1 Cor 7:9 let them ***m***...it is better to ***m*** than to burn
1 Cor 7:33 he that is ***m'ied*** careth for...things...of... world
1 Tim 5:14 that the younger women ***m,*** bear children, guide the house

MARTHA (the sister of Mary and Lazarus whom Jesus

rebuked because of her excessive worry about domestic duties). **Luke 10:38–42** • John 11:1–39; 12:2.

MARVEL [LED]

Matt 8:10 he [Jesus] ***m'led***...I have not found so great faith
Matt 8:27 ***m'led,*** saying, What manner of man [Jesus] is this
Matt 21:20 they [the disciples] ***m'led,*** saying, How soon is the fig tree withered
Mark 6:6 he [Jesus] ***m'led*** because of their unbelief
Mark 15:44 Pilate ***m'led*** if he [Jesus] were already dead
Luke 2:33 Joseph and his mother ***m'led*** at those things...spoken of him [Jesus]
John 3:7 ***M*** not that I [Jesus] said...Ye [Nicodemus] must be born again
John 7:15 Jews ***m'led***...How knoweth this man [Jesus] letters
Acts 4:13 they [religious leaders] ***m'led***...they [Peter and John] had been with Jesus
Gal 1:6 I [Paul] ***m*** that ye are...removed from him [Jesus] that called you
1 John 3:13 ***M*** not, my brethren, if the world hate you

MARVELLOUS

1 Chr 16:24 Declare his [God's] glory...his ***m*** works among all nations
Ps 31:21 he [God] hath showed me his ***m*** kindness
Ps 98:1 for he [God] hath done ***m*** things
Ps 139:14 I will praise thee [God]...***m*** are thy works
1 Pet 2:9 him [Jesus] who hath called you out of darkness into his ***m*** light
Rev 15:3 Great and ***m*** are thy works, Lord...Almighty

MARY

1. Earthly mother of Jesus. Matt 1:16,18,20; 2:11 • Mark 6:3 • **Luke 1:26–56;** 2:5,16,19, 34 • Acts 1:14.

2. A woman, called Mary Magdalene, who witnessed the crucifixion of Jesus and visited the empty tomb. **Matt 27:56,61;** 28:1 • Mark 15:40,47; 16:9 • Luke 8:2; 24:10 • John 19:25; **20:1–18.**

3. Sister of Martha and Lazarus. Luke 10:39,42 • John 11:1–45; 12:3.

MATHUSALA. See *Methuselah.*

MATTANIAH. See *Zedekiah.*

MATTHEW (a tax collector who became a disciple of Jesus and author of the Gospel that bears his name). Matt 9:9; 10:3 • Mark 3:18 • Luke 6:15 • Acts 1:13. *Levi:* Mark 2:13–17 • Luke 5:27–32.

MATTHEW, GOSPEL OF. One of the four Gospels written to show the Jewish people that Jesus was the Messiah promised in the Old Testament. Matthew's Gospel also emphasizes the teaching ministry of Jesus, particularly His instructions to His disciples in the Sermon on the Mount (5:1–7:29).

MATTHIAS (the person who replaced Judas as an apostle). Acts 1:15–26.

MEASURE [D, ING, S]

Deut 25:14 not have...divers ***m's,*** a great and a small

Deut 25:15 a perfect and just ***m*** shalt thou have

Job 38:5 Who hath laid the ***m's*** thereof, if thou knowest

Ps 39:4 LORD, make me to know...the ***m*** of my days

Isa 40:12 Who [God]...***m'd*** the waters...hollow of his hand

Ezek 40:3 a man...with a line of flax...and a ***m'ing*** reed

Hos 1:10 Israel shall be as the sand of the sea...cannot be ***m'd***

Mark 4:24 with what ***m*** ye mete, it shall be ***m'd*** to you

Luke 13:21 like leaven, which a woman took and hid in three ***m's*** of meal

2 Cor 11:23 in stripes above ***m,*** in prisons more frequent

Gal 1:13 beyond ***m*** I [Paul] persecuted the church

Eph 4:7 grace according to the ***m*** of the gift of Christ

Eph 4:13 all come...unto the ***m***... of the fulness of Christ

Rev 6:6 I [John] heard a voice... ***m*** of wheat for a penny

MEDES (descendants of Japheth who founded an ancient kingdom between the Tigris River and the Caspian Sea). Gen 10:2 • 2 Kgs 17:6 • Esth 1:3,19 • Isa 13:17 • Dan 5:30–31; 6:1–28 • Acts 2:9.

MEDIATOR

1 Tim 2:5 one God, and one ***m*** between God and men

Heb 8:6 he [Jesus] is the ***m*** of a better covenant

Heb 9:15 he [Jesus] is the ***m*** of the new testament

MEDITATE

Ps 1:2 in his [God's] law doth he ***m*** day and night

Ps 119:15 I will ***m*** in thy [God's] precepts

Ps 143:5 I ***m*** on all thy [God's] works

Luke 21:14 not to ***m*** before what ye shall answer

1 Tim 4:15 ***M*** upon these things; give thyself...to them

MEDITERRANEAN SEA. See *Great Sea*.

MEEK [NESS]
Num 12:3 the man Moses was very ***m,*** above all the men
Ps 37:11 But the ***m*** shall inherit the earth
Ps 147:6 LORD lifteth up the ***m***...casteth...wicked down
Isa 61:1 to preach good tidings unto the ***m***
Matt 5:5 Blessed are the ***m***... they shall inherit the earth
Matt 11:29 I [Jesus] am ***m*** and lowly in heart
Gal 5:23 ***M'ness,*** temperance: against such there is no law
Gal 6:1 restore...spirit of ***m'ness***...lest thou...be tempted
Col 3:12 Put on...kindness... ***m'ness,*** longsuffering
1 Pet 3:15 be ready always to give an answer...with ***m'ness*** and fear

MEGIDDO (a fortified city in the plain of Jezreel associated with the great battle in the end-time). Josh 12:21; 17:11 • Judg 1:27–28; 5:19–21 • 1 Kgs 4:12; 9:15–27 • 2 Kgs 23:29–30 • Rev 16:16. *Megiddon:* Zech 12:11.

MEGIDDON. See *Megiddo.*

MELCHISEDEC.
See *Melchizedek.*

MELCHI-SHUA. See *Malchi-shua.*

MELCHIZEDEK (king of Salem who received tithes from Abraham). **Gen 14:18–20** • Ps 110:4. *Melchisedec:* Heb 7:11.

MELITA (an island where Paul was shipwrecked while sailing to Rome). Acts 28:1–8.

MEMBER [S]
Job 17:7 eye...is dim...all my ***m's*** are as a shadow
Rom 12:5 So we...are one body in Christ, and every one ***m's*** one of another
1 Cor 6:15 your bodies are the ***m's*** of Christ
1 Cor 12:19 all one ***m,*** where were the body
1 Cor 12:26 one ***m*** suffer, all the ***m's*** suffer
Jas 3:5 tongue is a little ***m,*** and boasteth great things

MEMORIAL SUPPER. See *Jesus, Life and Ministry of; Lord's Supper.*

MENAHEM (a king of Israel who killed Shallum to assume the throne). 2 Kgs 15:14–22.

MEPHIBOSHETH (a son of Jonathan who was honored by King David). 2 Sam 4:4; **9:1–13;** 16:1–4; 19:24–30; 21:7. *Merib-baal:* 1 Chr 8:34.

MERCIFUL

Deut 21:8 Be ***m,*** O LORD, unto thy people Israel

Ps 41:4 I said, LORD, be ***m*** unto me: heal my soul

Ps 67:1 God be ***m*** unto us, and bless us

Ps 103:8 LORD is ***m*** and gracious, slow to anger

Matt 5:7 Blessed are the ***m:*** for they shall obtain mercy

MERCURIUS (Roman name for the pagan god Mercury and the name applied to Paul by the people of Lystra). Acts 14:12.

MERCY [IES]

Gen 39:21 LORD was with Joseph, and showed him ***m***

Ex 20:6 showing ***m*** unto... them that love me [God]

1 Chr 16:34 he [God] is good; for his ***m*** endureth for ever

Ps 6:2 Have ***m*** upon me, O LORD; for I am weak

Ps 13:5 But I have trusted in thy [God's] ***m***

Ps 23:6 ***m*** shall follow me all the days of my life

Ps 25:6 Remember, O LORD, thy tender ***m'ies***

Ps 40:11 Withhold not thou thy [God's] tender ***m'ies***

Ps 85:7 Show us thy ***m,*** O LORD...grant us thy salvation

Ps 94:18 My foot slippeth; thy ***m,*** O LORD, held me up

Ps 103:8 LORD is...slow to anger, and plenteous in ***m***

Ps 103:17 ***m*** of the LORD is from everlasting

Ps 119:77 Let thy [God's] tender ***m'ies*** come unto me

Ps 136:1 give thanks unto the LORD...***m*** endureth for ever

Isa 49:13 the LORD...will have ***m*** upon his afflicted

Hos 6:6 For I [God] desired ***m,*** and not sacrifice

Mic 6:8 LORD require of thee, but to...love ***m***

Matt 23:23 you [Pharisees]... have omitted the weightier matters of the law...***m,*** and faith

Luke 16:24 Abraham, have ***m***...and send Lazarus

Rom 12:1 ***m'ies*** of God...present your bodies a living sacrifice

2 Cor 1:3 Father of ***m'ies,*** and the God of all comfort

Eph 2:4 God, who is rich in ***m***...loved us

Col 3:12 Put on...bowels of ***m'ies,*** kindness

Titus 3:5 according to his [God's] ***m*** he saved us

Heb 4:16 obtain ***m,*** and find grace to help

1 Pet 2:10 had not obtained ***m,*** but now have obtained ***m***

Jude 21 ***m*** of our Lord Jesus Christ unto eternal life

MERIB-BAAL. See *Mephibosheth.*

MERODACH (a pagan Babylonian god of war). Jer 50:2.

MERODACH-BALADAN. See *Berodach-baladan.*

MERRY

Prov 15:13 A ***m*** heart maketh a cheerful countenance
Prov 17:22 A ***m*** heart doeth good like a medicine
Luke 15:23 bring...the fatted calf...let us eat, and be ***m***
Jas 5:13 Is any ***m?*** let him sing psalms

MESHACH (Daniel's friend who was thrown into the fiery furnace for refusing to worship an idol). Dan 1:7; 2:49; **3:13–30.**

MESOPOTAMIA (the territory between the Tigris and Euphrates rivers). Gen 24:10 • Deut 23:4 • Judg 3:8,10 • 1 Chr 19:6 • Acts 2:9; 7:2. *Padan-aram:* Gen 25:20.

MESSENGER

Prov 13:17 A wicked ***m*** falleth into mischief
Mal 3:1 I [God] will send my ***m***...he shall prepare the way
Luke 7:27 I send my [God's] ***m*** before thy face

MESSIANIC PROPHECIES OF THE OLD TESTAMENT AND THEIR FULFILLMENT IN JESUS CHRIST

1. Star out of Jacob (Num 24:17 • Luke 3:34)
2. Of the house of David (Isa 11:1–10 • Matt 1:1)
3. Son of man (Dan 7:13 • Mark 8:38)
4. Named Immanuel (Isa 7:14 • Matt 1:22–23)
5. Chief cornerstone (Ps 118:22 • 1 Pet 2:4,7)
6. A prophet like Moses (Deut 18:15–19 • Mark 6:14–15)
7. Bring in the new covenant (Jer 31:31–34 • Heb 12:24)
8. Call the Gentiles (Isa 11:10 • Rom 15:9–12)
9. Die for mankind's sin (Isa 53:4–6 • 1 Pet 1:18–20)
10. Born of a virgin (Isa 7:14 • Matt 1:18–25)
11. Born at Bethlehem (Mic 5:2 • Luke 2:4–7)
12. Flight into Egypt (Hos 11:1 • Matt 2:13–15)
13. Preceeded by a forerunner (Mal 3:1–2 • Mark 1:1–8)
14. Ministry of miracles (Isa 35:5–6 • Matt 11:4–5)
15. Meek and gentle (Isa 42:1–4 • Matt 12:15–21)
16. Full of wisdom and power (Isa 11:2 • Matt 3:16–17)
17. Anointed to preach God's good news (Isa 61:2–3 • Luke 4:43)

18. Triumphal entry into Jerusalem (Zech 9:9–10 • Matt 21:1–11)

19. Betrayed for thirty pieces of silver (Zech 11:12–13 • Matt 26:14–15)

20. Rejected by His own people (Isa 53:3 • John 1:11)

21. Crucified with criminals (Isa 53:12 • Matt 27:38)

22. Silent before His accusers (Isa 53:7 • Mark 15:4–5)

23. Mocked on the cross (Ps 22:6–8 • Matt 27:39–44)

24. No bones broken (Ps 34:20 • John 19:32–33,36)

25. Died for others (Isa 53:1–12 • 1 Pet 3:18)

26. Buried with the rich (Isa 53:9 • Matt 27:57–60)

27. Ascended to His Father (Ps 68:18 • Eph 4:8–10)

28. Makes intercession for believers (Zech 6:13 • Rom 8:34)

29. Serves as a heavenly high priest (Zech 6:12–13 • Heb 8:1–2)

30. Exalted above all (Ps 2:6–12 • Phil 2:9–11)

METHUSELAH (a son of Enoch who lived to the age of 969, the oldest recorded age in the Bible). **Gen 5:21–27** • 1 Chr 1:3. *Mathusala:* Luke 3:37.

MICAH (a prophet who denounced social injustices and author of the book that bears his name). Jer 26:18 • Mic 1:1.

MICAH, BOOK OF. A short prophetic book of the Old Testament known for its prediction that the Messiah would be born in Bethlehem (5:2).

MICAIAH (a prophet who predicted that King Ahab would be killed). **1 Kgs 22:8–28** • 2 Chr 18:7–27.

MICHAEL (an archangel who was thought to serve as a guardian over Israel). Dan 10:13,21; 12:1 • Jude 9 • Rev 12:7.

MICHAL (a daughter of King Saul and a wife of David). 1 Sam 14:49; 18:20–28; 19:9–17; 25:44 • 2 Sam 3:13–16; 6:16–23.

MIDIAN

1. A son of Abraham and founder of the Midianites. Gen 25:1–4 • 1 Chr 1:32–33.

2. A region in the Arabian desert occupied by the Midianites. Ex 2:15 • Judg 7:8–25; 8:3–28. *Madian:* Acts 7:29.

MIDIANITES (nomadic traders who occupied the land of Midian). Gen 37:28,36 • Num 31:2–7 • Judg 6:2–33; 7:1–25 • Ps 83:9.

MIDNIGHT

Ps 119:62 At ***m*** I will rise to give thanks unto thee [God]

Mark 13:35 know not when the master...cometh, at even, or at ***m***

Acts 16:25 at ***m*** Paul and Silas prayed, and sang praises

MIGHT

Gen 43:32 ***m*** not eat bread with the Hebrews...abomination unto the Egyptians

Deut 6:5 love the LORD thy God...with all thy ***m***

Judg 6:14 Go in this thy [Gideon's] ***m,*** and thou shalt save Israel

2 Sam 6:14 David danced... with all his ***m***

2 Chr 20:6 in thine [God's] hand is...power and ***m***

Job 23:3 Oh that I knew where I ***m*** find him [God]

Ps 119:11 Thy [God's] word have I hid in mine heart, that I ***m*** not sin against thee

Ps 145:6 the ***m*** of thy [God's] terrible acts

Eccl 9:10 hand findeth to do, do it with thy ***m***

Jer 9:1 I [Jeremiah] ***m*** weep day and night for...my people

Jer 9:23 neither let the mighty man glory in his ***m***

Zech 4:6 Not by ***m***...but by my [God's] spirit

Mark 14:35 if...possible, the hour ***m*** pass from him [Jesus]

John 3:17 the world through him [Jesus] ***m*** be saved

John 10:10 I [Jesus] am come that they ***m*** have life

John 20:31 that ye ***m*** believe that Jesus is the Christ

Rom 10:1 my [Paul's]... prayer...for Israel is, that they ***m*** be saved

1 Cor 9:22 all things to all men...I [Paul] ***m***...save some

2 Cor 4:10 life...of Jesus ***m*** be... manifest in our body

2 Cor 8:9 he [Jesus] became poor, that ye through his poverty ***m*** be rich

Gal 4:5 we ***m*** receive the adoption of sons

Eph 6:10 be strong in the Lord, and in the power of his ***m***

1 John 4:9 God sent his...Son... that we ***m*** live through him

MIGHTY

Ex 1:7 children of Israel... waxed exceeding ***m***

Deut 6:21 LORD brought us [Israelites] out...***m*** hand

2 Sam 1:27 How are the ***m*** fallen

1 Chr 11:11 number of the ***m*** men whom David had

Job 12:19 He [God]...overthroweth the ***m***

Job 34:24 He [God] shall break in pieces ***m*** men

Job 36:5 Behold, God...is ***m*** in strength and wisdom

Ps 24:8 LORD strong and ***m,*** the LORD ***m*** in battle

Ps 50:1 The ***m*** God, even the LORD, hath spoken
Ps 89:6 who among the...***m*** can be likened unto the LORD
Ps 150:2 Praise him [God] for his ***m*** acts...his...greatness
Isa 9:6 his [Jesus'] name shall be called...The ***m*** God
Ezek 20:34 I [God]...will gather you...with a ***m*** hand
Amos 5:24 let judgment run down as waters, and righteousness as a ***m*** stream
Matt 13:58 And he [Jesus] did not many ***m*** works... because of their unbelief
Acts 2:2 a sound from heaven as of a rushing ***m*** wind
1 Cor 1:26 not many ***m,*** not many noble, are called
1 Cor 1:27 weak things of the world to confound the...***m***
1 Pet 5:6 Humble yourselves... under the ***m*** hand of God

MILCOM (supreme god of the Ammonites). 1 Kgs 11:5,33 • 2 Kgs 23:13. *Molech:* Lev 20:2. *Moloch:* Acts 7:43.

MILETUS (a city where Paul met the leaders of the Ephesian church). Acts 20:15–38. *Miletum:* 2 Tim 4:20.

MILLO

1. A fortress at Shechem whose occupants proclaimed Abimelech as their king. Judg 9:6,20.

2. A defensive fortress tower built by David near Jerusalem and improved by Solomon. **2 Sam 5:9 • 1 Kgs 9:15,24;** 11:27 • 2 Kgs 12:20 • 1 Chr 11:8 • 2 Chr 32:5.

MIND [S]

Neh 4:6 the people had a ***m*** to work
Prov 29:11 A fool uttereth all his ***m***
Isa 26:3 keep him in perfect peace...***m*** is stayed on thee
Mark 12:30 love the Lord... with all thy ***m***
Luke 8:35 the man [demoniac]... clothed...in his right ***m***
Rom 1:28 God gave them over to a reprobate ***m***
Rom 8:5 they...after the flesh do ***m*** the things of the flesh
Rom 11:34 who hath known the ***m*** of the Lord
Rom 12:2 transformed by the renewing of your ***m***
Eph 4:17 walk not as other Gentiles...vanity of their ***m***
Phil 2:2 the same love, being of one accord, of one ***m***
Phil 2:3 but in lowliness of ***m*** let each esteem other better than themselves
Phil 2:5 this ***m*** be in you, which was also in Christ
Phil 4:7 peace of God...shall keep your hearts and ***m's***
2 Tim 1:7 God hath not given us the spirit of fear; but...of a sound ***m***

Heb 8:10 I [God] will put my laws into their ***m***

1 Pet 1:13 Wherefore gird up the loins of your ***m***

MINDFUL

1 Chr 16:15 Be ye ***m***...of his [God's] covenant

Ps 8:4 What is man, that thou [God] art ***m*** of him

Ps 115:12 LORD hath been ***m*** of us: he will bless us

MINISTER [ED, S]

Ps 9:8 he [God] shall ***m*** judgment to the people

Ps 103:21 Bless ye the LORD... ye ***m's*** of his

Matt 20:28 Son of man came not to be ***m'ed*** unto, but to ***m***

Mark 10:43 great among you, shall be your ***m***

Rom 15:16 I [Paul] should be... ***m*** of Jesus...to the Gentiles

1 Cor 3:5 Who then is Paul... Apollos, but ***m's*** by whom ye believed

2 Cor 11:23 Are they ***m's*** of Christ...I [Paul] am more

Eph 3:7 I [Paul] was made a ***m,*** according to...grace

1 Pet 4:10 even so ***m*** the same one to another

MINISTRY

Acts 6:4 we [the apostles] will give ourselves continually... to the ***m*** of the word

2 Cor 5:18 God...hath given to us the ***m*** of reconciliation

Eph 4:12 perfecting of the saints, for the work of the ***m***

2 Tim 4:5 work of an evangelist, make full proof of thy ***m***

Heb 8:6 now hath he [Jesus] obtained a more excellent ***m***

MIRACLE [S]

Mark 6:52 they [the disciples] considered not the ***m*** of the loaves

John 2:11 This beginning of ***m's*** did Jesus in Cana

John 3:2 no man can do these ***m's*** that thou [Jesus] doest, except God be with him

John 9:16 How can a man that is a sinner do such ***m's***

John 12:37 though he [Jesus] had done so many ***m's***...yet they believed not

Acts 6:8 Stephen...did great wonders and ***m's***

1 Cor 12:10 To another the working of ***m's***

MIRACLES OF JESUS. See *Jesus, Miracles of.*

MIRIAM (a sister of Moses who arranged for their mother Jochebed to care for him). **Ex 2:4–10;** 15:20–21 • Num 12:1–16; 20:1; 26:59 • Deut 24:9 • 1 Chr 6:3 • Mic 6:4.

MIZPAH (a place where Jacob and Laban made a covenant

and agreed to a friendly separation). Gen 31:44–53.

MIZRAIM (a son of Ham whose descendants settled in Egypt). Gen 10:6,13 • 1 Chr 1:8,11.

MNASON (a believer who accompanied Paul on his last visit to Jerusalem). Acts 21:16.

MOAB (a son of Lot and the name of the land inhabited by him and his descendants). Gen 19:33–37 • Num 21:11–29 • Judg 11:15–25 • Ruth 1:1–22 • Jer 48:1–47.

MOABITES (inhabitants of Moab who were pagan worshipers and enemies of the Israelites). Gen 19:37 • Num 22:4 • Deut 2:9,11,29 • Judg 3:28 • 2 Sam 8:2 • 1 Kgs 11:1, 33 • 2 Kgs 3:18,21–24; 23:13; 24:2 • 1 Chr 18:2 • Ezra 9:1.

MOCK [ED, ETH, ING]
1 Kgs 18:27 Elijah ***m'ed*** them [prophets of Baal]...Cry aloud...he is a god
Job 12:4 I [Job] am as one ***m'ed*** of his neighbour
Prov 14:9 Fools...***m*** at sin
Prov 17:5 Whoso ***m'eth*** the poor reproacheth his Maker
Jer 20:7 I am in derision daily, every one ***m'eth*** me
Mark 10:34 they shall ***m*** him [Jesus]...scourge him
Mark 15:31 chief priests ***m'ing*** said...himself he [Jesus] cannot save
Luke 18:32 he [Jesus] shall be delivered unto the Gentiles, and shall be ***m'ed***
Luke 23:36 the soldiers also ***m'ed*** him [Jesus]
Acts 2:13 ***m'ing*** said, These men [converts at Pentecost] are full of new wine
Gal 6:7 Be not deceived; God is not ***m'ed***

MODEL PRAYER OF JESUS. See *Lord's Prayer.*

MOLECH. See *Milcom.*

MOLOCH. See *Milcom.*

MORDECAI (a Jewish exile in Persia and a kinsman of Esther). Esth 2:5–23; 3:2–6; 4:1–17; 5:9–14; 6:2–13; 7:9–10; 8:1–15; 9:3–31; 10:2–3.

MOREH (a place near Shechem where Abraham built an altar after entering Canaan). **Gen 12:6–7** • Deut 11:30.

MORESHETH-GATH (birthplace of the prophet Micah). Mic 1:14.

MORIAH (a mountainous area near Jerusalem where Abraham was directed to sacrifice his son Isaac). **Gen 22:1–13** • 2 Chr 3:1.

MOSES (the great lawgiver and prophet who led the Israelites out of Egypt and guided their formative years as a nation). Moses is the central personality in the books of Exodus, Leviticus, Numbers, and Deuteronomy.

1. Hidden on the Nile River as a baby (Ex 2:1–5)
2. Reared in the house of Pharaoh (Ex 2:6–10)
3. Fled to the land of Midian (Ex 2:11–22)
4. Called to deliver the Hebrews from slavery (Ex 2:23–4:17)
5. Led Israelites out of Egypt (Ex 13:17–22)
6. Brought water out of a rock (Ex 17:3–6)
7. Received the Ten Commandments (Ex 19:3; 20:1–17)
8. Struck a rock in sin (Num 20:11–12)
9. Raised up a brass serpent (Num 21:8–9)
10. Joshua chosen as his successor (Num 27:18–23)
11. Death of Moses (Deut 34:1–8)

Moses is also mentioned in Josh 1:1–17; 8:31–35; 11:12–23; 13:8–33; 14:2–11; 22:4–9 • 2 Kgs 18:4–12 • 1 Chr 23:13–15 • Ps 106:16–32 • Isa 63:11–12 • Dan 9:11,13 • Matt 17:3–4 • Mark 9:4–5 • Luke 16:29–31 • John 7:19–23 • Acts 7:20–44 • Rom 10:5,19 • Heb 3:2–16; 11:23–24 • Rev 15:3.

MOURN [ETH, ING]

Job 2:11 Job's three friends...came...to ***m*** with him

Ps 38:6 I am troubled...I go ***m'ing*** all the day long

Ps 88:9 Mine eye ***m'eth*** by reason of affliction

Eccl 3:4 a time to ***m,*** and a time to dance

Isa 60:20 the days of thy ***m'ing*** shall be ended

Isa 61:2 to comfort all that ***m***

Amos 8:10 And I [God] will turn your feasts into ***m'ing***

Matt 5:4 Blessed are they that ***m***...shall be comforted

Matt 9:15 children...***m,*** as long as the bridegroom [Jesus] is with them

Jas 4:9 Be afflicted, and ***m***

MOVE [D, ING, TH]

Gen 1:2 Spirit of God ***m'd*** upon the...waters

Gen 9:3 Every ***m'ing*** thing that liveth shall be meat

Ps 16:8 he [God] is at my right hand, I shall not be ***m'd***

Ps 46:5 God is in the midst of her [Jerusalem]...not be ***m'd***

Ps 62:2 he [God] is my defence; I shall not be greatly ***m'd***

Ps 69:34 praise him [God], the seas, and every thing that ***m'th*** therein

Ps 96:10 the LORD reigneth: the world...shall not be ***m'd***

Isa 6:4 posts of the door ***m'd*** at the voice of him [God]

Mark 6:34 Jesus...was ***m'd*** with compassion toward them [the crowds]

John 5:3 multitude...waiting for the ***m'ing*** of the water

Acts 17:28 in him [God] we live... ***m***...have our being

Heb 12:28 a kingdom which cannot be ***m'd***

2 Pet 1:21 holy men...spake as...***m'd*** by the Holy Ghost

MULTITUDE [S]

Gen 32:12 thy [Jacob's] seed as the sand...which cannot be numbered for ***m***

Ex 12:38 mixed ***m*** went up... with them [Israelites]

Ps 69:13 O God, in the ***m*** of thy mercy hear me

Ps 109:30 I will praise him [God] among the ***m***

Joel 3:14 ***M's, m's*** in the valley of decision

Matt 5:1 seeing...***m's,*** he [Jesus] went...into a mountain

Matt 15:33 should we have... bread...fill so great a ***m***

Matt 22:33 ***m*** heard this, they were astonished

Mark 4:1 whole ***m*** was by the sea on the land

Mark 5:31 seest the ***m*** thronging thee [Jesus], and sayest... Who touched me

Luke 2:13 with the angel a ***m*** of the heavenly host

Luke 23:1 ***m***...arose, and led him [Jesus] unto Pilate

John 6:2 great ***m*** followed him [Jesus]...they saw his miracles

1 Pet 4:8 charity shall cover the ***m*** of sins

Rev 7:9 a great ***m,*** which no man could number

MURMUR [ED, ING, INGS]

Ex 15:24 the people ***m'ed*** against Moses

Num 14:27 I [God]...heard... ***m'ings*** of the children of Israel

Luke 5:30 Pharisees ***m'ed*** against his [Jesus'] disciples

John 6:41 ***m'ed***...because he [Jesus] said, I am the bread... from heaven

John 7:12 there was much ***m'ing*** among the people concerning him [Jesus]

Phil 2:14 Do all things without ***m'ings*** and disputings

MYSTERY [IES]

Mark 4:11 Unto you [the disciples] it is given to know the ***m*** of the kingdom

Luke 8:10 it is given to know the ***m'ies*** of the kingdom... but to others in parables

1 Cor 2:7 we speak the wisdom of God in a ***m***

1 Cor 4:1 ministers of Christ... stewards of the ***m'ies*** of God

1 Cor 13:2 though I [Paul]... understand all ***m'ies,*** and all knowledge

1 Cor 15:51 I show you a ***m;*** We shall not all sleep

Eph 5:32 a great ***m***...I [Paul] speak concerning Christ

1 Tim 3:9 Holding the ***m*** of the faith in a pure conscience

-N-

NAAMAN (a captain in the Syrian army who was healed of leprosy by the prophet Elisha). **2 Kgs 5:1–14** • Luke 4:27.

NABAL (a wealthy herdsman who refused to provide food for David and his army). **1 Sam 25:2–42** • 2 Sam 3:3.

NABOTH (an Israelite who was framed and killed by Jezebel so Ahab could take possession of his vineyard). **1 Kgs 21:1–23** • 2 Kgs 9:21–26.

NADAB

1. Aaron's son who was destroyed for offering "strange fire" to God. Ex 24:1,9–12; 28:1 • **Lev 10:1–7.**

2. A king of Israel who was assassinated and succeeded by Baasha. 1 Kgs 14:20; **15:25–31.**

NAHASH (a king of Ammon who befriended David). 2 Sam 10:1–2.

NAHUM (a prophet of Judah and author of the book that bears his name). Nah 1:1. *Naum:* Luke 3:25.

NAHUM, BOOK OF. A short prophetic book of the Old Testament that predicted the downfall of the pagan nation of Assyria because of the atrocities which it committed against God's people (3:7–19).

NAIN (a village near the Sea of Galilee where Jesus raised a widow's son from the dead). Luke 7:11–17.

NAIOTH (a place where David fled to escape from King Saul). 1 Sam 19:18–23; 20:1.

NAOMI (mother-in-law of Ruth). Ruth 1–4.

NAPHTALI (a son of Jacob and ancestor of one of the twelve tribes of Israel). Gen 30:8; 35:25; 46:24; 49:21 • Ex 1:4 • 1 Chr 2:2; 7:13 • Ezek 48:34. The tribe of Naphtali settled in northern Canaan. Josh 19:32–39.

NAPHTUHIM (inhabitants of central Egypt who were descendants of Mizraim, son of Ham). Gen 10:13.

NATHAN (a prophet who rebuked King David for his sin with Bathsheba). 2 Sam 7:2–17; **12:1–25** • 1 Kgs 1:8–45 • 1 Chr 17:1–15; 29:29 • 2 Chr 9:29; 29:25 • Ps 51:1.

NATHANAEL.
See *Bartholomew.*

NATION [S]

Gen 12:2 make of thee [Abraham] a great ***n***

Gen 17:5 a father of many ***n's*** have I [God] made thee [Abraham]

Gen 25:23 Two ***n's*** are in thy [Rebekah's] womb

Ex 19:6 ye [Israel] shall be unto me [God]...an holy ***n***

Deut 9:1 possess ***n's*** greater and mightier than thyself

Deut 28:1 God will set thee... above all ***n's*** of the earth

1 Sam 8:5 make us a king to judge us like all the ***n's***

2 Sam 7:23 what one ***n***...is like thy [God's] people

1 Chr 16:24 Declare...his [God's] marvellous works among all ***n's***

Ps 22:28 and he [God] is the governor among the ***n's***

Ps 33:12 Blessed is the ***n*** whose God is the LORD

Ps 67:2 thy [God's] way may be known...thy saving health among all ***n's***

Ps 72:11 all kings...all ***n's*** shall serve him [God]

Ps 82:8 judge the earth...thou [God]...inherit all ***n's***

Ps 96:5 For all the gods of the ***n's*** are idols

Ps 113:4 The LORD is high above all ***n's***

Prov 14:34 Righteousness exalteth a ***n***

Isa 2:4 ***n*** shall not lift up sword against ***n***

Isa 40:15 Behold, the ***n's*** are as a drop of a bucket

Isa 52:10 LORD hath made bare his...arm in...all the ***n's***

Isa 60:12 ***n***...that will not serve thee [God] shall perish

Jer 1:5 ordained thee [Jeremiah] a prophet unto the ***n's***

Jer 2:11 Hath a ***n*** changed their gods

Jer 50:41 a people shall come from the north, and a great ***n***

Ezek 12:15 I [God] shall scatter them among the ***n's***

Mic 4:3 ***n*** shall not lift up a sword against ***n***

Zeph 3:6 I [God] have cut off the ***n's***...towers are desolate

Hag 2:7 and the desire of all ***n's*** shall come

Zech 8:22 strong ***n's*** shall come to seek the LORD

Mal 3:9 ye have robbed me [God], even this whole ***n***

Matt 24:7 ***n*** shall rise against ***n***...kingdom against kingdom

Matt 24:14 gospel of the kingdom...preached...unto all ***n's***

Matt 25:32 before him [Jesus] shall be gathered all ***n's***

Matt 28:19 teach all ***n's,*** baptizing them

Luke 24:47 repentance... preached...among all ***n's***

John 11:50 one man should die...that the whole ***n*** perish not

Acts 2:5 devout men, out of every ***n*** under heaven
Acts 10:35 in every ***n*** he that feareth him [God]...is accepted with him
Acts 17:26 And [God] hath made of one blood all ***n's***
Phil 2:15 in the midst of a crooked and perverse ***n***
1 Pet 2:9 ye are a chosen generation...an holy ***n***
Rev 7:9 multitude, which no man could number, of all ***n's***

NATURAL
Deut 34:7 his [Moses'] eye...not dim, nor...***n*** force abated
1 Cor 2:14 ***n*** man receiveth not the things of the Spirit
1 Cor 15:44 It is sown a ***n*** body...raised a spiritual body

NATURE
Rom 1:26 women did change the natural use into that...against ***n***
Rom 2:14 Gentiles...do by ***n***...things contained in the law
2 Pet 1:4 ye might be partakers of the divine ***n***

NAUM. See *Nahum*.

NAZARETH (hometown of Jesus in the province of Galilee). Matt 2:20–23 • Luke 4:16–30.

NAZARITE (a person especially consecrated to God whose vows included abstaining from strong drink and not cutting his hair). Num 6:2–21 • Judg 13:5–7 • Lam 4:7 • Amos 2:11–12.

NEAPOLIS (a seaport where Paul landed during the second missionary journey). Acts 16:11.

NEBO
1. The highest point of Mount Pisgah where Moses died. Deut 32:49; 34:5–6.
2. Babylonian god of science and knowledge. Isa 46:1.

NEBUCHADNEZZAR (a king of Babylonia who captured Jerusalem and carried Judah into exile). **2 Kgs 25:1–26** • 2 Chr 36:7–13 • Jer 28:11–14 • Dan 1–4. *Nebuchadrezzar:* Jer 51:34.

NEBUCHADREZZAR. See *Nebuchadnezzar.*

NEBUZAR-ADAN (an officer in Nebuchadnezzar's army during the Babylonian siege of Jerusalem). 2 Kgs 25:8–20 • Jer 39:11–14.

NECHO, NECHOH. See *Pharaoh.*

NEED [ED, ETH, S]
Matt 3:14 I [John the Baptist] have ***n*** to be baptized of thee [Jesus]...comest...to me

Matt 6:8 Father knoweth what things ye have ***n*** of
Luke 5:31 They that are whole ***n*** not a physician
Luke 15:7 joy...over one sinner ...than over...just persons, which ***n*** no repentance
John 4:4 he [Jesus] must ***n's*** go through Samaria
Acts 2:45 sold...and parted them [possessions] to all men, as every man had ***n***
Acts 17:25 though he [God] ***n'ed*** any thing, seeing he... giveth…life
1 Cor 12:21 eye cannot say unto the hand...no ***n*** of thee
Phil 4:19 But my God shall supply all your ***n***
2 Tim 2:15 a workman that ***n'eth*** not to be ashamed
Heb 4:16 and find grace to help in time of ***n***
Heb 7:27 Who [Jesus] ***n'eth*** not daily...to offer up sacrifice, first for his own sins

NEEDY
Deut 15:11 open thine hand... to thy ***n,*** in thy land
Job 24:14 The murderer...killeth the poor and ***n***
Ps 37:14 The wicked have... bent their bow, to cast down the poor and ***n***
Ps 40:17 I am poor and ***n;*** yet the Lord thinketh upon me
Ps 82:3 do justice to the afflicted and ***n***
Ps 86:1 O LORD, hear me: for I am poor and ***n***
Prov 31:9 and plead the cause of the poor and ***n***
Amos 8:6 buy the poor for silver...***n*** for a pair of shoes

NEGLECT [ED]
Matt 18:17 if he shall ***n*** to hear them, tell it unto the church
Acts 6:1 widows were ***n'ed*** in the daily ministration
1 Tim 4:14 ***N*** not the gift that is in thee [Timothy]
Heb 2:3 How shall we escape, if we ***n*** so great salvation

NEHEMIAH (governor of Jerusalem who helped rebuild the city wall after the Exile and author of the book that bears his name). Neh 1:11; 2:1–6; 8:1–13.

NEHEMIAH, BOOK OF. An Old Testament historical book that records the rebuilding of Jerusalem's defensive wall after the Exile under the leadership of Nehemiah (1:1–7:73). The book also recounts the religious reforms undertaken by Nehemiah and Ezra.

NEIGHBOUR [S]
Ex 20:16 not bear false witness against thy ***n***
Lev 19:13 not defraud thy ***n,*** neither rob him

Lev 19:18 but thou shalt love thy ***n*** as thyself
Ps 79:4 We are become a reproach to our ***n's***
Prov 11:12 He that is void of wisdom despiseth his ***n***
Prov 14:20 The poor is hated even of his own ***n:*** but the rich hath many friends
Prov 24:28 Be not a witness against thy ***n*** without cause
Prov 27:10 better is a ***n*** that is near than a brother far off
Jer 31:34 they shall teach no more every man his ***n***
Zech 8:17 let none of you imagine evil...against his ***n***
Matt 22:39 Thou shalt love thy ***n*** as thyself
Luke 10:36 Which...of these three...was ***n*** unto him that fell among the thieves
Luke 15:6 he calleth...***n's,*** saying...Rejoice with me...I have found my sheep
Rom 13:10 Love worketh no ill to his ***n***
Gal 5:14 Thou shalt love thy ***n*** as thyself
Eph 4:25 speak every man truth with his ***n***
Jas 2:8 fulfil the royal law... love thy ***n*** as thyself

NERGAL (a Babylonian god of war). 2 Kgs 17:30.

NERGAL-SHAREZER (a Babylonian prince who released Jeremiah from prison). Jer 39:3–14.

NEW
Ex 1:8 there arose up a ***n*** king ...which knew not Joseph
Ps 40:3 And he [God] hath put a ***n*** song in my mouth
Ps 96:1 sing unto the LORD a ***n*** song...all the earth
Eccl 1:9 there is no ***n*** thing under the sun
Isa 1:14 Your ***n*** moons...my [God's] soul hateth
Isa 42:10 Sing unto the LORD a ***n*** song
Isa 65:17 I [God] create ***n*** heavens and a new earth
Lam 3:23 they [God's mercies] are ***n*** every morning: great is thy faithfulness
Ezek 36:26 a ***n*** spirit will I [God] put within you
Amos 8:5 ***n*** moon be gone, that we may sell corn
Matt 27:60 laid it [Jesus' body] in his [Joseph's] own ***n*** tomb
Mark 2:22 no man putteth ***n*** wine into old bottles
Luke 22:20 cup is the ***n*** testament in my [Jesus'] blood
John 13:34 A ***n*** commandment I [Jesus] give unto you
Acts 2:13 men [converts at Pentecost] are full of ***n*** wine
1 Cor 5:7 Purge out...the old leaven...may be a ***n*** lump
2 Cor 3:6 Who [Jesus]...made us able ministers of the ***n*** testament...of the spirit

2 Cor 5:17 any man be in Christ, he is a ***n*** creature
Eph 4:24 put on the ***n*** man
2 Pet 3:13 we...look for ***n*** heavens and a ***n*** earth
Rev 21:1 I [John] saw a ***n*** heaven and a ***n*** earth
Rev 21:5 Behold, I [Jesus] make all things ***n***

NEW BIRTH DISCUSSION OF JESUS WITH NICODEMUS. John 3:1–21.

NEW COVENANT
Jer 31:31 I [God] will make a ***n-c*** with the house of Israel
Heb 8:8 I [God] will make a ***n-c*** with the house of Israel
Heb 8:13 he [God] saith, A ***n-c,*** he hath made the first old
Heb 12:24 And to Jesus the mediator of the ***n-c***

NEW JERUSALEM
Rev 3:12 the city of my God, which is ***n-J***
Rev 21:2 I John saw the...***n-J,*** coming down from God

NEWNESS
Rom 6:4 even so we also should walk in ***n*** of life
Rom 7:6 serve in ***n*** of spirit... not in...oldness of the letter

NIBHAZ (an idol worshiped by the Avites, who settled in Samaria). 2 Kgs 17:31.

NICANOR (one of the seven men chosen as "deacons" in the church at Jerusalem). Acts 6:1–5.

NICODEMUS (a Pharisee who talked with Jesus about the new birth and helped prepare Jesus' body for burial). **John 3:1–21;** 7:50–52; **19:39–40.**

NICOLAITANES (an early Christian sect condemned for its false beliefs). Rev 2:6,15.

NICOLAS (one of the seven men chosen as "deacons" in the church at Jerusalem). Acts 6:1–5.

NIMROD (a son of Cush who became a powerful king and empire builder in Babylonia, or Shinar). Gen 10:8–12 • 1 Chr 1:8–10 • Mic 5:6.

NINEVE. See *Nineveh.*

NINEVEH (capital of Assyria where the prophet Jonah preached God's message of judgment). Gen 10:11–12 • 2 Kgs 19:36 • Isa 37:37 • **Jon 1–4** • Nah 1:1; 2:8; 3:7 • Zeph 2:13 • Matt 12:41. *Nineve:* Luke 11:32.

NISROCH (a false god worshiped by King Sennacherib of Assyria). **2 Kgs 19:36–37** • Isa 37:38.

NO (capital of upper Egypt). Jer 46:25 • Ezek 30:14–16 • Nah 3:8.

NOAH (a righteous man who was chosen by God to preserve life on earth by building an ark to escape the great flood). Gen 5:29–32; 6:8–22; **7:1–8:22;** 9:1–29; 10:1,32 • 1 Chr 1:4 • Isa 54:9 • Ezek 14:14,20 • Heb 11:7 • 1 Pet 3:20 • 2 Pet 2:5. *Noe:* Luke 17:26.

NOB (a city where David fled to escape King Saul's wrath). **1 Sam 21:1–9;** 22:9–23 • Neh 11:32 • Isa 10:32.

NOD (a region where Cain lived after murdering his brother Abel). Gen 4:16–17.

NOE. See *Noah.*

NOPH (an ancient royal city of the Egyptians). Isa 19:13 • Jer 2:16; 44:1; 46:14,19 • Ezek 30:13,16.

NORTHERN KINGDOM (ISRAEL) FALLS TO ASSYRIA. 2 Kgs 17.

NORTHERN TRIBES OF ISRAEL REVOLT. 1 Kgs 12:6–24.

NOTHING

Deut 2:7 forty years...God hath been with thee; thou hast lacked ***n***

Josh 11:15 he [Joshua] left ***n*** undone of all that the LORD commanded Moses

2 Sam 12:3 poor man had ***n***, save one little ewe lamb

Job 8:9 we...know ***n***, because our days...are a shadow

Ps 49:17 when he dieth he shall carry ***n*** away

Prov 13:7 There is that maketh himself rich, yet hath ***n***

Eccl 2:24 ***n*** better for a man, than that...his soul enjoy good in his labour

Isa 40:17 All nations before him [God] are as ***n***

Isa 44:10 a graven image that is profitable for ***n***

Jer 32:17 there is ***n*** too hard for thee [God]

Dan 4:35 inhabitants of the earth are reputed as ***n***

Matt 5:13 salt...is...good for ***n***, but to be cast out

Matt 17:20 ***n*** shall be impossible unto you

Mark 6:8 they [the disciples']... take ***n*** for their journey

Mark 7:15 ***n*** from without a man...can defile him

Mark 9:29 This kind can come forth by ***n,*** but by prayer
Luke 5:5 toiled all the night, and have taken ***n***
Luke 23:9 but he [Jesus] answered him [Pilate] ***n***
John 3:27 receive ***n,*** except it be given him from heaven
John 5:19 The Son [Jesus] can do ***n*** of himself
John 15:5 for without me [Jesus] ye can do ***n***
Acts 11:8 ***n***...unclean...entered into my [Peter's] mouth
Rom 14:14 I [Peter] know... there is ***n*** unclean of itself
1 Cor 1:19 I [God]...will bring to ***n*** the understanding of the prudent
1 Cor 7:19 Circumcision is ***n,*** and uncircumcision is ***n***
1 Cor 13:2 though I [Paul]... have not charity, I am ***n***
Phil 2:3 Let ***n*** be done through strife or vainglory
1 Tim 6:7 For we brought ***n*** into this world
Heb 7:19 For the law made ***n*** perfect

NUMBERS, BOOK OF. An Old Testament book that focuses on the Israelites in the wilderness of Sinai—a period of more than forty years between their departure from Egypt and their occupation of Canaan.

-O-

OATH [S]

Matt 5:33 perform unto the Lord thine ***o's***

Matt 26:72 And again he [Peter] denied with an ***o,*** I do not know the man [Jesus]

Heb 7:20 not without an ***o*** he [Jesus] was made priest

Jas 5:12 neither by any other ***o:*** but let your yea be yea

OBADIAH (a prophet of Judah and author of the book that bears his name). Obad 1.

OBADIAH, BOOK OF. A short prophetic book of the Old Testament that pronounces judgment against the Edomites because of their mistreatment of God's people, the Israelites.

OBED-EDOM (a Philistine in whose house the ark of the covenant was kept before its removal to Jerusalem). 2 Sam 6:10–12 • **1 Chr 13:13–14;** 15:24–25.

OBEDIENCE

Rom 5:19 so by the ***o*** of one [Jesus] shall many be made righteous

2 Cor 10:5 bringing into captivity every thought to the ***o*** of Christ

Heb 5:8 Though he [Jesus] were a Son, yet learned he ***o***

OBEDIENT

Isa 1:19 willing and ***o,*** ye shall eat the good of the land

Acts 6:7 company of the priests were ***o*** to the faith

Phil 2:8 he [Jesus] humbled himself...became ***o*** unto death

1 Pet 1:14 As ***o*** children, not... according to the former lusts

OBEY [ED, ETH, ING]

Gen 22:18 thou [Abraham] hast ***o'ed*** my [God's] voice

Ex 5:2 Who is the LORD, that I [Pharaoh] should ***o*** his voice

Deut 27:10 Thou shalt...***o*** the voice of the LORD

Josh 24:24 our God will we serve...his voice will we ***o***

1 Sam 15:22 Behold, to ***o*** is better than sacrifice

Jer 11:3 Cursed be the man... ***o'eth*** not...this covenant

Jer 26:13 amend your ways... and ***o*** the voice of the LORD

Mark 4:41 even the wind and the sea ***o*** him [Jesus]

Acts 5:29 We [the apostles]...***o*** God rather than men

Gal 3:1 bewitched you [Galatians]...not ***o*** the truth

Eph 6:1 Children, ***o*** your parents in the Lord

Col 3:20 Children, ***o*** your parents in all things

Heb 5:9 he [Jesus] became the author of...salvation unto all them that ***o*** him

Heb 11:8 he [Abraham]... ***o'ed***...not knowing whither he went

Jas 3:3 bits in the horses' mouths, that they may ***o*** us

1 Pet 1:22 purified your souls in ***o'ing*** the truth

OFFER [ED, ETH, ING, INGS]

Gen 4:4 LORD had respect unto Abel and to his ***o'ing***

Gen 22:2 ***o*** him [Isaac] there for a burnt ***o'ing***

Lev 10:1 And Nadab and Abihu ...***o'ed*** strange fire before the LORD

Ps 50:23 Whoso ***o'eth*** praise glorifieth me [God]

Ps 51:16 thou [God] delightest not in burnt ***o'ing***

Ps 96:8 bring an ***o'ing,*** and come into his [God's] courts

Ps 119:108 Accept...the freewill ***o'ings*** of my mouth

Hos 6:6 I [God] desired...the knowledge of God more than burnt ***o'ings***

Amos 5:22 neither will I [God] regard the peace ***o'ings***

Mal 3:8 have we robbed thee [God]? In tithes and ***o'ings***

Matt 5:24 be reconciled to thy brother, and then...***o*** thy gift

Mark 12:33 to love him [God] with all the heart...is more than...***o'ings*** and sacrifices

Luke 6:29 smiteth thee on the one cheek ***o*** also the other

Luke 11:12 if he shall ask an egg, will he ***o*** him a scorpion

Luke 21:4 all these have of their abundance cast in unto the ***o'ings*** of God

Luke 23:36 the soldiers also mocked him [Jesus]...***o'ing*** him vinegar

1 Cor 8:1 Now as touching things ***o'ed*** unto idols

Eph 5:2 Christ...hath given himself for us an ***o'ing***

2 Tim 4:6 I [Paul] am now ready to be ***o'ed***

Heb 7:27 he [Jesus] did once, when he ***o'ed*** up himself

Heb 9:28 Christ was once ***o'ed*** to bear the sins of many

Heb 10:10 sanctified through the ***o'ing***...of Jesus Christ

Heb 10:12 he [Jesus] had ***o'ed*** one sacrifice for sins for ever

Heb 11:4 Abel ***o'ed*** unto God a more excellent sacrifice

Heb 11:17 Abraham, when he was tried, ***o'ed*** up Isaac

Heb 13:15 let us ***o*** the sacrifice of praise to God

Jas 2:21 Was not Abraham our father justified...when he had ***o'ed*** Isaac his son

OFFSPRING

Job 5:25 seed...great, and thine [Job's] ***o*** as the grass

Acts 17:28 For we are also his [God's] ***o***

Acts 17:29 we are the ***o*** of God

Rev 22:16 I [Jesus] am the root and the ***o*** of David

OG (an Amorite king defeated by the Israelites at Edrei). **Num 21:32–35** • Deut 3:1,8, 10–13 • Josh 12:4 • Ps 135:11.

OLD MAN / NEW MAN. Eph 4:17–29.

OLIVES, MOUNT OF (a hill near Jerusalem where Jesus was betrayed on the night before His crucifixion). Zech 14:4 • Matt 21:1; 24:3; **26:30** • Mark 11:1; 13:3; 14:26 • Luke 19:29,37; 21:37; 22:39 • John 8:1. *Mount Olivet:* 2 Sam 15:30 • Acts 1:12.

OLIVET, MOUNT. See *Olives, Mount of.*

OMRI (a king of Israel who built Samaria as the capital city of the Northern Kingdom). **1 Kgs 16:23–28** • 2 Kgs 8:26 • 2 Chr 22:2 • Mic 6:16.

ON

1. A leader who rebelled against Moses in the wilderness. Num 16:1–35.

2. A city of lower Egypt noted as a center of sun worship. Gen 41:45,50. *Aven:* Amos 1:5.

ONAN (a son of Judah who failed to consummate a marriage union with Tamar). **Gen 38:8–10;** 46:12 • Num 26:19 • 1 Chr 2:3.

ONESIMUS (a slave who was converted under Paul's ministry). Col 4:7–9 • Phlm 10.

ONESIPHORUS (a believer who befriended Paul when he was a prisoner in Rome). 2 Tim 1:16–18; 4:19.

OPEN [ED, EST, ETH]

Gen 3:7 eyes of them [Adam and Eve] both were ***o'ed***

Job 11:5 that God would...***o*** his lips against thee

Ps 51:15 O Lord, ***o*** thou my lips

Ps 119:131 I ***o'ed*** my mouth, and...longed for thy [God's] commandments

Ps 145:16 Thou [God] ***o'est*** thine hand, and satisfiest the desire of every living thing

Ps 146:8 The LORD ***o'eth*** the eyes of the blind

Prov 13:3 he that ***o'eth*** wide his lips shall have destruction

Prov 27:5 ***O*** rebuke is better than secret love

Isa 35:5 Then the eyes of the blind shall be ***o'ed***

Isa 42:7 To ***o*** the blind eyes, to bring out the prisoners

Isa 53:7 he [God's servant]... ***o'ed*** not his mouth

Lam 3:46 enemies have ***o'ed*** their mouths against us
Ezek 3:2 I [Ezekiel] ***o'ed*** my mouth, and he [God] caused me to eat that roll
Mal 3:10 prove me [God]... herewith...if I will not ***o*** you the windows of heaven
Matt 3:16 heavens were ***o'ed*** unto him [Jesus]
Matt 7:7 knock, and it shall be ***o'ed*** unto you
Matt 27:52 graves were ***o'ed;*** and many bodies...arose
Mark 7:34 he [Jesus]...saith... Ephphatha, that is, Be ***o'ed***
Luke 24:31 eyes were ***o'ed,*** and they [Emmaus travelers] knew him [Jesus]
John 9:30 know not from whence he [Jesus] is, and yet he hath ***o'ed*** mine eyes
John 10:21 Can a devil ***o*** the eyes of the blind
Acts 9:8 when his [Saul's] eyes were ***o'ed,*** he saw no man
Acts 14:27 he [God] had ***o'ed*** the door of faith unto...Gentiles
Acts 26:18 To ***o*** their eyes, and to turn them from darkness
Rom 3:13 Their throat is an ***o*** sepulchre
1 Cor 16:9 a great door...is ***o'ed*** unto me [Paul]
1 Pet 3:12 the eyes of the Lord are over the righteous, and his ears are ***o***
Rev 3:7 write...he that ***o'eth,*** and no man shutteth
Rev 3:8 I [Jesus] have set before thee an ***o*** door
Rev 3:20 any man...***o*** the door, I [Jesus] will come in
Rev 4:1 door...***o'ed*** in heaven
Rev 5:9 worthy to take the book, and to ***o*** the seals

OPENLY

Matt 6:4 Father which seeth in secret...shall reward thee ***o***
Mark 8:32 he [Jesus] spake that saying [about his death] ***o***
John 11:54 Jesus...walked no more ***o*** among the Jews

OPHIR (a gold-producing region visited by the ships of Solomon and the Phoenicians). **1 Kgs 9:26–28;** 10:11; 22:48 • 1 Chr 29:4 • 2 Chr 8:18; 9:10 • Job 22:24; 28:16 • Ps 45:9 • Isa 13:12.

OPHRAH (Gideon's hometown where an angel assured him of God's guidance and protection). **Judg 6:11–14,24;** 8:27,32; 9:5.

ORDAIN [ED]

1 Chr 17:9 I [God] will ***o*** a place for my people Israel
Ps 8:3 moon and the stars, which thou [God] hast ***o'ed***
Jer 1:5 I [God] ***o'ed*** thee [Jeremiah] a prophet unto the nations

Mark 3:14 he [Jesus] ***o'ed*** twelve...they should be with him

John 15:16 I [Jesus] have chosen you, and ***o'ed*** you

Rom 13:1 the powers that be are ***o'ed*** of God

1 Cor 9:14 the Lord ***o'ed***... they...should live of the gospel

ORDINANCE [S]

Ex 12:43 LORD said...This is the ***o*** of the passover

Lev 18:4 Ye shall...keep mine [God's] ***o's***

1 Pet 2:13 Submit yourselves to every ***o*** of man

ORNAN. See *Araunah.*

OSEE. See *Hosea.*

OSHEA. See *Joshua.*

OTHNIEL (the first judge of Israel who defeated the king of Mesopotamia). Judg 3:9–11.

OUGHT

Matt 5:23 rememberest...thy brother hath ***o*** against thee

Luke 11:42 these ***o*** ye [Pharisees] to have done

Luke 12:12 Holy Ghost shall teach you...what ye ***o*** to say

Luke 18:1 men ***o*** always to pray, and not to faint

John 13:14 ye also ***o*** to wash one another's feet

John 19:7 and by our law he [Jesus] ***o*** to die

Acts 5:29 We [the apostles] ***o*** to obey God rather than men

Rom 12:3 think of himself more highly...he ***o*** to think

Rom 15:1 strong ***o*** to bear the infirmities of the weak

Eph 5:28 So ***o*** men to love... wives as their own bodies

Col 4:6 ye may know how ye ***o*** to answer every man

Heb 2:1 ***o*** to give...heed to... things...we have heard

Jas 3:10 My brethren, these things ***o*** not so to be

2 Pet 3:11 what manner of persons ***o*** ye to be

1 John 4:11 Beloved...we ***o*** also to love one another

OVERCOME [TH]

Num 13:30 for we are well able to ***o*** it [Canaan]

John 16:33 be of good cheer; I [Jesus] have ***o*** the world

Rom 12:21 Be not ***o*** of evil, but ***o*** evil with good

1 John 2:13 young men...ye have ***o*** the wicked one

1 John 5:4 and this is the victory that ***o'th*** the world

Rev 17:14 Lamb shall ***o*** them: for he is Lord of lords

Rev 21:7 He that ***o'th*** shall inherit all things

OWE [ST, TH]

Matt 18:28 he [servant] laid hands on him...saying, Pay me that thou ***o'st***

Luke 16:5 How much ***o'st*** thou unto my lord

Rom 13:8 ***O*** no man any thing, but to love one another

Phlm 18 he [Onesimus]...***o'th*** thee ought, put that on mine [Paul's] account

OZIAS. See *Uzziah.*

-P-

PADAN-ARAM.
See *Mesopotamia.*

PALESTINE (the territory of the Canaanites that became known as the land of the people of Israel). Joel 3:4. *Palestina:* Ex 15:14 • Isa 14:29,31.

PAMPHYLIA (a coastal region in Asia Minor visited by Paul). Acts 2:10; **13:13; 14: 24–25;** 15:38; 27:5.

PAPHOS (a city on the island of Cyprus where Paul blinded the magician Elymas). Acts 13:6–12.

PARABLES OF JESUS. See *Jesus, Parables of.*

PARDON [ED, ETH]
1 Sam 15:25 ***p*** my [Saul's] sin, and turn again with me
Neh 9:17 a God ready to ***p,*** gracious and merciful
Ps 25:11 O LORD, ***p*** mine iniquity; for it is great
Isa 40:2 her [Jerusalem's] iniquity is ***p'ed***
Jer 33:8 I [God] will ***p*** all their iniquities
Mic 7:18 Who is a God like unto thee, that ***p'eth*** iniquity

PARMENAS (one of the seven men chosen as "deacons" in the church at Jerusalem). Acts 6:1–5.

PARTHIANS (inhabitants of Parthia, a country north of Media and Persia). Acts 2:1,9.

PASHUR (a priest who had the prophet Jeremiah imprisoned). **Jer 20:3–6;** 38:1.

PASSOVER (a festival that commemorated the Exodus of Israel from Egypt). **Ex 12:11–48** • Num 9:2–14 • 2 Chr 30:1–18; 35:1–19 • Matt 26:2–19 • Mark 14:1–16 • Luke 22:1–15 • 1 Cor 5:7 • Heb 11:28.

PASTOR [S]
Jer 3:15 I [God] will give you ***p's*** according to mine heart
Jer 17:16 I [Jeremiah] have not hastened from being a ***p***
Jer 23:1 Woe be unto the ***p's*** that...scatter the sheep
Eph 4:11 he [God] gave some, apostles...and some, ***p's***

PATHROS (a name for upper Egypt). Isa 11:11 • Jer 44:1,15 • Ezek 29:14; 30:14.

PATIENCE
Rom 5:3 tribulation worketh ***p***
Rom 15:5 the God of ***p***...grant you to be likeminded
1 Thes 1:3 Remembering... your work of faith...and ***p*** of hope

1 Tim 6:11 follow after...faith, love, ***p,*** meekness
Heb 12:1 run with ***p*** the race that is set before us
Jas 1:3 that the trying of your faith worketh ***p***
Jas 5:7 husbandman waiteth for the...fruit of the earth, and hath long ***p*** for it

PATIENT [LY]
Ps 40:1 I waited ***p'ly*** for the LORD; and he inclined unto me
Eccl 7:8 the ***p*** in spirit is better than the proud in spirit
Rom 12:12 Rejoicing in hope; ***p*** in tribulation
1 Thes 5:14 support the weak, be ***p*** toward all men
Heb 6:15 And so, after he [Abraham] had ***p'ly*** endured, he obtained the promise
Jas 5:7 ***p*** therefore, brethren, unto the coming of the Lord

PATMOS (a desolate island where the apostle John was exiled and where he wrote the Book of Revelation). Rev 1:9.

PAUL (an apostle to the Gentiles who was converted from persecuting the Christian faith to proclaiming its truths). Also known as *Saul* (Acts 8:1), Paul is the central personality of the second half of the Book of Acts. Recognized as the author of thirteen epistles of the New Testament: Romans, 1 and 2 Corinthians, Galatians, Ephesians, Philippians, Colossians, 1 and 2 Thessalonians, 1 and 2 Timothy, Titus, and Philemon. See **Acts 13–28** for a sketch of Paul's life.

1. Consented to Stephen's death (Acts 7:59–8:1)
2. Converted on road to Damascus (Acts 9:1–9)
3. Ministered with Barnabas at Antioch (Acts 11:25–26)
4. First missionary journey (Acts 13:1–14:28)
5. Second missionary journey (Acts 15:36–18:23)
6. Third missionary journey (Acts 19:1–21:16)
7. Arrested in Jerusalem and detained in Caesarea (Acts 21:27–26:32)
8. Journey to Rome and shipwrecked (Acts 27:1–28:10)
9. Preached while under house arrest at Rome (Acts 28:16–31)

PAULUS, SERGIUS (Roman proconsul of Cyprus who was converted under Paul's ministry). Acts 13:4–12.

PAY [ED, ETH]
Ps 37:21 The wicked borroweth, and ***p'eth*** not again
Ps 66:13 I will ***p*** thee [God] my vows
Prov 7:14 this day have I ***p'ed*** my vows

Eccl 5:4 thou vowest a vow unto God, defer not to ***p*** it
Matt 18:34 his lord...delivered him to the tormentors, till he should ***p*** all
Matt 23:23 ye [scribes and Pharisees] ***p*** tithe of mint and anise and cummin
Rom 13:6 for this cause ***p*** ye tribute...are God's ministers

PEACE

Job 33:31 hold thy [Job's] ***p,*** and I [God] will speak
Ps 4:8 I will both lay me down in ***p,*** and sleep
Ps 34:14 seek ***p,*** and pursue it
Ps 55:18 He [God] hath delivered my soul in ***p***
Ps 83:1 hold not thy ***p,*** and be not still, O God
Ps 119:165 Great ***p*** have they which love thy [God's] law
Ps 122:7 ***P*** be within thy walls
Prov 17:28 a fool, when he holdeth his ***p,*** is counted wise
Eccl 3:8 a time of war, and a time of ***p***
Isa 9:6 his [Messiah's] name shall be called...Prince of ***P***
Isa 26:3 keep him in perfect ***p***...mind is stayed on thee [God]
Isa 48:22 no ***p,*** saith the LORD, unto the wicked
Isa 52:7 beautiful...the feet of him...that publisheth ***p***
Isa 53:5 chastisement of our ***p***...upon him [God's servant]
Jer 29:7 And seek the ***p*** of the city...for in the ***p*** thereof shall ye have ***p***
Matt 10:34 I [Jesus] came not to send ***p,*** but a sword
Mark 4:39 he [Jesus]...said unto the sea, ***P,*** be still
Luke 2:14 Glory to God...on earth ***p,*** good will toward men
Luke 10:5 whatsoever house ye enter...***P*** be to this house
John 14:27 my [Jesus'] ***p*** I give unto you
John 16:33 that in me [Jesus] ye might have ***p***
Rom 2:10 honour, and ***p,*** to every man that worketh good
Rom 5:1 we have ***p*** with God through...Jesus Christ
Rom 10:15 beautiful are the feet of them that preach the gospel of ***p***
Rom 14:19 follow after the things which make for ***p***
1 Cor 14:33 God is not the author of confusion, but of ***p***
Gal 5:22 fruit of the Spirit is love, joy, ***p,*** longsuffering
Eph 2:14 he [Jesus] is our ***p,*** who hath made both one
Eph 4:3 unity of the Spirit in the bond of ***p***
Phil 4:7 ***p*** of God, which passeth all understanding
Col 3:15 let the ***p*** of God rule in your hearts
2 Thes 3:16 Now the Lord of ***p*** himself give you ***p***

PECULIAR PEOPLE
Deut 14:2 LORD hath chosen thee [Israel] to be a ***p-p***
Titus 2:14 he [Jesus] might... purify unto himself a ***p-p***
1 Pet 2:9 ye [Christians] are... an holy nation, a ***p-p***

PEKAH (a king of Israel who assassinated Pekahiah to gain the throne). **2 Kgs 15:23–31** • 2 Chr 28:6 • Isa 7:1–9.

PEKAHIAH (a king of Israel who was assassinated and succeeded by Pekah, one of his military officers). 2 Kgs 15:23–26.

PELETHITES (a loyal unit of David's soldiers). 2 Sam 8:18; 15:14–18; 20:7,23 • 1 Kgs 1:38,44 • 1 Chr 18:17.

PENIEL (a place near the Jabbok River where Jacob wrestled with an angel). Gen 32:24–32. *Penuel:* Judg 8:8.

PENTECOST (a harvest festival being observed in Jerusalem when the Holy Spirit came in power upon the early believers). **Acts 2:1–47;** 20:16 • 1 Cor 16:8. *Feast of Harvest* or *Ingathering:* Ex 23:16. *Feast of Weeks:* Ex 34:22.

PENUEL. See *Peniel.*

PEOPLE OF GOD
Heb 4:9 There remaineth...a rest to the ***p-o-G***
Heb 11:25 Choosing...to suffer affliction with the ***p-o-G***
1 Pet 2:10 in time past were not a people...now the ***p-o-G***

PEOR. See *Baal-peor.*

PERCEIVE [D, ING, ST, TH]
Job 33:14 God speaketh... twice, yet man ***p'th*** it not
Job 38:18 Hast thou [Job] ***p'd*** the breadth of the earth
Isa 6:9 see ye indeed, but ***p*** not
Mark 7:18 not ***p,*** that whatsoever...entereth into the man...cannot defile
Luke 6:41 ***p'st*** not the beam that is in thine own eye
Luke 8:46 I [Jesus] ***p*** that virtue is gone out of me
Luke 9:47 Jesus, ***p'ing***...their heart, took a child
Acts 4:13 they [the Sanhedrin] ...***p'd*** that they [Peter and John] were unlearned ...men
Acts 10:34 I [Peter] ***p*** that God is no respecter of persons
1 John 3:16 ***p*** we the love of God, because he [Jesus] laid down his life

PERFECT [ED, ING, LY]
Gen 6:9 Noah was a just man and ***p*** in his generations
Job 1:1 that man [Job] was ***p*** and upright

Ps 18:30 his [God's] way is ***p***... word...is tried

Ps 18:32 It is God that... maketh my way ***p***

Ps 19:7 law of the LORD is ***p,*** converting the soul

Prov 4:18 path of the just... shineth...unto the ***p*** day

Matt 5:48 even as your Father which is in heaven is ***p***

Rom 12:2 prove what is that good...and ***p,*** will of God

1 Cor 1:10 ***p'ly*** joined together in the same mind

1 Cor 13:10 But when that which is ***p*** is come

2 Cor 12:9 My [Jesus'] grace is sufficient...strength is made ***p*** in weakness

Eph 4:12 ***p'ing*** of the saints, for the work of the ministry

2 Tim 3:17 That the man of God may be ***p***

Heb 5:9 And being made ***p,*** he [Jesus] became the author of eternal salvation

Heb 10:14 he [Jesus] hath ***p'ed***...them that are sanctified

Jas 1:17 good gift and every ***p*** gift is from above

1 John 4:12 If we love one another...his [God's] love is ***p'ed*** in us

1 John 4:18 but ***p*** love casteth out fear

PERFECTION

Ps 50:2 Out of Zion, the ***p*** of beauty, God hath shined

2 Cor 13:9 this also we wish, even your ***p***

Heb 6:1 let us go on unto ***p***

Heb 7:11 If...***p*** were by the Levitical priesthood

PERGA (capital of Pamphylia and a city visited by the apostle Paul). Acts 13:13–14; 14:25.

PERGAMOS (a city where one of the seven churches addressed by John in the Book of Revelation was located). Rev 2:12–17.

PERISH [ED, ETH, ING]

2 Sam 1:27 How are the mighty fallen, and the weapons of war ***p'ed***

Job 3:3 Let the day ***p*** wherein I [Job] was born

Job 33:18 He keepeth...his life from ***p'ing*** by the sword

Job 34:15 All flesh shall ***p*** together...man...unto dust

Ps 1:6 but the way of the ungodly shall ***p***

Ps 68:2 the wicked ***p*** at the presence of God

Prov 19:9 and he that speaketh lies shall ***p***

Prov 29:18 Where there is no vision, the people ***p***

Matt 18:14 that one of these little ones should ***p***

Mark 4:38 Master [Jesus], carest thou not that we [the disciples] ***p***

Luke 15:17 father's [servants] have bread...and I [prodigal son] ***p*** with hunger
John 3:16 whosoever believeth in him [Jesus] should not ***p***
John 6:27 Labour not for the meat which ***p'eth***
1 Cor 1:18 For the preaching of the cross is to them that ***p*** foolishness
2 Cor 4:16 outward man ***p,*** yet the inward man is renewed
2 Pet 3:9 The Lord...is longsuffering to us-ward, not willing that any should ***p***

PERIZZITES (descendants of Perez who were conquered by Joshua's forces). Gen 15:20; 34:30 • Ex 3:8,17; 23:23 • Deut 7:1; 20:17 • **Josh 3:10;** 12:8; 17:15; 24:11 • Judg 1:4–5; 3:5 • 1 Kgs 9:20 • 2 Chr 8:7 • Ezra 9:1 • Neh 9:8.

PERSECUTE [D, ING, ST]
Ps 7:1 O LORD...save me from all them that ***p*** me
Ps 31:15 deliver me...from them that ***p*** me
Ps 119:161 Princes have ***p'd*** me without a cause
Matt 5:10 Blessed are they... ***p'd*** for righteousness' sake
Matt 5:11 Blessed are ye, when men shall...***p*** you
Matt 5:44 Love...enemies... pray for them which...***p*** you
John 15:20 If they have ***p'd*** me [Jesus]...also ***p*** you
Acts 9:4 Saul, Saul, why ***p'st*** thou me [Jesus]
Rom 12:14 Bless them which ***p*** you: bless...curse not
1 Cor 15:9 I [Paul] ***p'd*** the church of God
2 Cor 4:9 ***P'd,*** but not forsaken; cast down, but not destroyed
Phil 3:6 Concerning zeal, ***p'ing*** the church

PERSECUTION
Lam 5:5 Our necks are under ***p:*** we...have no rest
Acts 8:1 a great ***p*** against the church...at Jerusalem
Rom 8:35 Who shall separate us from the love of Christ? shall...distress, or ***p***
2 Tim 3:12 all that will live... in Christ Jesus shall suffer ***p***

PERSIA (a great empire that conquered Babylonia and allowed the Israelites to return to their native land). **2 Chr 36:20–23** • Ezra 1:1–8; 3:7; 4:3–24; 6:14; 7:1; 9:9 • Esth 1:3–18; 10:2 • Ezek 27:10; 38:5 • Dan 8:20; 10:1–20; 11:2.

PERSUADE [D, ST, TH]
Luke 16:31 neither will they be ***p'd,*** though one rose from the dead
Acts 18:13 This fellow [Paul] ***p'th*** men to worship God contrary to the law

Acts 26:28 Almost thou [Paul] ***p'st*** me [Agrippa] to be a Christian
Rom 8:38 I [Paul] am ***p'd,*** that neither death, nor life
Rom 14:14 I [Paul]...am ***p'd***... that there is nothing unclean of itself
2 Cor 5:11 Knowing...the terror of the Lord, we ***p*** men
2 Tim 1:12 know whom I [Paul] have believed, and am ***p'd*** that he [Jesus] is able

PETER. See *Simon,* No. 1.

PETER, FIRST AND SECOND EPISTLES OF. Two short epistles, probably from the apostle Peter, written to encourage Christians who were experiencing persecution and discouragement (1 Peter) and to warn them against false teachers (2 Peter).

PHARAOH (title of the king of Egypt). The named pharaohs of the Bible are Shishak (1 Kgs 14:25–26), So (2 Kgs 17:4), Tirhakah (2 Kgs 19:9), Nechoh (2 Kgs 23:29; *Necho:* Jer 46:2) and Hophra (Jer 44:30).

PHARISEES (a Jewish sect whose traditional religious views brought them into conflict with Jesus and the apostles). Matt 12:14–34; 15:12–14; 16:1; 19:3; 22:15; 23:13–33 • Luke 7:36–50; 11:53–54 • Acts 5:34; 15:5; 23:5–8; 26:5 • Phil 3:5.

PHARPAR (a river of Damascus). 2 Kgs 5:9–12.

PHEBE (a believer commended by Paul for her support). Rom 16:1–2.

PHENICE (a Mediterranean coastal region north of Israel). Acts 11:19; 15:3. *Phenicia:* Acts 21:2.

PHENICIA. See *Phenice.*

PHILADELPHIA (a city where one of the seven churches addressed by John in the Book of Revelation was located). Rev 3:7–13.

PHILEMON (a believer to whom Paul wrote on behalf of Philemon's slave). Phlm 1,9–21.

PHILEMON, EPISTLE TO. A short book written by Paul to help Onesimus, a runaway slave. Paul encouraged Philemon to welcome Onesimus back as a Christian brother (v. 16).

PHILIP

1. One of the twelve apostles of Jesus. Matt 10:3 • Mark 3:18 • Luke 6:14 • John

1:43–48; 6:5–7; 12:20–22; 14:8–12 • Acts 1:13.

2. One of the seven men chosen as "deacons" in the church at Jerusalem and an evangelist in the early church. Acts 6:5; 8:5–40; 21:8.

3. A Roman ruler in northern Palestine. Luke 3:1. See also *Herod,* No. 4.

PHILIPPI (a city where Paul and Silas were miraculously released from prison). **Acts 16:12–34;** 20:6 • Phil 1:1 • 1 Thes 2:2.

PHILIPPIANS, EPISTLE TO THE. A short epistle written by Paul to the church at Philippi—a group for whom he expressed great appreciation and thanksgiving (1:1–11). Philippians has been called Paul's "epistle of joy" (4:4).

PHILISTIA (a coastal region beside the Mediterranean Sea that served as the land of the Philistines). Gen 21:32–34 • Ps 60:8; 87:4; 108:9.

PHILISTIM. See *Philistines.*

PHILISTINES (inhabitants of Philistia who were enemies of the Israelites, especially during the days of Saul and David). Gen 26:1–18 • Ex 13:17 • Josh 13:2–3 • Judg 14:1–4; 15:3–20; 16:5–31 • 1 Sam 17:8–57 • 2 Sam 21:15–19 • 1 Chr 10:1–12 • Jer 47:1–4 • Amos 6:2; 9:7. *Philistim:* Gen 10:14.

PHILISTINES, SEA OF THE. See *Great Sea.*

PHINEHAS

1. Aaron's grandson who became a high priest of Israel. 1 Chr 9:19–20.

2. A son of Levi and priest who corrupted his office through immoral behavior. 1 Sam 2:22–24.

PHRYGIA (a region of Asia Minor visited by Paul). Acts 2:10; **16:6.**

PHUT. See *Libya.*

PHYSICIAN [S]

Jer 8:22 Is there no balm in Gilead...no ***p*** there

Mark 5:26 [a certain woman] had suffered many things of many ***p's***

Luke 5:31 They that are whole need not a ***p***

Col 4:14 Luke, the beloved ***p,*** and Demas, greet you

PIERCE [D, ING, INGS]

Job 30:17 My [Job's] bones are ***p'd***...in the night

Prov 12:18 There is that speaketh like the ***p'ings*** of a sword

Zech 12:10 they shall look upon me [the Messiah] whom they have ***p'd***
Luke 2:35 sword shall ***p*** through thy [Mary's]... soul
John 19:34 one of the soldiers... ***p'd*** his [Jesus'] side
Heb 4:12 word of God is... sharper...twoedged sword, ***p'ing***...soul and spirit
Rev 1:7 he [Jesus] cometh... every eye shall see him, and they also which ***p'd*** him

PILATE (the Roman governor of Judea who presided at Jesus' trial). **Matt 27:2–65** • **Mark 15:1–44** • Luke 3:1; 13:1; **23:1–52** • **John 18:29–38; 19:1–38** • Acts 3:13; 4:27; 13:28 • 1 Tim 6:13.

PILLAR OF CLOUD AND FIRE LEAD ISRAEL. Ex 13:17–22.

PISGAH, MOUNT (a mountain peak in Moab from which Moses viewed Canaan before his death). Num 21:20; 23:14 • Deut 3:27; **34:1–6.**

PISIDIA (a mountainous district in Asia Minor visited by Paul). Acts 13:14; 14:24.

PISON (one of four rivers which flowed out of the Garden of Eden). Gen 2:10–14.

PITHOM (an Egyptian city built by Hebrew slaves). Ex 1:11.

PLAGUES AGAINST EGYPT

1. Water turned into blood (Ex 7:20–25)
2. Frogs (Ex 8:1–7)
3. Lice (Ex 8:16–19)
4. Flies (Ex 8:20–24)
5. Diseased livestock (Ex 9:3–7)
6. Boils (Ex 9:8–12)
7. Hail (Ex 9:13–25)
8. Locusts (Ex 10:1–15)
9. Darkness (Ex 10:21–23)
10. Death of Egyptian firstborn (Ex 12:1–36)

PLAIN, SEA OF THE. See *Salt Sea.*

PLEASE [D, ING]

1 Sam 12:22 ***p'd*** the LORD to make you his people
Ps 40:13 Be ***p'd,*** O LORD, to deliver me
Ps 69:31 This also shall ***p*** the LORD better than an ox
Isa 53:10 it ***p'd*** the LORD to bruise him [God's servant]
Mic 6:7 LORD be ***p'd*** with thousands of rams
Matt 17:5 my [God's] beloved Son, in whom I am well ***p'd***
Luke 3:22 my [God's] beloved Son; in thee I am well ***p'd***
John 8:29 I [Jesus] do always those things that ***p*** him [God]

Rom 8:8 they that are in the flesh cannot ***p*** God
1 Cor 1:21 it ***p'd*** God by the foolishness of preaching
Col 1:19 it ***p'd*** the Father that in him [Jesus] should all fulness dwell
Col 3:20 obey your parents... well ***p'ing*** unto the Lord
Heb 11:6 without faith it is impossible to ***p*** him [God]
1 John 3:22 do those things... ***p'ing*** in his [God's] sight

PLEASURE [S]
Job 22:3 any ***p*** to the Almighty, that thou art righteous
Job 36:11 If they obey...him [God], they shall spend their...years in ***p's***
Ps 147:11 The LORD taketh ***p*** in them that fear him
Ps 149:4 For the LORD taketh ***p*** in his people
Prov 21:17 He that loveth ***p*** shall be a poor man
Isa 44:28 He [Cyrus]...shall perform all my [God's] ***p***
Ezek 33:11 I [God] have no ***p*** in the death of the wicked
Mal 1:10 I have no ***p*** in you, saith the LORD of hosts
Luke 12:32 your Father's good ***p*** to give you the kingdom
Eph 1:9 his [Jesus'] good ***p***... he hath purposed in himself
2 Tim 3:4 lovers of ***p's*** more than lovers of God
Heb 11:25 Choosing rather to suffer affliction...than to enjoy the ***p's*** of sin
Rev 4:11 thou [God] hast created all things...for thy ***p*** they...were created

PONTUS (a coastal region along the Black Sea where Priscilla and Aquila settled). Acts 2:5,9; **18:2** • 1 Pet 1:1.

POOR
Lev 19:10 thou shalt leave them [grapes] for the ***p***
Deut 15:11 the ***p*** shall never cease out of the land
2 Sam 12:3 ***p*** man had nothing, save one little ewe lamb
Job 5:15 He [God] saveth the ***p*** from the sword
Job 30:25 was not my [Job's] soul grieved for the ***p***
Job 36:6 He [God]...giveth right to the ***p***
Ps 34:6 This ***p*** man cried, and the LORD heard him
Ps 40:17 I am ***p*** and needy; yet the Lord thinketh upon me
Ps 72:13 He [God] shall spare the ***p*** and needy
Ps 109:22 I am ***p*** and needy, and my heart is wounded
Prov 14:20 The ***p*** is hated even of his own neighbour
Prov 21:17 He that loveth pleasure shall be a ***p*** man
Prov 22:2 rich and ***p***...LORD is the maker of them all

Prov 22:22 Rob not the ***p,*** because he is ***p***
Eccl 4:13 Better is a ***p*** and a wise child than an old and foolish king
Isa 25:4 thou [God] hast been a strength to the ***p***
Amos 2:6 they [Israel] sold... the ***p*** for a pair of shoes
Matt 5:3 Blessed are the ***p*** in spirit
Mark 10:21 sell whatsoever thou [rich young ruler] hast, and give to the ***p***
Mark 14:7 For ye have the ***p*** with you always
Luke 4:18 anointed me [Jesus] to preach the gospel to the ***p***
Luke 14:13 makest a feast, call the ***p,*** the maimed
Luke 19:8 Behold, Lord, the half of my [Zacchaeus's] goods I give to the ***p***
1 Cor 13:3 though I [Paul] bestow...goods to feed the ***p***
2 Cor 8:9 he [Jesus] was rich, yet...he became ***p***
Jas 2:5 God chosen the ***p*** of this world rich in faith

POSSESSION [S]
Gen 17:8 I [God] will give... Canaan, for an everlasting ***p***
Gen 47:27 they [Israel] had ***p's*** therein [in Egypt], and grew, and multiplied
Ps 2:8 I [God] shall give thee [his Son]...the uttermost parts of the earth for thy ***p***
Mark 10:22 he [rich young ruler]...went away grieved: for he had great ***p's***
Acts 5:1 Ananias, with Sapphira his wife, sold a ***p***

POSSIBLE
Matt 19:26 but with God all things are ***p***
Matt 26:39 if it be ***p,*** let this cup pass from me [Jesus]
Mark 9:23 all things are ***p*** to him that believeth
Luke 18:27 things...impossible with men are ***p*** with God
Rom 12:18 If it be ***p***...live peaceably with all men
Heb 10:4 not ***p***...blood of bulls... should take away sins

POTIPHAR (an Egyptian official who had Joseph imprisoned). Gen 37:36; **39:1–20.**

POWER [S]
Ex 15:6 Thy right hand, O LORD, is...glorious in ***p***
1 Chr 29:11 Thine, O LORD, is the greatness, and the ***p***
Job 37:23 he [God] is excellent in ***p,*** and in judgment
Ps 49:15 redeem my soul from the ***p*** of the grave
Ps 68:35 he [God]...giveth strength and ***p*** unto his people
Ps 111:6 He [God] hath showed...the ***p*** of his works
Prov 18:21 Death and life are in the ***p*** of the tongue

Jer 32:17 thou [God] hast made...the earth by thy great ***p***

Nah 1:3 LORD is slow to anger, and great in ***p***

Zech 4:6 Not by might, nor by ***p,*** but by my [God's] spirit

Matt 6:13 thine [God's] is the kingdom, and the ***p***

Matt 24:30 Son of man coming in the clouds...with ***p***

Matt 28:18 All ***p*** is given unto me [Jesus]

Mark 13:25 the ***p's*** that are in heaven shall be shaken

Luke 4:32 his [Jesus'] word was with ***p***

Luke 9:1 he [Jesus]...gave them [disciples] ***p***...over... devils

Luke 24:49 tarry ye [the disciples]...until...endued with ***p***

John 1:12 gave he [Jesus] ***p*** to become the sons of God

John 19:11 no ***p*** at all against me [Jesus], except it were given thee [Pilate] from above

Acts 6:8 Stephen, full of faith and ***p,*** did great wonders

Rom 8:38 neither death, nor life...nor ***p's***

Rom 13:1 every soul be subject unto the higher ***p's***

1 Cor 4:20 kingdom of God is not in word, but in ***p***

Eph 6:10 be strong in the Lord, and in the ***p*** of his might

Eph 6:12 we wrestle...against principalities, against ***p's***

2 Tim 1:7 God hath not given us the spirit of fear; but of ***p***

Rev 4:11 Thou [God] art worthy...to receive glory...***p***

POWER OF GOD

Matt 22:29 not knowing the scriptures, nor the ***p-o-G***

Luke 22:69 Son of man sit on the right hand of the ***p-o-G***

Rom 1:16 it [the gospel] is the ***p-o-G*** unto salvation

1 Cor 1:18 the preaching of the cross...is the ***p-o-G***

1 Cor 2:5 your faith should... stand...in the ***p-o-G***

POWERFUL

Ps 29:4 voice of the LORD is ***p***

Heb 4:12 For the word of God is quick, and ***p***

PRAISE [D, ING, S]

1 Chr 16:25 great is the LORD, and greatly to be ***p'd***

1 Chr 29:13 we thank thee [God]...***p*** thy glorious name

Ps 18:3 call upon the LORD, who is worthy to be ***p'd***

Ps 21:13 so will we sing and ***p*** thy [God's] power

Ps 44:8 In God we boast...and ***p*** thy name for ever

Ps 47:7 sing ye [God's] ***p's*** with understanding

Ps 51:15 my mouth shall show forth thy [God's] ***p***

Ps 67:3 Let the people ***p*** thee, O God...all...***p*** thee

Ps 79:13 show forth thy [God's] ***p*** to all generations
Ps 84:4 they will be still ***p'ing*** thee [God]
Ps 92:1 a good thing...to sing ***p's*** unto thy [God's] name
Ps 100:4 Enter into his [God's] ...courts with ***p***
Ps 145:3 Great is the LORD, and greatly to be ***p'd***
Isa 42:10 Sing unto the LORD... his ***p***...the end of the earth
Luke 2:20 shepherds returned, glorifying and ***p'ing*** God
John 12:43 loved the ***p*** of men more than the ***p*** of God
Acts 16:25 Paul and Silas... sang ***p's*** unto God
1 Pet 2:9 show forth the ***p's*** of him [God] who hath called you out of darkness
Rev 19:5 ***P*** our God, all ye his servants...ye that fear him

PRAISE THE LORD
Ps 7:17 I will ***p-t-L*** according to his righteousness
Ps 107:15 Oh that men would ***p-t-L*** for his goodness
Ps 117:1 O ***P-t-L,*** all ye nations...all ye people
Ps 150:6 Let every thing that hath breath ***p-t-L***

PRAY [EST, ETH, ING]
2 Chr 7:14 my [God's] people... humble themselves, and ***p***
Ps 5:2 unto thee [God] will I ***p***
Ps 55:17 Evening, and morning, and at noon, will I ***p***
Jer 14:11 said the LORD unto me [Jeremiah], ***P*** not for this people for their good
Dan 6:11 these men...found Daniel ***p'ing***...before...God
Matt 6:6 when thou ***p'est,*** enter into thy closet
Matt 6:9 ***p*** ye: Our Father which art in heaven
Mark 6:46 he [Jesus] departed into a mountain to ***p***
Mark 11:25 when ye stand ***p'ing,*** forgive
Mark 13:33 watch and ***p:*** for ye know not when the time is
Luke 6:28 ***p*** for them which despitefully use you
Luke 11:1 Lord, teach us to ***p***
John 14:16 I [Jesus] will ***p*** the Father, and he shall give you another Comforter
John 17:9 I [Jesus] ***p***...for them [the disciples] which thou [God] hast given me
Acts 10:9 Peter went up upon the housetop to ***p***
Rom 8:26 we know not what we should ***p*** for as we ought
1 Cor 14:14 if I [Paul] ***p***... unknown tongue...spirit ***p'eth***
2 Cor 5:20 we ***p*** you...be ye reconciled to God
1 Thes 5:17 ***P*** without ceasing
Jas 5:13 Is any among you afflicted? let him ***p***
Jas 5:16 ***p*** one for another, that ye may be healed

PRAYER

2 Chr 7:12 I [God] have heard thy [Solomon's] ***p***

Ps 6:9 LORD will receive my ***p***

Ps 66:20 God...hath not turned away my ***p***

Ps 102:17 He [God] will regard the ***p*** of the destitute

Prov 15:29 The LORD...heareth the ***p*** of the righteous

Matt 21:22 whatsoever ye shall ask in ***p,*** believing, ye shall receive

Luke 19:46 My [God's] house is the house of ***p***

Acts 6:4 we [the apostles] will give ourselves...to ***p***

Rom 10:1 my [Paul's]...***p*** to God for Israel...they might be saved

Jas 5:15 the ***p*** of faith shall save the sick

Jas 5:16 fervent ***p*** of a righteous man availeth much

PREACH [ED, ING]

Isa 61:1 the LORD hath anointed me [God's servant] to ***p*** good tidings

Matt 3:1 John the Baptist, ***p'ing*** in the wilderness

Matt 4:17 Jesus began to ***p,*** and to say, Repent

Matt 24:14 gospel...shall be ***p'ed*** in all the world

Mark 1:4 John did baptize... and ***p***...repentance

Mark 3:14 that he [Jesus] might send them [the disciples] forth to ***p***

Luke 24:47 remission of sins... be ***p'ed*** in his [Jesus'] name

Acts 5:42 they [the apostles] ceased not to...***p*** Jesus Christ

Acts 8:4 they [believers]...went every where ***p'ing*** the word

Acts 8:5 Philip went down to... Samaria, and ***p'ed*** Christ

1 Cor 1:18 For the ***p'ing*** of the cross is to them that perish foolishness

1 Cor 1:21 it pleased God by the foolishness of ***p'ing*** to save them that believe

1 Cor 1:23 But we ***p*** Christ crucified

1 Cor 9:27 lest...when I [Paul] have ***p'ed*** to others, I myself should be a castaway

1 Cor 15:14 if Christ be not risen, then is our ***p'ing*** vain

2 Cor 4:5 we ***p*** not ourselves, but Christ Jesus

Eph 3:8 I [Paul] should ***p*** among the Gentiles

Phil 1:18 Christ is ***p'ed;*** and I [Paul]...do rejoice

2 Tim 4:2 ***P*** the word; be instant in season

1 Pet 3:19 he [Jesus] went and ***p'ed*** unto the spirits in prison

PREACH THE GOSPEL

Mark 16:15 Go ye into all the world, and ***p-t-g*** to every creature

Luke 4:18 he [God]...anointed me [Jesus] to ***p-t-g*** to... poor

Rom 1:15 I [Paul] am ready to ***p-t-g*** to you that are at Rome
Rom 10:15 beautiful are the feet of them that ***p-t-g***
1 Cor 1:17 For Christ sent me [Paul] not to baptize, but to ***p-t-g***
1 Cor 9:14 they which ***p-t-g*** should live of the gospel

PREACHER
Eccl 1:2 Vanity of vanities, saith the ***P***...all is vanity
Rom 10:14 and how shall they hear without a ***p***
2 Tim 1:11 I [Paul] am appointed a ***p***...of the Gentiles

PRECEPT [S]
Ps 119:27 me to understand the way of thy [God's] ***p's***
Ps 119:100 I understand... because I keep thy [God's] ***p's***
Isa 28:10 ***p*** upon ***p;*** line upon line...here a little
Dan 9:5 We have sinned... rebelled, even by departing from thy [God's] ***p's***
Mark 10:5 Jesus...said...For the hardness of your heart he [Moses] wrote you this ***p***

PRECIOUS
Ps 116:15 ***P*** in the sight of the LORD is...death of his saints
Ps 139:17 How ***p*** also are thy thoughts...O God
Prov 17:8 A gift is as a ***p*** stone in the eyes of him that hath it
Eccl 7:1 A good name is better than ***p*** ointment
Isa 28:16 a tried stone, a ***p*** corner stone
Matt 26:7 came...a woman having an alabaster box of very ***p*** ointment
1 Cor 3:12 if any man build upon this foundation gold, silver, ***p*** stones
Rev 21:19 foundations...were garnished with...***p*** stones

PREDESTINATE [D]
Rom 8:29 whom he [God] did foreknow, he also did ***p***
Eph 1:5 Having ***p'd*** us unto the adoption of children by Jesus Christ
Eph 1:11 ***p'd*** according to the purpose of him [God] who worketh all things

PRESENCE OF THE LORD
Gen 3:8 Adam and his wife hid...from the ***p-o-t-L***
Ps 114:7 Tremble, thou earth, at the ***p-o-t-L***
Jon 1:3 Jonah rose up to flee... from the ***p-o-t-L***
2 Thes 1:9 punished with... destruction from the ***p-o-t-L***

PRICE
1 Chr 21:24 I [David] will verily buy it [a threshingfloor] for the full ***p***
Job 28:18 the ***p*** of wisdom is above rubies

Prov 31:10 find a virtuous woman...***p***...above rubies
Isa 55:1 buy wine and milk without money and without ***p***
Matt 13:46 when he had found one pearl of great ***p***
Acts 5:2 [Ananias] kept back part of the ***p***
1 Cor 6:20 ye are bought with a ***p:*** therefore glorify God

PRIDE
Lev 26:19 I [God] will break the ***p*** of your power
Ps 10:2 wicked in his ***p*** doth persecute the poor
Ps 73:6 ***p*** compasseth them about as a chain
Prov 8:13 The fear of the LORD is to hate...***p***
Prov 16:18 ***P*** goeth before destruction
1 John 2:16 the lust of the eyes, and the ***p*** of life

PRINCIPALITY [IES]
Rom 8:38 neither death, nor life, nor angels, nor ***p'ies***
Eph 1:21 Far above all ***p,*** and power, and might
Eph 6:12 we wrestle...against ***p'ies,*** against powers
Col 2:15 having spoiled ***p'ies*** and powers, he [Jesus] made a show of them openly

PROCHORUS (one of the seven men chosen as "deacons" in the church at Jerusalem). Acts 6:1–5.

PROCLAIM [ED]
Lev 23:4 holy convocations, which ye shall ***p***
Prov 20:6 Most men will ***p*** every one his own goodness
Isa 61:1 the LORD...hath sent me [God's servant]...to ***p*** liberty to the captives
Jon 3:5 people of Nineveh believed God, and ***p'ed*** a fast
Luke 12:3 spoken in the ear in closets shall be ***p'ed*** upon the housetops

PROFANE [D]
Ezek 23:38 they have...***p'd*** my [God's] sabbaths
Ezek 44:23 teach...the difference between the holy and ***p***
Mal 2:11 Judah hath ***p'd*** the holiness of the LORD
1 Tim 4:7 refuse ***p*** and old wives' fables
2 Tim 2:16 But shun ***p*** and vain babblings

PROFESS [ING]
Matt 7:23 will I [Jesus] ***p***...I never knew you
Rom 1:22 ***P'ing*** themselves... wise, they became fools
Titus 1:16 ***p*** that they know God; but in works...deny him

PROFESSION
1 Tim 6:12 thou...hast professed a good ***p***
Heb 3:1 consider the...High Priest of our ***p,*** Christ Jesus

Heb 10:23 Let us hold fast the ***p*** of our faith

PROFIT [ETH]

Ps 30:9 ***p*** is there in my blood, when I go down to the pit

Eccl 1:3 What ***p*** hath a man of all his labour

Jer 2:11 changed their glory for that which doth not ***p***

Mark 8:36 ***p*** a man, if he... gain the whole world, and lose his own soul

John 6:63 spirit that quickeneth; the flesh ***p'eth*** nothing

Rom 3:1 or what ***p*** is there of circumcision

1 Cor 13:3 have not charity, it ***p'eth*** me nothing

Jas 2:14 doth it ***p***...though a man...have not works

PROMISE [D, S]

Josh 23:10 he [God]...fighteth for you, as he hath ***p'd***

2 Chr 1:9 thy [God's] ***p*** unto David...be established

Jer 33:14 I [God] will perform that...which I have ***p'd***

Luke 24:49 behold, I [Jesus] send the ***p*** of my Father

Rom 15:8 Jesus Christ was a minister...truth of God, to confirm the ***p's*** made

Gal 3:21 the law then against the ***p's*** of God

Gal 3:29 Abraham's seed, and heirs according to the ***p***

Gal 4:28 we, brethren...are the children of ***p***

Eph 3:6 Gentiles should be... partakers of his [God's] ***p***

Eph 6:2 Honour thy father... first commandment with ***p***

Titus 1:2 eternal life, which God, that cannot lie, ***p'd***

Heb 11:9 he [Abraham] sojourned in the land of ***p***

Jas 1:12 crown of life, which the Lord hath ***p'd***

2 Pet 3:4 Where is the ***p*** of his [Jesus'] coming

1 John 2:25 ***p*** that he [Jesus] hath ***p'd*** us, even eternal life

PROPHECIES ABOUT JESUS. See *Messianic Prophecies.*

PROPHECY [IES]

1 Cor 12:10 to another ***p;*** to another discerning of spirits

1 Cor 13:2 though I [Paul] have the gift of ***p***

1 Cor 13:8 whether there be ***p'ies,*** they shall fail

2 Pet 1:20 no ***p*** of the scripture is of...private interpretation

PROPHESY [IED, IETH]

Ezek 37:4 he [God] said...***P*** upon these bones...hear the word

Joel 2:28 your sons and your daughters shall ***p***

Amos 7:15 LORD said...Go, ***p*** unto my people Israel

Matt 7:22 have we not ***p'ied*** in thy [Jesus'] name

Mark 7:6 Well hath Esaias ***p'ied*** of you hypocrites

Acts 2:18 pour out...my [God's] Spirit...they shall ***p***

Rom 12:6 let us ***p*** according to the proportion of faith

1 Cor 13:9 we know in part, and we ***p*** in part

1 Cor 14:5 greater is he that ***p'ieth*** than he that speaketh with tongues

PROPITIATION

Rom 3:25 Whom [Jesus] God hath set forth...a ***p*** through faith

1 John 2:2 he [Jesus] is the ***p*** for our sins...not for ours only

1 John 4:10 God...sent his Son to be the ***p*** for our sins

PROUD

Job 40:12 Look on every one that is ***p,*** and bring him low

Ps 94:2 thou [God]...render a reward to the ***p***

Ps 119:69 The ***p*** have forged a lie against me

Prov 6:17 A ***p*** look, a lying tongue

Prov 16:5 one that is ***p*** in heart is an abomination

Eccl 7:8 the patient in spirit is better than the ***p*** in spirit

2 Tim 3:2 men shall be... covetous, boasters, ***p***

Jas 4:6 God resisteth the ***p,*** but giveth grace unto the humble

PROVE [D, TH]

Deut 13:3 God ***p'th*** you... whether ye love the LORD

Ps 26:2 Examine me, O LORD, and ***p*** me; try...my heart

Mal 3:10 ***p*** me now...saith the LORD of hosts

Rom 12:2 ***p*** what is that good, and...perfect, will of God

Gal 6:4 But let every man ***p*** his own work

1 Thes 5:21 ***P*** all things; hold fast that which is good

1 Tim 3:10 be ***p'd;*** then let them use the office of a deacon

PROVERBS, BOOK OF. A wisdom book of the Old Testament filled with pithy sayings on how to live with maturity and integrity under the watchful eye of God—the source of all wisdom.

PROVOKE [D, ING]

Deut 32:16 They ***p'd*** him [God]...with strange gods

Ps 78:17 sinned...against him [God] by ***p'ing***...most High

Ps 78:58 ***p'd*** him [God] to anger with their high places

1 Cor 10:22 Do we ***p*** the Lord to jealousy

1 Cor 13:5 [charity] is not easily ***p'd,*** thinketh no evil

Gal 5:26 not be desirous of vain glory, ***p'ing*** one another
Eph 6:4 fathers, ***p*** not your children to wrath
Heb 10:24 consider one another to ***p***...to good works

PSALMS, BOOK OF. A poetic book of the Old Testament filled with hymns of praise and prayers that probably were meant to be sung to the accompaniment of a musical instrument. King David of Judah wrote many of these psalms (see, for example, Pss 54; 59; 65).

PUBLIUS (a Roman official who entertained Paul on the island of Miletus after a shipwreck). Acts 28:7–8.

PUL. See *Tiglath-Pileser III.*

PUNISH [ED]
Isa 13:11 And I [God] will ***p*** the world for their evil
Jer 21:14 I [God] will ***p*** you according to...your doings
Jer 50:18 Behold, I [God] will ***p*** the king of Babylon
2 Thes 1:9 ***p'ed*** with everlasting destruction from the presence of the Lord

PURIFY [IED, IETH]
Titus 2:14 that he [Jesus] might...***p***...a peculiar people
Jas 4:8 and ***p*** your hearts, ye double minded
1 Pet 1:22 ***p'ied*** your souls in obeying the truth
1 John 3:3 every man that hath this hope...***p'ieth*** himself

PURPOSE [D, TH]
Eccl 3:1 a time to every ***p*** under the heaven
Dan 1:8 Daniel ***p'd***...that he would not defile himself
Rom 8:28 to them who are the called according to his ***p***
2 Cor 9:7 as he ***p'th*** in his heart, so let him give
Eph 3:11 eternal ***p*** which he ***p'd*** in Christ Jesus
1 John 3:8 For this ***p*** the Son of God was manifested

-Q-

QUAIL PROVIDED FOR ISRAEL IN THE WILDERNESS. Ex 16:1–13.

QUENCH [ED]

2 Chr 34:25 my [God's] wrath... shall not be ***q'ed***

Song 8:7 Many waters cannot ***q*** love

Jer 7:20 mine [God's] anger... shall not be ***q'ed***

Matt 12:20 A bruised reed shall he [God's servant] not break, and smoking flax shall he not ***q***

Mark 9:44 Where their worm dieth not...fire is not ***q'ed***

Eph 6:16 ye shall...***q*** all the fiery darts of the wicked

1 Thes 5:19 **Q** not the Spirit

QUICK [EN, ENED, ENETH, ENING]

Ps 71:20 Thou [God]...shalt ***q'en*** me

Ps 80:18 ***q'en*** us, and we will call upon thy [God's] name

Ps 119:88 ***Q'en*** me after thy [God's] lovingkindness

Ps 143:11 ***Q'en*** me, O LORD, for thy name's sake

Isa 11:3 make him [God's servant] of ***q*** understanding

John 5:21 Son ***q'eneth*** whom he will

John 6:63 the spirit that ***q'eneth***...flesh profiteth nothing

Acts 10:42 he [Jesus]...was ordained...Judge of ***q*** and dead

1 Cor 15:45 the last Adam was made a ***q'ening*** spirit

Eph 2:1 And you hath he ***q'ened,*** who were dead in trespasses and sins

2 Tim 4:1 Jesus Christ...shall judge the ***q*** and the dead

Heb 4:12 For the word of God is ***q,*** and powerful

-R-

RABBAH (capital city of the Ammonites captured by David's army). Josh 13:25 • **2 Sam 12:26–31** • 1 Chr 20:1 • Jer 49:2–3 • Ezek 25:5 • Amos 1:14. *Rabbath:* Ezek 21:20.

RABBATH. See *Rabbah.*

RACE
Eccl 9:11 I...saw...that the ***r*** is not to the swift
1 Cor 9:24 in a ***r*** run all, but one receiveth the prize
Heb 12:1 run with patience the ***r***...set before us

RACHAB. See *Rahab.*

RACHEL (Jacob's wife who died giving birth to Benjamin). Gen 29:6–31; 30:1–25; 31:4–34; 33:1–7; **35:16–24;** 46:19–25; 48:7 • Ruth 4:11 • Matt 2:18. *Rahel:* Jer 31:15–17.

RAHAB (a harlot who hid the spies sent by Joshua to scout the city of Jericho). **Josh 2:1–24;** 6:17–25 • Heb 11:31 • Jas 2:25. *Rachab:* Matt 1:5.

RAHEL. See *Rachel.*

RAINBOW AS GOD'S COVENANT SYMBOL. Gen 9:11–17.

RAISE [D, TH]
Judg 2:16 Nevertheless the LORD ***r'd*** up judges
Ps 41:10 LORD, be merciful unto me, and ***r*** me up
Ps 113:7 He [God] ***r'th*** up the poor out of the dust
Jer 23:5 I [God] will ***r*** unto David a righteous Branch
Amos 9:11 day will I [God] ***r*** up the tabernacle of David
Hab 1:6 I [God] ***r*** up the Chaldeans...bitter...nation
Matt 10:8 Heal the sick, cleanse the lepers, ***r*** the dead
Matt 16:21 he [Jesus] must... be killed, and be ***r'd*** again
John 2:19 Destroy this temple, and in three days I [Jesus] will ***r*** it up
John 5:21 as the Father ***r'th*** up the dead, and quickeneth them
Acts 10:40 Him [Jesus] God ***r'd*** up the third day
Rom 6:4 as Christ was ***r'd***... we...walk in newness of life
Rom 10:9 believe...God hath ***r'd*** him [Jesus] from the dead
1 Cor 6:14 God...will also ***r*** up us
1 Cor 15:16 if the dead rise not, then is not Christ ***r'd***
2 Tim 2:8 Jesus Christ...was ***r'd*** from the dead
Heb 11:19 God was able to ***r*** him [Jesus] up

RAMAH. See *Ramoth-gilead.*

RAMESES (a district of Egypt where Jacob and his descendants settled). **Gen 47:11** • Ex 12:37 • Num 33:3,5.

RAMOTH. See *Ramoth-gilead.*

RAMOTH-GILEAD (an Amorite city that became one of the six cities of refuge). Deut 4:43 • Josh 20:8 • 1 Chr 6:80. *Ramah:* 2 Kgs 8:29. *Ramoth:* 1 Kgs 22:3.

RANSOM

Prov 13:8 The ***r*** of a man's life are his riches

Hos 13:14 I [God] will ***r*** them from the power of the grave

Mark 10:45 the Son of man came...to give his life a ***r***

1 Tim 2:6 Who [Jesus] gave himself a ***r*** for all

READY

Ex 17:4 they be almost ***r*** to stone me [Moses]

Job 17:1 My [Job's] days are extinct...graves are ***r*** for me

Ps 86:5 thou, Lord, art good, and ***r*** to forgive

Mark 14:38 The spirit truly is ***r*,** but the flesh is weak

Luke 12:40 Be ye...***r***...the Son of man cometh...when ye think not

Luke 22:33 Lord, I [Peter] am ***r*** to go with thee

Rom 1:15 I [Paul] am ***r*** to preach...at Rome also

2 Tim 4:6 For I [Paul] am now ***r*** to be offered

1 Pet 3:15 be ***r*** always to give an answer to every man

REAP [ETH, ING]

Lev 19:9 not wholly ***r*** the corners of thy field

Job 4:8 they that...sow wickedness, ***r*** the same

Ps 126:5 They that sow in tears shall ***r*** in joy

Prov 22:8 He that soweth iniquity shall ***r*** vanity

Hos 8:7 they have sown the wind...***r*** the whirlwind

Matt 25:24 an hard man, ***r'ing*** where thou hast not sown

Luke 12:24 Consider...ravens: for they neither sow nor ***r***

John 4:37 One soweth, and another ***r'eth***

2 Cor 9:6 soweth bountifully shall ***r*** also bountifully

Gal 6:7 whatsoever a man soweth, that shall he also ***r***

Gal 6:9 shall ***r*,** if we faint not

REASON [ING]

Ps 90:10 if by ***r*** of strength they [days of our years] be fourscore years

Isa 1:18 Come now, and let us ***r*** together, saith the LORD

Luke 9:46 ***r'ing*** among them [the disciples], which... should be greatest

Acts 6:2 not ***r*** that we [the apostles] should leave... word of God...serve tables

1 Pet 3:15 asketh you a ***r*** of the hope that is in you

REBECCA. See *Rebekah.*

REBEKAH (wife of Isaac and mother of Jacob and Esau). Gen 22:23; 24:15–67; 26:7–8,35; 27:5–46; 28:5; 49:31. *Rebecca:* Rom 9:10.

REBUKE [D, S, TH]

Ps 6:1 O LORD, ***r*** me not in thine anger

Ps 119:21 Thou [God] hast ***r'd*** the proud that are cursed

Prov 27:5 Open ***r*** is better than secret love

Eccl 7:5 It is better to hear the ***r*** of the wise

Ezek 25:17 I [God] will execute... vengeance...furious ***r's***

Nah 1:4 He [God] ***r'th*** the sea, and maketh it dry

Matt 16:22 Peter took him [Jesus], and began to ***r*** him

Mark 8:33 he [Jesus] ***r'd*** Peter... Get...behind me, Satan

Luke 8:24 Then he [Jesus] arose, and ***r'd*** the wind

Titus 2:15 These things speak... and ***r*** with all authority

Rev 3:19 As many as I [Jesus] love, I ***r*** and chasten

RECEIVE [D, ING, TH]

Job 2:10 ***r*** good at the hand of God, and...not ***r*** evil

Prov 19:20 Hear counsel, and ***r*** instruction

Isa 40:2 Jerusalem...hath ***r'd*** of the LORD'S hand double

Mal 3:10 not be room enough to ***r*** it [God's blessing]

Matt 7:8 For every one that asketh ***r'th***

Matt 10:8 freely ye have ***r'd,*** freely give

Matt 11:5 blind ***r*** their sight, and the lame walk

Matt 18:5 whoso...***r*** one such little child...***r'th*** me [Jesus]

Matt 21:22 ask in prayer, believing, ye shall ***r***

Mark 10:15 Whosoever shall not ***r*** the kingdom of God as a little child

Luke 23:41 we [two thieves] ***r*** the due reward of our deeds

John 1:11 came unto his [Jesus'] own...own ***r'd*** him not

John 3:27 ***r*** nothing, except it be given him from heaven

John 14:3 come again, and ***r*** you unto myself [Jesus]

John 20:22 he [Jesus] breathed on them [the disciples]...***R*** ye the Holy Ghost

Acts 1:8 But ye [the apostles] shall ***r*** power

Acts 8:17 they [the Samaritans] ***r'd*** the Holy Ghost

Acts 17:11 they [the Bereans] ***r'd*** the word with...readiness

Acts 20:35 It is more blessed to give than to ***r***

Rom 8:15 ye have ***r'd*** the Spirit of adoption

1 Cor 2:14 natural man ***r'th*** not the things of the Spirit

1 Cor 3:14 If any man's work abide...he shall ***r*** a reward
Heb 11:8 called to...a place which he [Abraham] should after ***r*** for an inheritance
Heb 11:13 died in faith, not having ***r'd*** the promises
Jas 1:12 man...endureth temptation...***r*** the crown of life
Jas 4:3 Ye ask, and ***r*** not, because ye ask amiss
1 Pet 1:9 ***R'ing*** the end of your faith, even...salvation
1 Pet 5:4 ye shall ***r*** a crown of glory that fadeth not
Rev 4:11 Thou art worthy, O Lord, to ***r*** glory and honour

RECHAB (father of Jehonadab and ancestor of the Rechabites). 2 Kgs 10:15–23 • Jer 35:6–19.

RECKON [ED, ETH]
Matt 25:19 lord of those servants...***r'eth*** with them
Luke 22:37 he [Jesus] was ***r'ed*** among the transgressors
Rom 8:18 ***r*** that the sufferings... not worthy to be compared

RECONCILE [D, ING]
Matt 5:24 be ***r'd*** to thy brother...then...offer thy gift
2 Cor 5:19 God was in Christ, ***r'ing*** the world unto himself
2 Cor 5:20 in Christ's stead, be ye ***r'd*** to God
Eph 2:16 he [Jesus] might ***r*** both unto God...by the cross

RECONCILIATION
2 Chr 29:24 priests...made ***r*** with their [animals'] blood
2 Cor 5:18 God...hath given to us the ministry of ***r***
Heb 2:17 he [Jesus] might... make ***r***...sins of the people

RED SEA (a body of water that the Israelites crossed miraculously to escape the Egyptian army). Ex 10:19; **14:16–29; 15:4,22** • Num 33:10–11.

REDEEM [ED, ETH, ING]
Ps 26:11 ***r*** me, and be merciful unto me
Ps 34:22 The LORD ***r'eth*** the soul of his servants
Ps 49:15 But God will ***r*** my soul from...the grave
Ps 77:15 Thou [God] hast... ***r'ed*** thy people
Ps 107:2 Let the ***r'ed*** of the LORD say so
Isa 43:1 Fear not: for I [God] have ***r'ed*** thee [Israel]
Isa 50:2 Is my [God's] hand shortened...that it cannot ***r***
Isa 52:9 for the LORD...hath ***r'ed*** Jerusalem
Luke 1:68 the Lord...hath visited and ***r'ed*** his people
Gal 3:13 Christ hath ***r'ed*** us from the curse of the law
Gal 4:5 To ***r*** them that were under the law

Eph 5:16 ***R'ing*** the time, because the days are evil
Col 4:5 Walk in wisdom...***r'ing*** the time
Titus 2:14 he [Jesus] might ***r*** us from all iniquity

REDEMPTION
Ps 130:7 for with the LORD there is...plenteous ***r***
Rom 3:24 justified...through the ***r*** that is in Christ Jesus
Eph 1:7 we have ***r*** through his [Jesus'] blood
Heb 9:12 by his [Jesus'] own blood he...obtained...***r***

REGENERATION
Matt 19:28 ye which...followed me [Jesus], in the ***r***...sit upon twelve thrones
Titus 3:5 he [Jesus] saved us, by the washing of ***r***

REHOBOAM (son and successor of Solomon as king of Judah who refused to implement the reform measures called for by northern leaders). 1 Kgs 11:43; **12:1–24;** 14:21–31; 15:6 • 1 Chr 3:10 • 2 Chr 9:31; 10:1–18; 11:1–22; 12:1–16; 13:7. *Roboam:* Matt 1:7.

REIGN [ED, ETH]
Gen 37:8 Shalt thou [Joseph] indeed ***r*** over us
Judg 9:8 The trees...said unto the olive tree, ***R*** thou over us
2 Sam 5:4 David was thirty years old when he began to ***r***
1 Chr 29:26 David the son of Jesse ***r'ed*** over all Israel
Ps 47:8 God ***r'eth*** over the heathen
Ps 93:1 The LORD ***r'eth,*** he is clothed with majesty
Ps 146:10 LORD shall ***r*** for ever
Jer 23:5 a King shall ***r*** and prosper...execute judgment
Luke 1:33 he [Jesus] shall ***r*** over the house of Jacob for ever
Rom 5:14 death ***r'ed*** from Adam to Moses
Rom 6:12 Let not sin...***r*** in your mortal body
1 Cor 15:25 he [Jesus] must ***r,*** till...all enemies under his feet
Rev 11:15 Christ...shall ***r*** for ever and ever
Rev 19:6 Alleluia...the Lord God omnipotent ***r'eth***

REJECT [ED]
1 Sam 15:26 thou [Saul] hast ***r'ed*** the word of the LORD
Isa 53:3 he [God's servant] is despised and ***r'ed*** of men
Mark 7:9 ye [Pharisees] ***r*** the commandment of God
Mark 12:10 The stone which the builders ***r'ed***
Luke 17:25 must he [Jesus] suffer many things, and be ***r'ed*** of this generation

REJOICE [D, ING, TH]
Deut 30:9 for the LORD will again ***r*** over thee
1 Sam 2:1 My [Hannah's] heart ***r'th*** in the LORD
1 Chr 16:10 let the heart of them ***r*** that seek the LORD
Job 8:21 Till he [God] fill...thy lips with ***r'ing***
Ps 5:11 those that put their trust in thee [God] ***r***
Ps 19:8 statutes of the LORD are right, ***r'ing*** the heart
Ps 32:11 Be glad in the LORD, and ***r,*** ye righteous
Ps 40:16 Let all those that seek thee [God] ***r*** and be glad
Ps 63:7 in the shadow of thy [God's] wings will I ***r***
Ps 97:1 The LORD reigneth; let the earth ***r***
Ps 108:7 God hath spoken in his holiness; I will ***r***
Ps 118:24 day...LORD hath made; we will ***r*** and be glad
Ps 119:14 I have ***r'd*** in...thy [God's] testimonies
Ps 126:6 come again with ***r'ing,*** bringing his sheaves
Prov 5:18 and ***r*** with the wife of thy youth
Prov 15:30 The light of the eyes ***r'th*** the heart
Eccl 11:9 ***R,*** O young man, in thy youth
Isa 29:19 poor...shall ***r*** in the Holy One of Israel
Joel 2:21 be glad and ***r:*** for the LORD will do great things
Matt 2:10 they [the wise men] ***r'd*** with...great joy
Matt 5:12 ***R***...for great is your reward in heaven
Luke 15:6 ***R*** with me; for I have found my sheep
John 8:56 Abraham ***r'd*** to see my [Jesus'] day
Rom 12:12 ***R'ing*** in hope; patient in tribulation
Rom 12:15 ***R*** with them that do ***r***...weep with them that weep
Phil 1:18 Christ is preached; and I [Paul] therein do ***r***

REJOICE IN THE LORD
Ps 33:1 ***R-i-t-L,*** O ye righteous
Ps 97:12 ***R-i-t-L***...and give thanks at...his holiness
Hab 3:18 I will ***r-i-t-L,*** I will joy in...my salvation
Phil 3:1 Finally, my brethren, ***r-i-t-L***
Phil 4:4 ***R-i-t-L*** alway: and again I say, Rejoice

REMEMBER [ED, EST, ETH, ING]
Gen 8:1 God ***r'ed*** Noah, and every living thing
Gen 9:16 that I [God] may ***r*** the everlasting covenant
Ex 2:24 God heard their [Israel's] groaning, and...***r'ed*** his covenant
Ex 20:8 ***R*** the sabbath day, to keep it holy
Deut 8:18 thou shalt ***r*** the LORD thy God

Deut 15:15 ***r*** that thou [Israel] wast a bondman in...Egypt
Ps 20:7 we will ***r*** the name of the LORD our God
Ps 25:7 ***R*** not the sins of my youth, nor my transgressions
Ps 45:17 make thy [God's] name to be ***r'ed***
Ps 77:10 ***r*** the years of the right hand of the most High
Ps 78:39 he [God] ***r'ed*** that they were but flesh
Ps 98:3 He [God] hath ***r'ed*** his mercy...toward...Israel
Ps 103:14 For…he [God] ***r'eth*** that we are dust
Ps 137:1 we [Israelites] wept, when we ***r'ed*** Zion
Ps 137:7 ***R,*** O LORD, the children of Edom
Eccl 12:1 ***R*** now thy Creator in the days of thy youth
Jer 31:34 I [God] will ***r*** their sin no more
Jon 2:7 my [Jonah's] soul fainted...I ***r'ed*** the LORD
Matt 5:23 there [at the altar] ***r'est*** that thy brother hath ought against thee
Luke 22:61 And Peter ***r'ed*** the word of the Lord
Luke 23:42 Lord, ***r*** me [thief] when thou comest into thy kingdom
Luke 24:8 they [the disciples] ***r'ed*** his [Jesus'] words
John 16:21 as soon as she is delivered of the child, she ***r'eth*** no more the anguish
1 Thes 1:3 ***R'ing*** without ceasing your work of faith
2 Tim 2:8 ***R*** that Jesus Christ... was raised from the dead
Heb 10:17 their sins...will I [God] ***r*** no more

REMEMBRANCE

Ps 30:4 give thanks at the ***r*** of his [God's] holiness
Ps 102:12 endure for ever; and thy [God's] ***r*** unto all generations
Luke 22:19 This is my [Jesus'] body...this do in ***r*** of me
John 14:26 the Comforter... bring all things to your ***r***

REMISSION

Heb 9:22 without shedding of blood is no ***r***
Heb 10:18 where ***r***...is, there is no more offering for sin

REMISSION OF SINS

Matt 26:28 my [Jesus'] blood... is shed for many for the ***r-o-s***
Mark 1:4 John did baptize... preach the baptism of repentance for the ***r-o-s***
Luke 24:47 repentance and ***r-o-s*** should be preached...among all nations
Acts 2:38 be baptized...in the name of Jesus...for the ***r-o-s***
Acts 10:43 whosoever believeth in him [Jesus] shall receive ***r-o-s***

REMPHAN (a pagan Babylonian god worshiped by the Israelites). Acts 7:41–43.

RENDER [ED, ING]
Ps 38:20 They...that ***r*** evil for good are mine adversaries
Ps 116:12 ***r*** unto the LORD for all his benefits
Prov 12:14 and the recompence of a man's hands shall be ***r'ed*** unto him
Luke 20:25 ***R***...unto Caesar
Rom 2:6 Who [God] will ***r*** to... man according to his deeds
1 Cor 7:3 husband ***r*** unto the wife due benevolence
1 Thes 5:15 See that none ***r*** evil for evil unto any man
1 Pet 3:9 Not ***r'ing*** evil for evil...railing for railing

RENEW [ED, EST, ING]
Ps 51:10 clean heart, O God... ***r*** a right spirit within me
Ps 104:30 thou [God] ***r'est*** the face of the earth
Isa 40:31 they that wait upon the LORD...***r*** their strength
Rom 12:2 be ye transformed by the ***r'ing*** of your mind
2 Cor 4:16 yet the inward man is ***r'ed*** day by day

REPENT [ED, ETH]
Gen 6:6 it ***r'ed*** the LORD that he had made man
Job 42:6 I [Job] abhor myself... ***r*** in dust and ashes
Matt 4:17 Jesus began to preach, and to say, ***R***
Luke 15:7 joy...in heaven over one sinner that ***r'eth***
Luke 17:3 if he [your brother] ***r***, forgive him
Acts 2:38 Peter said...***R***, and be baptized every one of you
Rev 3:19 I [Jesus] rebuke... chasten: be zealous...and ***r***

REPENTANCE
Matt 9:13 I [Jesus] am...come to call...sinners to ***r***
Luke 24:47 ***r***...preached...among all nations
2 Cor 7:10 godly sorrow worketh ***r*** to salvation
2 Pet 3:9 all should come to ***r***

REPHAIM (a valley near Jerusalem where David defeated the Philistines). **2 Sam 5:18–25;** 23:13 • 1 Chr 11:15; 14:9 • Isa 17:5.

REPROACH [ED, ETH]
Ps 31:11 I was a ***r*** among all mine enemies
Ps 55:12 For it was not an enemy that ***r'ed*** me
Ps 102:8 Mine enemies ***r*** me all the day
Prov 14:31 He that oppresseth the poor ***r'eth*** his Maker
Prov 14:34 but sin is a ***r*** to any people
Heb 11:26 Esteeming...***r*** of Christ greater riches than... treasures in Egypt

Heb 13:13 go...unto him [Jesus]...bearing his ***r***
1 Pet 4:14 ye be ***r'ed*** for the name of Christ, happy are ye

REPROBATE [S]
Rom 1:28 God gave them over to a ***r*** mind
2 Cor 13:6 I [Paul] trust that ye...know...we are not ***r's***
2 Tim 3:8 men of corrupt minds, ***r*** concerning the faith

REPROVE [D, TH]
Ps 50:8 I [God] will not ***r*** thee for thy sacrifices
Prov 9:7 He that ***r'th*** a scorner getteth...shame
John 16:8 he [the Holy Spirit] will ***r*** the world of sin
Eph 5:13 all things that are ***r'ed*** are made manifest
2 Tim 4:2 ***r,*** rebuke, exhort with all longsuffering

REPUTATION
Phil 2:7 made himself [Jesus] of no ***r***...took...form of a servant
Phil 2:29 Receive him [Epaphroditus]...and hold such in ***r***

RESIST [ED, ETH]
Matt 5:39 I [Jesus] say unto you, That ye ***r*** not evil
Acts 7:51 ye do always ***r*** the Holy Ghost
Heb 12:4 Ye have not yet ***r'ed*** unto blood
Jas 4:6 God ***r'eth***...proud... giveth grace unto the humble
Jas 4:7 ***R*** the devil, and he will flee from you

RESPECT [ETH]
Gen 4:4 the LORD had ***r*** unto Abel and to his offering
Ps 40:4 Blessed is that man that...***r'eth*** not the proud
Ps 119:15 I will...have ***r*** unto thy [God's] ways

RESPECT OF PERSONS
Prov 24:23 not good to have ***r-o-p*** in judgment
Rom 2:11 For there is no ***r-o-p*** with God
Eph 6:9 neither is there ***r-o-p*** with him [Jesus]
1 Pet 1:17 who [God] without ***r-o-p*** judgeth...every man's work

RESTORE [TH]
Ps 23:3 He [God] ***r'th*** my soul
Ps 51:12 ***R*** unto me the joy of thy [God's] salvation
Luke 19:8 Behold, Lord...I [Zacchaeus] ***r*** him fourfold
Acts 1:6 Lord, wilt thou...***r*** again the kingdom to Israel
Gal 6:1 ***r*** such an one in the spirit of meekness

RESURRECTION
Matt 27:53 [the saints] came out of the graves after his [Jesus'] ***r***

Luke 20:33 Therefore in the ***r*** whose wife of them is she
John 11:25 I [Jesus] am the ***r***, and the life
Acts 4:33 gave the apostles witness of the ***r*** of...Jesus
Acts 17:32 they [philosophers] heard of the ***r***...mocked
1 Cor 15:13 no ***r*** of the dead, then is Christ not risen
Phil 3:10 I [Paul] may know him [Jesus]...power of his ***r***
1 Pet 1:3 a lively hope by the ***r*** of Jesus Christ
Rev 20:6 Blessed...is he that hath part in the first ***r***

RESURRECTION AND THE LIFE, JESUS AS. See *"I Am" Statements of Jesus.*

RESURRECTION OF JESUS. See *Jesus, Life and Ministry of.*

REUBEN (a son of Jacob and ancestor of one of the twelve tribes of Israel). Gen 29:32; 37:21–29; 42:22,37; 46:8–9; 48:5; 49:3. The tribe of Reuben settled east of the Jordan River along the Dead Sea. Num 32:1–25.

REUEL. See *Jethro.*

REVEAL [ED, ETH]
Job 20:27 heaven shall ***r*** his [man's] iniquity
Isa 40:5 glory of the LORD shall be ***r'ed***
Dan 2:28 there is a God in heaven that ***r'eth*** secrets
Matt 16:17 flesh and blood... not ***r'ed*** it unto thee [Peter]
Luke 10:21 hid these things from the wise and...***r'ed*** them unto babes
Luke 10:22 no man knoweth... who the Father is...and he to whom the Son will ***r*** him
Rom 1:17 righteousness of God ***r'ed*** from faith to faith
1 Cor 3:13 it [man's work] shall be ***r'ed*** by fire
Phil 3:15 God shall ***r*** even this
1 Pet 1:5 kept by the power of God through faith...ready to be ***r'ed*** in the last time
1 Pet 4:13 when his [Jesus'] glory shall be ***r'ed***

REVELATION
Gal 1:12 neither was I [Paul] taught it, but by the ***r*** of Jesus Christ
Eph 3:3 by ***r*** he [God] made known...the mystery
Rev 1:1 ***R*** of Jesus Christ, which God gave

REVELATION OF JOHN, BOOK OF THE. The last book of the New Testament that consists of a series of visions revealed by the Lord to the apostle John. These visions are considered by some interpreters to portray the end of the present age and the coming of God's kingdom.

REVERENCE

Lev 26:2 keep my [God's] sabbaths, and ***r*** my sanctuary

Luke 20:13 it may be they will ***r*** him [vineyard owner's son]

Heb 12:28 we may serve God... with ***r*** and godly fear

REVILE [D]

Matt 5:11 Blessed are ye, when men shall ***r*** you

Mark 15:32 And they [two thieves] that were crucified with him [Jesus] ***r'd*** him

1 Pet 2:23 Who [Jesus], when he was ***r'd, r'd*** not again

REWARD [ED, ETH]

Gen 15:1 I [God] am thy [Abraham's]...great ***r***

Ps 18:20 LORD ***r'ed*** me according to my righteousness

Ps 31:23 the LORD...plentifully ***r'eth*** the proud doer

Ps 58:11 Verily there is a ***r*** for the righteous

Ps 103:10 He [God] hath not... ***r'ed*** us according to our iniquities

Ps 127:3 and the fruit of the womb is his [God's] ***r***

Prov 17:13 Whoso ***r'eth*** evil for good, evil shall not depart from his house

Matt 5:12 great is your ***r*** in heaven: for so persecuted they the prophets

Matt 5:46 love them which love you, what ***r*** have ye

Luke 23:41 we [two thieves] receive...due ***r*** of our deeds

1 Cor 3:8 every man shall receive his own ***r***

Col 3:24 ye shall receive the ***r*** of the inheritance

1 Tim 5:18 The labourer is worthy of his ***r***

REZIN (a king of Syria who was killed in the conquest by the Assyrians). **2 Kgs 15:37; 16:5–9** • Isa 7:4,8; 8:6; 9:11.

RHODES (a Greek island that Paul's ship passed). Acts 21:1.

RIGHT HAND OF GOD

Mark 16:19 he [Jesus] was received up...and sat on the ***r-h-o-G***

Acts 7:55 he [Stephen]... saw...Jesus standing on the ***r-h-o-G***

Col 3:1 seek those things... above, where Christ sitteth on the ***r-h-o-G***

Heb 10:12 this man [Jesus]... sat down on the ***r-h-o-G***

1 Pet 3:22 Who [Jesus] is gone into heaven...on the ***r-h-o-G***

RIGHTEOUS [LY, NESS]

Gen 15:6 the LORD...counted it...for ***r'ness***

Gen 18:23 Wilt thou [God]... destroy the ***r*** with the wicked

Job 15:14 What is man...that he should be ***r***
Job 32:1 because he [Job] was ***r*** in his own eyes
Ps 1:6 For the LORD knoweth the way of the ***r***
Ps 9:8 And he [God] shall judge the world in ***r'ness***
Ps 19:9 judgments of the LORD are true and ***r***
Ps 23:3 he [God] leadeth me in the paths of ***r'ness***
Ps 35:28 my tongue shall speak of thy [God's] ***r'ness***
Ps 37:16 A little that a ***r*** man hath is better than...riches
Ps 37:29 The ***r*** shall inherit the land...dwell therein
Ps 45:7 Thou [God] lovest ***r'ness,*** and hatest wickedness
Ps 97:6 The heavens declare his [God's] ***r'ness***
Ps 119:137 ***R*** art thou, O LORD... upright...thy judgments
Ps 129:4 LORD is ***r:*** he hath cut...the cords of the wicked
Ps 145:17 The LORD is ***r*** in all his ways...holy in...works
Prov 10:11 The mouth of a ***r*** man is a well of life
Prov 14:34 ***R'ness*** exalteth a nation
Prov 15:29 The LORD...heareth the prayer of the ***r***
Prov 16:8 Better is a little with ***r'ness*** than great revenues
Prov 31:9 judge ***r'ly,*** and plead the cause of the poor
Isa 62:2 the Gentiles shall see thy [God's] ***r'ness***
Jer 23:5 I [God] will raise unto David a ***r*** Branch
Amos 5:24 let judgment run down as waters, and ***r'ness*** as a mighty stream
Mal 4:2 Sun of ***r'ness*** arise with healing in his wings
Matt 5:6 Blessed are they which...thirst after ***r'ness***
Matt 5:20 except your ***r'ness***... exceed...***r'ness*** of the scribes
Matt 6:33 But seek ye first the kingdom of God, and his ***r'ness***
Luke 5:32 I [Jesus] came not to call the ***r***...to repentance
Luke 23:47 Certainly this [Jesus] was a ***r*** man
Rom 1:17 ***r'ness*** of God revealed from faith to faith
Rom 3:10 As it is written, There is none ***r,*** no, not one
Rom 4:3 Abraham believed God...counted...for ***r'ness***
Rom 5:19 by the obedience of one [Jesus]...many be made ***r***
Rom 10:10 with the heart man believeth unto ***r'ness***
2 Cor 5:21 might be made... ***r'ness*** of God in him [Jesus]
2 Cor 6:14 what fellowship hath ***r'ness*** with unrighteousness
Eph 6:14 having on the breastplate of ***r'ness***
2 Tim 4:8 laid up for me [Paul] a crown of ***r'ness***
Jas 5:16 fervent prayer of a ***r*** man availeth much

1 Pet 3:12 For the eyes of the Lord are over the ***r***
1 Pet 3:14 if ye suffer for ***r'ness'*** sake, happy are ye

RIMMON (a pagan god worshiped by Naaman the leper). 2 Kgs 5:18.

ROBOAM. See *Rehoboam.*

ROMANS, EPISTLE TO THE. An epistle on the themes of righteousness and salvation, written by the apostle Paul to the Christians at Rome. The most systematic and theological of all of Paul's epistles, Romans expresses his conviction that the gospel is the power of salvation to all who believe (1:16–17).

ROME (capital city of the Roman Empire and the place where Paul was imprisoned during his final days). Acts 2:10; 18:2; 19:21; 23:11; **28:14–16** • Rom 1:7,15 • 2 Tim 1:17.

RUHAMAH (a symbolic name, meaning "having obtained favor," given by the prophet Hosea to his daughter to show that Israel would be forgiven). Hos 2:1.

RULE [ING, TH]
Gen 1:16 two great lights; the greater light to ***r*** the day
2 Sam 23:3 He that ***r'th*** over men must be just
Matt 2:6 a Governor, that shall ***r*** my people Israel
Col 3:15 let the peace of God ***r*** in your hearts
1 Tim 3:5 if a man know not how to ***r*** his own house
1 Tim 3:12 deacons...***r'ing***... their own houses well

RUN [NETH, NING]
Ps 23:5 my cup ***r'neth*** over
Eccl 1:7 All the rivers ***r*** into the sea...sea is not full
Isa 40:31 they shall ***r,*** and not be weary
Jer 5:1 ***R*** ye [Jeremiah] to and fro through...streets of Jerusalem
Amos 5:24 let judgment ***r*** down as waters
Hab 2:2 Write the vision...that he may ***r*** that readeth it
Matt 28:8 they [the women] departed...and did ***r*** to bring his [Jesus'] disciples word
Luke 6:38 pressed down... shaken together, and ***r'ning*** over
1 Cor 9:24 ***r*** all, but one receiveth the prize
Gal 5:7 Ye did ***r*** well; who did hinder you
Heb 12:1 let us ***r*** with patience the race...before us

RUTH (a Moabite woman who remained loyal to her Jewish mother-in-law Naomi after the death of their husbands). Ruth 1–4.

RUTH, BOOK OF. A short Old Testament book on the power of love in dismal circumstances. Love bound Ruth and her mother-in-law Naomi together, even after their husbands died (1:1–2:23).

-S-

SACKCLOTH AND ASHES

Esth 4:3 and many [Jews] lay in ***s-a-a***

Dan 9:3 seek [God] by prayer... with fasting, and ***s-a-a***

Matt 11:21 they [Tyre and Sidon] would have repented long ago in ***s-a-a***

SACRIFICE [S]

1 Sam 15:22 Behold, to obey is better than ***s***

Ps 4:5 Offer the ***s's*** of righteousness...trust in the LORD

Ps 51:17 The ***s's*** of God are a broken spirit

Ps 116:17 offer to thee [God] the ***s*** of thanksgiving

Prov 15:8 The ***s*** of the wicked is an abomination

Prov 17:1 Better is a dry morsel...than...***s's*** with strife

Hos 6:6 For I [God] desired mercy, and not ***s***

Jon 2:9 I will ***s*** unto thee [God] with...thanksgiving

Rom 12:1 present your bodies a living ***s***

Heb 7:27 Who [Jesus] needeth not daily...to offer up ***s***

Heb 11:4 Abel offered...a more excellent ***s*** than Cain

Heb 13:15 offer the ***s*** of praise to God continually

1 Pet 2:5 offer up spiritual ***s's,*** acceptable to God

SADDUCEES (a priestly aristocratic party of New Testament times that often opposed Jesus and His teachings). Matt 3:7; **16:1,6,11–12; 22:23–34 • Mark 12:18 • Luke 20:27 •** Acts 4:1–3; 5:17–18; 23:6–8.

SAINTS

2 Chr 6:41 let thy [God's] ***s*** rejoice in goodness

Ps 30:4 Sing unto the LORD, O ye ***s*** of his

Ps 89:7 God is greatly to be feared in...assembly of the ***s***

Ps 116:15 Precious in the sight of the LORD...death of his ***s***

Matt 27:52 bodies of the ***s*** which slept arose

Rom 12:13 Distributing to the necessity of ***s***

1 Cor 1:2 them...sanctified in Christ Jesus, called to be ***s***

Eph 3:8 Unto me [Paul], who am less than the least of all ***s***

Eph 4:12 perfecting of the ***s,*** for the work of the ministry

Rev 17:6 woman drunken with the blood of the ***s***

SAKE [S]

Ps 23:3 paths of righteousness for his [God's] name's ***s***

Matt 5:10 Blessed are they which are persecuted for righteousness' ***s***

Mark 8:35 lose his life for my [Jesus'] ***s*** and the gospel's

Luke 21:17 ye shall be hated... for my [Jesus'] name's ***s***

Acts 9:16 he [Paul] must suffer for my [Jesus'] name's ***s***
Rom 8:36 For thy [God's] ***s*** we are killed all the day long
1 Cor 4:10 We are fools for Christ's ***s***
2 Cor 8:9 for your ***s's*** he [Jesus] became poor
1 Tim 5:23 use a little wine for thy stomach's ***s***
1 Pet 3:14 suffer for righteousness' ***s,*** happy are ye

SALAMIS (a town on the island of Cyprus where Paul and Barnabas preached during the first missionary journey). Acts 13:4–5.

SALEM. See *Jerusalem.*

SALIM (a place near the Jordan River where John the Baptist baptized). John 3:23.

SALOME (a woman who witnessed the crucifixion of Jesus and visited His tomb). Mark 15:40–41; 16:1.

SALT
Job 6:6 Can that which is unsavoury be eaten without ***s***
Matt 5:13 Ye are the ***s*** of the earth
Col 4:6 Let your speech be... seasoned with ***s***

SALT SEA (a salt-saturated body of water, referred to today as the *Dead Sea,* into which the Jordan River empties in southern Palestine). Gen 14:3 • Josh 3:16. *East Sea:* Joel 2:20. *Sea of the Plain:* Deut 3:17.

SAMARIA (capital city of Israel, or the Northern Kingdom, that was captured by the Assyrians). 1 Kgs 16:24–29; 20:1–22 • **2 Kgs 17:3–24** • Amos 3:11–12.

SAMARITANS (inhabitants of the district of Samaria who were considered inferior by the Jews because of their mixed-blood ancestry). 2 Kgs 17:29 • Matt 10:5 • Luke 9:52; 10:33; 17:16 • John 4:9–40; 8:48 • Acts 8:25.

SAMOS (an island of Greece visited by the apostle Paul). Acts 20:15.

SAMOTHRACIA (an island in the Aegean Sea visited by the apostle Paul). Acts 16:11.

SAMSON (a judge of Israel with great physical strength who died when he destroyed a pagan Philistine temple). Judg 13:24; 14:1–20; 15:1–16; **16:1–31** • Heb 11:32.

SAMUEL (a prophet and the last judge of Israel who anointed the first two kings of Judah—Saul and David). 1 Sam 1:20; 2:18–26; 3:1–21; 4:1; 7:3–15; 8:1–22; **9:14–27; 10:1–25;** 11:7–14; 12:1–25; 13: 8–15; 15:1–35; **16:1–23;** 25:1; 28:3,11–20 • 1 Chr 6:28; 9:22; 11:3; 26:28; 29:29 • 2 Chr 35:18 • Ps 99:6 • Jer 15:1 • Acts 3:24; 13:20 • Heb 11:32. *Shemuel:* 1 Chr 6:33.

SAMUEL, BOOKS OF FIRST AND SECOND. Two historical books of the Old Testament named for the prophet Samuel, who anointed Saul and David as the first two kings of Israel. Their anointing marked the transition of the nation from a loose confederacy of tribes to a united kingdom under the leadership of a king.

SANBALLAT (a Samaritan who plotted to kill Nehemiah to stop his rebuilding projects). Neh 2:10,19; 4:1,7; 6:1–14; 13:28.

SANCTIFICATION
1 Thes 4:3 this is the will of God, even your ***s***
2 Thes 2:13 God hath...chosen you to salvation through ***s*** of the Spirit
1 Pet 1:2 Elect...through ***s*** of the Spirit

SANCTIFY [IED]
Gen 2:3 God blessed the seventh day, and ***s'ied*** it
Lev 20:7 ***S*** yourselves therefore, and be ye holy
Deut 5:12 Keep the sabbath day to ***s*** it
Josh 3:5 Joshua said unto the people, ***S*** yourselves
1 Chr 15:14 priests...***s'ied*** themselves to bring...the ark
Joel 1:14 ***S*** ye a fast, call a solemn assembly
John 17:17 ***S*** them [the disciples] through thy [God's] truth: thy word is truth
1 Cor 6:11 ye are washed...ye are ***s'ied***...ye are justified
1 Tim 4:5 it is ***s'ied*** by the word of God and prayer
1 Pet 3:15 But ***s*** the Lord God in your hearts

SAPPHIRA (a believer struck dead for lying and withholding money she had pledged to the church). Acts 5:1–11.

SARAH (wife of Abraham and mother of Isaac). Gen 17:15–21; 18:6–15; 20:2–18; 21:1–12; 23:1–19; 24:36; 25:10; 49:31 • Isa 51:2 • Rom 9:9 • *Sara:* Heb 11:11 • 1 Pet 3:6. *Sarai:* Gen 11:30; 12:5.

SARDIS (a city of Asia Minor and site of one of the seven churches addressed by John in the Book of Revelation). Rev 3:1–6.

SAREPTA. See *Zarephath.*

SARGON (a king of Assyria who captured Samaria and carried the Northern Kingdom into exile). Isa 20:1.

SARON. See *Sharon.*

SATAN (an evil being who opposes God; the devil). 1 Chr 21:1 • Job 1:6–12; 2:1–7 • Ps 109:6 • Zech 3:1–2 • Matt 4:10; 12:26; 16:23 • Mark 1:13; 3:23, 26; 4:15; 8:33 • Luke 4:8; 10:18; 11:18; 13:16; 22:3,31 • John 13:27 • Acts 5:3; 26:18 • Rom 16:20 • 1 Cor 5:5; 7:5 • 2 Cor 2:11; 11:14; 12:7 • 1 Thes 2:18 • 2 Thes 2:9 • 1 Tim 1:20; 5:15 • Rev 2:9,13,24; 3:9; 12:9; 20:2,7. *Belial:* 2 Cor 6:15. *Lucifer:* Isa 14:12.

SAUL

1. The first king of Israel who tried to kill David and was defeated by the Philistines. 1 Sam 9:1–31:12 • 1 Chr 10:2–13.

2. The original name of the apostle Paul. See *Paul.*

SAVE [D, ING, TH]

Ex 14:30 Lord ***s'd*** Israel...out of...hand of...Egyptians

Job 2:6 he [Job] is in thine [Satan's] hand; but ***s*** his life

Ps 7:1 ***s*** me from all them that persecute me

Ps 7:10 My defence is of God, which ***s'th*** the upright

Ps 44:6 not trust in my bow, neither shall my sword ***s*** me

Ps 55:16 I will call upon God; and the Lord shall ***s*** me

Ps 67:2 thy [God's] ***s'ing*** health among all nations

Ps 80:19 cause thy [God's] face to shine...we shall be ***s'd***

Ps 107:13 he [God] ***s'd*** them out of their distresses

Prov 20:22 wait on the Lord, and he shall ***s*** thee

Isa 45:22 be ye ***s'd,*** all the ends of the earth

Isa 59:1 Lord's hand is not shortened, that it cannot ***s***

Jer 8:20 summer is ended, and we are not ***s'd***

Matt 1:21 he [Jesus] shall ***s*** his people from their sins

Matt 10:22 he that endureth to the end shall be ***s'd***

Mark 8:35 whosoever will ***s*** his life shall lose it

Mark 10:26 Who...can be ***s'd***

Luke 19:10 Son of man is come to seek and to ***s*** that which was lost

Luke 23:35 He [Jesus] ***s'd*** others; let him save himself

John 3:17 the world through him [Jesus] might be ***s'd***
John 12:47 I [Jesus] came not to judge...but to ***s*** the world
Acts 2:21 whosoever shall call on...the Lord shall be ***s'd***
Acts 4:12 none other name... whereby we must be ***s'd***
Rom 5:10 we shall be ***s'd*** by his [Jesus'] life
Rom 10:13 whosoever shall call upon the name of the Lord shall be ***s'd***
1 Cor 1:21 it pleased God by the foolishness of preaching to ***s*** them that believe
1 Cor 9:22 I [Paul] am made all things to all men, that I might...***s*** some
Eph 2:8 by grace are ye ***s'd*** through faith
1 Tim 1:15 Christ Jesus came into the world to ***s*** sinners
2 Tim 1:9 Who [Jesus]...***s'd***... called us with an holy calling
Heb 7:25 he [Jesus] is able also to ***s*** them to the uttermost
Jas 2:14 though a man...have not works? can faith ***s*** him

SAVIOUR
2 Sam 22:3 The God of my rock ...is...my high tower...***s***
Isa 43:11 beside me [God] there is no ***s***
Luke 2:11 unto you is born...in the city of David a ***S***
1 John 4:14 Father sent the Son to be the ***S*** of the world

SCEVA (a Jewish priest whose sons tried to cast out evil spirits as Paul did). Acts 19:11–16.

SCRIPTURE [S]
Luke 4:21 This day is this ***s*** fulfilled in your ears
Luke 24:45 they [the disciples] might understand the ***s's***
John 5:39 Search the ***s's;*** for in them...ye have eternal life
John 20:9 as yet they [the disciples] knew not the ***s,*** that he [Jesus] must rise again
Acts 17:11 These [the Bereans]... searched the ***s's*** daily
Rom 4:3 what saith the ***s?*** Abraham believed God
1 Cor 15:3 Christ died for our sins according to the ***s's***
2 Tim 3:16 All ***s*** is given by inspiration of God
2 Pet 1:20 Knowing this...no prophecy of the ***s*** is of any private interpretation

SECOND COMING OF JESUS. Matt 25:32–46 • Luke 12:35–48 • John 14:3 • 1 Thes 4:13–18.

SECRET [S]
Deut 29:29 ***s*** things belong unto the LORD
Ps 44:21 God...knoweth the ***s's*** of the heart
Ps 91:1 dwelleth in the ***s*** place of the most High
Ezek 28:3 no ***s*** that they can hide from thee [God]

Dan 2:28 a God in heaven that revealeth ***s's***
Matt 6:6 pray to thy Father which is in ***s***
Rom 2:16 God shall judge the ***s's*** of men by Jesus Christ

SECUNDUS (a believer who accompanied Paul on his third missionary journey). Acts 20:4.

SEEK [ETH, ING]
2 Chr 7:14 If my [God's] people... pray, and ***s*** my face
Ps 40:16 those that ***s*** thee [God] rejoice and be glad
Ps 63:1 thou art my God; early will I ***s*** thee
Ps 105:4 ***S*** the LORD, and his strength: seek his face
Ps 119:2 Blessed are they... that ***s*** him [God] with the whole heart
Isa 55:6 ***S*** ye the LORD while he may be found
Lam 3:25 LORD is good...to the soul that ***s'eth*** him
Matt 7:7 ***s,*** and ye shall find
Matt 7:8 he that ***s'eth*** findeth
Mark 8:12 Why doth this generation ***s*** after a sign
Luke 12:31 But rather ***s*** ye the kingdom of God
Luke 17:33 Whosoever shall ***s*** to save his life shall lose it
Luke 19:10 Son of man is come to ***s*** and to save that which was lost
John 5:30 because I [Jesus] ***s***... the will of the Father
Rom 3:11 there is none that ***s'eth*** after God
1 Cor 1:22 and the Greeks ***s*** after wisdom
1 Cor 13:5 [charity] ***s'eth*** not her own
Col 3:1 ***s*** those things...above
1 Pet 5:8 devil...walketh... ***s'ing*** whom he may devour

SEEK THE LORD
1 Chr 16:11 ***S-t-L*** and his strength...continually
Ps 34:10 they that ***s-t-L*** shall not want any good thing
Prov 28:5 they that ***s-t-L*** understand all things
Amos 5:6 ***S-t-L,*** and ye shall live
Zech 8:22 nations shall come to ***s-t-L*** of hosts

SEM. See *Shem.*

SENIR. See *Hermon, Mount.*

SENNACHERIB (a king of Assyria who demanded tribute from King Hezekiah of Judah). **2 Kgs 18:13–16;** 19:16–36 • 2 Chr 32:1–22 • Isa 36:1; 37:17,21,37.

SEPARATE [D]
Prov 19:4 Wealth maketh... friends; but the poor is ***s'd*** from his neighbour
Isa 59:2 iniquities have ***s'd*** between you and your God
Matt 25:32 he [Jesus] shall ***s*** them one from another

Acts 13:2 **S** me Barnabas and Saul for the work
Rom 8:39 Nor height...shall... ***s*** us from the love of God
2 Cor 6:17 come out...and be ye ***s*,** saith the Lord

SEPHARVAIM (a city whose residents colonized the Northern Kingdom after Samaria fell to the Assyrians). 2 Kgs 17:24–31.

SERAIAH (a leader who carried Jeremiah's prophecy of doom for Judah to the city of Babylon). Jer 51:59–61.

SERMON ON THE MOUNT. Matt 5–7.

SERVANT [S]
Gen 9:25 a ***s*** of ***s's*** shall he [Canaan] be
Job 1:8 Hast thou [Satan] considered my [God's] ***s*** Job
Ps 31:16 Make thy [God's] face to shine upon thy ***s***
Ps 34:22 The LORD redeemeth the soul of his ***s's***
Ps 113:1 Praise, O ye ***s's*** of the LORD
Ps 116:16 I am thy [God's] ***s***... son of thine handmaid
Ps 119:125 I am thy [God's] ***s*;** give me understanding
Prov 14:35 The king's favour is toward a wise ***s***
Isa 42:1 Behold my [God's] ***s*,** whom I uphold
Isa 52:13 my [God's] ***s*** shall deal prudently
Dan 9:17 hear the prayer of thy [God's] ***s***
Mal 1:6 A son honoureth his father, and a ***s*** his master
Matt 10:24 disciple is not above his master, nor the ***s*** above his lord
Matt 23:11 he that is greatest... shall be your ***s***
Matt 25:21 Well done, thou good and faithful ***s***
Mark 9:35 the same shall be last of all, and ***s*** of all
Luke 12:37 Blessed are those ***s's*,** whom the lord...shall find watching
Luke 15:19 make me [the prodigal son] as one of thy hired ***s's***
John 8:34 Whosoever committeth sin is the ***s*** of sin
Rom 6:18 ye became the ***s's*** of righteousness
1 Cor 9:19 I [Paul] made myself ***s*** unto all
Gal 4:7 Wherefore thou art no more a ***s*,** but a son
Phil 2:7 took upon him [Jesus] the form of a ***s***

SERVANT SONGS OF ISAIAH. Isa 42:1–4; 49:1–6; 50:4–9; 52:13–53:12.

SERVE [D, ING, ST]
Gen 27:29 Let people ***s*** thee [God]...nations bow down
Gen 29:20 Jacob ***s'd*** seven years for Rachel

Deut 6:13 Thou shalt fear the LORD thy God, and ***s*** him
Ps 72:11 Yea...all nations shall ***s*** him [God]
Dan 3:17 our [Daniel's three friends'] God whom we ***s*** is able to deliver us
Dan 6:16 God whom thou [Daniel] ***s'st***...deliver thee
Matt 4:10 worship the LORD... him only shalt thou ***s***
Luke 16:13 No servant can ***s*** two masters
John 12:26 any man ***s*** me [Jesus], let him follow me
Acts 6:2 not reason that we [the apostles] should...***s*** tables
Rom 1:25 Who...worshipped and ***s'd*** the creature more than the Creator
Rom 12:11 fervent in spirit; ***s'ing*** the Lord
Gal 5:13 by love ***s*** one another

SERVE THE LORD

Josh 24:15 as for me [Joshua] and my house, we will ***s-t-L***
Ps 100:2 ***S-t-L*** with gladness
Jer 30:9 they [Israel and Judah] shall ***s-t-L***...and David their king

SERVICE

John 16:2 the time cometh... whosoever killeth you will think that he doeth God ***s***
Rom 12:1 present your bodies a living sacrifice...which is your reasonable ***s***
Rev 2:19 I know thy works... and ***s***, and faith

SEVEN CHURCHES, LETTERS TO

1. To Ephesus (Rev 2:1–7)
2. To Smyrna (Rev 2:8–11)
3. To Pergamos (Rev 2: 12–17)
4. To Thyatira (Rev 2:18–29)
5. To Sardis (Rev 3:1–6)
6. To Philadelphia (Rev 3: 7–13)
7. To Laodicea (Rev 3:14–22)

SEVEN LAST WORDS OF JESUS FROM THE CROSS

1. "Father, forgive them; for they know not what they do" (Luke 23:34)
2. "Verily I say unto thee, to day shalt thou be with me in paradise" (Luke 23:43)
3. "Woman, behold they son!...Behold thy mother!" (John 19:26–27)
4. "My God, my God, why hast thou forsaken me" (Matt 27:46 • Mark 15:34)
5. "I thirst" (John 19:28)
6. "It is finished" (John 19:30)
7. "Father, into thy hands I commend my spirit" (Luke 23:46)

SEVEN SIGNS OF JESUS IN JOHN'S GOSPEL

1. Turning of water into wine (John 2:1–11)

2. Healing of a nobleman's son (John 4:46–54)

3. Healing of a paralyzed man (John 5:1–9)

4. Feeding of the five thousand (John 6:5–14)

5. Walking on the water (John 6:15–21)

6. Healing of a man born blind (John 9:1–7)

7. Raising of Lazarus from the dead (John 11:38–44)

SEVENTY WEEKS VISION OF DANIEL. Dan 9:24–27.

SHADRACH (one of Daniel's friends who was miraculously delivered from the fiery furnace). Dan 1:7; 2:49; **3:1–28.**

SHALLUM. See *Jehoahaz,* No. 2.

SHALMANESER (an Assyrian king who defeated the Northern Kingdom and deported its people). **2 Kgs 17:3–6;** 18:9.

SHAME [D]

Ps 4:2 how long will ye turn my [God's] glory into ***s***

Ps 14:6 Ye have ***s'd*** the counsel of the poor

Ps 35:4 Let them be...put to ***s*** that seek after my soul

Ps 83:16 Fill their faces with ***s***... may seek thy [God's] name

Ps 119:31 O LORD, put me not to ***s***

Prov 3:35 ***s*** shall be the promotion of fools

Prov 13:18 ***s*** shall be to him that refuseth instruction

Prov 29:15 a child left to himself bringeth his mother to ***s***

1 Cor 14:35 it is a ***s*** for women to speak in the church

Phil 3:19 glory is in their ***s***

Heb 12:2 Jesus...endured the cross, despising the ***s***

SHAMEFULLY

Hos 2:5 she that conceived them hath done ***s***

Mark 12:4 and...they [husbandmen]...sent him [servant] away ***s*** handled

SHAMGAR (a judge who delivered Israel from the Philistines). **Judg 3:31;** 5:6.

SHARON (a fertile coastal plain along the Mediterranean Sea). 1 Chr 27:29 • Song 2:1 • Isa 33:9; 35:2; 65:10. *Saron:* Acts 9:35.

SHEAR-JASHUB (a symbolic name, meaning "a remnant shall return," given by Isaiah to his son to show God's promise to His people after their period of exile). Isa 7:3–4.

SHECHEM

1. A tribal leader killed by Simeon and Levi for seducing their sister Dinah. Gen 34:1–29.

2. A city of refuge in the territory of Ephraim. Josh 20:7 • Judg 9:1–57 • 1 Kgs 12:1,25. *Sichem:* Gen 12:6. *Sychem:* Acts 7:16.

SHEEP

1 Sam 15:14 What meaneth... this bleating of the ***s***

2 Sam 7:8 I [God] took thee [David] from the sheepcote, from following the ***s***

Ps 44:22 we are counted as ***s*** for the slaughter

Ps 74:1 why doth thine [God's] anger smoke against the ***s*** of thy pasture

Ps 95:7 people of his [God's] pasture, and the ***s*** of his hand

Ps 119:176 I have gone astray like a lost ***s***

Isa 53:6 All we like ***s*** have gone astray

Matt 10:16 send you forth as ***s*** in the midst of wolves

Matt 15:24 I [Jesus] am not sent but unto the lost ***s*** of the house of Israel

Mark 6:34 Jesus...saw... people...as ***s*** not having a shepherd

Luke 15:6 I have found my ***s*** which was lost

John 10:7 I [Jesus] am the door of the ***s***

John 10:11 good shepherd [Jesus] giveth his life for the ***s***

John 21:16 He [Jesus] saith unto him [Peter]...Feed my ***s***

1 Pet 2:25 For ye were as ***s*** going astray

SHEM (the oldest son of Noah who was preserved in the ark). Gen 5:32; 6:10; **7:13; 9:18–27;** 10:1–31; 11:10–11 • 1 Chr 1:4,17,24. *Sem:* Luke 3:36.

SHEMAIAH (a prophet of Judah who warned King Rehoboam not to attack Israel). **1 Kgs 12:22–24** • 2 Chr 11:2.

SHEMER (a man who sold King Omri of the Northern Kingdom a hill on which the city of Samaria was built). 1 Kgs 16:24.

SHEMUEL. See *Samuel.*

SHENIR. See *Hermon, Mount.*

SHEPHERD [S]

Gen 47:3 Thy servants [the Hebrews] are ***s's***

Ps 23:1 The LORD is my ***s;*** I shall not want

Isa 40:11 He [God] shall feed his flock like a ***s***

Ezek 34:2 Son of man, prophesy against the ***s's*** of Israel

Matt 9:36 were scattered abroad, as sheep having no ***s***

Luke 2:8 in the same country ***s's*** abiding in the field

John 10:11 I [Jesus] am the good ***s***...giveth his life

Heb 13:20 that great ***s*** [Jesus] of the sheep
1 Pet 5:4 when the chief ***S*** [Jesus] shall appear

SHESHACH. See *Babylonia.*

SHESH-BAZZAR. See *Zerubbabel.*

SHIELD
Gen 15:1 Fear not, Abram: I [God] am thy ***s***
2 Sam 22:3 in him will I trust: he [God] is my ***s***
Ps 5:12 wilt thou [God] compass him as with a ***s***
Ps 33:20 the LORD...is...our ***s***
Ps 84:11 For the LORD God is a sun and ***s***
Ps 115:11 the LORD: he is their help and their ***s***
Prov 30:5 he [God] is a ***s*** unto them...put their trust in him
Eph 6:16 Above all, taking the ***s*** of faith

SHILOAH. See *Siloam.*

SHILOH
1. A town in Ephraim where the Philistines captured the ark of the covenant. Josh 18:1–10 • Judg 21:12–23 • **1 Sam 4:3–11** • Jer 7:12,14.
2. A title of the coming Messiah that identified Him as a descendant of Judah. Gen 49:10.

SHIMEI (a man who insulted David when he was fleeing from Absalom). **2 Sam 16:5–13;** 19:16–23 • 1 Kgs 2:8–44.

SHINAR. See *Babylonia.*

SHINE [D, ING, TH]
Num 6:25 The LORD make his face ***s*** upon thee
Ps 31:16 Make thy [God's] face to ***s*** upon thy servant
Ps 67:1 God...bless us; and cause his face to ***s*** upon us
Prov 4:18 But the path of the just is as the ***s'ing*** light
Eccl 8:1 a man's wisdom maketh his face to ***s***
Isa 9:2 upon them [people in darkness] hath the light ***s'd***
Isa 60:1 Arise, ***s;*** for thy light is come
Matt 5:16 Let your light so ***s*** before men
Matt 17:2 and his [Jesus'] face did ***s*** as the sun
John 1:5 light ***s'th*** in darkness
John 5:35 He [Jesus] was a burning and a ***s'ing*** light
Acts 9:3 there ***s'd*** round about him [Paul] a light
2 Cor 4:6 For God...hath ***s'd*** in our hearts
Rev 21:23 And the city had no need of the sun...to ***s***

SHUSHAN (the wealthy and powerful capital city of Persia where Esther interceded for her people). Neh 1:1 • Esth

1:2,5; 2:3–8; 3:15; 4:8,16; 8:14–15; 9:6–19 • Dan 8:2.

SICHEM. See *Shechem,* No. 2.

SICKNESS [ES]

Matt 4:23 Jesus went about... healing all manner of ***s***

Matt 8:17 spoken by Esaias... Himself [Jesus] took our infirmities, and bare our ***s'es***

John 11:4 Jesus...said, This ***s*** is not unto death

SIDON (a Phoenician city founded by Sidon, oldest son of Canaan). **Gen 10:15,19** • Matt 11:21–22; 15:21 • Mark 3:8; 7:24,31 • Luke 4:26; 6:17; 10:13–14 • Acts 12:20; 27:3. *Zidon:* Josh 11:8.

SIGHT

Ex 3:3 I [Moses] will now turn aside, and see this great ***s***

Num 13:33 we were in our own ***s*** as grasshoppers

Judg 2:11 children of Israel did evil in the ***s*** of the LORD

1 Chr 29:25 the LORD magnified Solomon exceedingly in the ***s*** of all Israel

Ps 9:19 let the heathen be judged in thy [God's] ***s***

Ps 19:14 Let the words of my mouth...be acceptable in thy [God's] ***s,*** O LORD

Ps 78:12 Marvellous things did he [God] in the ***s*** of their fathers, in...Egypt

Ps 90:4 a thousand years in thy [God's] ***s*** are...as yesterday

Ps 116:15 Precious in the ***s*** of the LORD...death of his saints

Eccl 6:9 Better is the ***s*** of the eyes than the wandering of the desire

Matt 11:5 blind receive their ***s,*** and the lame walk

Luke 1:15 he [John the Baptist] shall be great...***s*** of the Lord

Luke 15:21 I [prodigal son] have sinned...in thy ***s***

Acts 9:9 And he [Paul] was three days without ***s***

Jas 4:10 Humble yourselves in the ***s*** of the Lord

SIGN [S]

Gen 1:14 let them [lights] be for ***s's,*** and for seasons

Deut 6:8 bind them [Scriptures] for a ***s*** upon thine hand

Isa 7:14 the Lord himself shall give you a ***s***

Dan 4:3 How great are his [God's] ***s's***

Matt 12:39 An evil...generation seeketh after a ***s***

Matt 24:3 what shall be the ***s*** of thy [Jesus'] coming

Luke 2:12 this shall be a ***s*** unto you...babe wrapped in swaddling clothes

1 Cor 1:22 the Jews require a ***s***

Rev 15:1 I [John] saw another ***s*** in heaven, great... marvellous

SIGNS AND WONDERS
Deut 6:22 LORD showed ***s-a-w***... upon Egypt
Mark 13:22 false prophets shall rise...show ***s-a-w***
John 4:48 Except ye see ***s-a-w,*** ye will not believe
Acts 5:12 by the hands of the apostles were many ***s-a-w*** wrought among the people

SIHON (an Amorite king who refused to allow the Israelites to pass through his territory). Num 21:21–30.

SILAS (a church leader imprisoned with Paul at Philippi). Acts 15:40–41; 16:19,23. *Silvanus:* 2 Cor 1:19 • 2 Thes 1:1.

SILENCE
Ps 39:2 I was dumb with ***s,*** I held my peace
Eccl 3:7 a time to keep ***s,*** and a time to speak
Hab 2:20 let all the earth keep ***s*** before him [God]
1 Cor 14:28 no interpreter, let him keep ***s*** in the church
1 Cor 14:34 Let your women keep ***s*** in the churches

SILOAH. See *Siloam.*

SILOAM (a water reservoir supplied through King Hezekiah's underground tunnel from a spring outside Jerusalem). 2 Kgs 20:20 • Luke 13:4 • John 9:7–11. *Shiloah:* Isa 8:6. *Siloah:* Neh 3:15.

SILVANUS. See *Silas.*

SIMEON
1. A son of Jacob and ancestor of one of the twelve tribes of Israel. Gen 29:33; 34:25,30; 35:23; 42:24,36; 43:23; 46:10; 48:5; 49:5 • Ex 1:2; 6:15. The tribe of Simeon settled in southern Canaan. Josh 19:1–9.
2. A righteous man who blessed the child Jesus in the temple at Jerusalem. Luke 2:25–35.

SIMON
1. Simon Peter, one of the twelve apostles or disciples of Jesus and the leader of the church in Jerusalem after the resurrection and ascension of Jesus. Matt 4:18; 10:2; 16:16–17; 17:25 • Mark 1:16–36; 3:16; 14:37 • Luke 5:4–10; 6:14; 22:31; 24:34 • John 1:40–42; 6:8,68; 13:6,9,24,36; 18:10,15,25; 20:2,6; 21:2–17 • Acts 10:5,18,32 • 2 Pet 1:1.
(1) A fisherman and brother of Andrew (Matt 4:18)
(2) Called by Jesus (Matt 4:18–22)
(3) Included among Jesus' twelve apostles (Matt 10:2–4)

(4) Walked on the water to meet Jesus (Matt 14:28–33)

(5) Confessed Jesus as the Son of God (Matt 16:13–19)

(6) Condemned by Jesus for refusing to believe that Jesus would die (Matt 16:21–23)

(7) Witnessed the transfiguration of Jesus (Matt 17:1–8 • 2 Pet 1:16–18)

(8) With Jesus in the Garden of Gethsemane (Mark 14:32–42)

(9) Denied Jesus three times (Matt 26:69–75)

(10) Cut off the ear of a slave when Jesus was arrested (John 18:10–11)

(11) Ran to inspect the empty tomb after Jesus was resurrected (John 20:1–8)

(12) Reinstated by Jesus and challenged to continue His work (John 21:15–22)

(13) Preached sermon on the day of Pentecost when three thousand people believed on Jesus (Acts 2:38–41)

(14) Became the key leader in the early church at Jerusalem (Acts 3:12–26)

(15) Preached the gospel to Gentiles (Acts 10:24–48)

2. Simon Zelotes or Simon the Canaanite, another of the twelve apostles or disciples of Jesus. Matt 10:4 • Mark 3:18 • Luke 6:15 • Acts 1:13.

SIMPLE

Ps 19:7 testimony of the LORD is sure, making wise the ***s***

Prov 8:5 O ye ***s***, understand wisdom

Prov 22:3 but the ***s*** pass on, and are punished

SIN [NED, NETH, S]

Gen 4:7 if thou [Cain] doest not well, ***s*** lieth at the door

Lev 16:34 make an atonement... for all their ***s's*** once a year

1 Sam 15:24 Saul said...I have ***s'ned***

2 Chr 7:14 then will I [God] hear...forgive their ***s***

Job 1:22 In all this Job ***s'ned*** not, nor charged God

Job 13:23 How many are mine iniquities and ***s's***

Ps 32:1 Blessed is he...whose ***s*** is covered

Ps 41:4 for I have ***s'ned*** against thee [God]

Ps 51:2 cleanse me from my ***s***

Ps 51:3 my ***s*** is ever before me

Ps 51:4 Against thee [God], thee only, have I ***s'ned***

Ps 51:9 Hide thy [God's] face from my ***s's***

Ps 103:10 He [God] hath not dealt with us after our ***s's***

Ps 119:11 Thy [God's] word have I hid in mine heart, that I might not ***s***

Prov 14:34 but ***s*** is a reproach to any people

Eccl 7:20 not a just man upon earth, that...***s'neth*** not

Isa 1:18 though your ***s's*** be as scarlet...white as snow

Isa 6:7 touched thy [Isaiah's] lips...iniquity is taken away...***s*** purged

Isa 40:2 she [Jerusalem] ...received...double for... her ***s's***

Jer 14:20 we have ***s'ned*** against thee [God]

Jer 31:34 I [God] will remember their ***s*** no more

Ezek 18:20 The soul that ***s'neth,*** it shall die

Mic 7:19 thou [God] wilt cast all their ***s's*** into the...sea

Matt 1:21 he [Jesus] shall save his people from their ***s's***

Matt 18:21 Lord, how oft shall my brother ***s*** against me, and I forgive him

Matt 26:28 my [Jesus'] blood... is shed for many for the remission of ***s's***

Luke 15:21 I [the prodigal son] have ***s'ned*** against heaven, and in thy [his father's] sight

Luke 24:47 remission of ***s's***... preached in his [Jesus'] name

John 1:29 Behold the Lamb of God, which taketh away the ***s*** of the world

John 8:7 He that is without ***s***... let him first cast a stone

John 9:2 who did ***s,*** this man, or his parents

John 16:8 he [Jesus] will reprove the world of ***s***

Rom 3:9 Jews and Gentiles... they are all under ***s***

Rom 3:23 all...***s'ned,*** and come short of the glory of God

Rom 4:7 Blessed are they... whose ***s's*** are covered

Rom 5:12 by one man [Adam] ***s*** entered into the world

Rom 6:1 continue in ***s,*** that grace may abound

Rom 6:12 Let not ***s***...reign in your mortal body

Rom 6:23 wages of ***s*** is death

Rom 7:17 no more I [Paul] that do it, but ***s***...in me

1 Cor 6:18 he...committeth fornication ***s'neth*** against his own body

1 Cor 15:17 Christ be not raised...yet in your ***s's***

2 Cor 5:21 he [God] hath made him [Jesus] to be ***s*** for us

Heb 9:28 Christ was...offered to bear the ***s's*** of many

Heb 10:4 not possible that the blood of bulls...should take away ***s's***

Heb 12:1 lay aside...the ***s*** which doth so easily beset us

Jas 4:17 knoweth to do good, and doeth it not, to him it is ***s***

1 John 1:7 blood of Jesus... cleanseth us from all ***s***

1 John 1:8 say that we have no ***s,*** we deceive ourselves

1 John 1:9 he [Jesus] is faithful...to forgive us our ***s's***

1 John 1:10 If we say that we have not ***s'ned,*** we make him [Jesus] a liar

1 John 2:1 these things write I unto you, that ye ***s*** not

1 John 2:2 he [Jesus] is the propitiation for our ***s's***

1 John 4:10 he [God]...sent his Son [Jesus] to be the propitiation for our ***s's***

SIN, WILDERNESS OF (a desert region where manna and quail were miraculously provided for the Israelites). Ex 16:1–8.

SINAI (a mountain peak where Moses received the Ten Commandments and other parts of the Law from God). Ex **19–23;** 24:16; 31:18; 34:2–32 • Lev 7:38; 25:1; 26:46 • Num 1:1,19; 3:1–14; 9:1,5; 10:12; 26:64; 28:6; 33:15–16 • Deut 33:2 • Judg 5:5 • Neh 9:13 • Ps 68:8,17 • Gal 4:24–25. *Sina:* Acts 7:30.

SINCERITY

Josh 24:14 serve him [God] in ***s*** and in truth

1 Cor 5:8 keep the feast...with the...bread of ***s***

2 Cor 8:8 I [Paul] speak...to prove the ***s*** of your love

SING [ING]

Ex 15:21 **S** ye to the LORD, for he hath triumphed

Ps 59:17 Unto thee...will I ***s:*** for God is my defence

Ps 67:4 let the nations be glad and ***s*** for joy

Ps 81:1 **S** aloud unto God our strength: make a joyful noise

Ps 92:1 It is a good thing...to ***s*** praises unto thy [God's] name

Ps 100:2 come before his [God's] presence with ***s'ing***

Ps 137:4 How shall we ***s*** the LORD's song in a strange land

Song 2:12 the time of the ***s'ing*** of birds is come

Isa 49:13 break forth into ***s'ing,*** O mountains

Isa 52:9 ***s*** together, ye waste places of Jerusalem

Col 3:16 ***s'ing*** with grace in your hearts to the Lord

Jas 5:13 Is any merry? let him ***s*** psalms

SING UNTO THE LORD

1 Chr 16:23 ***S-u-t-L,*** all the earth

Ps 13:6 I will ***s-u-t-L***...he... dealt bountifully with me

Ps 95:1 let us ***s-u-t-L***...the rock of our salvation

Ps 96:1 ***s-u-t-L,*** all the earth

Ps 98:1 O ***s-u-t-L*** a new song

Ps 104:33 I will ***s-u-t-L*** as long as I live

Isa 12:5 ***S-u-t-L;*** for he hath done excellent things

SINNED AGAINST THE LORD
Ex 10:16 I [Pharaoh] have ***s-a-t-L*** your God
Josh 7:20 I [Achan] have ***s-a-t-L*** God of Israel
2 Sam 12:13 I [David] have ***s-a-t-L***

SINNER [S]
Ps 1:1 Blessed is the man that walketh not...nor standeth in the way of ***s's***
Eccl 9:18 but one ***s*** destroyeth much good
Mark 2:17 I [Jesus] came...to call...***s's*** to repentance
Luke 5:30 Why do ye [Jesus] eat...with...***s's***
Luke 15:10 joy...over one ***s*** that repenteth
Luke 18:13 God be merciful to me [publican] a ***s***
Rom 5:8 while we were yet ***s's,*** Christ died for us
1 Tim 1:15 Christ...came into the world to save ***s's***
Jas 4:8 Cleanse your hands, ye ***s's***...purify your hearts

SION. See *Zion.*

SIRION. See *Hermon, Mount.*

SISERA (a Canaanite commander killed by Jael). Judg 4:2–22.

SLEEP [EST, ETH, ING]
Ps 13:3 lighten mine eyes, lest I ***s*** the ***s*** of death
Ps 44:23 Awake, why ***s'est*** thou, O Lord
Prov 6:9 How long wilt thou ***s,*** O sluggard
Prov 20:13 Love not ***s,*** lest thou come to poverty
Mark 5:39 the damsel is not dead, but ***s'eth***
Mark 13:36 coming suddenly he [Jesus] find you ***s'ing***
Mark 14:41 **S** on now, and take your [the disciples'] rest
John 11:11 he [Jesus] saith... Our friend Lazarus ***s'eth***
1 Cor 15:51 shall not all ***s,*** but we shall all be changed

SLEPT
Ps 3:5 I laid me down and ***s***
Matt 28:13 Say ye, His [Jesus'] disciples...stole him away while we ***s***
1 Cor 15:20 now is Christ...the firstfruits of them that ***s***

SMYRNA (a city north of Ephesus where one of the seven churches addressed by John in the Book of Revelation was located). Rev 2:8–11.

SOBER [LY, NESS]
Acts 26:25 I [Paul]...speak... words of truth and ***s'ness***
1 Thes 5:6 let us not sleep... but...watch and be ***s***

1 Tim 3:2 A bishop...must be blameless...vigilant, ***s***
Titus 2:12 we should live ***s'ly,*** righteously, and godly
1 Pet 5:8 Be ***s,*** be vigilant...the devil...walketh about

SODOM (a city destroyed by God because of its wickedness and often mentioned as a symbol of evil and as a warning to sinners). **Gen 19:1–28** • Isa 1:9 • Jer 49:18 • Ezek 16:46–49 • Amos 4:11 • Zeph 2:9 • Matt 11:23–24 • 2 Pet 2:6 • Jude 7 • Rev 11:8. *Sodoma:* Rom 9:29.

SODOMA. See *Sodom.*

SOLOMON (David's son and successor as king of Israel, known for his wisdom, wealth, and lavish lifestyle, and probable author of the books of Ecclesiastes and Song of Solomon). See **1 Kgs 1–11 • 2 Chr 1–9** for a sketch of Solomon's life.

1. Prayed for wisdom and insight (1 Kgs 3:1–28)
2. Governed efficiently and became wealthy (1 Kgs 4:1–30)
3. Encouraged trade and commerce (1 Kgs 10:14–29)
4. Built the temple in Jerusalem (1 Kgs 5–8)
5. Married pagan wives (1 Kgs 11:1–8)
6. Burdened his subjects with excessive taxes (1 Kgs 12:4)
7. Northern tribes rebelled against his policies (1 Kgs 11:14–40)
8. Death of Solomon (1 Kgs 11:41–43).

SON OF GOD
Matt 27:40 If thou [Jesus] be the ***S-o-G,*** come down from the cross
Matt 27:54 Truly this [Jesus] was the ***S-o-G***
Luke 1:35 that holy thing... shall be called the ***S-o-G***
Luke 4:3 If thou be the ***S-o-G,*** command this stone...be made bread
John 1:34 I [John the Baptist]... bare record that this [Jesus] is the ***S-o-G***
John 20:31 believe that Jesus is the Christ, the ***S-o-G***
1 John 4:15 Whosoever shall confess that Jesus is the ***S-o-G,*** God dwelleth in him
1 John 5:12 he that hath not the ***S-o-G*** hath not life

SON OF MAN
Ps 8:4 What is...the ***s-o-m,*** that thou [God] visitest him
Ezek 2:1 ***S-o-m*** [Ezekiel], stand upon thy feet
Matt 12:8 the ***S-o-m*** [Jesus] is Lord even of the sabbath day
Matt 16:13 Whom do men say that I [Jesus] the ***S-o-m*** am
Matt 24:44 an hour as ye think not...***S-o-m*** [Jesus] cometh

Mark 10:45 ***S-o-m*** [Jesus] came not to be ministered unto, but to minister
Luke 9:58 ***S-o-m*** [Jesus] hath not where to lay his head
Luke 22:48 But Jesus said... Judas, betrayest thou the ***S-o-m*** with a kiss
John 3:14 even so must the ***S-o-m*** [Jesus] be lifted up
John 12:23 The hour is come, that the ***S-o-m*** [Jesus] should be glorified

SONG OF DEBORAH. Judg 5:1–31.

SONG OF MARY. Luke 1:46–55.

SONG OF MIRIAM. Ex 15:20–21.

SONG OF MOSES. Deut 32:1–44.

SONG OF SOLOMON, BOOK OF. A short Old Testament book, probably written by Solomon, that is filled with expressions of affection between two lovers (1:13; 4:1–11; 7:2–10). Some interpreters insist the song symbolizes God's love for His people Israel, while others believe the book is a healthy affirmation of the joys of physical love between husband and wife.

SONG OF ZACHARIAS. Luke 1:67–79.

SOPATER (a believer who accompanied Paul on the third missionary journey). Acts 20:4.

SORROW [FUL, S]
Ps 18:5 The ***s's*** of hell compassed me about
Ps 38:17 my ***s*** is continually before me
Eccl 1:18 he that increaseth knowledge increaseth ***s***
Isa 53:3 man of ***s's***...acquainted with grief
Jer 45:3 for the LORD hath added grief to my ***s***
Matt 19:22 he [rich young ruler] went away ***s'ful***
Matt 24:8 All these are the beginning of ***s's***
Matt 26:38 My [Jesus'] soul is exceeding ***s'ful***
John 16:20 your ***s*** shall be turned into joy
2 Cor 7:10 godly ***s*** worketh repentance to salvation
Rev 21:4 no more death, neither ***s,*** nor crying

SOSIPATER (a kinsman of Paul whose greetings were sent to the church at Rome). Rom 16:21.

SOSTHENES (a ruler of the synagogue at Corinth who was beaten by a mob). Acts 18:17.

SOUL [S]
Gen 2:7 man became a living ***s***
Deut 6:5 thou shalt love the LORD thy God...with all thy ***s***
1 Sam 18:1 ***s*** of Jonathan was knit with the ***s*** of David
Job 19:2 How long will ye vex my [Job's] ***s***
Ps 19:7 law of the LORD is perfect, converting the ***s***
Ps 23:3 He [God] restoreth my ***s***
Ps 25:1 Unto thee, O LORD, do I lift up my ***s***
Ps 33:20 Our ***s*** waiteth for the LORD; he is our help
Ps 35:9 And my ***s*** shall be joyful in the LORD
Ps 42:2 My ***s*** thirsteth for God
Ps 42:5 Why art thou cast down, O my ***s***
Ps 56:13 thou [God] hast delivered my ***s*** from death
Ps 72:13 He [God]...shall save the ***s's*** of the needy
Ps 84:2 My ***s***...fainteth for the courts of the LORD
Ps 103:1 Bless the LORD, O my ***s***...bless his holy name
Ps 142:4 refuge failed me; no man cared for my ***s***
Prov 11:30 and he that winneth ***s's*** is wise
Prov 18:7 A fool's...lips are the snare of his ***s***
Lam 3:24 The LORD is my portion, saith my ***s***
Ezek 18:20 The ***s*** that sinneth, it shall die
Mic 6:7 shall I give...fruit of my body for the sin of my ***s***
Matt 10:28 but rather fear him which is able to destroy...***s*** and body
Matt 11:29 ye shall find rest unto your ***s's***
Matt 16:26 what shall a man give in exchange for his ***s***
Mark 14:34 My [Jesus'] ***s*** is... sorrowful unto death
John 12:27 Now is my [Jesus'] ***s*** troubled
Rom 13:1 every ***s*** be subject unto the higher powers
1 Pet 2:11 abstain from fleshly lusts, which war against the ***s***
1 Pet 2:25 returned unto the... Bishop of your ***s's***

SOUND [ING]
John 3:8 The wind bloweth... thou hearest the ***s***
Acts 2:2 ***s*** from heaven as of a... mighty wind
1 Cor 13:1 I [Paul] am become as ***s'ing*** brass
1 Cor 14:8 if the trumpet give an uncertain ***s***
1 Cor 15:52 trumpet shall ***s***, and the dead...raised
2 Tim 4:3 when they will not endure ***s*** doctrine

SOUTHERN KINGDOM (JUDAH) FALLS TO BABYLONIA. 2 Kgs 25.

SOW [ED, ETH]

Ps 126:5 They that **s** in tears shall reap in joy

Prov 22:8 He that ***s'eth*** iniquity shall reap vanity

Matt 13:24 kingdom...is likened unto a man which ***s'ed*** good seed

Luke 8:5 as he [a sower] ***s'ed,*** some fell by the way side

Luke 12:24 Consider the ravens...they neither **s** nor reap

John 4:37 One ***s'eth,*** and another reapeth

2 Cor 9:6 ***s'eth*** bountifully shall reap also bountifully

Gal 6:7 whatsoever a man ***s'eth,*** that shall he also reap

SOWN

Hos 8:7 they have **s** the wind, and...reap the whirlwind

Hag 1:6 Ye have **s** much, and bring in little

Mark 4:18 these are they which are **s** among thorns

1 Cor 15:42 It [the body] is **s** in corruption; it is raised in incorruption

SPAIN (a country in Europe that Paul expressed a desire to visit). Rom 15:24,28.

SPEECH

Gen 11:1 And the whole earth was...of one **s**

Ex 4:10 I [Moses] am slow of **s**

Prov 17:7 Excellent **s** becometh not a fool

Isa 28:23 Give ye ear...hearken, and hear my [God's] **s**

Mark 14:70 thou [Peter] art a Galilaean, and thy **s** agreeth

1 Cor 2:1 I [Paul]...came not with excellency of **s**

Col 4:6 Let your **s** be...seasoned with salt

SPIES SENT INTO CANAAN. Num 13:1–33.

SPIRIT [S]

1 Sam 28:7 Seek me [Saul] a woman that hath a familiar **s**

2 Kgs 2:9 let a double portion of thy [Elijah's] **s** be upon me [Elisha]

Job 32:8 there is a **s** in man

Ps 31:5 Into thine hand I commit my **s**

Ps 51:10 O God...renew a right **s** within me

Prov 16:18 Pride goeth before destruction...haughty **s** before a fall

Prov 25:28 He that hath no rule over his own **s**

Isa 32:15 Until the **s** be poured upon us from on high

Isa 42:1 I [God] have put my **s** upon him [God's servant]

Ezek 3:24 Then the **s** entered into me [Ezekiel]

Ezek 11:19 I [God] will put a new **s** within you

Dan 6:3 because an excellent ***s*** was in him [Daniel]
Joel 2:28 I [God] will pour out my ***s*** upon all flesh
Zech 4:6 Not by might...but by my [God's] ***s***
Matt 5:3 Blessed are the poor in ***s***
Matt 26:41 the ***s***...is willing, but the flesh is weak
Mark 6:7 he [Jesus]...gave them [the disciples] power over unclean ***s's***
Luke 23:46 Father, into thy hands I [Jesus] commend my ***s***...gave up the ghost
John 3:5 Except a man be born of water and of the ***S***
John 4:23 worship the Father in ***s*** and in truth
John 16:13 the ***S*** of truth [Holy Spirit], is come
Acts 17:16 his [Paul's] ***s*** was stirred in him
Rom 8:16 The ***S*** itself beareth witness with our ***s***
1 Cor 12:4 diversities of gifts, but the same ***S***
1 Cor 12:10 to another discerning of ***s's***
2 Cor 3:6 letter killeth, but the ***s*** giveth life
Gal 5:16 Walk in the ***S***
Gal 5:22 fruit of the ***S*** is love, joy, peace, longsuffering
Eph 4:3 unity of the ***S*** in the bond of peace
Eph 6:17 sword of the ***S***...the word of God
2 Tim 1:7 God hath not given us the ***s*** of fear
1 John 4:1 try the ***s's*** whether they are of God
Rev 2:7 hear what the ***S*** saith unto the churches

SPIRIT, FILLING OF, AT PENTECOST. Acts 2:1–21.

SPIRIT OF GOD
Gen 1:2 ***S-o-G*** moved upon the face of the waters
1 Sam 11:6 And the ***s-o-G*** came upon Saul
Job 33:4 The ***s-o-G*** hath made me [Job]
Matt 3:16 Jesus...saw the ***S-o-G*** descending like a dove
Rom 8:14 led by the ***S-o-G,*** they are the sons of God
1 Cor 3:16 Know ye not...that the ***S-o-G*** dwelleth in you
Eph 4:30 And grieve not the holy ***S-o-G***

SPIRIT OF THE LORD
Judg 6:34 the ***s-o-t-L*** came upon Gideon
1 Sam 16:13 the ***s-o-t-L*** came upon David
Isa 11:2 the ***s-o-t-L*** shall rest upon him [God's servant]
Isa 61:1 The ***s-o-t-L*** GOD is upon me [God's servant]
Luke 4:18 The ***S-o-t-L*** is upon me [Jesus]
Acts 8:39 the ***S-o-t-L*** caught away Philip

2 Cor 3:17 where the ***S-o-t-L*** is, there is liberty

SPIRITUAL [LY]

Rom 8:6 to be ***s'ly*** minded is life and peace

1 Cor 14:1 Follow after charity, and desire ***s*** gifts

1 Cor 15:44 It is sown a natural body...raised a ***s*** body

Eph 6:12 we wrestle...against ***s*** wickedness in high places

1 Pet 2:5 Ye also, as lively stones, are built up a ***s*** house

STAND [EST, ETH, ING]

Ex 3:5 the place...thou [Moses] ***s'est*** is holy ground

Ex 14:13 ***s*** still, and see the salvation of the LORD

Job 19:25 my [Job's] redeemer... shall ***s*** at the latter day

Ps 1:1 walketh not...nor ***s'eth*** in the way of sinners

Ps 24:3 who shall ***s*** in his [God's] holy place

Prov 12:7 the house of the righteous shall ***s***

Isa 40:8 but the word of our God shall ***s*** for ever

Mal 3:2 who shall ***s*** when he [God] appeareth

Matt 12:25 house divided against itself shall not ***s***

Acts 7:55 he [Stephen]...saw... Jesus ***s'ing*** on the right hand

Rom 14:10 all ***s*** before the judgment seat of Christ

1 Cor 10:12 thinketh he ***s'eth*** take heed lest he fall

1 Cor 16:13 Watch ye, ***s*** fast in the faith...be strong

Gal 5:1 ***S*** fast...in the liberty... Christ hath made us free

Eph 6:11 able to ***s*** against the wiles of the devil

2 Thes 2:15 Therefore, brethren, ***s*** fast

Rev 3:20 I [Jesus] ***s*** at the door, and knock

STATUTE [S]

Ex 27:21 a ***s*** for ever unto their generations

Lev 10:11 teach...Israel all the ***s's***...the LORD hath spoken

Lev 16:34 this shall be an everlasting ***s*** unto you

Deut 5:31 I [God] will speak unto thee [Moses] all the commandments...***s's***... judgments

1 Kgs 3:3 Solomon loved the LORD, walking in the ***s's*** of David his father

Ps 19:8 The ***s's*** of the LORD are right, rejoicing the heart

Ps 119:12 Blessed art thou, O LORD: teach me thy ***s's***

Ezek 20:19 walk in my [God's] ***s's,*** and keep my judgments

STEDFAST [LY, NESS]

Luke 9:51 he [Jesus] ***s'ly*** set his face to go to Jerusalem

1 Cor 15:58 Therefore...be ye ***s,*** unmoveable

Col 2:5 and the ***s'ness*** of your faith in Christ

Heb 3:14 hold the beginning of our confidence ***s*** unto the end

STEPHEN (a believer who became the first Christian martyr when he was stoned because of his testimony). Acts 6:5–9; **7:55–60;** 8:2; 11:19; 22:20.

STEWARD [S]
Matt 20:8 lord of the vineyard saith unto his ***s,*** Call the labourers...give them their hire
Luke 16:8 the lord commended the unjust ***s***
1 Cor 4:2 required in ***s's,*** that a man be found faithful
Titus 1:7 a bishop must be blameless, as the ***s*** of God
1 Pet 4:10 good ***s's*** of the manifold grace of God

STEWARDSHIP
Luke 16:2 give an account of thy ***s***...be no longer steward
Luke 16:3 my lord taketh away from me the ***s***

STONE [D, S, ST]
Gen 31:45 Jacob took a ***s,*** and set it up for a pillar
Ex 17:4 this people...be almost ready to ***s*** me [Moses]
Ex 31:18 two...tables of ***s,*** written with...finger of God
Lev 26:1 neither shall ye set up any image of ***s***
Josh 4:6 What mean ye by these ***s's***
1 Sam 17:50 David prevailed... with a sling and...a ***s***
Ps 118:22 ***s*** which the builders refused is become the head ***s***
Eccl 3:5 and a time to gather ***s's*** together
Isa 28:16 I [God] lay in Zion for a foundation...a tried ***s***
Matt 4:3 command that these ***s's*** be made bread
Matt 21:42 The ***s*** which the builders rejected
Matt 24:2 There shall not be left here one ***s*** upon another
Matt 27:66 they [soldiers]... made...sepulchre sure, sealing the ***s***
Mark 16:4 they [the women] saw...the ***s*** was rolled away
Luke 13:34 O Jerusalem... which killest the prophets, and ***s'st*** them
John 1:42 called Cephas...by interpretation, A ***s***
Acts 4:11 the ***s*** which was set at nought of you builders
Acts 7:59 they ***s'd*** Stephen
1 Pet 2:8 a ***s*** of stumbling, and a rock of offence
Rev 21:19 foundations...garnished with...precious ***s's***

STRAIGHT
Isa 40:3 make ***s*** in the desert a highway for our God
Luke 3:4 Prepare ye the way of the Lord, make his paths ***s***

Acts 9:11 go into the street which is called ***S***

STRANGER [S]

Deut 10:19 Love ye...the ***s***

Ps 54:3 For ***s's*** are risen up against me

Ps 69:8 I am become a ***s*** unto my brethren

Matt 25:35 I was a ***s***, and ye took me in

Eph 2:19 therefore ye are no more ***s's*** and foreigners

Heb 13:2 Be not forgetful to entertain ***s's***

STRENGTH

Ex 13:14 By ***s*** of hand the LORD brought us [Israel] out from Egypt

Ex 15:2 LORD is my ***s*** and song

Job 12:13 With him [God] is wisdom and ***s***

Ps 18:2 my God, my ***s***, in whom I will trust

Ps 19:14 words of my mouth... be acceptable...my ***s***, and my redeemer

Ps 27:1 the LORD is the ***s*** of my life

Ps 43:2 For thou art the God of my ***s***

Ps 46:1 God is our refuge and ***s***, a...help in trouble

Ps 71:9 forsake me not when my ***s*** faileth

Ps 84:5 Blessed is the man whose ***s*** is in thee [God]

Ps 90:10 if by reason of ***s*** they [days of our years] be fourscore years

Ps 118:14 The LORD is my ***s*** and song...my salvation

Isa 12:2 LORD JEHOVAH is my ***s*** and my song

Isa 30:15 in quietness and in confidence shall be your ***s***

Isa 40:31 they that wait upon the LORD shall renew their ***s***

Hab 3:19 LORD God is my ***s***

Mark 12:30 love the Lord thy God...with all thy ***s***

2 Cor 12:9 my [Paul's] ***s*** is made perfect in weakness

STRENGTHEN [ED, ETH, ING]

Ps 27:14 he [God] shall ***s*** thine heart: wait...on the LORD

Luke 22:43 there appeared an angel...***s'ing*** him [Jesus]

Phil 4:13 do all things through Christ which ***s'eth*** me [Paul]

2 Tim 4:17 the Lord stood with me [Paul], and ***s'ed*** me

STRIPES

Isa 53:5 with his [God's servant's] ***s*** we are healed

2 Cor 11:24 five times received I [Paul] forty ***s***

1 Pet 2:24 by whose [Jesus'] ***s*** ye were healed

STRIVE [D, ING, TH]

Luke 13:24 ***S*** to enter in at the strait gate

Rom 15:20 so have I [Paul] ***s'd*** to preach the gospel

1 Cor 9:25 every man that ***s'th*** for the mastery is temperate in all things

Phil 1:27 one mind ***s'ing*** together for...the gospel

2 Tim 2:24 the servant of the Lord must not ***s***

STRONG [ER]

Deut 31:6 Be ***s*** and of a good courage, fear not

Ps 24:8 The LORD ***s*** and mighty ...mighty in battle

Ps 71:7 but thou [God] art my ***s*** refuge

Ps 89:8 who is a ***s*** LORD like unto thee

Prov 18:10 The name of the LORD is a ***s*** tower

Eccl 9:11 the race is not to the swift, nor the battle to the ***s***

Luke 2:40 child [Jesus] grew, and waxed ***s*** in spirit

Rom 15:1 ***s*** ought to bear the infirmities of the weak

1 Cor 1:25 the weakness of God is ***s'er*** than men

2 Cor 12:10 when I [Paul] am weak, then am I ***s***

Eph 6:10 Finally, my brethren, be ***s*** in the Lord

STUMBLINGBLOCK [S]

Jer 6:21 I [God] will lay ***s's*** before this people

Rom 14:13 no man put a ***s***...in his brother's way

1 Cor 1:23 Christ crucified, unto the Jews a ***s***

1 Cor 8:9 liberty...become a ***s*** to them that are weak

SUBMISSION TO OTHERS IN THE LORD. 1 Pet 3:1–12.

SUBMIT [TING]

Eph 5:21 ***S'ting*** yourselves one to another...fear of God

Eph 5:22 Wives, ***s*** yourselves unto your own husbands

Jas 4:7 ***S*** yourselves therefore to God. Resist the devil

1 Pet 5:5 ye younger, ***s*** yourselves unto the elder

SUCCOTH-BENOTH (an idol set up in Samaria by the people who colonized the area after the Northern Kingdom fell to the Assyrians). 2 Kgs 17:29–30.

SUFFER [ED, ETH, INGS]

Ps 55:22 he [God] shall never ***s*** the righteous to be moved

Matt 16:21 Jesus...must go... and ***s*** many things

Matt 19:14 ***S*** little children, and forbid them not

Luke 24:26 Ought not Christ to have ***s'ed*** these things

Luke 24:46 thus it behoved Christ to ***s***

Acts 9:16 he [Paul] must ***s*** for my [Jesus'] name's sake

Rom 8:18 ***s'ings***...not worthy to be compared with the glory...revealed
1 Cor 10:13 God...will not ***s*** you to be tempted above that ye are able
1 Cor 13:4 Charity ***s'eth*** long, and is kind...envieth not
Phil 3:10 the fellowship of his [Jesus'] ***s'ings***
2 Tim 2:12 If we ***s,*** we shall also reign with him [Jesus]
Heb 5:8 learned he [Jesus] obedience by the things which he ***s'ed***
1 Pet 4:13 ye are partakers of Christ's ***s'ings***

SUKKIIMS (an African or Ethiopian tribe allied with Pharaoh Shishak of Egypt when he invaded Judah). 2 Chr 12:3.

SUN STANDS STILL AT AJALON. Josh 10:12–14.

SUSANNA (a woman who provided food and lodging for Jesus). Luke 8:2–3.

SWEAR
Lev 19:12 ye shall not ***s*** by my [God's] name falsely
Matt 5:34 I [Jesus] say unto you, ***S*** not at all
Mark 14:71 he [Peter] began to curse and to ***s***

SYCHAR (a city of Samaria where Jesus talked to the woman at Jacob's well). John 4:5–42.

SYCHEM. See *Shechem,* No. 2.

SYNAGOGUE [S]
Matt 4:23 Jesus went about all Galilee, teaching in their ***s's***
Mark 5:22 one of the rulers of the ***s,*** Jairus by name
Mark 13:9 in the ***s's*** ye shall be beaten
Luke 4:16 he [Jesus] went into the ***s***...stood up for to read

SYRACUSE (a city in Sicily visited by Paul). Acts 28:12.

SYRIA (a nation northeast of Israel which was a persistent enemy of the Jews across several centuries). Judg 10:6 • 2 Sam 8:11–13 • 1 Kgs 20:1–34 • 2 Kgs 13:3–24 • Isa 17:1–3 • Luke 2:2 • Acts 15:23,41. *Aram:* Num 23:7.

SYRIA-DAMASCUS. See *Damascus.*

-T-

TABERNACLE BUILT IN THE WILDERNESS. Ex 36:8–38:21.

TABITHA (a widow, also known as *Dorcas,* whom Peter restored to life). Acts 9:36–40.

TABOR, MOUNT (a mountain from which the judge Deborah sent Barak to defeat the Canaanites). Josh 19:22 • **Judg 4:6–14;** 8:18 • Ps 89:12 • Jer 46:18 • Hos 5:1.

TAMAR (Absalom's sister who was sexually assaulted by her half brother Amnon). **2 Sam 13:1–32** • 1 Chr 3:9.

TARPELITES (a tribe which colonized Samaria after the Northern Kingdom fell to Assyria). Ezra 4:9.

TARSUS (capital city of the Roman province of Silicia and the place where Paul was born). Acts 9:11,30; 11:25; 21:39; 22:3.

TARTAK (a pagan god worshiped by the Avites, a people who colonized Samaria after the Northern Kingdom fell to the Assyrians). 2 Kgs 17:31.

TATNAI (a Persian official who tried to stop the Jews from rebuilding the temple in Jerusalem). Ezra 5:3–17.

TAUGHT

Ps 119:102 thy [God's] judgments: for thou hast ***t*** me

Isa 54:13 all thy children shall be ***t*** of the LORD

Mark 1:22 he [Jesus] ***t*** them as one that had authority

Mark 4:2 he [Jesus] ***t*** them many things by parables

John 8:28 but as my Father hath ***t*** me [Jesus], I speak these things

2 Thes 2:15 hold the traditions which ye have been ***t***

TEACH [EST, ETH, ING]

Deut 6:7 thou shalt ***t*** them [God's commands] diligently unto thy children

Job 21:22 Shall any ***t*** God knowledge

Job 36:22 God exalteth by his power: who ***t'eth*** like him

Ps 25:4 Show me thy ways, O LORD; ***t*** me thy paths

Ps 51:13 Then will I ***t*** transgressors thy [God's] ways

Ps 86:11 ***T*** me thy way, O LORD...walk in thy truth

Ps 90:12 So ***t*** us to number our days

Prov 16:23 heart of the wise ***t'eth*** his mouth

Jer 31:34 they shall ***t*** no more every man his neighbour

Matt 21:23 elders...came unto him [Jesus] as he was ***t'ing***
Matt 28:19 Go ye therefore, and ***t*** all nations
Matt 28:20 ***T'ing*** them to observe all things
Mark 8:31 he [Jesus] began to ***t***...Son of man must suffer
Luke 11:1 Lord, ***t*** us [the disciples] to pray
Luke 12:12 Holy Ghost shall ***t*** you...what ye ought to say
John 14:26 the Comforter...he shall ***t*** you all things
Rom 2:21 Thou therefore which ***t'est*** another, ***t'est*** thou not thyself
Col 3:16 ***t'ing***...one another in psalms and hymns
1 Tim 3:2 A bishop...given to hospitality, apt to ***t***

TEACHER [S]
Ps 119:99 I have more understanding than all my ***t's***
John 3:2 know...thou [Jesus] art a ***t*** come from God
1 Cor 12:29 are all prophets? are all ***t's***
Eph 4:11 he [God] gave some, apostles...some...pastors ...***t's***

TEARS
Ps 6:6 water...couch with my ***t***
Ps 126:5 They that sow in ***t*** shall reap in joy
Jer 9:1 Oh that my [Jeremiah's] head were waters, and...eyes a fountain of ***t***
Rev 21:4 God shall wipe away all ***t*** from their eyes

TEKOA (a fortress city near Bethlehem and hometown of the prophet Amos). 2 Chr 11:6; 20:20 • Jer 6:1 • Amos 1:1. *Tekoah:* 2 Sam 14:2,4,9.

TEKOAH. See *Tekoa.*

TEL-ABIB (a Babylonian city where the prophet Ezekiel lived with the other Jewish captives). Ezek 3:15.

TEMPERANCE
Gal 5:23 Meekness, ***t:*** against such there is no law
2 Pet 1:6 And to knowledge ***t;*** and to ***t*** patience

TEMPERATE
1 Cor 9:25 And every man that striveth for the mastery is ***t*** in all things
Titus 1:8 a lover of good men, sober, just, holy, ***t***
Titus 2:2 That the aged men be sober, grave, ***t***

TEMPT [ED, ING]
Deut 6:16 Ye shall not ***t*** the LORD your God
Ps 78:41 Yea, they turned back and ***t'ed*** God
Matt 4:1 was Jesus led...into the wilderness to be ***t'ed***
Matt 4:7 Thou shalt not ***t*** the Lord thy God

Mark 8:11 seeking of him [Jesus] a sign...***t'ing*** him
John 8:6 ***t'ing*** him [Jesus]...to accuse him
1 Cor 7:5 Satan ***t*** you not for your incontinency
1 Cor 10:13 God...will not suffer you to be ***t'ed*** above that ye are able
Heb 4:15 high priest [Jesus]... was...***t'ed*** like as we are
Jas 1:13 Let no man say...I am ***t'ed*** of God

TEMPTATION [S]
Matt 6:13 lead us not into ***t***
Luke 4:13 when the devil had ended all the ***t,*** he departed from him [Jesus] for a season
1 Cor 10:13 no ***t*** taken you but such as is common to man
Jas 1:2 count it all joy when ye fall into divers ***t's***
Jas 1:12 Blessed is the man that endureth ***t***
2 Pet 2:9 Lord knoweth how to deliver...out of ***t's***

TEMPTATIONS OF JESUS. See *Jesus, Life and Ministry of.*

TEN COMMANDMENTS. Ex 20:1–17 • Deut 5:7–21.

TERAH (father of Abraham). **Gen 11:24–32** • Josh 24:2 • 1 Chr 1:26. *Thara:* Luke 3:34.

TERTULLUS (a Jewish lawyer who accused Paul of desecrating the temple). Acts 24:1–8.

TESTIFY [IED, IETH, ING]
Num 35:30 one witness shall not ***t*** against any person to cause him to die
Isa 59:12 our sins ***t*** against us
John 4:44 Jesus...***t'ied***...a prophet hath no honour in his own country
Acts 20:21 ***t'ing***...to the Jews, and...Greeks, repentance
Acts 23:11 Paul...hast ***t'ied*** of me [Jesus] in Jerusalem
Heb 7:17 he [God] ***t'ieth,*** Thou art a priest for ever
1 John 4:14 we...do ***t*** that the Father sent the Son
1 John 5:9 the witness of God... hath ***t'ied*** of his Son
Rev 22:20 He [Jesus] which ***t'ieth***...saith...I come quickly

TESTIMONY [IES]
Deut 6:20 What mean the ***t'ies***...which...God hath commanded you
Ps 19:7 ***t*** of...LORD is sure, making wise the simple
Ps 119:24 Thy [God's] ***t'ies*** also are my delight
Mark 6:11 shake off the dust... for a ***t*** against them
John 21:24 and we know that his ***t*** is true
2 Tim 1:8 Be not...ashamed of the ***t*** of our Lord

THADDAEUS. See *Judas.*

THANK

Matt 11:25 I [Jesus] ***t*** thee... Lord of heaven and earth

Luke 18:11 Pharisee... prayed...God, I ***t*** thee, that I am not as other men

Phil 1:3 I [Paul] ***t*** my God upon...remembrance of you

THANKS

1 Chr 16:34 give ***t*** unto the LORD; for he is good

Ps 92:1 It is a good thing to give ***t*** unto the LORD

Ps 107:1 give ***t*** unto the LORD, for he is good

Luke 22:19 And he [Jesus] took bread, and gave ***t***

1 Cor 11:24 he [Jesus] had given ***t,*** he brake it [bread]

1 Cor 15:57 ***t*** be to God, which giveth us the victory

2 Cor 9:15 ***T*** be unto God for his unspeakable gift

1 Thes 5:18 In every thing give ***t***...this is...will of God

THARA. See *Terah.*

THEBEZ (a fortified city where Abimelech was killed). **Judg 9:50–55** • 2 Sam 11:21.

THEOPHILUS (a friend to whom Luke addressed the Gospel of Luke and the Book of Acts). Luke 1:3 • Acts 1:1.

THESSALONIANS, FIRST AND SECOND EPISTLES TO THE. Two epistles written by the apostle Paul to the believers in the church at Thessalonica. The theme of both letters is the second coming of Christ.

THESSALONICA (a city on the Macedonian coast where Paul preached and founded a church). Acts 17:1–13 • 1 Thes 1:1.

THIEF [VES]

Matt 6:20 where ***t'ves*** do not break through nor steal

Mark 14:48 Are ye come out, as against a ***t***

Mark 15:27 with him [Jesus] they crucify two ***t'ves***

Luke 10:30 A certain man... fell among ***t'ves***

Luke 19:46 ye have made it [God's house] a den of ***t'ves***

John 10:10 The ***t*** cometh not, but for to steal

John 12:6 This he [Judas] said...because he was a ***t***

1 Thes 5:2 the day of the Lord so cometh as a ***t*** in the night

2 Pet 3:10 the day of the Lord will come as a ***t*** in the night

THINK [EST, ETH]

Prov 23:7 as he ***t'eth*** in his heart, so is he

Jer 29:11 I [God] know the thoughts that I ***t*** toward you

Matt 6:7 heathen...***t***...they shall be heard for...much speaking
Matt 24:44 such an hour as ye ***t*** not the Son of man cometh
Luke 10:36 Which...of these... ***t'est*** thou, was neighbour
John 16:2 that whosoever killeth you will ***t*** that he doeth God service
Rom 12:3 not to ***t*** of himself... highly than he ought to ***t***
1 Cor 10:12 ***t'eth*** he standeth take heed lest he fall
1 Cor 13:5 [charity] is not easily provoked, ***t'eth*** no evil
Gal 6:3 For if a man ***t*** himself to be something, when he is nothing
Eph 3:20 unto him [Jesus] that is able to do...above all that we ask or ***t***
Phil 4:8 if there be any praise, ***t*** on these things

THOMAS (a disciple of Jesus who insisted on indisputable proof that Jesus was alive). Matt 10:3 • Mark 3:18 • Luke 6:15 • John 11:16; 14:5; **20:24–29;** 21:2 • Acts 1:13.

THORN IN THE FLESH, PAUL'S. 2 Cor 12:7–10.

THOUGHT [S]
Gen 50:20 ye ***t*** evil against me [Joseph]; but God meant it unto good
Job 21:27 Behold, I [God] know your ***t's***
Job 42:2 no ***t*** can be withholden from thee [God]
Ps 92:5 O LORD...thy ***t's*** are very deep
Prov 16:3 Commit thy works unto the LORD, and thy ***t's*** shall be established
Isa 55:8 For my [God's] ***t's*** are not your ***t's***
Jer 29:11 I [God] know the ***t's*** that I think toward you
Matt 6:27 Which of you by taking ***t*** can add one cubit unto his stature
Mark 7:21 out of the heart of men, proceed evil ***t's***
1 Cor 3:20 The Lord knoweth the ***t's*** of the wise
1 Cor 13:11 I [Paul] understood as a child, I ***t*** as a child
Phil 2:6 Who [Jesus]...***t*** it not robbery to be equal with God
Heb 4:12 the word of God...is a discerner of the ***t's*** and intents of the heart

THRONE
Ps 45:6 Thy ***t,*** O God, is for ever and ever
Ps 97:2 righteousness and judgment are the habitation of his [God's] ***t***
Prov 20:28 his [the king's] ***t*** is upholden by mercy
Isa 6:1 I [Isaiah] saw also the Lord...upon a ***t***
Isa 66:1 Thus saith the LORD, The heaven is my [God's] ***t***

Jer 33:17 David shall never want a man to sit upon the ***t*** of the house of Israel
Lam 5:19 thy [God's] ***t*** from generation to generation
Matt 19:28 Son of man shall sit in the ***t*** of his glory
Matt 25:31 shall he [Jesus] sit upon the ***t*** of his glory
Luke 1:32 God shall give unto him [Jesus] the ***t*** of...David
Heb 4:16 Let us...come boldly unto the ***t*** of grace
Rev 4:2 one [Jesus] sat on the ***t***

THRONE OF GOD
Heb 12:2 Jesus...is set down at the right hand of the ***t-o-G***
Rev 7:15 before the ***t-o-G,*** and serve him day and night
Rev 22:1 water of life...proceeding out of the ***t-o-G***

THYATIRA (hometown of Lydia and site of one of the seven churches addressed by John in the Book of Revelation). Acts 16:14 • Rev 1:1; 2:18,24.

TIBERIAS
1 A city near the Sea of Galilee built by Herod Antipas and named for the Roman emperor Tiberius. John 6:1,23; 21:1.
2. Another name for the Sea of Galilee. See *Galilee, Sea of.*

TIGLATH-PILESER III (an Assyrian king who defeated the Northern Kingdom and carried Jewish captives to Assyria). 2 Kgs 15:29; 16:1–10. *Pul:* 1 Chr 5:26. *Tilgath-pilneser:* 2 Chr 28:20.

TILGATH-PILNESER. See *Tiglath-pileser III.*

TIMON (one of the seven men chosen as "deacons" in the church at Jerusalem). Acts 6:1–5.

TIMOTHEUS. See *Timothy.*

TIMOTHY (a young believer, also called *Timotheus,* who traveled with Paul and briefly shared his imprisonment at Rome). **Acts 16:1–3; 17:14–15; 18:1–5;** 19:22; 20:4 • Rom 16:21 • 1 Cor 4:17; 16:10 • 2 Cor 1:1,19 • **Phil 1:1; 2:19,23** • Col 1:1 • 1 Thes 1:1; 3:2,6 • 2 Thes 1:1 • 1 Tim 1:2,18; 6:20 • 2 Tim 1:2 • Phlm 1 • Heb 13:23.

TIMOTHY, FIRST AND SECOND EPISTLES TO. Two short epistles of the apostle Paul to his friend and fellow missionary, Timothy. The first epistle is practical in scope, instructing Timothy on how to lead a church. In 2 Timothy Paul expresses tender affection for the young minister (1:1–2:26) and speaks of the possibility of his own execution (4:6–22).

TIRZAH (capital of the Northern Kingdom before Samaria was built). 1 Kgs 14:17; 15:21,33; 16:6–23 • 2 Kgs 15:14–16 • Song 6:4.

TITHE [S]
Lev 27:30 all the ***t*** of the land... is the LORD'S
Deut 14:22 Thou shalt...***t*** all the increase of thy seed
Neh 13:12 Then brought all Judah the ***t*** of the corn
Mal 3:8 have we robbed thee [God]? In ***t's*** and offerings
Mal 3:10 Bring ye all the ***t's*** into the storehouse
Luke 11:42 ye [Pharisees] ***t*** mint and rue and...herbs
Heb 7:6 he [Melchisedec]... received ***t's*** of Abraham

TITUS (a church leader and traveling companion of Paul). 2 Cor 2:13; 7:6–14; 8:6,16,23; 12:18 • Gal 2:1–3 • 2 Tim 4:10 • Titus 1:4–3:11.

TITUS, EPISTLE TO. A short epistle from the apostle Paul to Titus in which he deals with several practical church matters (1:5–16) and the behavior of Christians in an immoral world (3:1–11).

TOBIAH (an Ammonite who opposed Nehemiah's reconstruction of Jerusalem's wall). Neh 2:10,19; 4:3,7; 6:1–19; 13:4,7–8.

TOLA (a minor judge of Israel). Judg 10:1–2.

TONGUE, POWER OF. Jas 3:1–12.

TONGUES, SPEAKING IN. 1 Cor 14:7–40.

TOOTH FOR A TOOTH
Matt 5:38 An eye for an eye, and a ***t-f-a-t***

TOPHET (a place of human sacrifice in the Valley of Hinnom near Jerusalem). Jer 7:31–32.

TOWER OF BABEL. Gen 11:1–9.

TRADITION [S]
Matt 15:6 commandment of God of none effect by your [Pharisees'] ***t***
Mark 7:5 Why walk not thy [Jesus'] disciples according to the ***t*** of the elders
2 Thes 2:15 hold the ***t's*** which ye have been taught

TRANSFIGURATION OF JESUS. See *Jesus, Life and Ministry of.*

TRANSGRESS [ED, ETH]

Deut 26:13 I have not ***t'ed*** thy [God's] commandments

Jer 2:29 all have ***t'ed*** against me, saith the LORD

Matt 15:2 Why do thy [Jesus'] disciples ***t*** the tradition of the elders...wash not their hands

1 John 3:4 Whosoever committeth sin ***t'eth*** also the law

TRANSGRESSION [S]

1 Chr 10:13 Saul died for his ***t***...against the LORD

Job 13:23 make me [Job] to know my ***t*** and my sin

Ps 32:1 Blessed is he whose ***t*** is forgiven

Ps 32:5 I will confess my ***t's*** unto the LORD

Ps 51:3 I acknowledge my ***t's***

Prov 12:13 The wicked is snared by the ***t*** of his lips

Prov 29:6 In the ***t*** of an evil man there is a snare

Isa 53:5 he [God's servant] was wounded for our ***t's***

Amos 1:3 For three ***t's*** of Damascus, and for four

TRANSGRESSOR [S]

Ps 51:13 Then will I teach ***t's*** thy [God's] ways

Prov 22:12 he [God] overthroweth the words of the ***t***

Mark 15:28 he [Jesus] was numbered with the ***t's***

TREASURE [S]

Ex 19:5 ye [Israel] shall be a peculiar ***t*** unto me [God]

Ps 135:4 LORD hath chosen... Israel for his peculiar ***t***

Prov 10:2 ***T's*** of wickedness profit nothing

Prov 15:16 Better is little with the fear of the LORD than great ***t*** and trouble

Matt 2:11 they [the wise men] had opened their ***t's***

Matt 6:20 lay up for yourselves ***t's*** in heaven

Matt 13:44 kingdom of heaven is like unto ***t*** hid in a field

Luke 12:34 where your ***t*** is, there will your heart be also

2 Cor 4:7 we have this ***t*** in earthen vessels

Col 2:3 In whom [Jesus] are hid all the ***t's*** of wisdom

TREE OF KNOWLEDGE OF GOOD AND EVIL (a tree in the Garden of Eden declared off-limits for Adam and Eve by the Lord). Gen 2:9–17.

TREE OF LIFE (a tree in the Garden of Eden whose fruit would bring eternal life). Gen 2:9 • Rev 22:2.

TRESPASS [ED, ES]

Ezra 9:15 we are before thee [God] in our ***t'es***

Ezek 15:8 they have committed a ***t***, saith the Lord GOD

Ezek 39:23 Israel went into captivity...because they ***t'ed*** against me [God]
Matt 6:14 if ye forgive men their ***t'es,*** your...Father will also forgive you
Mark 11:25 your Father...may forgive you your ***t'es***
Luke 17:3 If thy brother ***t*** against thee, rebuke him
2 Cor 5:19 God was...not imputing their ***t'es*** unto them
Eph 2:1 hath he [Jesus] quickened, who were dead in ***t'es***

TRIBULATION [S]
Matt 24:21 then shall be great ***t***
John 16:33 In the world ye shall have ***t***
Rom 5:3 knowing that ***t*** worketh patience
Rom 8:35 Who shall separate us...shall ***t,*** or distress
2 Cor 1:4 Who [Jesus] comforteth us in all our ***t***
Eph 3:13 I [Paul] desire that ye faint not at my ***t's*** for you

TRIUMPHAL ENTRY OF JESUS. See *Jesus, Life and Ministry of.*

TROAS (a city on the coast of Mysia where Paul received a vision). **Acts 16:8–11;** 20:5–6 • 2 Cor 2:12 • 2 Tim 4:13.

TROPHIMUS (a believer who accompanied Paul on the third missionary journey). Acts 20:4; 21:29 • 2 Tim 4:20.

TROUBLE [D, TH]
1 Sam 16:14 an evil spirit from the LORD ***t'd*** him [Saul]
1 Kgs 18:17 Art thou [Elijah] he that ***t'th*** Israel
Job 14:1 Man...is of few days, and full of ***t***
Ps 9:9 The LORD...will be a refuge...in times of ***t***
Ps 31:9 Have mercy upon me, O LORD, for I am in ***t***
Ps 38:6 I am ***t'd;*** I am bowed down greatly
Ps 46:1 God is...a very present help in ***t***
Ps 77:2 In the day of my ***t*** I sought the Lord
Ps 90:7 by thy [God's] wrath are we ***t'd***
Ps 108:12 Give us help from ***t***
Prov 15:27 He that is greedy of gain ***t'th*** his own house
Jer 8:15 We looked for peace... and for a time of health, and behold ***t***
Matt 2:3 he [Herod] was ***t'd,*** and all Jerusalem with him
Luke 1:29 she [Mary] was ***t'd*** at his [the angel's] saying
John 12:27 Now is my [Jesus'] soul ***t'd***...what shall I say
John 14:1 Let not your heart be ***t'd***...believe...in me
2 Cor 4:8 We are ***t'd*** on every side...not distressed
Gal 1:7 some that ***t*** you, and would pervert the gospel

2 Thes 1:6 recompense tribulation to them that ***t*** you

TRUE

Ps 19:9 judgments of the LORD are ***t*** and righteous

Zech 7:9 Execute ***t*** judgment, and show mercy

John 1:9 the ***t*** Light [Jesus]... lighteth every man

John 6:32 my [Jesus'] Father giveth you the ***t*** bread

John 15:1 I [Jesus] am the ***t*** vine...Father...the husbandman

John 21:24 we know that his [John's] testimony is ***t***

Rom 3:4 let God be ***t,*** but every man a liar

TRUE VINE, JESUS AS. See *"I Am" Statements of Jesus.*

TRUST [ED, ETH, ING]

Deut 32:37 Where are their gods...in whom they ***t'ed***

2 Sam 22:3 The God of my rock; in him will I ***t***

Job 13:15 Though he [God] slay me [Job]...I ***t*** in him

Ps 13:5 I have ***t'ed*** in thy [God's] mercy

Ps 16:1 Preserve me...for in thee [God] do I put my ***t***

Ps 26:1 I have ***t'ed***...in the LORD...I shall not slide

Ps 34:8 blessed is the man that ***t'eth*** in him [God]

Ps 37:5 ***t***...in him [God]...he shall bring it to pass

Ps 56:3 What time I am afraid, I will ***t*** in thee [God]

Ps 112:7 his heart is fixed, ***t'ing*** in the LORD

Ps 118:8 better to ***t*** in the LORD than...confidence in man

Prov 3:5 ***T*** in the LORD with all thine heart

Prov 11:28 He that ***t'eth*** in his riches shall fall

Mark 10:24 hard is it for them that ***t*** in riches to enter... the kingdom

1 Tim 1:11 According to the glorious gospel...which was committed to my [Paul's] ***t***

TRUTH

1 Sam 12:24 serve him [God] in ***t*** with all your heart

Ps 25:5 Lead me in thy [God's] ***t,*** and teach me

Ps 33:4 all his [God's] works are done in ***t***

Ps 86:11 Teach me...I will walk in thy [God's] ***t***

Ps 100:5 his [God's] ***t*** endureth to all generations

Ps 119:30 I have chosen the way of ***t***

John 1:17 grace and ***t*** came by Jesus Christ

John 4:24 must worship him [God] in spirit and in ***t***

John 8:32 know the ***t,*** and the ***t*** shall make you free

John 14:6 I [Jesus] am the way, the ***t,*** and the life

John 16:13 the Spirit of ***t***... will guide you into all ***t***

John 18:38 Pilate saith unto him [Jesus], What is ***t***
Acts 10:34 Of a ***t*** I [Peter] perceive that God is no respecter of persons
1 Cor 13:6 [charity] rejoiceth in the ***t***
Gal 4:16 Am I [Paul]...enemy, because I tell you the ***t***
Eph 4:15 speaking the ***t*** in love
1 Tim 2:4 Who [God] will have all men...come unto the knowledge of the ***t***
1 Tim 3:15 the church...the pillar and ground of the ***t***
2 Tim 2:15 workman...needeth not to be ashamed, rightly dividing the word of ***t***
1 John 1:8 If we say that we have no sin...***t*** is not in us
3 John 4 no greater joy than to hear that my [John's] children walk in ***t***

TYRANNUS (a citizen of Ephesus who allowed Paul to use his lecture hall). Acts 19:8–10.

TYRE (an ancient Phoenician city and thriving trade center north of Palestine). Josh 19:29 • 1 Kgs 5:1–12 • Joel 3:4–6 • Matt 15:21–28. *Tyrus:* Ezek 26:1–21; 27:1–36 • Amos 1:10.

TYRUS. See *Tyre.*

-U-

UNBELIEF

Mark 9:24 Lord, I believe; help thou mine ***u***

Heb 3:12 lest there be in any of you an evil heart of ***u***

Heb 4:11 lest any man fall after the same example of ***u***

UNBELIEVERS

1 Cor 6:6 brother goeth to law with brother...before the ***u***

2 Cor 6:14 Be ye not unequally yoked together with ***u***

UNBELIEVING

Acts 14:2 But the ***u*** Jews stirred up the Gentiles

1 Cor 7:14 the ***u*** husband is sanctified by the wife

Titus 1:15 unto them that are defiled and ***u*** is nothing pure

UNCIRCUMCISED

1 Sam 17:26 this ***u*** Philistine [Goliath], that he should defy...the living God

Ezek 44:9 No stranger, ***u*** in heart...shall enter into my [God's] sanctuary

Acts 7:51 stiffnecked and ***u*** in heart and ears

UNCIRCUMCISION

1 Cor 7:19 Circumcision is nothing, and ***u*** is nothing

Gal 5:6 neither circumcision availeth any thing, nor ***u***

Col 3:11 neither Greek nor Jew, circumcision nor ***u***

UNCLEAN [NESS]

Num 19:11 He that toucheth the dead body...***u*** seven days

Isa 6:5 because I [Isaiah] am a man of ***u*** lips

Isa 64:6 But we are all as an ***u*** thing

Mark 6:7 And he [Jesus]...gave them [the disciples] power over ***u*** spirits

Acts 10:14 I [Peter] have never eaten any thing...***u***

Rom 1:24 God also gave them up to ***u'ness***

Rom 14:14 persuaded...that there is nothing ***u*** of itself

Gal 5:19 works of the flesh are manifest...Adultery, fornication, ***u'ness***

1 Thes 4:7 God hath not called us unto ***u'ness***

UNDEFILED

Ps 119:1 Blessed are the ***u***... walk in the law of the LORD

Heb 7:26 high priest [Jesus]... who is holy, harmless, ***u***

Jas 1:27 Pure religion and ***u*** before God and the Father

UNDERSTAND [EST, ETH, ING]

1 Kgs 4:29 God gave Solomon wisdom and ***u'ing***

Job 26:12 by his [God's] ***u'ing*** he smiteth...the proud

Job 28:28 and to depart from evil is ***u'ing***

Job 32:9 neither do the aged ***u*** judgment

Ps 119:27 Make me to ***u*** the way of thy [God's] precepts

Ps 119:34 Give me ***u'ing,*** and I shall keep thy [God's] law

Ps 147:5 Great is our Lord... his ***u'ing*** is infinite

Prov 2:2 and apply thine heart to ***u'ing***

Prov 2:5 Then shalt thou ***u*** the fear of the LORD

Prov 3:5 and lean not unto thine own ***u'ing***

Prov 4:7 and with all thy getting get ***u'ing***

Prov 10:13 a rod is for...him that is void of ***u'ing***

Prov 14:6 knowledge is easy unto him that ***u'eth***

Prov 17:28 he that shutteth his lips is...a man of ***u'ing***

Isa 40:28 there is no searching of his [God's] ***u'ing***

Isa 44:18 he [God] hath shut their eyes...and...hearts, that they cannot ***u***

Dan 9:22 come forth to give thee [Daniel] skill and ***u'ing***

Dan 10:14 make thee [Daniel] ***u*** what shall befall thy people

Matt 15:16 Are ye [the disciples] also yet without ***u'ing***

Mark 8:21 How is it that ye [the disciples] do not ***u***

Luke 24:45 opened he [Jesus] their [Emmaus travelers'] ***u'ing***...might ***u*** the scriptures

Acts 8:30 Philip...said, ***U'est*** thou [Ethiopian eunuch] what thou readest

Rom 3:11 none that ***u'eth***... none that seeketh after God

1 Cor 13:2 though I [Paul]...***u*** all mysteries

1 Cor 14:19 I [Paul] had rather speak five words with my ***u'ing***...than...unknown tongue

Phil 4:7 peace of God, which passeth all ***u'ing***

Heb 11:3 we ***u***...worlds were framed by the word of God

UNDERSTOOD

Job 13:1 mine [Job's] ear hath heard and ***u*** it

Job 42:3 I [Job] uttered that I ***u*** not; things too wonderful

Isa 40:21 have ye not ***u*** from the foundations of the earth

John 12:16 These things ***u*** not his [Jesus'] disciples

1 Cor 13:11 When I [Paul] was a child...I ***u*** as a child

UNGODLY [INESS]

Ps 1:1 man that walketh not in the counsel of the ***u***

Prov 16:27 An ***u*** man diggeth up evil

Rom 1:18 wrath of God is revealed...against all ***u'iness***

Rom 5:6 in due time Christ died for the ***u***

Titus 2:12 denying ***u'iness***... we should live soberly

Jude 18 mockers...should walk after their own ***u*** lusts

UNJUST

Matt 5:45 he [God]...sendeth rain on the just and...***u***

Luke 16:8 the lord commended the ***u*** steward

1 Pet 3:18 Christ...suffered for sins, the just for the ***u***

UNKNOWN

Acts 17:23 altar with this inscription, TO THE ***U*** GOD

1 Cor 14:4 speaketh in an ***u*** tongue edifieth himself

1 Cor 14:19 I [Paul] had rather speak...with...understanding...than...in an ***u*** tongue

UNRIGHTEOUS [NESS]

Ps 92:15 and there is no ***u'ness*** in him [God]

Isa 55:7 Let the wicked forsake his way, and the ***u*** man his thoughts

Rom 1:18 wrath of God is revealed from heaven against all...***u'ness*** of men

1 Cor 6:9 the ***u*** shall not inherit the kingdom of God

2 Cor 6:14 what fellowship... righteousness with ***u'ness***

1 John 1:9 he [Jesus] is faithful...to cleanse us from all ***u'ness***

UNSEARCHABLE

Ps 145:3 Great is the LORD... his greatness is ***u***

Rom 11:33 how ***u*** are his [God's] judgments

Eph 3:8 I [Paul] should preach... the ***u*** riches of Christ

UR OF THE CHALDEES (a city in Mesopotamia where Abraham spent his early life before going to Canaan). **Gen 11:28,31;** 15:7 • Neh 9:7.

URIAH (a Hittite warrior whom David had killed after his affair with Uriah's wife). **2 Sam 11:1–26;** 12:9–10; 23:39 • 1 Kgs 15:5 • 1 Chr 11:41. *Urias:* Matt 1:6.

URIAS. See *Uriah.*

URIJAH (a prophet killed by King Jehoiakim for predicting God's judgment on Judah). Jer 26:20–23.

URIM AND THUMMIN (two objects in the breastplate of the high priest which were cast as lots to help determine God's will). Ex 28:30 • Lev 8:8 • Num 27:21 • Deut 33:8 • Ezra 2:63 • Neh 7:65.

UZ (a place west of the Arabian desert where Job lived). **Job 1:1** • Jer 25:20.

UZZA (an Israelite struck dead for touching the ark of the covenant). 1 Chr 13:7–11.

UZZIAH (a king of Judah who contracted leprosy as a divine punishment for assuming duties that belonged to the priesthood). 2 Kgs 15:13–34 • **2 Chr 26:1–23;** 27:2 • Isa 1:1; 6:1; 7:1 • Hos 1:1 • Amos 1:1 • Zech 14:5. *Azariah:* 2 Kgs 14:21. *Ozias:* Matt 1:8.

-V-

VAIN

Ex 20:7 not take the name of the LORD...in ***v***

Ps 2:1 Why do...the people imagine a ***v*** thing

Ps 60:11 ***v*** is the help of man

Ps 127:1 Except the LORD build the house, they labour in ***v*** that build it

Prov 31:30 Favour is deceitful, and beauty is ***v***

Matt 6:7 when ye pray, use not ***v*** repetitions

1 Cor 3:20 The Lord knoweth the thoughts of the wise, that they are ***v***

1 Cor 15:14 if Christ be not risen, then is our preaching ***v***

2 Tim 2:16 But shun profane and ***v*** babblings

VANITY [IES]

Job 35:13 God will not hear ***v,*** neither…regard it

Ps 31:6 I have hated them that regard lying ***v'ies***

Ps 39:5 every man at his best state is altogether ***v***

Ps 94:11 LORD knoweth the thoughts of man...they are ***v***

Ps 144:4 Man is like to ***v:*** his days are as a shadow

Eccl 1:2 ***v*** of ***v'ies;*** all is ***v***

Isa 41:29 they are all ***v;*** their works are nothing

Acts 14:15 Sirs [people of Lystra]...turn from these ***v'ies***

Eph 4:17 walk not...in the ***v*** of their mind

VASHTI (the queen of Ahasuerus of Persia who was replaced by Esther). Esth 1:9–12; 2:1–4,15–17.

VENGEANCE

Ps 94:1 God, to whom ***v*** belongeth, show thyself

Isa 61:2 To proclaim...the day of ***v*** of our God

Luke 21:22 these be the days of ***v***...things...may be fulfilled

Rom 12:19 ***V*** is mine; I will repay, saith the Lord

VICTORY

Isa 25:8 He [God] will swallow up death in ***v***

1 Cor 15:55 O grave, where is thy ***v***

1 Cor 15:57 God...giveth us the ***v*** through...Jesus Christ

1 John 5:4 this is the ***v*** that overcometh the world

VINE [S]

Judg 9:12 said the trees unto the ***v***...reign over us

Song 2:15 the little foxes, that spoil the ***v's***

Mic 4:4 sit every man under his ***v*** and under his fig tree

Luke 22:18 I [Jesus] will not drink of the fruit of the ***v***

John 15:5 I [Jesus] am the ***v***, ye are the branches

VINE OF SODOM (a plant which produced a beautiful fruit that was unfit to eat—a fitting description of Israel's idolatry). Deut 32:32.

VIRTUE

Mark 5:30 Jesus...knowing... that ***v*** had gone out of him

Phil 4:8 if there be any ***v***... think on these things

2 Pet 1:5 add to your faith ***v***; and to virtue knowledge

VIRTUOUS

Ruth 3:11 all the city...doth know...thou art a ***v*** woman

Prov 12:4 A ***v*** woman is a crown to her husband

Prov 31:10 Who can find a ***v*** woman...price...above rubies

VISION [S]

Prov 29:18 Where there is no ***v***, the people perish

Ezek 1:1 heavens...opened, and I [Ezekiel] saw ***v's***

Ezek 11:24 the spirit...brought me [Ezekiel] in a ***v***...into Chaldea

Dan 2:19 Then was the secret revealed...in a night ***v***

Joel 2:28 your young men shall see ***v's***

Hab 2:2 Write the ***v***, and make it plain upon tables

Luke 1:22 he [Zacharias] had seen a ***v*** in the temple

Acts 16:9 a ***v*** appeared to Paul in the night

Acts 26:19 I [Paul] was not disobedient unto the heavenly ***v***

VOICE [S]

Gen 22:18 thou [Abraham] hast obeyed my [God's] ***v***

Ex 5:2 Who is the LORD, that I [Pharaoh] should obey his ***v***

Josh 24:24 our God will we serve...his ***v*** will we obey

1 Kgs 19:12 and after the fire a still small ***v***

Job 40:9 canst thou thunder with a ***v*** like him [God]

Ps 27:7 Hear, O LORD, when I cry with my ***v***

Ps 66:8 make the ***v*** of his [God's] praise to be heard

Ps 116:1 he [God] hath heard my ***v*** and my supplications

Isa 40:3 The ***v*** of him that crieth in the wilderness

Jon 2:2 and thou [God] heardest my [Jonah's] ***v***

Matt 3:3 The ***v*** of one crying in the wilderness

Matt 3:17 a ***v*** from heaven... my [God's] beloved Son

Mark 9:7 a ***v*** came out of the cloud...This is my [God's] beloved Son

Luke 23:46 when Jesus had cried with a loud ***v***

John 10:27 My [Jesus'] sheep hear my ***v***...I know them

Acts 9:4 a ***v*** saying...Saul, why persecutest...me [Jesus]

1 Cor 14:10 There are...so many...***v's*** in the world

Heb 3:15 To day if ye will hear his [God's] ***v***

Rev 1:10 I [John]...heard behind me a great ***v***

Rev 3:20 any man hear my [Jesus'] ***v,*** and open the door

VOICE OF THE LORD

Gen 3:8 they [Adam and Eve] heard the ***v-o-t-L***

Deut 13:18 thou shalt hearken to the ***v-o-t-L***

1 Sam 15:22 Hath the LORD as great delight in... sacrifices, as in obeying the ***v-o-t-L***

Ps 29:4 the ***v-o-t-L*** is powerful... full of majesty

Isa 6:8 I [Isaiah] heard the ***v-o-t-L***...Whom shall I send

VOW [ED, EST, S]

Judg 11:30 Jephthah ***v'ed*** a ***v*** unto the LORD

Ps 50:14 and pay thy ***v's*** unto the most High

Ps 116:14 I will pay my ***v's*** unto the LORD

Eccl 5:4 ***v'est*** a ***v*** unto God, defer not to pay it

Jon 1:16 the men...offered a sacrifice...and made ***v's***

Jon 2:9 I will pay that that I have ***v'ed***

-W-

WAGES

Lev 19:13 ***w*** of him...shall not abide with thee all night

Hag 1:6 earneth ***w*** to put it into a bag with holes

Rom 6:23 the ***w*** of sin is death

WAIT ON THE LORD

Ps 27:14 **W-o-t-L:** be of good courage...strengthen thine heart

Ps 37:34 **W-o-t-L,** and keep his way...he shall exalt thee

Prov 20:22 ***w*-o-t-L,** and he shall save thee

WALLS OF JERUSALEM REBUILT AFTER THE EXILE. Neh 6:15.

WANDERING IN THE WILDERNESS BY ISRAEL. Num 14:20–35.

WATCH [ED, ETH, ING]

Job 14:16 dost thou [God] not ***w*** over my sin

Ps 90:4 For a thousand years in thy [God's] sight are...as a ***w*** in the night

Ps 141:3 Set a ***w,*** O LORD, before my mouth

Matt 24:42 **W** therefore: for ye know not what hour

Mark 14:37 couldest not thou [Peter] ***w*** one hour

Luke 2:8 shepherds...keeping ***w*** over their flock

Luke 12:37 Blessed are those... the lord...find ***w'ing***

Luke 12:39 goodman...had known...thief would come, he would have ***w'ed***

1 Pet 4:7 be ye...sober, and ***w*** unto prayer

Rev 16:15 I [Jesus] come as a thief. Blessed is he that ***w'eth***

WATER [EST, ETH, S]

Gen 1:2 the Spirit of God moved upon...the ***w's***

Gen 7:24 the ***w's*** prevailed upon the earth

Gen 9:11 neither shall all flesh be cut off any more by the ***w's*** of a flood

Ex 7:18 Egyptians shall loathe to drink of the ***w*** of the river

Ex 14:22 ***w's*** were a wall unto [the Israelites]

Num 20:11 Moses...smote the rock...and...***w*** came out

Josh 9:27 Joshua made them [Gibeonites]...drawers of ***w***

1 Kgs 18:38 fire of the LORD fell...and licked up the ***w***

Job 5:10 Who [God]...sendeth ***w's*** upon the fields

Ps 1:3 like a tree planted by the rivers of ***w***

Ps 22:14 I am poured out like ***w***...bones are out of joint

Ps 23:2 he [God] leadeth me beside the still ***w's***

Ps 63:1 flesh longeth for thee [God] in a dry and thirsty land, where no ***w*** is

Ps 65:9 Thou [God] visitest the earth, and ***w'est*** it

Ps 69:14 let me be delivered... out of the deep ***w's***

Ps 119:136 Rivers of ***w's*** run down mine eyes

Prov 5:15 Drink ***w's*** out of thine own cistern

Prov 25:21 if he [one's enemy] be thirsty, give him ***w***

Eccl 11:1 Cast thy bread upon the ***w's***

Song 8:7 Many ***w's*** cannot quench love

Isa 11:9 earth shall be full of the knowledge of the LORD, as the ***w's*** cover the sea

Isa 40:12 Who [God] hath measured the ***w's*** in...his hand

Isa 55:1 every one that thirsteth, come ye to the ***w's***

Jer 2:13 forsaken me [God] the fountain of living ***w's***

Jer 9:1 Oh that my [Jeremiah's] head were ***w's***

Ezek 7:17 all knees shall be weak as ***w***

Ezek 12:18 drink thy [Ezekiel's] ***w*** with trembling

Amos 5:24 let judgment run down as ***w's***

Hab 2:14 earth...filled with... the glory of the LORD, as the ***w's*** cover the sea

Mark 1:8 I [John the Baptist]... have baptized you with ***w***

Luke 8:24 he [Jesus]...rebuked... the raging of the ***w***

John 3:5 Except a man be born of ***w*** and of the Spirit

John 4:14 drinketh of the ***w*** that I [Jesus] shall give him

Acts 1:5 John...baptized with ***w;*** but ye shall be baptized with the Holy Ghost

Acts 8:36 here is ***w;*** what doth hinder me [Ethiopian eunuch] to be baptized

1 Cor 3:7 neither he that ***w'eth;*** but God that giveth the increase

Rev 22:17 whosoever will, let him take the ***w*** of life freely

WAY [S] OF THE LORD

2 Sam 22:22 I have kept the ***w's-o-t-L***

2 Kgs 21:22 he [Amon]...walked not in the ***w-o-t-L***

Ps 18:21 For I have kept the ***w's-o-t-L***

Ps 138:5 they shall sing in the ***w's-o-t-L***

Isa 40:3 Prepare...the ***w-o-t-L***

Jer 5:4 they are foolish: for they know not the ***w-o-t-L***

Ezek 33:17 the...people say, The ***w-o-t-L*** is not equal

Hos 14:9 for the ***w's-o-t-L*** are right, and...just

Mark 1:3 Prepare...the ***w-o-t-L,*** make his paths straight

Acts 13:10 wilt thou [Elymas]... pervert the right ***w's-o-t-L***

WAY OF THE SEA (a road that ran from Phoenicia to Egypt, passing through Palestine). Isa 9:1.

WAY, THE TRUTH, AND THE LIFE, JESUS AS. See *"I Am" Statements of Jesus.*

WAYS

Deut 10:12 what doth...God require...to walk in all his ***w***

1 Sam 18:14 David behaved... wisely in all his ***w***

2 Chr 7:14 If my [God's] people... shall...turn from their wicked ***w;*** then will I hear

Job 34:21 his [God's] eyes are upon the ***w*** of man

Ps 25:4 Show me thy ***w,*** O LORD, teach me thy paths

Ps 128:1 Blessed is every one... walketh in his [God's] ***w***

Prov 3:6 In all thy ***w*** acknowledge him [God]

Prov 14:12 the end thereof are the ***w*** of death

Prov 28:18 he that is perverse in his ***w*** shall fall

Isa 55:8 neither are your ***w*** my ***w,*** saith the LORD

Lam 3:40 search and try our ***w,*** and turn...to the LORD

Rom 11:33 how unsearchable are his [God's] judgments... his ***w*** past finding out

Jas 1:8 A double minded man is unstable in all his ***w***

WEAK [ENED]

Ps 6:2 Have mercy upon me, O LORD; for I am ***w***

Ps 102:23 He [God] ***w'ened*** my strength in the way

Matt 26:41 the spirit...is willing, but the flesh is ***w***

Acts 20:35 so labouring ye ought to support the ***w***

1 Cor 1:27 God hath chosen... ***w*** things of the world to confound the...mighty

1 Cor 9:22 became...***w,*** that I [Paul] might gain the ***w***

WEAKNESS

1 Cor 1:25 the ***w*** of God is stronger than men

1 Cor 15:43 it [the body] is sown in ***w***...raised in power

2 Cor 12:9 my [Jesus'] strength is made perfect in ***w***

WICKED [LY, NESS]

Gen 6:5 God saw that the ***w'ness*** of man was great

Gen 18:23 Wilt thou [God]... destroy...righteous with the ***w***

Job 4:8 they that...sow ***w'ness,*** reap the same

Job 18:5 Yea, the light of the ***w*** shall be put out

Job 27:4 My [Job's] lips shall not speak ***w'ness***

Ps 10:2 ***w*** in his pride doth persecute the poor

Ps 34:21 Evil shall slay the ***w***

Ps 58:3 The ***w*** are estranged from the womb

Ps 71:4 Deliver me, O my God, out of the hand of the ***w***

Ps 84:10 rather be a doorkeeper...than to dwell in the tents of ***w'ness***

Ps 94:3 LORD...how long shall the ***w*** triumph

Ps 106:6 committed iniquity, we have done ***w'ly***

Ps 129:4 he [God] hath cut asunder the cords of the ***w***

Prov 4:17 they [evil men] eat the bread of ***w'ness***

Prov 15:29 The LORD is far from the ***w***

Isa 53:9 he [God's servant] made his grave with the ***w***

Jer 4:14 O Jerusalem, wash thine heart from ***w'ness***

Jer 17:9 The heart is...desperately ***w:*** who can know it

Hos 10:13 Ye have plowed ***w'ness***...reaped iniquity

Jon 1:2 their [Ninevites'] ***w'ness*** is...before me [God]

Matt 16:4 A ***w***...generation seeketh after a sign

Eph 6:12 we wrestle...against spiritual ***w'ness***

Eph 6:16 able to quench all the fiery darts of the ***w***

WICKED ONE

Matt 13:19 cometh the ***w-o***... catcheth...which was sown

Matt 13:38 the tares are the children of the ***w-o***

1 John 2:14 and ye have overcome the ***w-o***

1 John 3:12 Cain...was of that ***w-o,*** and slew his brother

1 John 5:18 begotten of God... that ***w-o*** toucheth him not

WILL OF GOD

Mark 3:35 do the ***w-o-G,*** the same is my brother

Rom 12:2 what is that good... and perfect, ***w-o-G***

1 Thes 4:3 this is the ***w-o-G***... abstain from fornication

1 Thes 5:18 give thanks...this is the ***w-o-G*** in Christ Jesus

1 John 2:17 he that doeth the ***w-o-G*** abideth for ever

WINE

Job 32:19 my belly is as ***w*** which hath no vent

Prov 4:17 they...drink the ***w*** of violence

Prov 20:1 **W** is a mocker, strong drink is raging

Isa 5:22 Woe unto them that are mighty to drink ***w***

Mark 2:22 no man putteth new ***w*** into old bottles

John 2:3 mother of Jesus saith...They have no ***w***

Acts 2:13 men [believers at Pentecost] are full of new ***w***

Eph 5:18 be not drunk with ***w***

1 Tim 3:8 deacons be grave... not given to much ***w***

1 Tim 5:23 use a little ***w*** for thy stomach's sake

WISDOM

1 Kgs 4:29 God gave Solomon ***w*** and understanding

Job 28:28 Behold, the fear of the Lord, that is ***w***

Job 34:35 his [Job's] words were without ***w***

Ps 90:12 number our days... apply our hearts unto ***w***

Ps 111:10 fear of the LORD is the beginning of ***w***

Prov 2:2 So that thou incline thine ear unto ***w***

Prov 4:7 **W** is the principal thing; therefore get ***w***

Prov 10:13 In the lips of him that hath understanding ***w*** is found

Prov 23:4 Labour not to be rich: cease from thine own ***w***

Eccl 1:18 For in much ***w*** is much grief

Isa 11:2 the spirit of ***w*** and understanding

Jer 9:23 Let not the wise man glory in his ***w***

Luke 2:52 And Jesus increased in ***w*** and stature

Acts 6:3 seven men...full of the Holy Ghost and ***w***

1 Cor 1:20 hath not God made foolish the ***w*** of this world

1 Cor 1:22 Jews require a sign... Greeks seek after ***w***

1 Cor 3:19 ***w*** of this world is foolishness with God

Col 3:16 word of Christ dwell in you richly in all ***w***

Jas 1:5 If any of you lack ***w***, let him ask of God

WISE

Ps 19:7 testimony of the LORD is sure, making ***w*** the simple

Prov 3:7 Be not ***w*** in thine own eyes: fear the LORD

Prov 6:6 consider her [the ant's] ways, and be ***w***

Eccl 4:13 Better is a poor and a ***w*** child than an old and foolish king

Isa 5:21 Woe unto them that are ***w*** in their own eyes

Jer 9:23 Let not the ***w*** man glory in his wisdom

Matt 2:1 when Jesus was born... came ***w*** men from the east

Matt 7:24 a ***w*** man, which built his house upon a rock

Matt 10:16 ***w*** as serpents, and harmless as doves

Matt 11:25 thou [God] hast hid these things from the ***w***

Matt 25:8 foolish said unto the ***w***, Give us of your oil

Rom 12:16 Be not ***w*** in your own conceits

1 Cor 1:20 Where is the ***w?*** where is the scribe

1 Cor 1:26 not many ***w*** men after the flesh...are called

WISE MEN VISIT THE CHILD JESUS. Matt 2:1–12.

WITNESS [ES]

Ex 20:16 not bear false ***w*** against thy neighbour

Ps 35:11 False ***w'es*** did rise up

Prov 19:9 A false ***w*** shall not be unpunished

Matt 24:14 gospel...preached... for a ***w*** unto all nations
Mark 14:56 many bare false ***w*** against him [Jesus]
John 1:8 He [John the Baptist] ...was sent to bear ***w*** of that Light [Jesus]
Acts 1:8 and ye shall be ***w'es*** unto me [Jesus]
Acts 22:15 thou shalt be his [Jesus'] ***w*** unto all men
Rom 8:16 The Spirit itself beareth ***w*** with our spirit
Heb 12:1 compassed about with so great a cloud of ***w'es***

WIVES
Matt 19:8 Moses...suffered you to put away your ***w***
Eph 5:22 ***W,*** submit...unto your own husbands
Eph 5:25 Husbands, love your ***w***...as Christ...loved the church
Col 3:18 ***W,*** submit...unto your own husbands
Col 3:19 Husbands, love your ***w***...be not bitter
1 Tim 4:7 But refuse profane and old ***w'*** fables
1 Pet 3:1 ***w,*** be in subjection to your own husbands

WOMAN AT THE WELL TALKS WITH JESUS. John 4:5–42.

WONDERS
Ps 77:14 Thou art the God that doest ***w***
Ps 96:3 Declare his [God's]...***w*** among all people
John 4:48 Except ye see signs and ***w,*** ye will not believe
Acts 2:43 ***w*** and signs were done by the apostles
Acts 6:8 Stephen, full of faith and power, did great ***w***

WORD [S]
Job 8:2 ***w's*** of thy [Job's] mouth be like a strong wind
Ps 12:6 The ***w's*** of the LORD are pure ***w's:*** as silver
Ps 19:14 Let the ***w's*** of my mouth...be acceptable in thy [God's] sight
Ps 119:11 Thy [God's] ***w*** have I hid in mine heart
Ps 119:81 I hope in thy [God's] ***w***
Ps 119:105 Thy [God's] ***w*** is a lamp unto my feet
Prov 15:1 but grievous ***w's*** stir up anger
Prov 15:23 a ***w*** spoken in due season, how good is it
Isa 40:8 the ***w*** of our God shall stand for ever
Jer 1:9 I [God]...put my ***w's*** in thy [Jeremiah's] mouth
Dan 12:9 Go thy way, Daniel: for the ***w's*** are closed up
Mal 2:17 have wearied the LORD with your ***w's***
Matt 12:36 That every idle ***w*** that men shall speak, they shall give account
Matt 24:35 my [Jesus'] ***w's*** shall not pass away

Luke 1:38 And Mary said...be it unto me according to thy [God's] ***w***

Luke 4:32 his [Jesus'] ***w*** was with power

Luke 5:5 at thy [Jesus'] ***w*** I [Peter] will let down the net

John 1:1 In the beginning was the ***W***...***W*** was God

John 6:68 thou [Jesus] hast the ***w's*** of eternal life

John 17:17 Sanctify them... thy [God's] ***w*** is truth

Acts 8:4 they that...scattered abroad went every where preaching the ***w***

1 Cor 2:4 my [Paul's] preaching was not with enticing ***w's***

2 Cor 5:19 committed unto us the ***w*** of reconciliation

Col 3:17 And whatsoever ye do in ***w*** or deed

2 Tim 2:15 a workman...rightly dividing the ***w*** of truth

Jas 1:22 doers of the ***w,*** and not hearers only

1 John 3:18 let us not love in ***w***...but in deed

WORD OF GOD

Prov 30:5 Every ***w-o-G*** is pure

Luke 4:4 not live by bread alone, but by every ***w-o-G***

Luke 5:1 people pressed upon him [Jesus] to hear the ***w-o-G***

Luke 8:21 my [Jesus'] brethren are these which hear the ***w-o-G,*** and do it

Acts 4:31 place was shaken... filled with the Holy Ghost... spake the ***w-o-G***

Rom 10:17 faith cometh by hearing...hearing by the ***w-o-G***

Eph 6:17 the sword of the Spirit, which is the ***w-o-G***

Heb 4:12 the ***w-o-G*** is quick, and powerful

Heb 11:3 the worlds were framed by the ***w-o-G***

WORD [S] OF THE LORD

Ps 33:6 By the ***w-o-t-L*** were the heavens made

Amos 8:11 not a famine of bread...but of hearing the ***w's-o-t-L***

Acts 19:10 all...in Asia heard the ***w-o-t-L***

1 Pet 1:25 the ***w-o-t-L*** endureth for ever

WORK [ETH, ING]

Gen 2:2 on the seventh day God ended his ***w***

Ex 23:12 Six days thou shalt do thy ***w***

Neh 4:6 for the people had a mind to ***w***

Ps 8:3 consider thy [God's] heavens, the ***w*** of thy fingers

Ps 77:12 I will meditate also of all thy [God's] ***w***

Ps 90:17 establish thou [God] the ***w*** of our hands

Ps 115:4 Their idols are...the ***w*** of men's hands

Eccl 12:14 God shall bring every ***w*** into judgment
John 4:34 My [Jesus'] meat is...to finish his [God's] ***w***
John 5:17 My [Jesus'] Father ***w'eth***...and I ***w***
John 6:29 the ***w*** of God, that ye believe on him [Jesus]
John 9:4 night cometh, when no man can ***w***
John 17:4 I [Jesus] have finished the ***w*** which thou [God] gavest me to do
Acts 13:2 Separate me Barnabas and Saul for the ***w***
Rom 8:28 we know...all things ***w*** together for good
Rom 13:10 Love ***w'eth*** no ill to his neighbour
1 Cor 3:14 If any man's ***w*** abide...receive a reward
1 Cor 12:10 To another the ***w'ing*** of miracles
Eph 4:12 perfecting of the saints...***w*** of the ministry
Phil 1:6 he [God] which hath begun a good ***w*** in you
Phil 2:13 God...***w'eth*** in you... to do of his good pleasure
1 Tim 3:1 office of a bishop, he desireth a good ***w***
Heb 13:21 ***w'ing*** in you that which is wellpleasing in his [God's] sight

WORK [S] OF GOD
Ps 64:9 all men...shall declare the ***w-o-G***
Ps 66:5 Come and see the ***w's-o-G***
Ps 78:7 not forget the ***w's-o-G,*** but keep his commandments
Eccl 7:13 Consider the ***w-o-G***
Eccl 8:17 Then I beheld all the ***w-o-G***
John 6:28 that we might work the ***w's-o-G***
Acts 2:11 hear them speak... the wonderful ***w's-o-G***

WORK [S] OF THE LORD
Ps 77:11 I will remember the ***w's-o-t-L***...thy wonders
Ps 118:17 I shall...declare the ***w's-o-t-L***
Jer 48:10 Cursed be he that doeth the ***w-o-t-L*** deceitfully
Jer 51:10 declare in Zion the ***w-o-t-L*** our God
1 Cor 15:58 stedfast, unmoveable, always abounding in the ***w-o-t-L***

WORKERS
Ps 6:8 Depart from me, all ye ***w*** of iniquity
1 Cor 12:29 are all teachers? are all ***w*** of miracles
Phil 3:2 Beware of dogs, beware of evil ***w***

WORKS
1 Chr 16:9 talk ye of all his [God's] wondrous ***w***
1 Chr 16:24 Declare his [God's] glory...marvellous ***w*** among all nations
Job 37:14 consider the wondrous ***w*** of God

Ps 33:4 all his [God's] ***w*** are done in truth

Ps 40:5 Many, O LORD...are thy wonderful ***w***

Ps 92:5 O LORD, how great are thy ***w***

Ps 143:5 I meditate on all thy [God's] ***w***

Ps 145:9 his [God's] tender mercies are over all his ***w***

Matt 5:16 see your good ***w,*** and glorify your Father

Matt 13:58 he [Jesus] did not many mighty ***w*** there

John 6:28 that we might work the ***w*** of God

John 9:3 ***w*** of God should be made manifest in him [Jesus]

John 14:12 greater ***w*** than these shall he do

Gal 2:16 man is not justified by the ***w*** of the law

Eph 2:9 Not of ***w,*** lest any man should boast

2 Tim 3:17 That the man of God may be perfect... furnished unto all good ***w***

Titus 3:5 Not by ***w*** of righteousness...we have done

Jas 2:17 faith, if it hath not ***w,*** is dead, being alone

Rev 3:8 I [Jesus] know thy [church at Philadelphia's] ***w***

WORSHIP [PED, PETH]

Ps 95:6 ***w*** and bow down [before God]

Ps 99:5 ***w*** at his [God's] footstool; for he is holy

Jer 25:6 go not after other gods...to ***w*** them

Dan 3:6 whoso falleth not down and ***w'peth*** shall...be cast into the...furnace

Dan 3:18 we [Daniel's three friends] will not...***w*** the golden image

Matt 2:2 we [the wise men]... are come to ***w*** him [Jesus]

John 4:24 they...must ***w*** him [God] in spirit and in truth

Acts 17:23 Whom...ye ignorantly ***w,*** him [God] declare I [Paul] unto you

Acts 17:25 Neither is [God] ***w'ped*** with men's hands

Rom 1:25 Who [ungodly people]...***w'ped***...served... creature more than... Creator

Rev 7:11 all the angels...fell before the throne on their faces, and ***w'ped*** God

WORSHIP THE LORD

1 Chr 16:29 ***w-t-L*** in the beauty of holiness

Ps 96:9 O ***w-t-L*** in the beauty of holiness

Luke 4:8 ***w-t-L*** thy God, and him only shalt thou serve

WRATH

Ex 32:11 why doth thy [God's] ***w*** wax hot

Job 5:2 For ***w*** killeth the foolish man

Ps 21:9 LORD shall swallow them up in his ***w***

Ps 90:7 by thy [God's] ***w*** are we troubled

Prov 14:29 He that is slow to ***w*** is of great understanding

Matt 3:7 warned you [Pharisee] to flee from the ***w***

Rom 5:9 we shall be saved from ***w*** through him [Jesus]

Eph 4:26 let not the sun go down upon your ***w***

Eph 6:4 fathers, provoke not your children to ***w***

Rev 6:17 the great day of his [God's] ***w*** is come

WRATH OF GOD

Ps 78:31 The ***w-o-G***...slew the fattest of them

John 3:36 believeth not the Son...***w-o-G*** abideth on him

Rom 1:18 ***w-o-G*** is revealed... against all ungodliness

Rev 16:1 pour out the vials of the ***w-o-G*** upon the earth

-Y-

YIELD [ED, ING]

Gen 1:11 earth bring forth grass, the herb ***y'ing*** seed

Num 17:8 rod of Aaron... budded...***y'ed*** almonds

Ps 67:6 Then shall the earth ***y*** her increase

Matt 27:50 Jesus...***y'ed*** up the ghost

Rom 6:13 but ***y*** yourselves unto God

Rev 22:2 the tree of life...***y'ed*** her fruit every month

YOKE

Deut 28:48 he [God] shall put a ***y*** of iron upon thy neck

1 Kgs 19:19 Elisha...was plowing with twelve ***y*** of oxen

2 Chr 10:14 My [Rehoboam's] father made your ***y*** heavy

Jer 28:2 I [God] have broken the ***y*** of...Babylon

Matt 11:30 my [Jesus'] ***y*** is easy, and my burden is light

Gal 5:1 be not entangled again with the ***y*** of bondage

YOUTH

1 Sam 17:33 thou [David] art but a ***y***, and he [Goliath] a man of war

Ps 25:7 Remember not the sins of my ***y***

Ps 71:17 O God, thou hast taught me from my ***y***

Prov 5:18 rejoice with the wife of thy ***y***

Eccl 12:1 Remember now thy Creator in the days of thy ***y***

Matt 19:20 All these things have I kept from my ***y*** up

1 Tim 4:12 Let no man despise thy ***y***

-Z-

ZABULON. See *Zebulun.*

ZACCHAEUS (a tax collector who met Jesus and vowed to give half of his wealth to the poor and make restitution to those whom he had cheated). Luke 19:1–10.

ZACHARIAH (a king of Israel who ruled only about three months before being assassinated). 2 Kgs 14:29; 15:8–11.

ZACHARIAS (father of John the Baptist). Luke 1:5–79.

ZAMZUMMIMS (a race of giants who lived in the region later occupied by the Ammonites). Deut 2:20–21.

ZAREPHATH (a coastal town of Phoenicia where Elijah restored a widow's son to life). **1 Kgs 17:9–24** • Obad 20. *Sarepta:* Luke 4:26.

ZEAL
Ps 69:9 the *z* of thine house hath eaten me up
John 2:17 written, The *z* of thine house hath eaten me up
Phil 3:6 Concerning *z*, persecuting the church

ZEALOUS
Acts 21:20 Jews...which believe...are all *z* of the law
Acts 22:3 I [Paul]...was *z* toward God, as ye all are
Titus 2:14 purify unto himself [God] a peculiar people, *z* of good works

ZEBAH (a Midianite king killed by Gideon's army). Judg 8:4–28.

ZEBEDEE (father of James and John, disciples of Jesus). Matt 4:21–22; 10:2; 20:20; 26:37; 27:56 • Mark 1:19–20; 3:17; 10:35 • Luke 5:10 • John 21:2.

ZEBOIIM. See *Zeboim.*

ZEBOIM (a city destroyed along with Sodom and Gomorrah because of its sin). Gen 10:19 • **Deut 29:23** • Hos 11:8. *Zeboiim:* Gen 14:2,8.

ZEBULUN (a son of Jacob and ancestor of one of the twelve tribes of Israel). Gen 30:20; 35:23; 46:14; 49:13 • Ex 1:3 • 1 Chr 2:1. The tribe of Zebulun settled in northern Canaan. Josh 19:10–16. *Zabulon:* Matt 4:13.

ZECHARIAH (a prophet after the Exile and author of the book that bears his name). Ezra 5:1.

ZECHARIAH, BOOK OF. A prophetic book of the Old

Testament written to encourage the Jewish people during the difficult years after they returned from the Exile. Zechariah encouraged the people to complete the task of rebuilding the temple in Jerusalem.

ZEDEKIAH (the last king of Judah who ruled as a puppet king under King Nebuchadnezzar of Babylonia and who was often condemned by the prophet Jeremiah). **2 Kgs 24:15–20;** 25:2–7 • 1 Chr 3:15 • 2 Chr 36:10–11 • **Jer 21–52.** *Mattaniah:* 2 Kgs 24:17.

ZELOPHEHAD (an Israelite whose five daughters petitioned for the right to inherit his property because he had no sons). Num 26:33; **27:1–8.**

ZELOTES (a political-religious party of Jesus' time whose aim was to overthrow Roman rule and establish a Jewish theocracy). Luke 6:15.

ZEPHANIAH (a priest and friend of the prophet Jeremiah and author of the book that bears his name). 2 Kgs 25:18 • Jer 21:1; 29:25,29; 37:3; 52:24.

ZEPHANIAH, BOOK OF. A short prophetic book of the Old Testament known for its portrayal of the certainty of God's judgment against the nation of Judah (1:1–2:15). The prophet Zephaniah also declared that God would spare a faithful remnant (3:13), through which His promise of a future Messiah would be accomplished.

ZERUBBABEL (a Jewish leader who supervised the rebuilding of the temple in Jerusalem after the Exile). Hag 2:21–23 • **Zech 4:6–10.** *Sheshbazzar:* Ezra 5:14. *Zorobabel:* Matt 1:12–13.

ZIBA (a former servant of King Saul who helped David locate Jonathan's son Mephibosheth). 2 Sam 9:2–11.

ZIDON. See *Sidon.*

ZIKLAG (a city where David hid from King Saul). 1 Sam 27:5–6.

ZILPAH (Leah's maid who became a concubine of Jacob and bore two of his twelve sons, Gad and Asher). Gen 30:9–13.

ZIMRI (a chariot commander who assassinated King Elah of Israel and assumed the throne). 1 Kgs 16:8–20.

ZIN (a desert wilderness near the Dead Sea through which the Israelites passed). Num 13:21; 20:1; 27:14; 33:36; 34:3–4 • Deut 32:51 • Josh 15:1–3.

ZION (another name for the city of Jerusalem, particularly used in the Psalms). Pss 48:2, 11–12; 102:13–21; 137:1,3; 149:2 • Lam 2:1–18. *Sion:* Rev 14:1.

ZIPH (a city where David hid from King Saul). 1 Sam 23:14–18.

ZIPPORAH (wife of Moses). Ex 2:21–22; 4:25; 18:2.

ZOAR (a city destroyed along with Sodom and Gomorrah because of its sin). **Gen 19:20–25** • Deut 34:3 • Isa 15:5 • Jer 48:34. *Bela:* Gen 14:2.

ZOBAH (a Syrian kingdom that warred against King Saul). 1 Sam 14:47. *Hamath-zobah:* 2 Chr 8:3. *Zoba:* 2 Sam 10:6,8.

ZOPHAR (one of the three friends who comforted Job). His speeches appear in Job 11:1–20; 20:1–29.

ZOROBABEL.
See *Zerubbabel.*

Ways to save money

① Ebates.com

② Extrabux.com

③ hukkster.com